ORGANIZED CRIME

ORGANIZED CRIME

A Global Perspective

Edited by

ROBERT J. KELLY

ROWMAN & LITTLEFIELD
PUBLISHERS

ROWMAN & LITTLEFIELD

Published in the United States of America in 1986
by Rowman & Littlefield, Publishers
(a division of Littlefield, Adams & Company)
81 Adams Drive, Totowa, New Jersey 07512

Copyright © 1986 by Rowman and Littlefield

Library of Congress Cataloging-in-Publication Data
Main entry under title:

Organized crime.

  Includes index.
  1. Organized crime — Cross-cultural studies.
I. Kelly, Robert J.   II. Title.
HV6441.074   1986   364.1'06   85-26141
ISBN 0-86598-085-3
ISBN 0-8476-7559-9 (pbk.)

88 87 86
10 9 8 7 6 5 4 3 2

Printed in the United States of America

For
Edward Sagarin

Contents

    Georgian Jews in Israel
      Menachem Amir

11 Organized Crime as It Emerges in Regions of Africa   192
      James S. E. Opolot

12 Organized Crime in Japan   208
      Hiroaki Iwai

13 Organized Crime in Australia: An Urban History   234
      Alfred W. McCoy

    Name Index   287

    Subject Index   295

    Contributors   301

Tables and Figures

Acknowledgments

This book, as the contents show, is a collective enterprise. It reflects the comments and suggestions received from many colleagues and associates. We have profited particularly from the advice of Edward Sagarin, whose idea inspired this book; from Charles Tilly, University of Michigan; Irving Louis Horowitz and Gerhard Mueller, Rutgers University, for contacts in Europe and Latin America; Denis Sazbo, University of Montreal; Judge Jean Cosson, Supreme Court of Appeals, Paris; David Critchelely, United Kingdom; Minoru Shikita, Director, Asian and Far East Institute, United Nations; R. W. Burnham, Vienna International Centre, United Nations; A. Brossard, Secretary-General of INTERPOL; many thanks to Hans-Georg Raeder of Muenchen, West Germany for the translation of chapter 7.

1

Overview

Humbert S. Nelli
University of Kentucky

As a native of Chicago and an Italian-American, my concepts about underworld figures and their activities were profoundly shaped by the articles I read in newspapers and the motion pictures I have seen. This is true for other Americans as well.

Much of what has been written on the subject of organized crime is either inaccurate or distorted. Nothing illustrates this fact more clearly than the research I conducted in the early 1970s on the origins and growth of the Italian-American crime syndicates. At the time, the generally accepted view of the emergence of the syndicates was that on September 11, 1931 the younger generation of criminals, led by Charles "Lucky" Luciano, overthrew the old-timers or, as they were called at the time, the "greaseballs." According to underworld lore, on September 11th, Luciano ordered the assassination of Salvatore Maranzano, then the reigning "boss of bosses," in his Park Avenue office in New York, and at the same time (according to some sources, within twenty-four hours or forty-eight hours), the elimination of Maranzano's allies and friends all over the country. Thus, according to former syndicate member Joseph Valachi, Maranzano's murder was "part of an intricate, painstakingly executed mass extermination." The number of murdered "greaseballs" varied according to the writer and ranged from 39 to nearly 200.[1] However, no one attempted to verify the story.

While doing research in cities in various parts of the country, I found that the "purge day" story was inaccurate in at least two important respects: Maranzano's murder took place on September 11 — actually, it occurred on the 10th; and Luciano, leader of the anti-Maranzano forces, had ordered the liquidation of "greaseballs" (or "moustache Petes") throughout America. The facts do not support the theory that the Maranzano killing formed part of a nationwide purge. The events that New York criminals recalled as taking place in September 1931 applied only to that city and were not repeated elsewhere. Italian syndicate criminals did not at that time, or since, kill quietly or unobtrusively when the purpose was not only to eliminate rivals but also to impart a message. In the Maranzano case the message stated clearly that any oldtimers still permitted to live had better accept and adjust to the new order. According to legend, "several" associates and allies of Maranzano in the New York area were eliminated at about the time of his death. Because of the bizarre manner in which syndicate killers carried out their tasks, such murders would quickly have become known to authorities and newspapers. Although reporters have generally used the descriptor "several" to indicate the number of "moustache Petes" eliminated on this occasion, they have cited only three victims as substantiation. The bound bodies of Louis Russo and Samuel Monaco were dumped in the Hackensack River, and James La Pore was shot in front of a Bronx barbershop. All died on September 10th. These deaths, reported in the daily press, appear to have been the extent of the "purge day" bloodbath in the New York area.[2]

A careful examination of newspapers issued during September, October, and November of 1931 in Boston, Philadelphia, Pittsburgh, Baltimore, New Orleans, Cleveland, Detroit, Chicago, Kansas City, Denver, Los Angeles, and San Francisco turned up evidence of only one killing that occurred at about the time Maranzano died, and that might have been linked to the death of the "Boss of Bosses." Denver, where this killing took place, contained gangs that routinely used violence to settle disputes, so that the timing of the murder to coincide with events in New York might not have been intentional. Moreover, the leaders of the two rival factions were Calabrians and not Sicilians; Luciano and Maranzano were Sicilians.[3]

Interestingly enough the "purge day" story originated not with journalists or the police, but with the Jewish criminals who Luciano allegedly employed to eliminate Maranzano. They, in turn, told the story to Dixie Davis, who was Dutch Schultz's lawyer, and he gave it to the world in a 1939 series of articles in *Collier's Magazine*. The story was later repeated, and embellished, by Joe Valachi in testimonies before the McClellan Committee in 1963.[4] This sequence underscores another fact regarding organized crime: syndicate members are the firmest believers in the myths and half truths that are so numerous in the past as well as the present of organized crime. They are, in fact, the original sources of many, if not most, of the myths.

Syndicate members are also among the biggest fans of crime books and movies. Thus when Philadelphia mob boss Philip "Chicken Man" Testa was murdered in March 1981 outside the front door of his house, FBI agents searched the house. Among other things they found a videotape of *The Godfather*, and a copy of the *The Last Mafioso* by Jimmy "The Weasel" Fratianno. And, as those familiar with the underworld are aware, every syndicate member has one burning ambition—to publish his autobiography. This ambition is probably at least in part due to the widespread popularity and huge financial success enjoyed by a work of fiction, *The Godfather*. The images presented in the novel and later in the two-part movie have reinforced many widely accepted but often inaccurate perceptions regarding organized crime in this country, including among others, the "purge day" myth.[5]

In recent years scholars have attempted to expose the myths and misconceptions and to present a more accurate and balanced picture of organized crime. In *Organized Crime in the USA*, Peter Lupsha very effectively outlines the extensive amount of work he and others have done on American syndicate activities in the formative period prior to World War II.

The post-World War II period has been a golden age for criminal syndicates in the United States. Economic opportunities have been unlimited in traditional lines of activity such as gambling, loan sharking, labor and business racketeering, and narcotics. In addition, a number of new moneymaking enterprises have been tapped, including arson for hire, credit card and real estate frauds, the pornography business, the theft and sale of securities, and bootlegging of a variety of items (among them cigarettes, electrical appliances and aspirin). And, of course, there has been a significant penetration into legitimate business.

The syndicates emerged from the war in strong financial condition. During hostilities, the criminal entrepreneurs catered to public demands for a wide variety of illegal services, and commodities in short supply. Such items as gasoline, meat, automobiles, tin, and rubber were provided — for a price. In addition to black market operations, the war proved to be a boon to underworld gambling operations. People played the numbers and flocked to horse and dog tracks, gambling casinos and bookmakers. Black market and gambling operations continued into the post-war era, and underworld syndicates maintained a tight grasp on both.

By the early 1950s, gambling — syndicate crime's greatest source of income — brought an estimated $20 million a year with annual net pofits of approximately $7 million. Although most of the money came from such illegal operations as slot machines, bookmaking, and illegal numbers and lotteries, illicit entrepreneurs also discovered the opportunities offered by legal gambling in Nevada.[6]

At the time it opened in December 1946, Bugsy Siegel's creation, the "fabulous Flamingo Hotel," appeared to be a 6 million dollar miscalculation. As events soon proved, of course, it was a stroke of genius. Unfortunately Siegel did not live to enjoy the benefits of his vision. On June 20, 1947, Siegel was murdered in Los Angeles, apparently on orders from east coast and middle west syndicate leaders who believed he had wasted or misused their money. Meyer Lansky and Frank Costello of New York; Cleveland leaders Moe Dalitz, Sam Tucker, Thomas J. McGinty, and Morris Kleinman; Hyman Abrams of Boston; New Jersey's "Doc" Stacher; Pete Licavoli of Detroit; Miami's Edward Levinson; Isadore "Kid Cann" Blumenfeld of Minneapolis; and Chicago's Tony Accardo and numerous other syndicate leaders quickly recognized the opportunities in Las Vegas and invested (either openly or through fronts) in the casino-hotels that sprang up during the fifties. In the process they turned Las Vegas into "the most lucrative gambling spa in the world."[7]

By 1967, when the President's Commission on Law Enforcement and Administration of Justice presented its findings on the extent of organized crime in the United States, profits from illegal wagering on horse races, lotteries, and sporting events reached a minimum of at least $20 billion a year, of which criminal syndicates received perhaps $6 or $7 billion, and remained a major source of underworld revenue. In 1978 New York City police estimated that just *one* crime family in the city, the Vito Genovese family, netted more than $100 million annually just from Super Bowl bets in the New York-New Jersey area.[8]

Labor and business racketeering, which made its appearance in the midst of the bootlegging era of the 1920s, was by the following decade a major source of syndicate income as well as a means to enter legitimate business and organized labor. As it developed in the 1920s and 1930s it was "a system whereby, through the creation of a so-called trade association, by the connivance, cooperation, or control of a labor union, and the use of the strong-arm squad, a process of shaking down merchants or other industrialists was smoothed out to machine efficiency."[9]

In the following years, racketeering grew to such proportions that the Senate Permanent Subcommittee on Investigations under the chairmanship of Senator John McClellan conducted a three-year inquiry into corrupt practices in labor-management relations. Conditions were found to be so serious that in 1959 Congress passed the Landrum-Griffin Act, which assigned the Department of Labor a big role in removing the influence of organized crime in labor unions. In 1978, the permanent subcommittee published the findings of a new investigation. In it Senator Charles Percy observed that "it is now all too apparent that labor-management racketeering has not disappeared in the twenty years since those hearings." Percy noted that the corrupt practices of racketeers "rob the union rank and file of their hard-earned rights and benefits. They force the American consumer to pay a duty tax to racketeers for essential goods and services. In effect, consumers and laborers alike are subsidizing organized crime."[10]

Loan sharking has since the 1930s been another major illicit enterprise for criminal organizations. Simply stated, loan sharking involves lending money at a higher rate of interest than that charged by legal lending institutions. Interest rates vary from 1 to 150 percent a week, according to the size of the loan, the potential for repayment, the intended use of the money, and the relationship between borrower and lender. Customers are willing to pay exorbitant interest rates because they are considered to be poor credit risks by legitimate lenders. Customers include gamblers and bookmakers who borrow to pay gambling losses, small businessmen with cash problems, and narcotics users who borrow to buy heroin.

A study conducted by the Russell Sage Foundation in the mid-1930s found that the gross annual income from loan sharking in New York City was in excess of $10 million. By the 1960s the President's Commission on Law Enforcement judged the loan sharking business to be "in the multi-billion dollar range" and noted that the profit margins it provides are higher than those obtained from gambling operations.[11]

During the 1960s organized crime tapped a new source of revenue — stolen securities. Although Italian syndicates played a prominent role, "a number of other groups, syndicates and combinations of criminals in a loosely organized confederation" participated extensively in the crimes. Securities were generally obtained in one of two ways: either through inside operators in banks or stockbrokerage houses, or by theft or registered mail at airports. In 1971 a congressional committee investigating the involvement of syndicate crime in the stolen securities business found that the securities were disposed of "through confidence men, stockbrokers and attorneys of shady reputation, fences, and other persons who have the ability, technical knowledge, skill, and contacts to sell the securities or to place them advantageously as collateral in financial transactions." The National Crime Information Center estimated the value of government and private securities stolen in 1970 to be at least $227 million, a figure other authorities considered to be short of the mark.[12]

In recent decades criminal entrepreneurs have devoted increasingly more attention to legitimate business. There is some disagreement among authorities as to whether this focus represents an effort to use profits obtained from illegal activities as a means to infiltrate and corrupt legitimate enterprises, or an attempt on the part of upwardly mobile entrepreneurs to leave a sordid life and gain respectability. The Kefauver Committee, which subscribed to the former theory, noted the presence of syndicate figures in "approximately 50 areas of business enterprise." These included advertising, appliances, the automobile industry, banking, coal, construction, drug stores and drug companies, electrical equipment, florists, food (meat, sea food, dairy products, groceries, cheese, olive oil, fruits), the garment industry, import-export business, insurance, the liquor industry, news services, newspapers, the oil industry, paper products, radio stations, ranching, real estate, restaurants, the scrap business, shipping, steel, television, theaters, and transportatation.[13]

The desire to "go legitimate" has continued to the present. A congressional investigation in 1980 found that profits obtained from illicit enterprises are "over time" invested in legitimate businesses which cover "the whole gamut of our private enterprise system." Businesses infiltrated through the use of "laundered" profits cover some 70 areas of economic activity and "include liquor, transportation, entertainment, sports, hotels and motels, brokerage houses, labor unions, insurance companies, construction firms, vending machines, the food industry, trade associations, trucking, waste collection, parking lots, garment manufacturing, resorts and casinos, holding and finance companies, and real estate development." An estimated 85 percent of the syndicate criminals in America have invested at least a part of their "ill-gotten gain" in legitimate business ventures.[14]

A significant portion of the enormous profits accruing to criminal organizations has in recent years come from the traffic in illegal narcotics. Thus according to Howard Kohn, the Washington director for the Center for Investigative Reporting, the earnings from cocaine, marijuana, amphetamines, heroin, barbiturates, and other illegal drugs "amount by the DEA's (Drug Enforcement Administration) estimate to a total of $80 billion a year in unreported business transactions."[15] Contrary to popular belief, this is not a recent phenomenon but rather an organized enterprise that dates from at least the 1920s or 1930s. Nevertheless, the illegal narcotics business has taken on a significantly greater importance in the years since World War II.

In 1973, *Newsday*, a Long Island daily, printed a 32-part report that traced the flow of narcotics from the poppy fields of Turkey to the streets of New York. The investigative study noted that New York is the center of America's heroin industry with more than half of the industry's customers believed to be living in the five boroughs along with many of the suppliers, wholesalers, retailers, and street peddlars. "In dollar terms, it may be one of the city's biggest industries, with annual sales of $1 billion or more." Control of the business had shifted over the decades from Jewish criminals in the 1930s, to Italians in the next two decades. In the late 1950s, however, a new federal conspiracy law went into effect which permitted prosecution of bosses who never actually handled the drugs. "Shortly afterward, around 1960, the five New York crime families prohibited their members from dealing in narcotics." The decision was apparently based in large part on the fear that those given long prison terms would turn informer to lighten their sentences. Although not all Italians moved out of the business, enough did to create the opportunity for Cuban groups to move in. The Cubans, unlike their black competitors, "had connections throughout Latin America and Europe, the sources of the drugs."[16]

At least as early as 1972 federal agents noted, and warned of, the increasing involvement of Latin Americans as well as the emergence of South Florida as a major center of drug traffic. Thus a May 1, 1972 article in *The New York Times*, based on information provided by "federal law enforcement officials," maintained that "enterprising Frenchmen, South Americans, Puerto Ricans, and Cuban refugees are turning southern Florida into the premier American entry point for smuggled heroin and cocaine." At the time this situation reflected the increasing use of South America as a stopover and dispersion point for European-refined heroin as well as "the growing popularity of South American-grown cocaine in the United States and an infusion of new Latin elements in the high-profit, high-risk business."[17]

Rapid changes took place throughout the 1970s in the nature of drug trafficking. Strong action by American authorities disrupted the traffic in heroin from Turkey as well as trade routes that had been formed during the Vietnam War to Thailand, Laos, and Cambodia. To fill the void created by these law enforcement activities, heroin production increased in Mexico, and Colombia became a major source of marijuana and cocaine. A new element emerged to tap the lushly profitable Colombian Connection. Doctors, lawyers, businessmen and other ostensibly honest and respectable professionals provided financial backing for individual entrepreneurs (most of them white, middle class young men) to purchase and transport the drugs by sea or air to the United States. Profits are so enormous that those at the lower end of the drug smuggling ladder pick up for a single venture what ordinary citizens would consider to be substantial sums. Thus the off-loaders receive $10,000 to $15,000 for one night's work in unloading a boatload of marijuana while airplane pilots are paid $50,000 to $100,000 for a round trip to Colombia to transport a planeload of marijuana.[18]

The enormous amounts of money generated by this illicit enterprise — and all transactions are in cash — has created a serious problem — how to dispose of the profits. This difficulty is illustrated by an incident that occurred in an Atlanta bank in November 1983. Two Internal Revenue Service agents were in a downtown Atlanta bank talking with bank officials when "a teller discreetly joined the conversation. The IRS agents might just be interested in small conversation taking place just a few feet away," the teller suggested. The agents looked. They saw two Hispanic men buying cashiers' checks in an exchange for a pile of currency that, in the words of one of the agents, was " 'at least six inches high.' The low-key afternoon drama," resulted in a "ten-count federal indictment against three Mexican men. The three were charged with laundering $148,000 in alleged narcotics profits at seventeen Atlanta banks over a two-day period."[19]

This incident uncovered one of the small money laundering operations conducted by cocaine traffickers in their efforts to convert cash profits which, the DEA estimated, exceeded $35 *billion* in 1983. According to Howard Kohn there are three basic laundering options available. "They can hoard their cash burying it in the yard, cramming it into a wall safe, spending it as needed. However, once they begin laying out cash for a houseboat or a fleet of cars, red flags may run up at IRS." A second option is to smuggle the money out of the United States and open a foreign bank account. Unfortunately for the smuggler, it is generally easier to get cocaine into the country than it is to get money out, because of the greater bulk of the cash. That leaves the third option which, Kohn continued, is the one most dealers prefer: "They take their money to a friendly bank, deposit it in an account, wire it to a foreign account that may or may not have their name on it (but that they control), then loan the money to a U.S. company that they also control." This laundering or money-washing procedure "can be accomplished through brokerage firms or money exchange houses, [but] for sheer convenience banks are best."[20] As the Atlanta experience of the three Mexicans demonstrates, however, things do not always work out as planned.

In recent years other groups have entered the scramble for narcotics dollars. Colombians have expanded roles developed during the 1960s and early 1970s as producers and couriers for other distribution networks to the actual trafficking and distribution of the Colombian-produced marijuana and cocaine in the United States. Although until 1979 outlaw motorcycle gangs such as the Hells Angels, Bandidos, Pagans, and the Outlaws were viewed by authorities mostly as "local nuisances" they now are considered to display "all the characteristics of the more traditional organized crime groups. They also have a formal, recognized rank structure that delineates authority and privilege." In addition to drug trafficking, the motorcycle gangs are involved in welfare frauds, auto and motorcycle theft, and murder.[20] Even the Italian syndicates (or Mafia) which, according to the *Wall Street Journal* "once viewed motorcycle gangs with contempt" now make "increasing use of them for arson, extortion and contract killings."[21]

While the outlaw bikers have been compared by the press to the Itlaian criminal syndicates, a confederation of drug smugglers, pimps, pornography peddlars, burglars, car thieves, and killers-for-hire operating in Florida, Georgia, Alabama, Virginia, Tennessee, Kentucky and other Southern states have been named the "Dixie Mafia" by law enforcement authorities.[22]

The complicated nature of the organized crime situation, especially with regard to the illicit traffic in narcotics, led a Senate subcommittee investigating the current state of the underworld to conclude in 1980 that "there is no one specific ethnic stereotype that is synonymous with 'organized crime.' The composition of organized crime syndicates varies from place to place, from year to year, and from drug to drug."[23] It must be emphasized that the Italian syndicate leaders are not encouraging the changes that are taking place in the world of organized crime nor are they pleased with these changes. Rather, they have made prodigious efforts to maintain the status quo, but as the most highly publicized and visible element in the underworld they have found this to be a difficult task.

Pressures from law enforcement agencies, the advancing age of syndicate leaders, and an inability to attract new local talent combined with increasing competition from blacks, Hispanics, and others may signify the beginning of the decline of the Italian American syndicates in other fields of economic activity and also in the highly competitive New York area. Increasingly, criminal syndicates have found it extremely difficult to attract able, intelligent, ambitious Italian Americans of the younger generation. As a result they have found it necessary to import ambitious young toughs from Sicily to provide needed manpower in the scramble for narcotics dollars.[24]

Although the Italian syndicates are not as powerful as they once were, their organizations are far from dead. They and their new competitors will continue to prosper by supplying and exploiting the seemingly endless need of the American public for illegal products and services.[25]

As the essays in this volume make amply clear, the desire and need for illegal products is not limited to the United States. Instead it is a fact and a problem of world-wide dimensions.

Notes

1. Peter Maas, *The Valachi Papers* (New York, 1968), p. 111. Also see Craig Thompson and Allen Raymond, *Gang Rule in New York: The Story of a Lawless Era* (New York, 1940), chap. 12; J. Richard "Dixie" Davis, "Things I Couldn't Tell Till Now," *Colliers* 104 (August 5, 1939), p.

44; and Donald R. Cressey, *Theft of the Nation: The Structure and Operations of Organized Crime in America* (New York, 1969), p. 44.

2. Maas, *The Valachi Papers,* pp. 115–116; *The New York Times,* September 11th and 15th, 1931; *The New York Daily News,* September 11, 1931.

3. For a full discussion see Humbert S. Nelli, *The Business of Crime: Italians and Syndicate Crime in the United States* (New York, 1976), pp. 183–184.

4. U.S. Congress, Senate, *Hearings Before the Permanent Subcommittee on Investigations of the Committee on Government Operations. Organized Crime and Illicit Traffic in Narcotics,* 88th Congress, 1st Session, pt. 1.

5. Mario Puzo, *The Godfather* (New York, 1969).

6. U.S. Congress, Senate, *Second Interim Report of the Special Committee to Investigate Organized Crime in Interstate Commerce,* 82nd Cong., 1st Sess., pp. 13–14.

7. Frank Browning and John Gerassi, *The American Way of Crime* (New York, 1980), p. 441.

8. *The Challenge of Crime in a Free Society. A Report by the President's Commission on Law Enforcement and Administration of Justice* (Washington, 1967), p. 189; *The Washington Post,* January 16, 1978.

9. Thompson and Raymond, *Gang Rule in New York,* p. 219.

10. U.S. Congress, Senate, *Hearings Before the Permanent Subcommittee on Investigations of the Committee on Government Operations. Labor Management Racketeering,* 95th Congress, 2nd Session, p. 6.

11. *The New York Times,* December 4, 1935; *President's Commission on Law Enforcement,* p. 189.

12. U.S. Congress, Senate, *Hearings Before the Permanent Subcommittee on Investigations of the Committee on Government Operations. Organized Crime—Stolen Securities,* 92nd Congress, 1st Session, p. 2–5.

13. U.S. Congress, Senate, *Third Interim Report,* pp. 170;71.

14. U.S. Congress, Senate, *Hearings Before the Permanent Subcommittee on Investigations of the Committee on Government Operations. Organized Crime and Use of Violence,* 96th Cong., 2nd Sess., p. 13; Jeff Gerth, "Nixon and the Mafia," *Sundance,* 1(3), p. 30.

15. Howard Kohn, "Cocaine: You Can Bank on It," *Esquire,* 100 (October 1983), p. 80.

16. The Staff and Editors of *Newsday, The Heroin Trail* (New York, 1974), pp. 198–200.

17. *The New York Times,* May 1, 1972.

18. U.S. Congress, Senate, *Hearings Before the Permanent Subcommittee on Investigations of the Committee on Government Operations. Illegal Narcotics Profits,* 96th Congress, 2nd Session, p. 18.

19. *Journal and Constitution,* November 19, 1983.

20. Howard Kohn, "Cocaine: You Can Bank on It," pp. 77–78.

21. "A Menace . . . Today's Motorcycle Gangs Rival the Mafia," *The Lexington Herald Leader,* September 2, 1981; *The Wall Street Journal,* January 11, 1984; U.S. Congress, Senate, *Organized Crime an Use of Violence,* p. 61.

22. "Dixie Mafia Thrives on High-Stakes Crime in Bullish Sun Belt," *The Louisville Courier-Journal,* December 19, 1982.

23. U.S. Congress, Senate, *Organized Crime and Use of Violence,* p. 61.

24. Nicholas Pileggi, "Anatomy of the Drug War," *New York Magazine,* 6 (January 8, 1973), p. 36; Staff and Editors of *Newsday, The Heroin Trail,* pp. 207–209.

25. It is ironic that as they decrease in importance, the Italian American criminal organizations have spawned a veritable cottage industry, consisting of films, television shows, novels, journalistic accounts, scholarly studies, and federal and state investigative reports which recount in loving or lurid detail the exploits of Italian American crime families.

2

Criminal Underworlds: Looking Down on Society from Below

Robert J. Kelly
City University of New York

In recent years, technical advances in the study of organized crime have progressed. Innovations and sophisticated research techniques such as network analysis, computer simulations, and the application of macroeconomic models of illegal market dynamics, among others have appeared to augment rather than replace more traditional treatments based on law enforcement pictures of organized crime. Consequently, the logical geography of the phenomenon and the knowledge we possess about it have been greatly modified.

As with any new special area of study experiencing growing pains, organized crime research has been marred by disputes and controversies over the very definition of the phenomenon itself. Debates have raged about the application of the term to various types of crime and to specific kinds of criminal groups and organizations. Organized crime has been defined in various ways (Maltz, 1976), and in a sense, we are still trying to come to grips with it conceptually, empirically, and as a social problem. Since the term gained currency in the twentieth century, widely different views on organized crime, in everyday language as well as in the scientific idiom, have had their staunch supporters. For many people, organized crime is synonymous with "Mafia," or "Cosa Nostra." For others, organized crime was and remains one of the several ways by which vigorous minorities bypass the traditional and orthodox routes to power, acceptance, and celebrity in American life. For still others, the term stands for a national conspiracy of formidable criminal confederations and associations that operate with the power and influence of another, invisible government.[1] Mainstream American social scientific thinking about organized crime has been deeply affected by the theoretical mixture of alien conspiracy theory with notions about centralizing tendencies among underworld groups. The results of such theorizing have been to posit a trend towards consolidation among criminal groups producing a monolithic organization which saps the economic and political vitality of the country (Cressey, 1967a; Salerno & Tompkins, 1969).

Organized crime in the United States is a more complex and subtle social reality than that suggested by fanciful conspiracy theories which depict the major criminal groups as ruthless Sicilians or other desperate foreigners. The implications of such thinking free Americans from the obligation to confront the political and economic contradictions in the social milieu which promote racketeering, corruption, and the provision of illicit goods and services. In the alien conspiracy perspective, America is the victim of foreign depredations and the forms of organized criminality that are prevalent may be attributed to minorities, ethnics, and others who are not part of the dominant cultural skein and ethos.

Consequently, and until fairly recently, the controversial and emotion-laden subject of organized crime has been more a field for ideological polemics than for critical analysis. Spawned by government-sponsored studies, much of the debate has focused on whether or not the set of activities described as "organized crime" is dominated by one or more particular ethnic groups. In addition to this, American folklore is replete with the legendary exploits of criminal societies such as the "Black Hand," "Murder, Inc.," "The Mafia," "La Cosa Nostra," and, no less ominously, "The National Syndicate." The sensational accounts of such groups and their successors have filled newspaper headlines intermittently and their words and deeds are further thrust upon us through paperback novels, films, and television. In short, the phenomenon of organized crime portrayed in official studies and announcements, and reinforced by the mass media has become embedded in the popular lore and has stimulated the public imagination to an unprecedented degree.

It is scarcely an exaggeration to say that organized crime is not just another social problem. It is enveloped in secrecy; data concerning its participants, spread, and infiltration into legitimate businesses are often closely guarded by law enforcement groups, and deception and dissimulation pose serious issues for both students, enforcement agencies, and public officials. Methodological difficulties and other impediments to research are not limited to analysts of American organized crime but pester researchers in other societies as weil. The major sources of information for researchers in the United States and elsewhere are government agencies. But this creates problems because these data possess inherent weaknesses from the standpoint of the analyst. Ianni has observed that:

> The files of government law enforcement agencies were never intended as research sources; they are police intelligence files focusing on the types of information necessary to seek indictments and hopefully obtain convictions of individual criminals. They tell little about how crime activists organize themselves and nothing of the relationship between organized crime and other sectors of American society. As a result, law enforcement agencies continue to seek out

individual organized crime figures in much the same way that they seek out perpetrators of street crime (Ianni, 1973:336).

This is a problem for organized crime researchers but it is not unique to them. Official records and data are collected and recorded for specific bureaucratic purposes by those working within the framework of complex, legal, and administrative regulations. The rules and proscriptions that shape the nature and flow of information are not designed with researchers in mind. Thus, there are intrinsic limitations in the relevance of official files for the student who is studying crime phenomena. Perhaps the chief obstacle, though, is the lack of access to organized crime groups. Ironically, many racketeers are well known to their clients, the police, other criminals, and to the public at large. Their need for connections with other underworld sources of power and prestige; their need to make reputations as ruthless individuals in order to insure compliance with agreements others enter into with them; and their need to command loyalty and obedience from subordinates—all these exigencies by which an individual emerges as a person of power and influence demand public posture, however circumscribed by the illegal nature of his activities. In some cases, the criminal label and its ramifications are mitigated by the benevolent and philanthropic roles inhabited by the individual with a criminal reputation. In the United States, because of his high-level political connections and charity work on behalf of the poor and indigent, it came as something of a shock to hear Frank Costello described as a notorious hoodlum directing a national syndicate of gangsters and murderers. In Sicily, the natural death of Calogero ·Vizzini, reputed capomafioso of the central province, was the occasion for a massive public procession involving civil officials, wealthy landowners, churchmen, and thousands of peasants and townspeople whom he had helped throughout a career that law enforcement agencies would have described as anything but benign and peaceful. Similarly, upon the death of Kazuo Taoka, the leader of Japan's largest organized crime group, high-level government members and people from the entertainment industry attended the funeral services.[2] Thus, many powerful organized crime figures are impervious to prosecution and reliable information about their activities is limited or suppressed because of their liaisons with influential individuals in the upper-world.

Other significant problems confront the researcher. Police and other law enforcement officials are often reluctant to make known their positions on questions concerning the extent or power of organized crime groups (Albini, 1976). Because of the corruption of law enforcement agencies by the underworld, data may not be available or, when it is, it may be unreliable (Panteleone, 1966). At least in the United States, access to criminal justice agencies is sometimes circumscribed by the politics of the organizations so that independent tests of their interpretations of the crime scene which they disseminate cannot be done adequately (Ianni, 1973; Cressey, 1967b).

The secrecy and confidentiality of information that characterizes enforcement agency practices is not solely or mainly attributable to the intrusions of underworld groups into the criminal justice process. There are good reasons why access to data that have to do with the very purposes and functions of law enforcement activities is limited. Given the nature of organized crime enterprises and activities, intelligence work, and undercover surveillance, the use of wiretaps and other electronic eavesdropping devices are important instruments and techniques for gathering information and evidence. In order to make cases, information must be protected since disclosure by government could well result in dismissals, libel and slander suits, and even political reprisals. Policemen and investigators are in delicate positions — they want to "educate" the public about organized criminality, and, perhaps, even supply data — primary data — to social scientists; but they are inhibited by the law and by their responsibilities as law enforcement officals to protect evidence and the rights of the accused. It must be noted that similar conditions affect social scientists in other countries who wish to study organized crime activity: most of their data derive from archives and official files that are no longer active, or from police investigations and prosecutions that have been closed or concluded. These facts of life — the reluctance of law enforcement to freely disseminate information and the purported impenetrability of organized crime groups — pose serious problems for the student of the phenomenon.

Other research techniques, particularly variations of participant observation methods widely employed in anthropological studies, have been used by some investigators. Ianni, for instance, supplemented his archival analysis with limited observations of a crime "family" but acknowledges that he could never have been an insider with the group he studied but only a part of the larger Italian-American social setting in which it operated (Ianni and Reuss-Ianni, 1973; Chambliss 1975), in commenting on the lack of original research on subjects that cannot be easily investigated, ascribes the dearth of primary research data on problems like organized crime to a "myopic research vision" based on a widespread unchallenged belief that such efforts are futile. Based on his field experiences, Chambliss thinks that such excursions are both possible and profitable as a corrective to the law enforcement view of things. Other attempts at field research (Kelly, 1982) indicate that entry into criminal settings and into the network of organized and professional criminals is very tricky and not likely to result in fruitful outcomes.

While an "on the streets" field work approach may be able to generate a body of data that is otherwise unavailable, most researchers lack the fortitude and agility to negotiate the insuperable difficulties likely to be encountered in settings that are prone to violence. Other procedures have emerged, mainly outside the United States, where social scientists often tend to play more vigorous roles in public affairs and appear to be more readily accepted as indispensable aids in handling societal problems. In his study of the mafia of a Sicilian village, Blok spent nearly three years living in the area among the patrons and clients of local Mafiosi (Blok, 1974). In other instances researchers have had access to relatively raw data as advisors and consultants to governmental investigative commissions and legislative bodies (Amir, this volume); or they have had close consultative contacts with police and law enforcement agencies (Iwai, this volume); or worked professionally in law enforcement (Tremblay & Kedzior, this volume).

The difficulties in obtaining reliable data about organized crime have not deterred others—popular writers, journalists, and organized crime figures themselves—from producing a vast literature on the subject. Biographies, gossipy exposés—a whole genre of books and articles have appeared offering static, but sometimes brilliantly vivid snapshots of life in the sordid and glamorous underworld. The trouble with so much of what is published is that it usually amounts to nothing more than a loose sequence of isolated events and scenes, written without much regard for tidiness, logical coherence, or the facts. The need for economy, for order in the presentation of the subject, does not seem to have made much of an impression on many writers in the pulp genre. This fact is especially obvious in the readily available paperback market of criminal biographies with their fast-moving narratives and well-edited dislays of gruesome photographs. One of the distressing realities students of organized crime face is that they must work in the shadow of this sensationalist literature which has more than peripheral influence and which has molded much of the public image and conception of organized crime while the few serious works lay, by comparison, neglected.

As the essays in this volume demonstrate, organized crime is hardly a Sicilian or an American invention. It flourishes in many different kinds of societies—those different politically, economically, and culturally. And even with many variations in origin and in form, organized crime is intimately linked with the political structures and economic infrastructures in those countries where it appears.[3] Historically, the majority of American accounts of organized crime or criminal underworlds have focused on the internal structure of criminal groups or on their ethnic bases. The study of organized crime has suffered from a lack of focus and attention to its myriad forms in other societies and cultures. One consequence of this gap in the literature is that many of the theories and perspectives emerging from the existing body of knowledge are too ad hoc and narrow. A more serious consequence is the lack of cooperation and mutual criticism among different groups of experts in the field.

There is much to be said in extentuation for this state of affairs, for many of the relevant research monographs and papers are scattered in foreign journals and periodicals, untranslated, often difficult to obtain, and somewhat unintelligible to an American audience immersed in the Cosa Nostra mystiques characteristic of North American work. To fill this lacuna, the present volume of essays by students from a number of countries seeks to offer a more comprehensive picture of the current state of thinking about the problem. Further, the volume may serve to stimulate some fresh considerations as to the international links, alliances and coalitions among organized criminal groups that are occurring.

As the essays indicate, in some parts of the world, organized crime is so deeply embedded in social institutions as to constitute a cultural tradition; in others, its composite features are novel and seem to have arisen out of the convulsions and turmoil of rapid social and economic transformations; and in still others, organized crime appears evanescent: a spontaneous reaction of mobile and newly-formed social groups which fade as they acculturate and are assimilated into their host societies.

From a purely scientific standpoint the presentation of work by scholars from other countries may have salutary effects on research programs in general by permitting some cross-fertilization of theory, empirical data, and historical analysis. Another advantage in a collection of this sort is that it may furnish some presumptive evidence that the atmosphere in which organized crime investigations are conducted in the United States preempts the analysis of other types of data and is intolerant of Marxist-oriented theory whose results might produce radically different conclusions from those attained so far. For scholars in this country, exposure to other ways of thinking about organized crime may encourage new ways of handling social facts rather than escaping from them.

The essays trace the rise, growth, and structure of organized crime and its variations in several societies. Not every society or nation-state with a palpable presence of organized criminality is covered here. Naturally, it does not mean that in those societies not included in the discussions, organized crime is non-existent or not a problem warranting the attention of scholars and law enforcement agencies. Rather, it may be a reflection of a lack of concern or resources to cope with crime that is conspiratorial, rooted in the problems of the political economy, and indicative of a corrupt symbiosis among ruling élites in the political, social, and economic sectors of that state.[4] The political systems in many countries may be too fragile to absorb the shocks of disclosure and recognition that criminality is diffused throughout their legal, administrative, and economic spheres. Or, in societies that are "closed," that guard data on crime as if it were a state secret, scholars understandably are denied access, and must assume that queries regarding the extent and frequency of certain types of criminal behavior constitute serious challenges to the integrity of the state. In other cases, legal authorities and scholars may have uncritically and too readily embraced American Cosa Nostra models of organized crime with the consequence that they are not able to find evidence of monolithic, national criminal conspiracies, and therefore conclude (perhaps disingenuously) that organized crime does not exist in their countries. The fact that Italian-American domination of syndicate criminality is an overheated thesis which leads to the preposterous conslusion that domination and centralization of racketeering activities is in the hands of some twenty-four or so "crime families" made up exclusively of Americans of Sicilian heritage may have escaped the notice of foreign observers. Much of what has been written in the United States (but not all, to be sure) about organized crime is overstatement based on slender evidence; sifting through FBI files and plucking hypotheses from them has led to conclusions that are simplistic, venomous, malicious xenophobic attacks on specific ethnic groups (Block & Chambliss, 1981; Smith, 1975; Schiavo, 1962; Galliher & Cain, 1974).

The fact is that legitimate power has historically surrounded itself with criminal instruments. The political use of gangs as agents provocateurs, as servants of the machinery of repressive power, as labor "mediators" is a fact of the twentieth century in the United States and elsewhere, and was a grim reality well before the spectacle of a Mafia or Cosa Nostra infatuated and frightened the public (Peterson, 1983; Lippmann, 1931). After World War I, these practices acquired more sophisticated and pernicious dimensions. Political parties and trade unions were infiltrated by career criminals and racketeers; thugs were regularly recruited as strike-breakers, or as goons to intimidate businessmen; a subrosa police emerged which functioned as a force capable of controlling and insuring the efficient operation of illicit circuits of profit in prohibited goods and services (Block, 1983; Nelli, 1976; Albini, 1971). During a period in which uprooted urban masses struggled for sheer survival, and in which businesses and industries squirmed under the impacts of a capricious economy stumbling under the effects of war demobilization and rapid growth at the same time, conditions were favorable for organized crime which offered protection and organization for both elements. The underworld did not merely prey; in some measure it also served its victims in innumerable ways by arranging for employment, by securing labor agreements, by influencing police and prosecutors on behalf of young delinquents, by providing the licit and illicit products and services society craves but has from time to time prohibited. These relationships tend to blunt the sharp distinctions between crime and civilized society. When organized crime is viewed in this fashion, it seems very unlikely that some manifestation of it is not present in major urban centers in most countries. In Paris and Marseilles, for example, cities located at the core of the French political economy, with many racial and ethnic groups with a class structure as highly crystallized as that in any industrial society, "Mafias" may be found among the Vietnamese, Algerians, Corsicans, Senegalese migrants, and among the metropolitan native French, catering to vices, and engaging in racketeering enterprises remarkably similar to those in the United States and Canada (Cosson, 1982). These criminal groups may not be as wealthy or as powerful as their counterparts in the United States but structurally they are virtually interchangeable.[5]

The essays in this volume describe situations in which organized crime networks generate wealth and exercise power and influence over segments of the political and law enforcement structures of their societies. In Australia (McCoy, this volume), in Sicily (Hess, this volume), in the Caribbean (Albini, this volume), as well as in the United States, crime networks are known to influence an election, deliver a vote, fund a political candidate, and dabble in union affairs and legitimate businesses. Since these underworlds are not limited to the developed countries but may be found in Third World and in Warsaw Pact nations (Marek, this volume) as well, it cannot be argued that organized crime is merely an outcome of the dynamics of capitalist economies and their politics. Nor can it be claimed that American versions of organized crime have spilled over into neighboring countries, or that its forms have been exported and adopted by criminal groups in other countries. The weight of the evidence suggests that criminal networks or underworlds evolve in response to conditions unique to the political economies of their host societies. However, the sophistication and affluence of national crime networks enables them, in a manner which is unprecedented, to establish links and connections which transcend national boundaries, cultural differences, political ideologies, and different economies.

What criminal networks share in common is a strategy to establish and sustain their activities in the face of opposition. Whether dealing in ivory in Africa, in marijuana in the Caribbean, in portable radios in Poland, in contraband cigarettes in Naples, or in stolen securities and bonds in the United States, each crime network attempts to build a coercive monopoly and to implement that system of control through at least two other criminal activities—corruption of public and private officials, and violent terrorism in order to enforce its discipline.

Some sixty years ago in the United States, the illegal liquor cartels warred with each other as one group moved into the territory of another. Each responded with gunfire and mayhem, and each sought to neutralize police and federal agents through bribery, compromise, and financial support for the political careers and ambitions of compliant public officials. Likewise, in many Latin American countries today, drug cartels and syndicates struggle with each other for control of the manufacturing, processing, and trafficking of heroin and cocaine. Although the drug "Mafias" are content to exercise power from backstage—especially in Florida, the narcotics supermarket for the United States (Lernoux, 1984b)—in other locales such as Colombia and Bolivia, they have not hesitated to bully governments and threaten coups. The various criminal organizations that have emerged to service the insatiable drug appetites of Americans are basically regional in their domestic operations but are international in scope. In some respects, cocaine, heroin, and marijuana are today what illegal liquor was in the twenties. Then, distillers in Canada, Great Britain and elsewhere peddled whisky to criminal groups in the United States (Kobler, 1971; Bonanno, 1983).

There are, however, some important differences in the structure of modern drug trafficking and the context in which it is carried on. Borders and distances have melted away. Cocaine, for example, is cultivated in the fields in Peru, Bolivia, Colombia, and Ecuador. Abetted by corrupt politicians and law enforcement officials, it is then processed in jungle labs and shipped from its refining centers by boat and aircraft to transshipment points in Central America, Mexico, and the Caribbean where it is prepared for movement into Florida, Texas, California, and other Gulf entry points (Lupsha & Schlegel, 1980; Lupsha, 1981; Lernoux, 1984a).

Similarly, the heroin networks in Southeast Asia and in the Mediterranean have developed intricate methods for moving multi-kilo loads with relative impunity across several countries. Elements of the Sicilian Mafia, the Singapore Triads, Indochinese warlords, Calabrians based in southeast Asia and Australia not only ship narcotics but have established themselves as distributors in those countries for which the drugs are destined. In the United States, the dominance of the traditional crime families has been challenged by these drug entrepreneurs. Until fairly recently, it was thought by law enforcement officials in the United States that the crime families left the drug trade to others. They may have financed it, but they let others do the dirty work — blacks, Cubans, Chinese, Mexicans, Colombians, and Puerto Ricans (McCoy, 1980; Meow & Gee, 1978). Now, however, the traditional families and other groups that are emerging in the United States, such as outlaw motorcycle gangs, have moved into drug trafficking themselves. To an extent, they had no choice. The Latin, European, Asian, and Middle Eastern syndicates pose a serious threat: they have the clout and financial resources to operate on their own. The southern Florida economy is fueled by narco-dollars generated by Colombian cocaine dealers and Cuban marijuana smugglers. The Herrera organization which controls the bulk of the heroin trade from Mexico is entrenched in Chicago with its own operatives who arrange distribution in the United States; the reach of the Sicilian mafia and its allies in the Middle East and France extends to Toronto, New York, Detroit, and many major cities in the United States; Triads and Tongs have located themselves in the Chinese communities throughout Western Europe, Canada, and the United States operating drug trafficking syndicates and extortion rackets within the ethnic community (Pileggi, 1982; Bresler, 1980).

The flood of narco-dollars in many comunities in the United States and Western Europe, the main demand centers, has simply overwhelmed law enforcement, compromised many banking institutions, and drastically inflated the real estate markets in many places. The transnational nature of these criminal syndicates and their rationalization of the trade in drugs, with some assuming command of marijuana and others that of the cocaine market, has been accompanied by internecine wars and has also produced cooperation and détente among the criminal protagonists. That, perhaps, is its most sinister threat. Armed with huge amounts of drug money, many of the newly organized crime syndicates have invested in legitimate businesses in order to further insulate themselves from detection and arrest. The "underworld economy" that has emerged from the drug trade has profoundly altered the character of organized crime worldwide. Especially in third world countries that supply narcotics, their political structures and economies, almost without exception, have been twisted by the exponential growth in criminal profits.

So far, in the United States, organized crime's infiltration of legitimate businesses seems to have been limited to small companies and firms — cash businesses where possible — through which money can be hidden and laundered, and where some nominal tax exposure can be generated (Cook, 1980).

But given its enormous cash flow from drug dealing and the ceaseless pressures to find outlets for it beyond the Swiss and off-shore banks, sooner or later it must find its way into large corporations, into businesses on a scale commensurate with that cash flow. In less developed countries in Latin America (Bolivia for instance), drug traffickers ran the government between 1980 and 1982 according to Lernoux (1984b). In Colombia, the leaders of the key cocaine cartels offered to pay off the country's thirteen billion dollar foreign debt in order to avoid extradition to the United States (Whitaker, 1985).

Throughout the rest of this century it is likely that organized crime on a scale inconceivable a decade ago will thrive. And it will become even more difficult to eradicate as it spreads across national boundaries and takes on the characteristics of multinational corporations committed only to themselves and their profits.

The work reported in this volume does not take up the issues of the internationalization of organized criminality directly—that is not the purpose of the individual essays. Rather, each seeks to describe in detail the status of criminal networks and groups, their emergence, activities, composition, and structure within a particular country. Peter Lupsha lays out the history of organized crime in the United States, charting its evolution from small, predatory gangs to large, hierarchically structured underworld businesses and influential élites participating in the political and economic life of the nation's communities. His essay is supplemented by Alan Block's analysis of the interrelationships of organized criminals, law enforcement authorities, and government officials during the height of World War II. In this period, according to Block, the government feared espionage activities on the waterfronts and in the coastal areas of the country and resorted to the expedient of consulting with underworld figures who had expert knowledge and influence among dock workers, especially on the eastern coast. Block offers a concrete example of cooperation between criminals and political figures which is often alluded to in the literature, but rarely documented in the depth he provides.

Canada is closely tied to the United States even in its criminal forms. As in the United States, Tremblay & Kedzior indicate that organized criminality parallels its counterpart; there is a vigorous illegal activity in contraband goods, provision of illicit services such as prostitution and gambling; drug dealing, extortion, and infiltration of legitimate businesses. Moreover, Canadian criminals, organized into crime families in cities like Montreal (which is the focus of the essay), have attempted to expand their operations into the United States. The considerable profits earned in drug trafficking are finding their way into real estate and business ventures outside the country.

In the first part of Joseph Albini's article on organized crime in Great Britain and the Caribbean, he notes that in England there are no criminal syndicates of the size and scope of those in the United States. The reasons for this are mainly economic. Great Britain's legislators and law enforcement officials have recognized the public demand for certain goods and services (gambling and drugs) in a highly administered manner which has taken the market away from criminal organizations that would have developed to fill the gap. Criminals in Great Britain tend to work in small groups but, nonetheless, maintain extensive networks of contacts through which they can procure wider services. Whether tendencies towards centralization and expansion are likely to develop seems likely to depend upon a combination of determinants that apply not only to criminal activity but to upperworld economic enterprises as well. As in the United States, small-scale criminal activity appears (like many small-scale businesses) preponderantly in environments in which there exists a high degree of uncertainty. To the extent that law enforcement activities could be influenced in the United States through corruption and bribery, rackets expanded; on the other hand, in criminal activities entailing more risks from the law, the police, and other criminal competitors, criminals choose to work in scaled down operations so that they can respond flexibly to changes as they occur. In contrast to the situation in Great Britain, the Ras Boys syndicate in the Caribbean has deep links and connections with the political system and law enforcement agencies. It is, thus, well organized, not very secretive about its illicit activities, and operates with little concern about police interventions. Here the risks are minimal and the monopolistic character of the Ras Boys is evident. Albini, Block, and Lupsha show that to the degree that law enforcement can be neutralized, crime can be organized and operated like a business; and it depends, perhaps, in a way that is unique to criminal activity, upon establishing relations with noncriminal sectors of the society over time. In this sense, organized criminals are hardly different from legitimate businessmen with whom relationships are developed.

Relations with clients, with important sections of the ruling elites and their law enforcement agencies are constructed subtly and patiently over time and become an integral part of the political and economic system of Sicilian society, according to Henner Hess. Mafiosi are not a residue of a state of lawlessness; they are not bandits and outlaws; Mafia groups are not outside the mainstream of social life living on its margins; rather they belong to, and often occupy, prominent positions in a reliable, protective and successful chain of patron-client relationships. They are above the law, the codified law, and conform to subcultural norms. The Mafiosi emerge in Sicily not in criminal acts alone — although they are not above violence and predatory crime. It is in the transition of the society from feudal structures into modern bureaucratic forms where the state has failed to exploit and legitimate its power and authority over all sectors of society that the Mafia emerges to fill the gaps.

In their roles as mediators between economic elites and oppressed workers, Mafiosi resemble local party bosses operating the urban political machines which for votes and support return favors and provide a range of services that the large municipal and state governments are incapable of performing. But the Mafioso is more than that: he manipulates the economic dynamics of his locale, deriving an income for his services. The willingness to use violence or the threat of violence to insure the success of his enterprises, whether these are purely economic or political, is the distinguishing characteristic of the Mafia phenomenon. Another point Hess makes, and it is an important observation in demystifying the Mafia, is that there has never been a centralized criminal organization called the "Mafia." Networks of Mafiosi, factions either loosely or tightly structured, whose cohesion is dependent largely upon kinship and commonality of parochial interests, constitute the phenomenon of the Mafia.

The apparatus of criminal gangs with inducted members, some discernible division of labor, and a hierarchical pattern of authority is characteristic of the Neopolitan Camorra rather than the Mafia as it has evolved in Sicily. According to Walston, Camorra, composed of the poor, is a distinctly urban entity that is parasitic upon all classes. More than Mafia, Camorra parallels organized criminal groups in the United States as they are currently structured. Its relations with formal governmental agencies are reciprocally exploitative. For political protection it provides electoral support — not unlike criminal networks in the United States, Australia, Japan, Canada, and Israel.

Andrzej Marek's essay is of special interest because it gives us a glimpse of organized criminality in a society that, under ordinary circumstances, does not permit data to be collected and analyzed, much less widely distributed on existing crime conditions. What has appeared over the years about crime in the Soviet Bloc nations are impressionistic, anecdotal accounts usually written by embittered defectors and emigrés forced out of their countries because of their political allegiances and treacheries. Marek's work gives us a peek, one which is long overdue, into the eastern European nations within the political orbit of the USSR.

Marek tells us that the study of organized criminality is hampered by several actors in Poland. For one, the government does not encourage scholars; secondly, the insulation of the Polish social scientific community from contact with colleagues in the West and elsewhere has meant that they possess only fragmentary and hazy notions of "organized crime" as the term is understood and applied in Western scientific writing. The effort at criminological analysis has, therefore, been on those individuals involved in the misappropriation of government and private property who are employed in state-owned enterprises. Clearly, a black market thrives in Poland in conjunction with fairly sophisticated smuggling rings in currency and valuable goods — that is, items which are scarce such as clothes, television sets, auto parts, and the like. Ironically, the reluctance of the government to support vigorous efforts to study the problems has produced a lack of reliable quantitative data so that policies designed to curb such activity tend to be inadequate. Further, what studies do exist suggest that the nexus of the numerous and extensive black markets and smuggling organizations lies in government agencies. Unlike many kindred criminal enterprises in the West where such individuals operate outside the government, in Poland (and it is reasonable to believe in other Eastern societies as well), they inhabit key roles in state bureaucracies.

In their official capacities, these criminal entrepreneurs are able to success-fully mask widespread stealing through bribery and the manipulation of offi-cial records. Marek aptly refers to them as "white-collar gangsters."

Menachem Amir's study of the Georgian Jews in Israel may represent a test case of what is known as the "ethnic succession theory" in organized crime. Briefly, the argument holds that, among other things, organized crime may be understood as a social mobility mechanism used by oppressed, impov-erished, newcomers to a society as a way out of the slums and the oblivion of a cruel and grinding life of discrimination and rejection. The evidence for the theory's confirmation in the United States is strong. The Irish and the Jews are perhaps the best examples of the process working in the United States. Systematic research has been fragmentary (Ianni and Reuss-Ianni, 1973). What has raised the issues in the theory to the level of acrimonious argument have been government studies which suggest the permanence and uniqueness of Italian-American participation and dominance in criminal syndicates in the United States.

It appears that the Irish were the first major immigrant group to enter into organized criminality in large numbers. As they succeeded, they acquired wealth and political power which provided respectability, prestige and entry into legitimate businesses and occupations. Then the Jewish immigrants moved into organized crime, and like the Irish, began to move out of it as they achieved more legitimate means of attaining economic and social mobil-ity. The Italians, in turn, had just begun their movement out of organized crime when government investigations and hearings were mounted to study the problem. Unfortunately, the conclusions emerging from the Kefauver Hearings and others indicated that Italian-Americans dominated the rackets and criminal syndicates in the country. The association of organized crime and Italian-American involvement and control became fixed in the popular and official view of the problem. An historical accident has resulted in what amounts to an ineradicable blemish on the reputations of millions of Ameri-cans of Italian heritage and ethnicity. The really valuable opportunity the theory of ethnic succession affords for social policy as to the causes of partic-ipation in criminal behavior among migrant groups and among the poor has been lost in the furor and recriminations of the public discussion.

Amir's discussion of the plight of the Georgian Jews in Israeli society sug-gests that they are perceived in large measure as an outcast group unwilling or unable to adjust to Israeli culture and the institutional structure of the soci-ety. Consequently, many drift into a life of crime and are abetted in these ac-tivities by family members and relatives who themselves exist marginally in the cracks and seams of Israeli political and economic life which, with its high levels of inflation, scarcities, and corruption, stimulates the perpetuation of black markets in consumer goods and the formation of criminal syndicates catering to public demands for goods and services. Conditions are, therefore, ripe for criminal careers which inhibit the assimilation of the Georgian Jews into the mainstream of Israeli society. The implication of Amir's ethnography of the Georgian Jews for Israeli criminal justice policy and for societies in general with significant groups of immigrants and urban poor is clear. More importantly for our purposes, Amir's study belies the widespread belief that organized crime is based on a general conspiracy. Rather it shows the relationships between ethnicity and organized crime; it reveals the dilemma ethnic groups not fully acculurated into their host society face: how does one gain acceptance and approval when the traditional routes to these desired goals are either closed off or sharply circumscribed by cultural values within the ethnic group? Crime is a way out but it is one enveloped in risks and high personal costs.

In several African countries, organized crime is in its incipient stages of development and refinement. Tribal divisions, traditional ethnic hostilities, poorly defined national boundaries, and state-formation processes have spawned the rise of predatory gangs that smuggle, steal, and extort from local villages and towns in tribal zones. They constitute a machine of "law and order" which serve in many instances as substitutes for the State.

Many of these groups in the rural sectors of the countryside operate as "Mafias" not unlike the sects and gangs that developed in Vietnam during the period of colonization by the French (McLane, 1971). With the increasing decay of village and tribal life, people are set in motion, their lives lose the symbolic consistency provided by custom which preserves meanings and structures events. In short, the social system verges on collapse. The gangs that prowl the countryside arise in times of crisis and transition as in the nineteenth-century "wild west" of the United States which experienced much the same thing: organized bands of outlaws raiding, stealing, and controlling pioneers and settlers through fear and intimidation. In many places in Africa, the "frontier" is equally precarious as gangs subjugate and exploit the peasants through direct terror and violence. Developing African states that have consciously created their programs of growth on Western models constitute a recapitulation of history—a scarred and painful history of struggle and disorder. On the other hand, in the more developed sectors of the economies, as Opolot describes it, a set of criminal conditions exist which again are reminiscent of Western development patterns: here we see the collusions among officials, workers, criminals (often interchangeable in their respective roles) and consumers to subvert the formal systems of taxation, distribution, and control over the political economy.

With the Yakuza, Hiroaki Iwai exposes us to "mizu shobei"—that side of Japanese life in which crime, show-business, prostitution, and high-stakes gambling rub together. But we also glimpse aspects of Japanese life other than the activities of criminals. The clue to understanding the elusive but nevertheless formidable Yakuza organized criminal groups lies in Japanese culture itself. Historically, organized criminals in Japan have not been seen as misunderstood or deprived individuals, nor have they been viewed as the products of broken homes left to shuffle for themselves but as monsters who reject the social rules and obligations and as individualists in a society that has tended to suppress individualism since the period in which the Shoguns clamped on the country one of the world's most pervasive police states.

For the Japanese in general, the Yakuza, the "Boryokudan" ("the organizations or gangs which habitually commit violent illegal actions") are the crux of the crime problem (Takahashi & Becker, 1984). The gangs and organizations are composed of the deviants of Japanese life: the dropouts, the failures, and those who cannot or will not accommodate the pressures of a highly competitive and culturally structured lifestyle. Despite the negative societal reactions against members of the Yakuza, they persist and even thrive because of several factors. First, is the history of vice in Japan. For centuries, gambling and prostitution flourished and prospered under government protection and patronage and only in the last twenty-five years were they declared illegal. Hence, there is much ambivalence in Japan about the strong sanctions against activities that were formerly permitted, a situation similar to the passage of the Volstead Act in the United States.

Second, connected to the recent trends towards prohibition of certain social activities, there emerged in Japan in the course of its history outcaste groups which formed societies that proved useful to leaders in the legitimate sectors of the society. They naturally developed power and prestige over time and established strong connections with government officials, businessmen and legislators. Much like Mafia cosche, Yakuza performed indispensable services for incumbent leaders in government and have consequently enjoyed some protection in an environment that is largely but not exclusively at the illegitimate end of the spectrum of economic activity.

Third, and perhaps most importantly, intermingled with the stern and pitiless pressures to conform in this highly competitive society is the concept of "Wa" (harmony), an integral part of the Japanese cultural temperament. The ramifications of the concept for the persistence of the Yakuza in the light of strict laws and strong social sanctions may be understood in terms of how it relates the individual to the group with which he identifies. The basic social unit in Japan has been neither the individual nor the family, but the village-like group who work together. This can be anything from an organized criminal network to the engineering department in one of the large automotive firms. Commitment will be two-way: member to group and vice versa. Loyalty is based on it, and those outside the reference group may be treated with hostility. It is "Wa" that lubricates social interactions among different groups; harmony enables a society of infinitely diverse groups to tolerate each other and to cooperate with each other while acknowledging tacitly that their interests are not identical, and, in fact, often conflict. Thus, judiciously applied, among those Japanese who have been excluded or rebuffed by legitimate society as incompetents and failures and who embrace the Yakuza way of life, they make intense identifications with it, but at the same time are able to put aside their abiding hatreds of the society that has rejected them in order to exploit it and provide for its illicit needs. The cultural scheme produces a society that is composed of many socially atomized groups that are tenaciously united but very flexible in dealing with each other. Yakuza are consequently tolerated informally, at least.

Alfred McCoy concludes his essay on organized crime in Australia with the observation that what has happened there may very well portend a global integration of criminal syndicates. He points out that what has occurred in the large cities of Australia, particularly in Sydney, may be indicative of trends throughout most of the megalopolises in the world. Political and economic conditions throughout most of the twentieth century have combined to create conditions ideal for organized criminal activity. The tendency towards the systematic suppression of vices that were tolerated throughout much of the nineteeth century mainly in Western governments (although there is evidence that the same practices of prohibition and abstinence have been implemented in Eastern bloc and Asian societies as well) has not abolished them, to be sure. Prohibition and delegalization of alcohol, gambling, narcotics, and prostitution have in many instances transferred their production, distribution and control to vice overlords with the will and skill to sustain them. Subsequent to the gang wars for control over these illicit goods and services, surviving groups have sought to impose syndicate structures on the underworld through which the scope of organized-crime activities could be widened and expanded. This trend has been exacerbated through the exploitation of contacts with foreign criminal organizations and through the corruption of law enforcement officials and political leaders with the enormous profits centralization of criminal activities produces.

Large profits and cash enable syndicates to develop the means by which to insulate themselves from interdiction, disruption, and dissolution. Moreover, available capital assets provide opportunities for diversification into other criminal and non-criminal enterprises. Stimulated by the drug trade, organized crime in Australia has spread considerably. Likewise in the United States, Canada, and Western Europe, police and law enforcement methods in general, designed to cope with and eliminate organized criminal acivity, provide opportunities for the corruption of the law enforcers by the violators. With unemployment in Western capitalist societies especially prevalent among the young, the attractions of drugs and their easy availability can only strengthen rather than weaken organized crime.

"Il fenomeno Mafioso" is a chilling phrase that makes organized crime appear to be nothing less than a force of nature. The Sicilian Mafias originated in the rural, oppressed regions of southern Italy, and the form and structure has been identified in other regions of the world, so that indigenous "Mafias" have sprung to life in countries and states where the processes of economic development and modernization have produced socially and culturally chaotic conditions for sizeable segments of the population.[6]

However, while "Mafias" may provide the cultural prerequisites for the evolution of a full-blown underworld, hostility and suspicion towards the police and political authority in general, and the rule of silence, at least three other conditions must emerge to sustain a large group of professional criminals that can be integrated into syndicates situated in a mature criminal milieu: the expansion of the economy; the criminalization of some of its products; and improvements in the technological base of the society which contribute to the efficient organization of criminal enterprises. Together, these conditions enable criminals to exploit the commercial opportunities created by restrictive and prohibitive local or national policies, and they facilitate the consolidation of industries in illicit goods and services (as well as the provision of licit goods and services through illegal means). Further refinements in the operations of the illegal sector may eventuate in the rationalization of criminal activities with a division of labor among and within criminal enterprises. This may take the form of illegal product specialization (drug trafficking, illegal liquor, numbers, gambling, and so on) or mediation and brokerage activities with law enforcement (corruption, bribery), accompanied by the penetration into legitimate environments in the upperworld through racketeering and extortion activities.

The dynamics of growth and development within an underworld are rife with violence — gang wars, assassinations, and episodes of open warfare with law enforcement. Violence, murder, and mayhem represent perhaps a failure to bring about conditions favorable to the stabilization of syndicate operations. Contrary to popular belief, violence as a means of conflict resolution is a costly and least desirable method for the achievement of deviant objectives.

In all of the countries and societies surveyed in these essays, potential or actual violence is a crucial ingredient in the criminal process. Other factors which are critical to the emergence of organized crime are not present to the same degree and have produced variations and differences in the types of criminality which are identified as "organized." However, in African states, in the Caribbean, in regions of Italy, and in more affluent countries with uneven economic prosperity which produces scarcities in goods and periods of high inflation and unemployment, impoverished slum dwellers and the rural poor see crime as an economic necessity. In other states such as Poland, Israel, and Canada with a somewhat more equitable distribution of desired goods and services but with strong prohibition policies, anti-law enforcement sentiments develop and crime proliferates. And in Japan, the United States, and Australia, all of these requirements appear to converge along with a law enforcement establishment incapable of checking the spread of organized crime.

The conditions favoring the development and growth of petty criminality into organized crime may seem universal and endemic to societies grappling with the problem. Further, conditions on the international level — especially in the enormously lucrative drug markets — favor the elaboration of transnational criminal conspiracies and syndicates. Conflict and struggle among national criminal syndicates to gain control of international markets may result in criminal coalitions, alliances and pacts among them. With law enforcement efforts on the international level still in nascent stages of cooperation, the prospects for effective control seem remote. The most effective forms of control are, paradoxically, not increases in the vigilance of, and cooperation of, national police forces but internal interventions into the matrix of forces that produce the poverty, corruption, alienation, and antagonism that are the breeding grounds of organized crime worldwide. The technological improvements in fast, international travel; the migrations of millions of people from different parts of the world to the more affluent countries in the West; and the rise in the criminalization of desired goods and services in many states have created conditions in which criminal groups, formerly limited in scope to their own countries, are looking for opportunities in other parts of the world. In New York, Los Angeles, Jerusalem, Tokyo, Montreal, London, Paris, Warsaw and in other major metropolitan centers, previously isolated and sometimes racially and ethnically hostile criminal groups are operating in confederations with each other or have settled into détentes, putting aside their grievances for the sake of profits.

Unless and until economic and social improvements can be engineered so that most groups are reconnected to their communities and feel that their lives can be enhanced by participation in the legitimate structure of their societies, organized criminality will persist even if law enforcement efforts at the international level achieve some degree of sophistication in crime control.

Notes

1. Actually, both positions are right — and both are wrong. If the term, "organized crime" is merely a stipulative definition, a convention or an agreemeent to use it in a particular, unvarying way, then it is a term that has no other meaning than that given arbitrarily to it, and as such it is neither true nor false. In these circumstances, if "organized crime" is a *nominal definition* then there can be no question that the adoption of a precise notion at the initiation of research is desirable in order to outline and delimit research work. On the other hand, if "organized crime" is thought of as a *real definition,* a term with empirical referents in the world that are verifiable, then it is necessary to rely upon investigation in order to determine whether or not the properties the definition ascribes to the concept actually do belong to it; whether, in short, the definition is true or false. It is a mistake to assume about an historical phenomenon such as organized crime that it possesses structural durabilities that are unaffected by time, by accident, and by particular social and political contingencies. Organized crime in the 1930s is hardly comparable to criminal firms operating in the 1980s. The findings of the Kefauver Committee of the 1950s, for example, on the extent of syndicate national operations in illicit goods and services ought to be thought of as descriptions and characterizations of groups and their structures that were the outcome of specific influences of time and place. To formulate a perspective or a research program on premises and concepts that emerged from investigations conducted thirty years ago is bound to produce ineffectual control policies and research findings that bear little resemblance to the realities of contemporary forms of organized crime.

Finally, there is another aspect of the elusive and fugitive notion of organized crime which deserves mention. Different and sometimes conflicting views as to the nature of organized crime, its structure and function, may stem in no small measure from the fact that not only are data neither fixed nor stable for all observers and analysts, but that disagreements among experts may arise in part because they are exposed to different sets of data. Research has shown that experts (i.e. law enforcement specialists at local and national levels, journalists, and social scientists) located in different professional settings do not always share equal access to data nor do they conduct their work on similar data bases (Kelly, 1978). Since the Kefauver hearings and the President's Task Force (1967) when organized crime as a major criminal problem in the United States was recognized and characterized as mainly an alien conspiracy dominated by Sicilian Mafiosi, our thinking about it is deeply ingrained with imagery of ethnics and foreigners. This had led some researchers (Haller, 1975) to abandon the term organized crime in favor of more neutral notions such as "illegal enterprises."

Despite the prejudicial and pejorative connotations surrounding the term organized crime and the circumscribed meanings attributed to it by official governmental investigative bodies, it may be retained and broadened to encompass dynamics of illegal activity that modern research has uncovered. One recent definition that has appeared seems concise enough and comprehensive enough to work as a useful explanation of what organized crime is about. According to Block and Scarpitti (1985), quoting Smith, organized crime, "should be viewed as 'the extension of legitimate market activities into areas normally proscribed for the pursuit of profit and in response to latent illicit demand.' As a result, organized crime has now come to be thought of as a series of mutually beneficial relationships among professional criminals, upper-world clients and politicians." (1985:64)

Many writers on organized crime have lamented the fact that no precise widely-agreed upon definition of organized crime exists either in the popular, academic or official literature. In a well-received recent book, it is noted that "[L]egislation to deal with organized crime, even including the major federal act with the title, Organized Crime Control Act, fails to provide any clear definition." (Reuter, 1983:175) Other prominent writers in the field similarly regard the problem of definition as a serious flaw in research programs and in policy efforts to curb organized crime (Cressey, 1967b; Ianni, 1973; Albini, 1971; Nelli, 1976; Block and Chambliss, 1981; Smith 1975). Indeed, it is maintained that it is important and necessary to have clearly articulated definitions of concepts so that we may know what we are talking about. But the issue which seems so fundamental and basic is more complex than it appears. Do we adopt an operational definition of organized crime in which the meaning of the concept would always be closely associated with the procedures employed in investigating the phenomenon, and in which controversies over meanings would thereby be avoided and research progress accordingly enhanced? Or, on the contrary, is it more advantageous to allow a definition to emerge as one of the results and consequences of inquiry? Perhaps a clear and accurate definition of organized crime can neither be given nor constructed at the beginning of research; that in scientific procedures it is not always desirable to have exact definitions because they have a dampening effect on research by closing off other lines of inquiry. It is unrealistic, therefore, to insist that the term, "organized crime," be clear and precise at the beginning of the research process. A definiton that is increasingly accurate and concrete will flow out of research through successive approximations and empirical confirmations.

2. These extraordinary displays of respect (and curiosity) suggest not only a grotesquely garish sense of mourning but also that many underworld bosses have nimbly and deftly insulated and shielded themselves from the police, and have precipitated in the public more embarrassment and awe than rancorous anger and disillusionment with such spectacles. More importantly, the veil is lifted on the intimate linkages among those in the under- and upperworlds. What is revealed to some extent by these events is the nature of the arrangements successful underworld barons must necessarily forge with law enforcement, with a compromised political apparatus, and a flinching, legitimate business community.

3. American scholars are being weaned away from alien conspiracy theories and the Capone-type gangster imagery which enthralled them for so long. However, the legacy of that orientation still persists somewhat. Structural-functional models of organized crime with their blend of corporate business analogies and foreign, mafia-based origins that emerged in the 1950s and 1960s in the United States may have few if any identifiable parallels in other societies. Thus, denials that "organized crime" in the American sense of that term is not a factor in the crime scene in many countries may be true and may not be an evasion or a subterfuge to avoid embarrassment at the prospect that little is being done to eradicate it or study it closely. Further, the connotations of American studies, both official and scholarly, may have seriously thwarted comparative research efforts and international cooperation among scholars. To be charitable to those countries whose official policies have precluded the admission of the existence of organized criminality, there is some recognition that criminal underworlds exist and perhaps thrive. Contemporary efforts by American scholars to substitute other terms for "organized crime" with its Cosa Nostra image, such as "criminal firm" and "illicit enterprise," may merely deepen the confusion. "Un-

derworld" by comparison is a term that seems clear to most criminologists in Europe, Asia, and Latin America; it is a term with a coherent meaning that suggests distinctive organizational patterns of criminal behavior that go beyond references to bandit groups, outlaws, and cliques of professional criminals. The term "underworld" refers to criminals tightly or loosely organized — that operate parasitically by preying on the social system in which they are entrenched through extortion, racketeering, corruption and controlling black markets that provide legal and illegal goods and services.

Not only is "underworld" an apt way of characterizing American types of criminality which preceded the Italian-American dominance of the 1940s and 1950s, but it also opens up the possibility of research and analysis in other societies. The work of Hobsbawm (1959), McIntosh (1975), Walston (this volume), and Arlacchi and Schneider (1985) suggest that the rise and perpetuation of criminal underworlds, in Europe at least, can be studied in conjunction with state formation processes and modernization trends.

4. In one of the few studies of public opinion about the prevalence and nature of organized crime that touch upon questions concerning public impressions and reactions, the Illinois survey commissioned by the Chicago Crime Commission found that organized crime persists in Illinois because it meets the needs of the citizens, and because the public at large believes that a complex system of corruption involving police, public officials, politicians, and racketeers continues. In the Household Survey part of the study, more than 60% of those interviewed throughout the state thought that organized crime has corrupted law enforcement officials and local politicians in order to operate its various enterprises. (ITT Research Institute & Chicago Crime Commission, 1971).

5. In her detailed but controversial study of a "crime family" in the United States, Anderson concluded that the enormous wealth attributed to membership in such an organization is largely a myth. Some few individuals do acquire sizeable fortunes — and these are not always the men reputedly at the top of the organization. For most, however, modest incomes and a great deal of fretting over unpaid bills seem to be their destiny (Anderson, 1979). A personal memoir published by an alleged former member of the New England crime family of Raymond Patriarca says much the same: there are some imaginative individuals who are "money makers" and there are the rest, no matter their rank or prestige in the organization, who barely survive on small-scale scams and extortion rackets (Teresa and Renner, 1973).

6. Mafia, or, in the United States its hybrid criminal cousin, La Cosa Nostra, has served as a convenient explanatory *deus ex machina* for an understanding of crime, drugs, corruption and a host of problems afflicting society. Its mystiques of "omerta" (silence), unquestioned loyalty and fealty to one's "family" (criminal association) are awesome. Yet, no matter how grotesque the actual activities and attitudes of such criminals may be, depictions of mafiosi have taken on epic qualities that tend to glorify them in an unseemly way. For one reason or another, there seems to be an unwillingness to confront the masks of the Mafia that have concealed it or that have been imposed on it. For the members of the Cosa Nostra (assuming such a clandestine organization exists) and the Mafias of Italy, the notoriety of the "friends of the friends," as it is referred to in native Sicily, becomes a valuable publicity asset in the criminal worlds of the United States and elsewhere.

As Reuter (1983) points out, through their intense preoccupation with the Mafia or La Cosa Nostra, the police and the press enhance their reputation as far-reaching organizations that are all-powerful. The death of an alleged, prominent Mafioso triggers in-depth press and TV coverage along with titillating speculations as to the ensuing power struggle likely to erupt. By comparison, other criminals who may be as sinister remain utterly obscure. But this may be an advantage for the latter who lack the celebrity and public image.

The liability of a reputation and high public profile is that law enforcement activity will tend to concentrate its efforts in the direction of those groups with whom the public has identified as the arch enemy of law and order. Within the criminal underworlds themselves, the Mafia is perceived with some ambivalence. Some individal members ("made men") are held in contempt for their lack of toughness and deviant competence. However, overall the consensus is that Cosa Nostra commands unique resources and for that reason alone deserves respect. The durability of the Cosa Nostra and the Mafia accrues to their reputations as stable, on-going enterprises. Where other ethnically homogeneous criminal groups have come and gone, the mafia continues despite intense pressures to eliminate it. Being identified as a Mafioso provides a comparative advantage for one in the underworld. In general, to be Mafioso insures prestige, however tainted.

References

Albini, Joseph L. (1976) "Public and Personal Reactions to the Questioning of the Mafia Myth" Paper presented to the American Sociological Association, New York.

_____ (1971) *The American Mafia: Genesis of a Legend*. NY: Appelton-Century-Crofts.

Anderson, Annelise (1979) *The Business of Organized Crime*. Stanford: Hoover Institute Press.

Arlacchi, Pino and Peter Schneider (April, 1985) "Urbanization, Modernization and Transformations of Rural Mafias." Ph.D. colloquium on the Mafia and Organized Crime in Europe. Graduate School, City University of New York.

Block, Alan A. (1983) *Eastside-Westside: Organizing Crime in New York, 1930-1950*. New Brunswick: Transaction Books.

Block, Alan A. and William Chambliss (1981) *Organizing Crime*. Elsevier, North Holland Science Publishers.

Block, Alan A. and Frank Scarpitti (1985) *Poisoning For Profit: The Mafia and Toxic Waste in America*. New York: William Morrow.

Blok, Anton (1974) *The Mafia of a Sicilian Village: A Study in Violent Peasant Entrepreneurs*. NY: Harper & Row Publishers.

Bonanno, Joseph [with S. Lalli] (1983) *A Man of Honor: The Autobiography of Joseph Bonanno*. New York: Simon & Schuster.

Bresler, Fenton (1980) *The Chinese Mafia*. New York: Stein & Day.

Chambliss, William (1975) "On the Paucity of Original Research on Organized Crime: A Footnote to Galliher and Cain." *The American Sociologist* 10:36–39.

Cook, James (1980) "The Invisible Empire: Part 2" *Forbes* 126, No. 8.

Cosson, Jean (1982) "The Collusion of White-Collar and Organized Crime." Private communication.

Cressey, Donald (1967a) "The Functions and Structure of Criminal Syndicates" Appendix A., Task Force on Organized Crime, *The President's Commission on Law Enforcement and Administration of Justice*. Washington, D.C.: Government Printing Office.

_____ (1967b) "Methodological Problems in the Study of Organized Crime as a Social Problem" *The Annals of the American Academy of Political and Social Science*. Vol. 374.

Galliher, John F. & James A. Cain (1974) "Citation Support for the Mafia Myth in Criminology Textbooks." *The American Sociologist* 8:68–74.

Haller, Mark H. (1975) "The Rise of Criminal Syndicates." Paper read at the Columbia University Seminar on the City.

Hobsbawn, E. J. (1959) *Primitive Rebels: Studies in Archaic Forms of Social Movements in the 19th & 20th Centuries*. New York: W.W. Norton.

Ianni, Francis A. J. (1973). *Ethnic Succession in Organized Crime: Summary Report*. U.S. Dept. of Justice, Law Enforcement Assistance Administration, National Institute of Law Enforcement and Criminal Justice. Washington, D.C.: U.S. Government Printing Office.

Ianni, Francis A. J. and E. Reuss-Ianni (1973) *A Family Business: Kinship and Social Control in Organized Crime* New York: Mentor Books.

ITT Research Institute & The Chicago Crime Commission (1971) *A Study of Organized Crime in Illinois*, Illinois Law Enforcement Commission.

Kelly, Robert J. (1982) "Field Research Among Deviants: A Consideration of Some Methodological Recommendations" *Deviant Behavior* Vol. 3, No. 2

_____ (1978) "Organized Crime: A Study in the Production of Knowledge by Law Enforcement Specialists" (unpublished Ph.D. dissertation, City University of New York.)

Kobler, John (1971) *Capone: The Life and World of Al Capone*. Greenwich: Fawcett Crest Books.

Lernoux, Penny (1984a) *In Banks We Trust* Garden City: Doubleday, Anchor.

_____ (1984b) "Trying to Uproot the Drug Trade," *Newsday* September 30.

Lippmann, Walter (1931) "The Underworld as Servant." *Forum* (January/February)

Lupsha, Peter (1981) "Drug Trafficking: Mexico and Colombia in Comparative Perspective." *Journal of International Affairs* Vol. 35, No. 1 (Spring/Summer)

Lupsha, Peter & Kip Schlegel (1980) "The Political Economy of Drug Trafficking: The Herrera Organization (Mexico and the United States). Working Paper #2, The Latin American Institute, University of New Mexico.

Maltz, Michael D. (1976) "On Defining 'Organized Crime'." *Crime & Delinquency*. Vol. 22, No. 3 (July) pp. 338–346.

McCoy, Alfred W. (1980) *Drug Traffic: Narcotics and Organized Crime in Australia*. New York: Harper & Row, Publishers.

McIntosh, Mary (1975) "New Directions in the Study of Criminal Organization." H. Bianchi, M. Simondi, & I. Taylor, eds. *Deviance and Social Control in European Group for the Study of Deviance & Social Control*. London: John Wiley & Sons.

McLane, John R. (1971) "Archaic Movements and Revolution in South Vietnam" N. Miller & R. Aya, eds. *National Liberation: Revolution in the Third World*. New York: Free Press.

Meow, Seah and Ag Gee (1978) "Secret Societies Today." *Singapore Police Life Annual*.

Nelli, Humbert, S. (1976) *The Business of Crime: Italians and Syndicate Crime in the United States*. New York: Oxford University Press.

Panteleone, Michele (1966) *The Mafia and Politics: The Definitive History of the Mafia*. New York: Coward, McCann.

Peterson, Virgil (1983) *The Mob: 200 Years of Organized Crime in New York*. Ottawa: Green Hill Publishers.

Pileggi, Nicholas (1982) "There's No Business Like the Drug Business." *New York Magazine* (December)

President's Commission on Law Enforcement and Administration of Justice (1967). *The Challenge of Crime in a Free Society*. Washington, D.C.: Government Printing Office.

Reuter, Peter (1983) *Disorganized Crime: The Economics of the Visible Hand*. Cambridge: The MIT Press.

Salerno, Ralph and John Tompkins (1969) *The Crime Confederation: Cosa Nostra and Allied Operations in Organized Crime*. New York: Popular Library.

Schiavo, Giovanni (1962) *The Truth About the Mafia and Organized Crime in America*. New York: The Vigo Press.

Smith, Dwight (1975) *The Mafia Mystique*. New York: Basic Books.

Teresa, Vincent and Thomas Renner (1973) *My Life in the Mafia*. Garden City: Doubleday Books.

Takahashi, Sadahiko and Carl Becker (1984) "Organized Crime in Japan." *The Law Review of Kin-ki University,* Vol. XXXII, No. 1 (August).

Whitaker, M. et. al. (1985) "The Evil Empire: Special Report" *Newsweek* February 25.

3

Organized Crime in the United States

Peter A. Lupsha
University of New Mexico

"The spirit of graft and lawlessness is the American spirit."
— Lincoln Steffens, *Shame of the Cities*

Organized crime in the United States of America is a topic much abused in the literature, both popular and academic. It is also subject to sensationalism, exaggeration, myth, romance, and falsehood, in addition to numerous attempts at factual reporting, empirical and theoretical analysis. Unfortunately, the attention to organized crime has often been myopic and monocular, focusing narrowly on Italian-American crime groups, referred to as the Mafia or La Cosa Nostra, when in fact organized crime is a process which can occur within any ethnic group or social system.

This chapter will examine the history and evolution of organized crime in the USA and examine both its operations and enterprises, as well as the concepts and frameworks that have been brought to the study of this phenomenon. There can be little doubt that organized crime represents one of the more paradoxical, yet critical problems facing complex societies in the last decades of the twentieth century. Its direct and indirect impact on citizens, its corrosive influence on government, and its insidious corruption of values threatens the quality of life, liberty, and choice of all Americans. Its transnational impact, especially on Third World nation-states, their people, and economies is a subject deserving global attention.

Organized Crime: A Conceptual Overview

Commentators and analysts place different dates on the beginnings of organized crime in America. Virgil Peterson finds it in the origin of Tammany Hall in the early nineteenth century (Peterson 1983). Others cite Prohibition as the fountainhead marking the emergence of organized crime as we know it. Still others assign some specific date, event, person or group, to mark and pinpoint its beginnings.

My perspective is that organized crime is a process — an activity possessing certain attributes and characteristics. As such it cannot be identified with any single temporal starting point.

From this perspective the key conceptual attributes of organized crime are:

— Ongoing interaction by a group of individuals over time.
— Patterns in that interaction: role, status, and specialization.
— Patterns of corruption of public officials, their agents, and individuals in private positions of trust.
— The use or threat of use of violence.
— A lifetime careerist orientation among the participants.
— A view of criminal activity as instrumental, rather than an end in itself.
— Goal direction toward the long term accumulation of capital, influence, power, and untaxed wealth.
— Patterns of complex criminal activity involving long term planning, and multiple levels of execution and organization.
— Patterns of operation that are interjurisdictional, often international in scope.
— Use of fronts, buffers, and "legitimate" associates.
— Active attempts at the insulation of key members from risks of identification, involvement, arrest and prosecution.
— Maximization of profits through attempts at cartelization or monopolization of markets, enterprises and crime matrices.

By looking for constellations of these attributes in criminal endeavors, one can trace organized crime to the very beginnings of this nation and its colonial period. Thus organized crime, as Lincoln Steffens suggests, is indeed as American as apple pie. It is rooted in our value system, freedom, and the inventiveness of the human spirit in attempting to maximize profits while seeking to minimize risks of sanction.

One hallmark of organized crime, compared with other types of criminal activity, is that it not only seeks to exploit market disparities, such as supply-demand inequities caused by government decision, over- or underregulation, but that it cannot exist without active interaction with the political system, its agents and institutions. For organized crime to prosper, it needs close ties to the body politic. Without the protection and risk minimization of the political system, the organized criminal cannot operate. Such a symbiotic relationship exists in many areas of the United States, as well as in economic and political systems quite alien to the USA. As has been pointed out by several authors, prior to Prohibition organized crime tended to exist in a subservient position to the politician and political machine. The capital and influence accumulation of that era often served to reverse this balance. (Hammer 1975, 87; Peterson 1983, 426–29). Prohibition also contributed to the expansion of organized crime into legitimate sectors of our society, as well as giving it a legitimacy of its own in our popular culture.

It is important to underscore the fact that no attributes cite ethnicity as a relevant conceptual variable. This is because organized crime can be found in every ethnic group, and thus a statement about it is of little use in understanding this phenomenon as process. What one can note about ethnicity is that like family or blood tie, it is a useful trust variable. If a group all speaks the same language, has the same village roots, possesses the same myth and culture norms, then it can function as a unit with greater trust and understanding. Also because the push and pull of history and events may cause certain groups to be uprooted from their native soil at a given point, the effect is that ethnic cohorts may migrate to a place like the United States almost as a unit and within a limited span of time. Thus in the United States we can note a progression of different ethnic groups in crime, "WASP," Irish, German, Jewish, Italian, Russian; now Soviet, Afro-American, Cuban, Mexican, Syrian-Lebanese, Asian, and so on.[1] At times, one can subdivide the essentially structural or organizational variable of ethnicity into clan, tong, dialect, or city of origin. But it is the organizational need for trust, loyalty, intimate knowledge of character, security, sense of courage, prowess, honesty, ease of understanding, communication and control, that makes ethnicity, kinship, blood-tie, language, and race important variables for group bonding, organization and identification. Ethnicity plays its role in group structuring and interaction, not in the process or activity that makes such groups an identifiable as a part of organized crime. Too often the identifier of ethnicity has been placed ahead of the attributes defining the organized criminal activity, thus creating distortions both in law enforcement and analysis as well as understanding of organized crime.

Given the needed link between the organized criminal system and the political system, such mono-ethnic emphasis and distortion has been politically useful, distracting attention from the politically influential in crime, while mobilizing media attention and law enforcement resources toward some outside group also engaged in crime.

Change and regime alternation and evolution within a social system as dynamic as the United States over the past 175 years naturally leads to a similar alternation in activity levels and dominance in criminal organization. Thus, the pattern of apparent ethnic succession in organized crime is as regular as the apparent patterns of upward mobility. The word apparent should not be overstressed here, for both succession and mobility are real; they are however often exaggerated.

Organized crime is a primitive and predatory form of elementary entrepeneurial capitalism and rudimentary power politics. As such, like economics and politics it is situationally both flexible and adaptable. As we shall see, the relative standings of ethnic organized criminal groups have in some 200 years of American history ebbed and flowed like the fortunes of other enterprises, industries, sports teams, political parties and nations. Yet the patterns and process of the enterprise have remained relatively the same.

The long term goal of organized crime is monopoly control with accompanying maximization of influence and minimization of risk. But it faces basic competition from other criminal groups and enterprises. Organized crime entrepreneurs, if they are to succeed, must always seek some edge, or advantage either in traditional or new markets, as well as some margin in the manipulation of law enforcement, the criminal justice system and powers that be. They must, therefore, seek to corrupt and manipulate the system. Such manipulation, however, requires leadership, management skills, innovation, and technical expertise that may not be available in traditional crime circles. Thus organized crime is constantly innovative and reaching out for both new markets and new talent to maintain its basic competitive edge.

Organized Crime: Some Evolving Academic and Law Enforcement Perspectives

Some twenty years ago, FBI director J. Edgar Hoover publicly acknowledged the existence of organized crime.[2] The Bureau of Narcotics and Dangerous Drugs (BNDD) had done so several decades earlier, but their reputation was at times in question.[3] A handful of local law enforcement agencies, private commissions, and academics had also been trumpeting this clarion callout with little recognition. It was only after a group of Italian gansters held a "summit meeting" in the woods at Apalachin, New York, that organized crime, "Mafia" style, riveted national attention for years to come.

The Chicago Crime Commission, Virgil Peterson, John Landesco, Professor Charles Merriam, and his students V. O. Key, Harold Lasswell and others had sought to understand organized crime in Chicago, but their work and that of the Chicago school of Sociology were little recognized at that time.[4] Thus, sustained academic and law enforcement interest in organized crime is still a relatively new phenomenon in these United States.

This activity has been influenced, for good and ill, by the press and media, which has publicly cataloged various organized crime groups, often romanticizing and sensationalizing their activities and members. At times in the U.S., even for organized criminals themselves, it appears that it is difficult to determine whether life is imitating art or art imitating life. Yet the contributions of journalists have too often been publicly denigrated while the results of their research fill rows of file cabinets in police agencies. They toiled long and hard in the vineyard, and if at times they were fooled and perpetuated myth so have others. The fact is that their work has increased both knowledge and concern.[5]

Chicago, the city Carl Sandberg described as "Stormy, husky, brawling," is thought of as the town of Capone, the First Ward, Jane Byrne, and police scandals too numerous to mention. It is also the city of some of the earliest studies of organized crime, and much latter-day investigation of the subject.[6] Some researchers have gone on to study organized crime elsewhere and so further added to our understanding. Alan Block's, *East Side-West Side* stands out as one such contribution (Block, 1983).

One of the most influential of such academic studies is Daniel Bell's classic article, "Crime as an American Way of Life" first published in the *Antioch Review* (1953) and later reprinted in his major book *The End of Ideology* (Bell, 1967). This article gave foundation to the view that organized crime was merely a "queer ladder" of social mobility. It gave rise to the concept of "ethnic succession," namely, the perspective that each social group in a dynamic social system must pass through crime on its road to social acceptance. This view is in appearance similar to yet, in fact, quite different from Balzac's prescient recognition that "Behind every great fortune there lies a crime." Bell's work, however, received also universal acceptance, for it fit the dominant structural-functionalist academic fashion of the time.[7]

The Apalachin meeting of November 14, 1957 wrapped theories in the cloth of hard but overblown and often myopically distorted fact. The result was a spate of law enforcement and Congressional hearings, commissions and analyses. Estes Kefauver had brought organized crime into American living rooms in 1951, as he and his committee used the medium of television to bring real gangsters and gamblers into our consciousness. The Apalachin episode reawakened public and offical concern and generated the most comprehensive hearings and detailed law enforcement analysis yet. This event set the stage for the direct assault on organized crime in the Hoffa trials and Valachi hearings of 1963. (U.S. Senate, Permanent Subcommittee on Investigations, 88th Congress: First Session, 1963).

Much has been written about the reality and myth of organized crime as told by Joseph Valachi (Peterson 1983, Part II). Regardless of the veracity of his account, or consensus on it, Valachi's testimony represents the culmination of a line of law enforcement investigation stretching from Kefauver through Apalachin and the McClellan hearings to the era of the Kennedy brothers, and the focusing of all federal attention on the Italian-American, or what Valachi called "La Cosa Nostra" crime groups.

Throughout history, politicians have ridden sensational events and crises into office. The investigation of organized crime is one such easy vehicle for political recognition. Thomas Dewey's work against "Dutch" Schultz and Charles "Lucky" Luciano assisted his entry into the Governor's office and national politics. Senator Estes Kefauver became a Presidential contender as a result, in part, of televised organized crime hearings. And, had a dark fate not intervened, Bob Kennedy's war on the mob would have enhanced his brother's 1964 reelection bid, and his own career.

This reality may have been in Eliot Lumbard's thoughts when, as Governor Nelson Rockefeller's special assistant, he had the governor call for a pooling of academic and law enforcement expertise to "chart new and concerted measures against the national criminal conspiracy" (Oyster Bay, 1976). Whatever may have motivated the action, the Oyster Bay Conferences on Organized Crime marked another turning point in the study of organized crime in the United States, and brought together, for the first time individuals from law enforcement and the academic world who would go on to contribute meaningfully to our knowledge of organized crime. The participants at Oyster Bay spent much of their time attempting to define organized crime, and eventually agreed on the term and concept of "confederation" to underscore the loose and open nature of organized crime group interactions. (Cressey 1969, 17–20). This important concept has tended, however, to be overlooked in the years and in the investigations that followed.

Many of the participants at Oyster Bay came together again two years later on the Organized Crime Task Force, which was part of the President's Commission on Law Enforcement and the Administration of Justice. The commission staff included Charles Rogovin, and such consultants as G. Robert Blakey, Donald Cressey, John Gardiner, Rufus King, Ralph Salerno and Gus Tyler, along with such law enforcement experts as William Duffy, Aaron Kohn, Eliot Lumbard, Henry Peterson, Virgil Peterson, and Alfred Scotti. At no other time have so many experts from both the academic and law enforcement communities gathered together to focus on the issue of organized crime (U.S. Dept. of Justice 1967, iv–v). Their report and the spate of books and articles that followed from it profoundly influenced the study and analysis of organized crime in the United States.

The task force report itself was more notable for its appendices than for its text, as each of the appendices either as books, articles, or legislation would help structure the present understandings of the subject of organized crime. Appendix A can be found in expanded form as Donald Cressey's, *The Theft of the Nation*; a structural-functional sociological paradigmatic analysis that would be a textbook classic for over a decade (Cressey, 1969). The second appendix reached book form as John Gardiner's *The Politics of Corruption,* an examination of corruption and organized crime in Reading ("Wincanton") Pennsylvania (1970). Appendix C, by Prof. G. Robert Blakey, took legislative form in the Racketeer Influenced Corrupt Organizations statute, better known as RICO. The fourth and final appendix was Thomas Shelling's widely reprinted article, "Economic Analysis of Organized Crime," which is the foundation of much of the public policy, and economic analysis of complex criminal enterprises (in Kaplan and Kessler 1976, 367–99).

At the same time that task force consultants produced their own views and interpretations of organized crime, Ralph Salerno wrote *The Crime Confederation,* which complements Cressey's book. Salerno's book, which was widely accepted, highlighted the tightly-structured, hierarchical view of organized crime of most law enforcement officials (1969). Thus, from this one group came the many intellectual streams that would define and influence the topic well into the 1970s.

The impact of this work was considerable, particularly in the case of

Cressey and Salerno, who presented a model of organized crime based on New York City data that stressed the structurally rigid, bureaucratic organizational aspects of criminal groups and focused attention on Italian-American crime groups of "La Cosa Nostra." In time their work was rigorously criticized by other interpreters, but their contribution should neither be forgotten nor underestimated, for it provided a systematic, unsensationalized, overview of the subject that paved the way for serious academic and law enforcement analysis.

One important reaction to the structuralist approach of Cressey and Salerno was Joseph Albini's book, *American Mafia: Genesis of a Legend* (1971). Albini presents an anthropological analysis of organized crime, in which the roles of kinship, friendship, and most importantly, the web of patron-client relationships are stressed. Rather than a rigid formal corporate entity, syndicated crime is viewed as a loose, informal system of effective and instrumental interaction and relationships.

It is noteworthy that the existential experience and data set on which Albini developed his analysis was Detroit, Michigan. His model was rooted in the interaction of Detroit crime groups with others in Canada, Western New York State, Pennsylvania and Ohio. Aided by law enforcement experts, Vincent Piersante and Robert Earhart, Albini's study worked with a reality that was more open, loosely structured and fragmented than the New York city data set of Cressey and Salerno.

In 1972 a second book took this same anthropological perspective. Francis A. J. Ianni's, *A Family Business: Kinship and Control in Organized Crime,* written apparently without knowledge of or reference to Albini's work, stresses the hypothesis that organized crime is evolving from criminal to legitimate business endeavors, that ethnic succession is taking place in Italian-American crime groups (Ianni, 1972). Based on actual interviews and anthropological field work with an organized criminal "family," Ianni's book represents an important research first. His reinforcement of Albini's patron-client network ties, and the affective type of open organizational norms, made this work an important counterweight to the structuralist approaches.

Ianni followed up with a monographic essay, "Ethnic Succession in Organized Crime: A Summary Report" (1973), and later on the same theme, *Black Mafia* (1975). Both these works present a more developed analysis of ethnic succession theory. Most observers agree that in many criminal groups ethnic succession is apparently occurring. This is particularly true in areas where organized crime groups are increasingly hidden behind multiple legitimate corporate fronts, or where, because of law enforcement pressures, they are leaving high risk tactical street endeavors such as drug retailing and bookmaking to new ethnic groups and concentrating instead on financing, laundering, and well-buffered behind-the-scenes influence and control.

Two years after Ianni's work, historian Humbert Nelli's book *The Business of Crime* was published (1976). This detailed history not only debunked many of the earlier folk theories about the Mafia and organized crime in

America, it lent further factual support to the idea that apparent ethnic succession was occurring in organized crime.

Annelise Anderson's work, *The Business of Organized Crime* (1979) is a study of the "Benguerra family" (actually the Angelo Bruno group in Philadelphia, Pennsylvania). After analyzing their numbers business, loansharking, and legitimate enterprises, she concludes that they are inefficient, loosely organized, and non-violent, making for a rather benign delivery of illicit services. More recent events, including Bruno's murder and some 20 other "hits" and "near-hits," as well as court-released wire surveillance recordings of conversations, indicate that her view is at best naive and short-sighted (Pennsylvania Crime Commission 1983, 12–17). The violence and volatility of the events in Philadelphia should alert us to the malleability of organized crime groups and the need to root our theorizing in long term sustained, systematic and longitudinal research.

Concurrent with academic studies, a number of journalistic accounts and biographies have been published. *The Valachi Papers* (Maas, 1968) and Vincent Teresa's, *My Life in the Mafia* (1973) provided two insider views.

More recently this genre of studies has been capped by an Israeli press team's biography of Meyer Lansky (Eisenberg and Landu 1976), Jonathan Kwitny's important book *Vicious Circles* (1979), Ovid Demaris's biography of Jimmy Fratianno (1981), and Joseph Bonanno's autobiography (1983). These books, while lacking theoretical or analytical rigor, do provide descriptive and historical insights and information. They must be carefully sifted and mined, however, for often — particularly in the case of the autobiographical volumes — these accounts are self serving, exaggerated, biased, and at times full of error deliberate or accidental. When properly evaluated, however, they can provide insights into personalities, value structures, attitudes, perceptions and events that would be difficult to acquire by other means.

An important academic direction that has greatly contributed toward understanding the phenomenon of organized crime in the United States was inaugurated in the task force work of Thomas Shelling and developed by the economists and public policy experts that have followed him. Harold Lasswell and Jeremiah McKenna broke ground with their study of organized crime's impact on a single neighborhood, Bedford-Stuyvesant, Brooklyn, New York (Lasswell and McKenna 1970). Others have studied the heroin market and law enforcement practices as a problem of political economy (see, for example, Moore 1977); still others have examined the street level realities of bookmaking and numbers gambling (Reuter and Rubinstein 1978, 45–68); the vending and solid waste carting industries (Reuter, Rubinstein and Wynn 1983); and the whole issue of disorganized crime (Block and Chambliss 1981; Reuter 1983).

These policy studies, employing economic market models and perspectives, looking into situational inducements and constraints, supply-demand factors, opportunities and risk analysis, have increased our knowledge and dispelled myths and overly romantic interpretations of organized crime.

Thus, in the two decades since Valachi, the study and analysis of organized criminal groups and markets has made great strides. New methodologies, conceptual approaches, and theoretical models are emerging and old arguments, definitional disagreements, and emotional ethnic debates are being laid to rest. Empirical studies and efforts at quantification are pointing the way toward new date collection techniques and research possibilities (Lupsha 1983a). This more rigorous mode of analysis now emerging leads to better informed hypothesis-formation and improved theory development and understanding. The success of these new methods depends, however, upon an open and cooperative partnership between law enforcement practitioners and academic researchers. Both sides need to get to know one another better and recognize mutual needs, agreements, and opportunities for mutually productive collaboration.

It would be ingenuous to imagine that the object of study remains oblivious to this work and the concerted efforts of the criminal justice system to control and erradicate it. As law enforcement knowledge and sophistication increases, it can be safely assumed that so does the knowledge and skill of organized criminal groups and enterprises. Each side learns from the other; as law enforcement methods change so do those of the sophisticated criminal. Indeed, at times both appear to be engaged in a dance, a spiraling interaction of learning, technology, and innovation in which each new step by one party is matched by the inventiveness of the other. Yet, the dance continues. To illustrate this more clearly we will turn to an examination of the history and evolution of organized crime in America.

A History of Organized Crime in the United States

There are those who state that they can precisely date the emergence of organized crime, at least the Italian-American "Mafia," "La Cosa Nostra" version of it (Chandler 1975, 77). Others identify the beginning of organized crime with the waves of foreign immigration, or with Prohibition (Hammer 1975, 3–7). From my perspective, where one cares to draw a line or place a date is not important, for as stated earlier, organized crime is a process that can be present at any place or time in complex communities and social relationships.

Organized crime has appeared at various times throughout American history. Prostitution and organized criminal fencing rings, for example, are reported as early as the 1680s in the records of Suffolk County (Boston) Massachusetts Bay Colony (Browning and Gerassi 1980). (This is not surprising when one recalls that many early colonists were products of England's jails.) Just prior to the American Revolution, well-financed and organized criminal enterprises, using corporate buffers, bribery, political payoffs and corruption, quite similar as a process to modern organized crime, operated in the major port cities of the colonies. The most notorious of these organizations was led by Thomas Hancock and his son John, who would go on to be the first and most legible signer of our Declaration of Independence. The Hancocks not only controlled wharves and warehouses in Boston, they also had fleets of merchant ships plying the seas between Holland, Spain, London and the Caribbean. Under this commercial cover, they were among the premier contraband smugglers in the colonies, violating British law and evading taxation with a boldness and impunity rarely matched by modern organized criminals.

Through the selective use of bribery and political and charitable contributions John Hancock made himself one of the most popular men in Boston. When the crown finally indicted him and his associates for smuggling over a ton of French wines valued at over 300,000 British pounds, the letters and testimonials of support from Boston's business, religious and local political community was such that the British prosecutor was advised to drop the charges for fear of open riot and rebellion on Hancock's behalf (Baxter 1945).

Two hundred years later another waterfront entrepreneur, International Longshoremen's Association (ILA) official Anthony "Tony" Scotto, paraded a similar stellar array of community leaders, church, business and political elite before the witness stand in his behalf (U.S. Senate 1981: *Waterfront Corruption,* 429–45). Hancock was never "known" as an organized criminal and was not convicted. Scotto, on the other hand, was a known member of an organized crime group, but the patterns remain the same.

It is not my intent to draw overly tight, distinct or strong comparisons between Hancock and Scotto. My purpose rather is to underscore the need to focus on organized criminal enterprise as activity or process in which similarities in action, method, patterns of risk-taking and avoidance appear, and which transcend any analysis based on a case study or ethnic variable perspective.

After the Revolution, land fraud and illegal land speculations rivaled anything modern Sunbelt real estate scam artists have engaged in. The most famous of these early enterprises was the Yazoo land fraud of 1795. Like so many modern organized crime enterprises, this fraud fell into the grey area between the legal and the illegal, requiring political corruption and the connivance of those sworn to protect the commonwealth. But it surpassed many modern organized crime capers in the prominence, ambition and shrewdness of the men involved. These included two United States Senators, James Gunn (Georgia) and Robert Morris (Pennsyvlania); U.S. Congressmen Thomas Carnes (Georgia) and Robert Harper (South Carolina); U.S. Supreme Court Justice James Wilson; Federal District Court Justice Nathaniel Pendleton; Georgia Superior Court Justice William Smith. In addition, more than a dozen Massachusetts and Connecticut bankers and businessmen were listed as co-conspirators (Magrath).

By bribing the Georgia legislature, these men obtained title to 35 million acres of state and Indian lands at the bargain price of one-half cent per acre.

For an investment of $200,000 plus bribe monies, the group reaped a profit of over $4 million. Despite the tremendous outcry from both public and press, with indictments and trials moving up to the U.S. Supreme Court, the conspirators and the myriad of dummy companies they hid behind escaped penalty (Magrath 1966, 217–30).

During the Civil War another corruption scam involving federal corruption, again rivaling anything organized crime could concoct today, occurred when directors of the Union Pacific Railroad, members of the Lincoln Cabinet, and key members of Congress formed the Credit Mobilier Corporation of America (Browning and Gerassi 1980, 216–17). This holding company had the stated purpose of coordinating and overseeing the construction of the transcontinental railroad. In fact it operated to falsify invoices, overcharge, engage in kickbacks, issue dummy contracts, and bilk the taxpayers out of some $23 million dollars. And, as in the Yazoo example, despite the outcry, most of the principals escaped any harsh retribution or penalties.

These examples are illustrative of why it is foolish to place a date or ethnic label on organized crime. They are also, hopefully, suggestive of a pattern or process, which makes the anatomy of organized crime subject to empirical analysis and dissection.

Street Gangs: One Vehicle for the Emergence of Organized Crime

The street gang serves as an excellent incubator for future organized criminals. While most street gang members grow beyond it, into ordinary law-abiding lines, for some it serves as a training ground for skill enhancement and career development. At times, environmental events and structures, such as the political machine in the nineteenth century or Prohibition, can enhance the potential of the street gang as a vehicle for a career in organized crime. Thus we must give some attention to it.

The potato famines that swept Ireland in the 1830s and 1840s brought tens of thousands of Irish immigrants to the streets and tenements of New York and other East Coast cities. Even earlier in the century, new immigrants had formed self-defense gangs against other groups, old-timers or outsiders. While many of the new immigrants would find work and success, others would carve out criminal careers in the streets (Peterson: 24–32).

The street gangs of the nineteenth century came to serve as recruiting grounds for many who would rise in machine politics through Tammany Hall or its equivalent in other cities, or in organized criminal groups. In street gang activity reputations and alliances were forged, and skills in leadership and depersonalized violence honed.

The first popular direct election for mayor of New York in 1834 provides an example of the growing use of street gangs to assist partisan politics. The election was set to last three days to allow all to vote, and by the third day the State Militia had to be called in to restore some semblance of order (Browning and Gerassi 1980). This election pitted Tammany Hall against older White-Anglo-Saxon, Protestant, English, and Dutch "Native Americans." Both parties recruited street gangs to vote early and often, and to intimidate the opposition, with resulting bloodshed, injury and deaths on both sides.

Tammany's supremacy at the polls in New York City over the next several decades was in part accomplished by the use of street gangs. More importantly, an alliance that would last well into the third quarter of the 20th century was forged over the years between the Democratic party machine in New York and those who would rule various organized crime groups (Peterson 1983, 294–359). New York City is not unique in this respect: organized crime held sway over First Ward politics and often the governance of the city of Chicago for more than eighty years (U.S. Senate 1983: *Organized Crime in Chicago*).

As waves of immigration from Southern and Eastern Europe swept across our shores in the last decades of the nineteenth century, new ethnic groups replaced the Irish and Germans in the street gangs. But while ethnicity changed, the ties between crime and politics remained firm and secure.

By 1890 the Five Points gang was headed by Paul Kelly, an Italian whose real name was Paolo Antonio Vaccarelli. His gang, actually a confederation of neighborhood street gangs, had some 1,500 members. Between 1898 and 1904 this gang engaged in a bloody rivalry with another large gang, run by Monk Eastman (Nelli 1976, 107–9). And by this time, associated with Kelly were such future organized crime luminaries as John Torrio, Salvatore "Charles Lucky" Luciano, Alphonse Caponi (Al Capone).

While Paul Kelly moved uptown to join the Morello brothers and Ciro Terranova in East Harlem, organizing the rag-pickers union and extorting monies from businessmen and rag-pickers alike, Torrio would move to Brooklyn to work for Unione Siciliana leader Frankie Uale (also known as Yale) later setting up Al Capone as one of Yale's bouncers (Nelli 1976, 163).

Kelly's control over the rag-pickers association is similar to modern organized crime's control over private carting, and its unions and trade associations in the New York Metropolitan area (U.S. Senate 1957). Kelly's skills did not go unnoticed, however, and by 1919 he had become International Vice-President of the International Longshoremen's Association. The comparatively high daily wage of the dockworker, the use of the "shape-up" as a hiring technique, as well as the nature of commerce, created a situation of dependence on the part of shippers and ship owners and opened up tremendous opportunities for extortion, kickbacks, theft, gambling, and loansharking that were not likely to be lost on a man of Paul Kelly's background. Other well known organized criminals associated with it were Albert Anastasia, his brother Anthony Anastasio, and his son-in-law Anthony Scotto, Anthony and Dominick Strollo, John M. "Cockeye" Dunn, Eddie McGrath and Michael Clemente.

It should now be clear that organized crime in the United States (1) is not some random or episodic thing; but a patterned and structured activity; (2)

finds and exploits opportunities for illicit gain; and (3) operates across time regardless of individual changes in personnel or leadership.

John Torro's career provides us with further examples. Familial ties and obligations caused him to leave New York to assist his aunt, who, with her husband "Big Jim" Colosimo, ruled the brothels and vice dens of Chicago's levee (Landesco 1929, 191–205). He turned the unprofitable brothels he supervised into money makers and expanded the family's prostitution empire. According to one report, there were some 192 brothels on the Chicago levee grossing an estimated $15 million annually (1910) from prostitution, liquor and drug sales (Bell 1980, 338).

The first decades of this century marked the progressive era in the United States. It was a time of political ferment, change and reform. The Mann Act, making it a federal crime to transport women in interstate commerce for immoral purposes, became law in 1910. In 1914, the Harrison Act, restricting the sale and use of narcotics, became law. In 1917, the U.S. Congress passed the Eighteenth Amendment banning the manufacture, sale and transportation of alcoholic beverages. By 1919 this amendment had been ratified by 36 states, bringing Prohibition and its enforcement machinery, the Volstead Act, into being at midnight January 16, 1920, marking perhaps the high point of moral reform fervor in this country. At the same time it created the leadtime and incentives for a vast black market and huge profits in crime.

The Prohibition Period

The two-year period between Congress's passage of the Eighteenth Amendment and the final ratification and enforcement of the law gave a variety of hoodlums, gangsters, and racketeers the necessary lead-time to acquire investment capital, and to establish the necessary networks and infrastructure to make large profits in bootlegging once the law was in place.

We would not have organized crime as we know it in the United States, if not for the period of Prohibition. While we have always had organized crime and criminal enterprises in the United States — from John Hancock's contraband empire to Ciro Terranova's monopoly over artichoke distribution and sales to Paul Kelly's influence over the rag-picker trade to Big Jim Colosimo and John Torrio's oligopoly in vice — all of the living pre-Prohibition mobsters, extortionists, racketeers and criminals would have remained in the lower depths without the passage of the Eighteenth Amendment. Prohibition not only gave them opportunity, it gave them a respectability and legitimacy. Through it they could parlay their skills in crime, violence, and corruption, and their working environment of saloons, brothels, and gambling dens, into platforms for creating huge fortunes, and a patina of respectability, status, and power. Prohibition not only provided a means of making vast sums of money, it created a need for organization, cooperation and syndication.

As in any new market situation, Prohibition began with fairly free and open competition in the marketplace. Immigrant communities with backyard stills for making wine and cordials, were soon producing rotgut whiskey and bathtub gin. Once-legal breweries were operating with new management in new locations. Street gangsters and gamblers now had new employment opportunities in transporting, guarding, and distributing shiploads of "booze." Saloons closed and reopened as speakeasies, while most urban Americans continued to drink and began to patronize places they normally would not have entered. The "Roaring Twenties" became part of our history.

In the early days of Prohibition, like the early days of Colombian drug trafficking in the 1970s, free competition created bloody conflicts as the market and its aggressive entrepreneurs sought to increase their profits and control. In Chicago, "Big Jim" Colosimo had made his fortune and wanted no part of this new enterprise. He shed his wife for a new young bride and moved uptown, rejecting John Torrio's pleas to get into bootlegging. It did not do any good as he was gunned down on May 11, 1920. His funeral illuminated the ties between politics and organized crime in Chicago. Included in the burial party as active and honorary pallbearers were two United States Congressmen, five judges, a State Senator, and nine Chicago Aldermen. (*Chicago American,* May 15, 1920).

Torrio, like Arnold Rothstein in New York City, when he saw Prohibition coming, bought up trucks and breweries. He established, with considerable business acumen, contacts for Canadian liquor. He placed his friend Alphonse Caponi (Al Capone) in Chicago, and attempted to end the violent competition among competing gangs by drawing up territories and franchising exclusive distribution rights and routes, through negotiation and compromise, so that all the Chicago gangs would get a share of the action.

Torrio had attempted to reduce the lethal conflicts of the free market, and Capone eventually succeeded in doing so, but only through using even greater violence to eliminate all competition. By then Torrio had returned to New York leaving Chicago to Capone, but the need for order, combination and cooperation that Torrio foresaw would subsequently become one of the hallmarks of organized crime. For example, in the 1980s, the stress toward order and cooperation is one point of contention between the older organized crime leadership and some of the "youngsters" in the business, and between old-line Italian-American groups and some outlaw motorcycle gangs (U.S. Senate 1983, *Profile of Organized Crime in the Middle Atlantic States).*

Torrio was not the only crime figure to recognize the need for cooperation and coordination, if all were to prosper, during Prohibition. In 1928, police broke up a meeting of Unione Siciliana members in Cleveland. Among those present were, Joseph Profaci, Joseph Magliocco and Vincent Mangano, who would become bosses of New York City crime "families" after the "Castellamaresse War." In the following year Enoch "Nuckey" Johnson, the political boss of Atlantic City, hosted a meeting of multi-ethnic gangsters from across the country. From New York City came Charles "Lucky" Luciano, Meyer Lansky, Frank Costello, John Torrio, Albert Anastasia, Philip Mangano, Frank Scalise, Dutch Schultz and Louis "Lepke" Buchalter. Chicago was represented by Al Capone, Jacob Guzik, Frank Nitti, Frank McErlane, Joe Saltis and Frank Rio. From Philadelphia came Nig Rosen, "Boo Boo" Hoff, Sam Lazer, and Charles Schwartz. From Boston, "King" Solomon joined the group, while Abe Bernstein represented Detroit's Purple Gang. Cleveland was significant in that in the group was Charles Polizzi, who had been born Leo Berkowitz but was adopted into an Italian family, and represented the interassociation of the Italians and Jews present. With him from Cleveland came Meyer Lansky's other business partners, Moe Dalitz, and Lou Rothkopf. New Jersey was represented by Willie Moretti and Abner "Longie" Zwillman (Nelli 1976, 215; Peterson 1983, 157–58). According to various reports, the purpose of this meeting was to discuss ways of achieving cooperation, ordering markets, solving supply and distribution problems and ways to curtail the violence, such as that which had recently occurred on St. Valentine's Day in Chicago. Violence was attracting both law enforcement and press attention and interfering with business. Notably absent from this meeting were the men Valachi saw as the top leaders of organized crime in New York at this time: Joseph Masseria and Salvatore Maranzano (Maas 1969, 84–87).

In 1933 there was a meeting at the Franconia Hotel in New York City which consisted only of Jewish organized crime figures. Benjamin "Bugsy" Siegel, Louis "Lepke" Buchalter, Jacob Shapiro, Joseph "Doc" Stacher, Harry Titlebaum, Louis Kravitz, Harry Greenberg, Philip Kovolik and Hyman Holtz were all arrested in a raid on this occasion (Reid and Demaris 1963, 116–17). The meeting's purpose has never been discovered, although it is likely that it was to discuss post-Prohibition gambling issues, and problems related to "Murder Inc.," for certainly many of those present would play roles in the national syndication of gambling and "Murder Inc." trials.

In historical perspective, these meetings toward the end of Prohibition served not only immediate ends, but also served to build contacts and networks as opportunities for interaction, combination and future cooperation going far beyond the individual urban power bases that these organized crime figures possessed. Indeed, in the long view, organized crime in the United States can be seen in stages: first, the ghetto ethnic settlement base, prior to Prohibition; second, the city-metropolitan area base, occasioned by Prohibition; third, the nationalization of organized crime with the syndication of illicit gambling; and fourth, the further nationalization and incipient internationalization of organized crime with legitimate casino gambling, drug trafficking and off-shore money laundering.

Prohibition opened the door of opportunity for many young street gang members (many of whom were born or came to the United States as small children), and when they eventually assumed their roles of leadership in organized crime, they were equipped with American values and attitudes. John Torrio came to the United States when he was two years of age. Frank Costello when he was four; and Charles "Lucky" Luciano when he was ten years old. Many others, Al Capone, Dutch Schultz, and Willie Moretti were born in the United States (Lupsha 1981a, 9). These were the new men who would mature through Prohibition into long term leadership in organized crime.

In contrast, the old leaders — the entrenched ghetto "Dons," such as Morello, Ciro Terranova, Joseph Masseria, Gaetano Reina, and the newcomers pushed from Italian and Sicilian criminal groups by the rise of Fascism in the late 1920s (Salvatore Maranzano, Peter Magaddino, Joseph Bonanno) and their old line cohorts Joseph Profaci, Stefano Magaddino, Vito Bonventre — were rooted in the old ways of extortion, money-lending, and the monopolization of ghetto businesses such as ice, coal, trash collection, and vital "old world" necessities like artichokes, olive oil, imported cheese, fish and produce (Bonanno 1983, 52).

The premier "Don" who controlled New York's "Little Italy" on Manhattan's lower east-side was "Joe the Boss" Masseria. He controlled all the "Little Italy" rackets and had extended his influence into East Harlem, where Peter Morello and his brother-in-law Ciro Terranova paid a "street tax" tribute to Joe Masseria. Masseria had come to the United States from Sicily as an adult, age 26. He was set in old world ways and did not seek any city-wide influence in bootlegging until the mid-1920s, and when he chose to expand he did it by bringing Charles "Lucky" Luciano's group into his orbit by threats and by promising them a share of his rackets (Gosch and Hammer 1974, 69–71).

A successful bootlegging enterprise requires sources of supply, a means of collection — ships, offloading boats, landing sites, trucks, drivers, guards, warehouses — and bars, clubs, restaurants, speakeasies, and other means of distribution. In addition, bribes have to be paid, lawyers must be on call, dummy corporations established to launder funds, and accountants and bookkeepers hired to maintain accounts and disbursements. Such an enterprise required a broader metropolitan orientation, which many of the older ghetto "Dons" lacked. Thus the Luciano group with its multi-ethnic make-up and associates in a variety of cities and states had the advantage of metropolitanism over the old-time "Dons" and was wooed by them. Yet Luciano's ties to non-Italians like Meyer Lansky, Ben Siegel, Frank Erickson and Phil Kastel, and non-Sicilians like Frank Costello and Joe Doto (known as Adonis) made him suspect in the old-timers' traditionalist eyes (Gosch and Hammer 1974, 65–67). New evidence of the hostility of the traditionalists to the Luciano group with its Lansky-"Jewish connection" has recently surfaced in Joseph Bonanno's autobiography. Bonanno repeatedly criticizes Luciano for not being a traditional "man of honor," for associating with people who were "outside the pale of our tradition," and for being too "avant-garde" (Bonanno 1983, 150).

So much has been written about the rivalry between Joseph Masseria, the old ghetto "Don" and Salvatore Maranzano, the newcomer from Castellammarese del Golfo, and what has become known as the "Castellammarese War" that there is no need to repeat that here. (See Maas 1968; Gosch and

Hammer 1974; Hammer, 1975; Nelli, 1976). It is important to note, however, that this conflict marked an important turning point in Italian-American groups and in the further Americanization of organized crime in the United States. When the smoke had cleared, the new men of the Luciano group were in the dominant positions, and the Italian-American crime "families" organizational and coordinating structures were modernized and increasingly democratized (Lupsha 1981a, 8–12). The greater autonomy and flexibility that had existed in organized crime groups elsewhere now came to New York City (Chicago Crime Commission 1983, 4–15).

The reader should not conclude that the old influences of the traditionalists, or the Unione Siciliana, completely disappeared. Rather two things should be understood. First, as the evidence and historical record suggests, organized crime in the United States is truly an American phenomenon, rooted in the culture, values and attitudes of the United States (Lupsha, 1981a, 1981b). Second, the Italian-American organized crime groups, which make up only one segment of all of organized crime in the United States, have more slowly become Americanized, and the pendulum has swung in various groups and cities back and forth between more traditionalist versus more "avant garde" methods.

After the Castellammarese War, while the influence of the traditionalists was diminished, it was not eclipsed by the new men. Luciano appears to have compromised and come to terms with the more traditional elements. The existence of Joseph Bonanno and Joseph Profaci as leaders of two New York crime "families" points to this, as does the long term survival of Gaetano "Thomas" Gagliano, and Philip and Vincent Mangano as leaders of other New York crime "families." Both Profaci and Bonanno were traditionalists steeped in the mores and customs of Sicily, while the Manganos and Gagliano were moderates who merely leaned in a traditionalist direction. The latter, however, had "new men" such as Albert Anastasia and Thomas Lucchese as key leaders, associating with Luciano's organization (Bonanno 1983). Luciano's patterns of association indicate that he preferred to associate with the more assimilated, younger men in these groups and his own, than with the traditionalists (Lupsha, 1983b). Luciano's alliance with the Lansky-Siegel group, and non-Sicilians like political fixer and corrupter Frank Costello and his underboss Vito Genovese, reinforces this opinion.

The New Men: Organized Crime After Prohibition

After Prohibition, many who had accumulated fortunes during that era simply stayed in the liquor business. Frank Costello and Phil Kastel set up Alliance Distributors, exclusive agent for King's Ransom and House of Lords Scotch. Later, they bought controlling interest in J. G. Turney, the holding company for these scotch liquors. John Torrio bought into Prendergast and Davies Co. Ltd., also a scotch importer and wholesaler, while Lansky, Luciano, Siegel, Adonis, Costello and others controlled Capitol Wine and

Spirits, a major distributor of French wines, Scotch and Canadian whiskies. Samuel Bronfman of Seagram and Lewis Rosenstiel of Schenley settled quietly with IRS for any Prohibition misdeeds these Canadian liquor magnates may have incurred and went on to rich and influential public lives in both countries (Hammer 1975, 130–31; Gosch and Hammer 1974, 174–75).

Other Prohibition gangsters returned to the old ways, strike-breaking for management and unions in the garment district (Leichter 1982; Peterson 1983; 308), hijacking, loansharking, narcotics trafficking, and prostitution, as well as the penetration and infiltration of legitimate businesses. The key leadership, however, turned to the national syndication of gambling and control of the wire services.

The difference in organized crime before and after Prohibition was that before they were subservient to politics and those with political clout, while now they had the organization, the networks, and the capital to call the shots and turn the tables. They also had the vast influence of judicial, law enforcement and political corruption that they had amassed in city halls and state capitols over the period of Prohibition.

Liquor, like money, has always been a part of the mother's milk of politics, influencing its ebb and flow, its compromises and decisions. The link between crime and politics was further cemented in the United States after Prohibition as ex-bootleggers sought out partners for legitimate liquor and business operations from that political cadre that had helped them get rich during Prohibition.

After Prohibition, the new men put their energies back into an old mainstay: gambling. The 1930s witnessed an expansion of "sawdust joints" illegal gambling parlors and card rooms for the working class, and "rug joints" for the elite. These gambling houses sprang up just over city lines, as in the case of the fancy houses of Joe Adonis and Willie Moretti across the George Washington bridge in New Jersey, and they also opened across state lines, for example in Covington, Kentucky across the river from Cincinnati, Ohio, and in elite resort areas like Saratoga Springs, New York and Hot Springs, Arkansas.

Prohibition had provided the incentive to develop contacts and connections across the United States, from the Atlantic seaboard through the Midwest and Great Lakes region, Chicago, Minneapolis, Kansas City, down through the South to New Orleans, and Florida's sunny shores. All that was needed was a reason, a mutually beneficial cause, to weld this loose acquaintanceship and net of prior association into a nationally cooperative syndicate. That cause came into being in the person of Moses Annenberg, and the U.S. Congress's legislative decision to end the transmission of racing information and results via Western Union (Eisenberg and Landu 1979, 145, 157; Gosch and Hammer 1974, 112–13).

Moses "call me Max" Annenberg, began his career as circulation manager for the *Chicago Tribune* under publisher Colonel Robert R. McCormick. In the late 1920s Al Capone was spreading his influence across the rackets, including labor racketeering, and the newsboy's union was only one of many he controlled. Annenberg used Capone muscle to make sure the Hearst paper stayed on top during the regular circulation wars. Indeed, at one point Annenberg got McCormick and Capone together to call off a strike against the *Tribune* (Kobler, 1971; 225). Moses Annenberg realized the significance of the vacuum created by the loss of Western Union's wire service to gamblers, and with financial assistance from Meyer Lansky and Frank Erickson, organized a national wire-service for the transmission of racing and sports information. When Annenberg went to jail for tax evasion in 1940, he sold the service to his partner James Ragen and Arthur McBride who renamed it the Continental Press Service (Messick 1972, 26–27; Reid and Demaris 1963, 13–14). Annenberg's operation, and later Ragen's Continental Press Service was a subsidiary of the Luciano-Lansky-Erickson coalition, which did not appease the Italian groups, particularly the Chicago group which had apparently felt that Annenberg's operations were within their orbit. Lansky's biographers have him calling Annenberg "a good friend" whom he helped establish (Eisenberg and Landu 1979, 157) while Luciano's biographer states, "As far as Annenberg was concerned, he could've never operated without us. He needed us and we needed him. It was a good thing all around" (Gosch and Hammer 1974, 128).

The Capone group, led by Frank Nitti and Jake Guzik, set up Trans-America Wire Service. It is unclear how the Luciano group worked with Trans-America, but less than a year after Annenberg was jailed associates of Meyer Lansky began working for Trans-America. Ben Siegel was sent to represent Trans-America in California, while Moe Sedway organized Nevada, and Gus Greenbaum, who had been paying a "street tax" to Nitti and Guzik for the privilege of running Trans-America in Arizona, fell under the Siegel-Lansky orbit (Reid and Demaris 1963, 34). Whatever the differences, they expired with James Ragen who was gunned down in Chicago and died some days later. He was recovering from his wounds but succumbed to mercury poisoning, while hospitalized and guarded by the Chicago Police (Hammer 1975, 220).

While nationalizing gambling the new men did not shun politics. They attended the Democratic convention in Chicago in 1932 where Luciano roomed with Albert Marinelli (Tammany leader in the Second Assembly District), and Costello stayed with Tammany boss, Jimmy Hines. Abner Longie Zwillman of New Jersey also attended the convention as did several members of the Capone group (Peterson 1983, 307). Out of this convention came Franklin Roosevelt's nomination, but more important for the new men was a contact with Louisiana Governor Huey Long and his associates.

After the convention Roosevelt turned against New York City's mayor Jimmy Walker and his mob supporters (Gosch and Hammer 1974, 167). Reform Mayor Fiorello La Guardia came to office, and inadvertently assisted the Luciano groups' national expansion by cracking down on slot machines, and displacing this Costello-Kastel enterprise to New Orleans (Wolf with DiMona 1974; 108–109).

Meyer Lansky too, was vigorously expanding his enterprises at this time. Having become familiar with Florida and the Caribbean during Prohibition, he now moved into Anthony "Little Augie" Carfano's Miami territory by settling with his brother Jake in neighboring Broward County and nearby Havana. He also placed his representattives in New Orleans (Messick 1971, 83–89). With his friends from Cleveland, Moe Dalitz, Sam Tucker, and Charles Polizzi, he had incorporated Molaska Corporation behind the cover of its President Jacob Stein (also known as John Drew) and his father-in-law Moses Citron some ten days before Louisiana ratified the 21st Amendment. Molaska Corporation, hiding behind its stated purpose of converting Caribbean molasses into a sugar substitute, was the largest illegal alcohol still in the United States. Its main still in Zanesville, Ohio turned out more than 5,000 gallons of 190 proof alcohol every 24 hours (Eisenberg and Landu 1979, 159–60; Messick 1971, 169–70). Just because Prohibition had ended was no reason to close down an efficient plant, or its sister plant in Elizabeth, New Jersey. Both operated until discovered by Treasury agents in 1935 (Messick 1972, 119–25; Hammer 1975, 132–33).

Figure 3.1 presents a chart of the major mid-thirties organized crime leaders, including their influence and association. This figure shows what much of the literature on organized crime in the United States overlooks, that after Prohibition organized crime in the United States tended to be dominated by a Italian-American-Jewish coalition. Alan Block's study (1983) also develops this perspective, but his focus is on New York City and Murder Inc. and does not suggest the overview presented here.

Charles "Lucky" Luciano's group appeared paramount over all other so-called "La Cosa Nostra" groups, and with its multi-ethnic leadership mix, it acted as the link connecting Jewish and Italian organized crime across the United States.

Even though Luciano faced complex legal problems, his group contained a number of talented managers. It appears that Meyer Lansky supervised overall expansion planning, development and money movement and laundering, while Frank Costello oversaw liaison with the Italian-American "families," political fixing and corruption. With Luciano's imprisonment in 1936, it would appear that Joe Doto (known as Adonis) played a larger role in liaison and management of gambling operations. Frank Erickson, who fell heir to Arnold Rothstein's gambling empire, apparently assisted with expansion and, under Costello, also assumed control over New York City gambling. He in turn was assisted by Phil Kastel, who acted as steward for Lansky interests, just as Italian-American Vincent "Jimmy Blue Eyes" Aloi worked on an almost daily basis with Lansky, but was also a soldier and then Capo under Vito Genovese. Had Genovese not left for Naples in 1937, this multi-ethnic partnership might not have prospered. But since he did not return until after

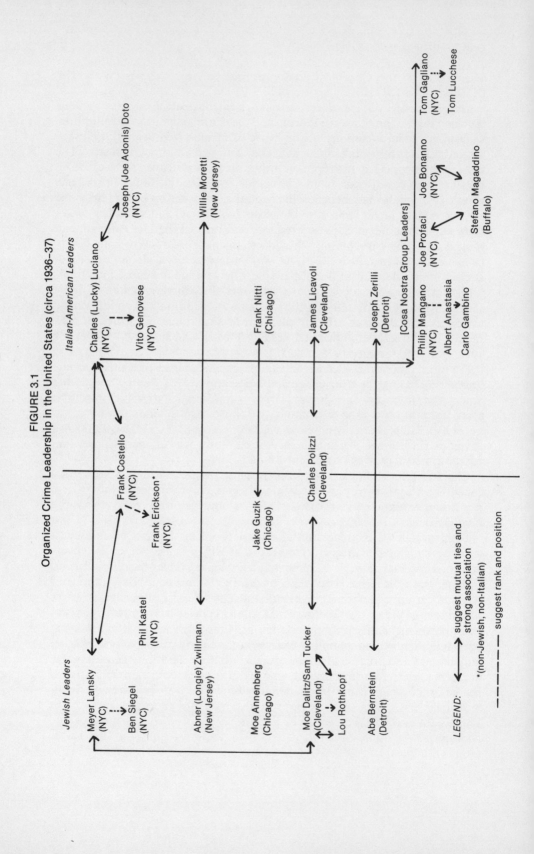

FIGURE 3.1

Organized Crime Leadership in the United States (circa 1936–37)

World War II, just before Luciano's deportation, and long after Lansky had decided that legalized casino gambling in Las Vegas and elsewhere represented the wave of the future for organized crime, Genovese did not affect them.

The four other New York City groups which came to be known as crime "families" played only supporting roles in the national expansion of organized crime. The Mangano-Anastasia-Gambino group controlled the Brooklyn waterfront, area drugs, hijacking and gambling. They also played a part, with Jewish criminals, in Murder Inc. The Joseph Profaci group concentrated on such old-time ghetto monopolies as olive oil, local real estate, funeral parlors, bars and restaurants. The Bonanno group, also following these traditional activities, had various legitimate enterprises—the B & D Coat Co., the Morgan Coat Co., the Anello and Bonanno Funeral Home, the Brunswick Laundry, and the Grande Cheese Co.—in addition to gambling and drug trafficking run by subordinate Carmine Galante (Bonanno 1983, 152). The Gagliano-Lucchese combination focused on labor racketeering in the garment district, and along with the Gambino family maintained businesses in private carting, loansharking, hijacking, trucking enterprises, and various corruption extortion rackets. All of these families tended to center their activities within a 50-mile radius of their home bases. They tended to intermarry, and, in recent years, bring in illegal "greenies" from Sicly and Italy. These are characteristic old-style methods, less efficient and more cumbersome than the corporate business oriented approaches of the new men.

Technological innovation played a vital role in the expansion of organized criminal enterprises. The national wire services not only facilitated the nationwide syndication of gambling, and the dependency of local independent bookmakers on organized crime for racing information and sports lines, it greatly increased the opportunities for citizens to gamble. As professional and college sports were brought into the home, first by radio in the 1930s and in the 1950s by television, popular interest increased tremendously. The result was a proportionate expansion of bookmaking opportunities and profits.

The late 1940s and the 1950s saw the growth of casino gambling in Las Vegas, and the manipulation of the Teamster Central States pension funds to provide capital for casino projects. It also increased the influence of the Chicago "Outfit" in the Teamsters Union. Today they are considered the most powerful family of the midwest, controlling organized crime markets and activities in many areas of the midwest and western United States (Chicago Crime Commission 1983, 16–20, 44).

During the 1950s and 1960s, security thefts and stock frauds increased, and the internationalization of organized crime continued, or money laundering and drug trafficking kept organized criminals on the move between the United States, Canada, Europe and the Bahamas. The International Longshoremen's Association was subject to waterfront hearings, yet this union, along with locals of the Teamsters Union, and locals of the Laborers Union,

Culinary Workers, and others, continues to have mob involvement in the 1980s (U.S. Senate 1981, *Government's Ability to Combat Labor Management Racketeering.*

Organized Crime in the Last Decades of the 20th Century

On January 15, 1983 Meyer Lansky died and with the exception of Joseph Bonanno, all of the leaders surviving the Castellammarese War are dead. In 1983, however, the President found it necessary to establish another Presidential Commission on Organized Crime.

Because organized crime is an activity and process, and the causal conditions, values and attitudes in which this process is rooted persist, it thus remains with us regardless of changes in personnel or group ethnicity. Today, there are black, Mexican, Cuban, Colombian, Asian, Middle Eastern, and many WASP crime groups flourishing in the United States. Despite legislation like RICO, electronic surveillance statutes, sophisticated long-term undercover operations and complex "sting" methods, organized criminal activity and criminals remain an integral part of our social, political and economic landscape.

The "new FBI" under Judge Webster has made significant inroads on traditional organizations: hundreds of indictments have been handed down, and many organized criminals convicted and jailed. Use of forfeiture laws, enhanced sentencing statutes for continuing criminal enterprise cases, and complex financial investigations to track and take away illicit profits are beginning to be used throughout the United States with some effect, yet the process and activity of organized crime continues.

Today, we see new groups, a continuing of the old crimes, and expansion into new enterprises. Pornography and massage-sex parlors have become more common than street prostitution and brothels in most areas. "Chopshops" have become the centerpiece of stolen car rings. Medicaid and Medicare and other "deep pocket," public purse frauds are becoming common and associated with traditional bankruptcy bustouts. Toxic waste haulage and dumping have become a part of the mob's private carting empire (U.S. Senate 1983, *Profile of Organized Crime in the Middle Atlantic States,* 402–55). Outlaw motorcycle gangs and prison gangs are forming new organized crime groups in their own right and providing services, especially violence, to older traditional crime groups.

In the New York City area, the five traditional Italian American organized crime "families" appear to be in disarray. Three of them are led by "acting" bosses and two of these have been disrupted both by law enforcement penetrations and the separation, death or incapacitation of traditional leaders. In 1983 the Gambino group, led by Paul Castellano, appeared to be the largest and most powerful New York "family," followed by the old Genovese and Lucchese groups. The New York Bonanno group and the Colombo "family" appear to be in the greatest distress, and according to some observers have been placed in "receivership" under the guidance of the more stable and powerful famiies (Lupsha 1983c).

Perhaps the most worrisome aspects of organized crime both now and in the future are: (1) the growth and expansion of all forms of drug trafficking and use; and (2) the continued penetration, and often acceptance of, organized crime in the marketplace. Organized crime's main threat to any society is the way it infects the body politic, corrupting officials, institutions, and ordinary citizens. Both drug trafficking and marketplace enterprise contain the potential for this because of their vast profits, as well as their need for corruption to obtain protection and market control. Acceptance of their commonplace reality by large segments of the population leads to further erosion of the whole of social community.

The study of the phenomenon of organized crime in the United States, and our knowledge and understanding of it, has made tremendous strides in the 20 years since the Valachi hearings, but the challenges before us are equally great, and much more work and research is needed. The new complex enterprise and marketplace crimes often require years of effort to unravel and analyze. The complexity of transnational organized crime, particularly drug trafficking and its effects on supplier and consumer nations and their peoples, is another area requiring lengthy research. Policy analysis and initiatives have thus far proved inadequate in dealing with the scope and complexity of these problems. As we approach the twenty-first century, about all that seems certain is that the process and activity of organized crime groups and their entrepreneurs will continue in the United States.

Notes

1. Immigrants and immigration patterns play an important role in many theories about organized crime (see Bell 1953; Ianni 1972). For others, events like Prohibition are viewed as critical (Kobler 1971; Wolf with DiMona 1974). Both should be viewed as environmental context variables that facilitate opportunity structures for the development of organized crime.
2. For a number of years John Edgar Hoover, Director of the Federal Bureau of Investigation, chose not to admit the existence of organized crime. Only after the Valachi hearings in 1963 did this agency begin reporting "La Cosa Nostra" organized crime groups.
3. The Bureau of Narcotics and Dangerous Drugs under Harry Anslinger, in annual reports since the 1930s, had written about "Mafia" organized crime groups trafficking drugs.
4. The University of Chicago school of sociology sought to study empirical reality by having its faculty and students do urban field research and investigations. Sociologist Robert Park and political scientist Charles Merrriam, who chaired the Chicago Crime Commission in the late 1920s, were two of its major exponents.
5. Hank Messick's many books include *Lansky* (1971) and *Mobs and the Mafia* (1972). Sandy Smith's work includes the September 1967 *Life Magazine* series, "The Mob." Bob Greene, who is one of the deans of investigative reporting, headed the IRE team investigating the bombing death of Arizona reporter Dan Bolles. Tom Renner is the prize-winning *Newsday* reporter who wrote *My Life in the Mafia* with Vincent Teresa (1973). J. Kwitny is best known for his work on organized crime's penetration of the legitimate business sector (1979). Jim Drinkhall, a *Wall Street Journal* reporter, is one of the leading experts on the Teamsters Union and its relationship to Las Vegas gambling.

6. Landesco's work for the Chicago Crime Commission in 1929 and the Chicago Vice Commission Report of 1910 are two early and important analyses of organized crime in the United States.

7. The role of the structural-functionalist theory in analyzing social phenomenon can be best seen in Robert Merton's *Social Theory and Social Structure* (1967).

References

Albini, J. 1971. *The American Mafia: Genesis of a Legend.* New York: Appleton-Century Crofts.

Anderson, A. G. 1979. *The Business of Organized Crime.* Stanford, Calif.: Hoover Institution Press.

Baxter, W. T. 1945. *The House of Hancock: Business in Boston 1724–1775.* Cambridge, Mass.: Harvard University Press.

Bell, D. 1953. "Crime as an American Way of Life." *Antioch Rev.* Summer: 131–45.

————. 1967. *The End of Ideology.* Glencoe, Ill.: The Free Press.

Bell, E. A. 1980. *War on the White Slave Trade.* Toronto, Canada: Coles Publishing Co. Ltd.

Block, A. 1983. *East Side—West Side: Organizing Crime in New York, 1930–1950.* New Brunswick, N.J.: Transaction Books.

Block, A., and Chambliss, W. 1981. *Organizing Crime.* New York: Elsevier Publishers.

Bonanno, J. 1983. *A Man of Honor: The Autobiography of Joseph Bonanno.* New York: Simon & Schuster.

Browning, F., and Gerassi, J. 1980. *The American Way of Crime.* New York: G. P. Putnam's Sons.

Chandler, L. 1975. *Brothers in Blood.* New York: E. P. Dutton & Co.

Chicago Crime Commission. 1983. *Testimony before the U.S. Senate Permanent Subcommittee on Investigations.* Chicago, Ill.: Chicago Crime Commission. Mimeographed.

Cressey, D. 1969. *Theft of the Nation.* New York: Harper & Row.

Demaris, O. 1981. *The Last Mafioso.* New York: New York Times Books Inc.

Eisenberg, D., Dan, U., and Landu, E. 1976. *Meyer Lansky: Mogul of the Mob.* New York: Paddington Press Ltd.

Gardiner, J. 1970. *The Politics of Corruption.* New York: Russell Sage Foundation.

Gosch, M., and Hammer, R. 1974. *The Last Testament of Lucky Luciano.* New York: Dell Publishing.

Hammer, R. 1975. *Playboy's Illustrated History of Organized Crime.* Chicago, Ill.: Playboy Press Inc.

Ianni, F. A. J. 1973. *Ethnic Succession in Organized Crime: A Summary Report.* Washington, D.C.: National Institute of Law Enforcement and Criminal Justice.

————. 1972. *A Family Business.* New York: Russell Sage Foundation.

————. 1975. *Black Mafia: Ethnic Succession in Organized Crime.* New York: Simon & Schuster.

Kaplan, L., and Kesler, D. 1976. *An Economic Analysis of Crime: Selected Readings.* Springfield, Ill.: Charles Thomas Publishers.

Kobler, J. 1971. *Capone: The Life and World of Al Capone.* New York: G. P. Putnam's Sons.

Kwitny, J. 1979. *Vicious Circles: The Mafia in the Marketplace.* New York: W. W. Norton.

Landesco, J. 1929. *Organized Crime in Chicago.* The Illinois Crime Survey. Reprinted, Chicago, Ill.: University of Chicago Press.

Lasswell, H., and McKenna, J. 1970. "The Impact of Organized Crime on an Inner City Community." New York: The Policy Center Inc. Mimeographed

Leichter, F. 1982. *Sweatshops to Shakedowns: Organized Crime in New York's Garment District.* New York State Legislative Report. March. Mimeographed.

Lupsha, P. 1981a. "Individual Choice, Material Culture and Organized Crime" *Criminology* 19. No. 1 (May) 3:24.

———— 1981b. "American Values and Organized Crime: Suckers versus Wiseguys." In Girgus, S., ed., *The American Self.* Albuquerque, NM: University of New Mexico Press.

_____. 1983a. "Networks versus Networking: An Analysis of an Organized Crime Group." In Waldo, G., ed., *Career Criminals*. Beverly Hills, Cal.: Sage Publishers.

_____. 1983b. "A Content Analysis Approach to Network Analysis of the Associational Ties Among Major Organized Crime Figures." Mimeographed.

_____. 1983c. "A Survey of Italian-American Crime Leadership—1983." (Chart and report) Mimeographed.

Maas, P. 1968. *the Valachi Papers*. New York: Bantam Books.

Magrath, C. P. 1966. *Yazoo: Law and Politics in the New Republic*. Providence, RI: Brown University Press.

Merton, Robert K. 1967. *Social Theory and Social Structure*. New York: Free Press.

Messick, H. 1971. *Lansky*. New York: G. P. Putnam's Sons.

_____. 1972. *The Mobs and the Mafia*. New York: Thomas Y. Crowell Co.

Moore, M. 1977. *Buy or Bust*. Lexington, Mass.: Lexington Books.

Nelli, H. 1976. *The Business of Crime*. New York: Oxford University Press.

Oyster Bay. 1976. *Conferences on Combatting Organized Crime 1975–1976*. New York State Report. Mimeographed.

Pennsylvania Crime Commission. 1983. *Annual Report*. St. Davids, Pa.: Commonwealth of Pennsylvania Publication.

Peterson, V. W. 1983. *The Mob: 200 Years of Organized Crime in New York*. Ottawa, Ill.: Green Hill Publishers Inc.

Reid, E., and Demaris, O. 1963. *The Green Felt Jungle*. New York: Pocket Books Inc.

Reuter, P. and Rubinstein, J. 1978. "Fact, Fancy and Organized Crime." *The Public Interest* 53 (Fall) 45:68.

_____ and Wynn, S. 1983. *Racketeering in Legitimate Industries: Two Case Studies*. Washington, D.C.: National Institute of Justice.

Reuter, P. 1983. *Disorganized Crime: The Economics of the Visible Hand*. Cambridge, Mass.: Mass. Institute of Technology Press.

Salerno, R. 1969. *The Crime Confederation*. New York: Popular Library.

Teresa, V. 1973. *My Life in the Mafia*. Greenwich, Conn.: Fawcett Books, Inc.

Tyler, G. 1969. *Organized Crime in America*. Ann Arbor, Mich.: University of Michigan Press.

U.S. Dept. of Justice. 1967. *Task Force Report: Organized Crime*. Washington, DC.: U.S. Government Printing Office.

U.S. Senate. 1957. *Investigation of Improper Activities in the Labor or Management Field*. Judiciary Committee Hearings. Washington, D.C.: U.S. Government Printing Office.

U.S. Senate. 1963. *Investigation of Narcotics Trafficking in Interstate Commerce*. Judiciary Committee Hearings. Washington, D.C.: U.S. Government Printing Office.

U.S. Senate. 1963. Permanent Subcommittee on Investigations. Washington, D.C.: U.S. Government Printing Office.

U.S. Senate. 1981. *Waterfront Corruption: Hearings of the Permanent Subcommittee on Investigations*. 97th Congress, 1st Session). Feb. 17–21. Washington, D.C.: U.S. Government Printing Office.

U.S. Senate. 1981. *Government's Ability to Combat Labor Management Rackateering: Hearings of the Permanent Subcommittee on Investigations*. 97th Congress, 1st Session. Oct.–Nov. Washington, D.C.: U.S. Government Printing Office.

U.S. Senate. 1983. *Profile of Organized Crime in the Middle Atlantic States: Hearings of the Permanent Subcommittee on Investigations*. 98th Congress, 1st Session. Feb. 15–24. Washington, D.C.: U.S. Government Printing Office.

U.S. Senate. 1983. *Organized Crime in Chicago: Hearings of the Senate Permanent Subcommittee on Investigations. 98th Congress, 1st Session. March 4. Washington, D.C.: U.S. Government Printing Office.*

Wolf, George with DiMona, Joseph. 1974. *Frank Costello: Prime Minister of the Underworld*. New York: William Morrow & Co.

4

A Modern Marriage of Convenience: A Collaboration Between Organized Crime and U.S. Intelligence

Alan A. Block
Pennsylvania State University

> Haydon also took it for granted that secret services were the only real measure of a nation's political health, the only real expression of its subconscious.
>
> — John Le Carré,
> *Tinker, Tailor, Soldier, Spy*

It is somewhat trite to note that organized crime is as much a political phenomenon as a social one. There are so many books and articles documenting the ties between American municipal government and professional criminal syndicates that it would be ludicrous to dare deny the fact. Among the abler works in the field is John A. Gardiner's study of Reading, Pennsylvania, which demonstrates the innumerable links between municipal government and organized crime (Gardiner 1970). Gardiner begins his chapter on "The Consequences of Corruption" by neatly summarizing the connections.

> Crime has not only corrupted American government for its own purposes; it has also tended to immobilize government for many other purposes. The problems of the American city . . . are not going to be solved by the dimwits whose campaigns are financed by the syndicates. And is there any reason to suppose that the leaders of organized crime are incapable of perceiving that they will be better off if American municipal government remains fragmented, uncoordinated, and in the hands, as much as possible, of incompetents? [p. 77]

Clearly enough, both the structure of American municipal government as well as the "dimwits" in office are responsible for the many ties.

What I want to suggest, however, is that organized crime's involvement in the political world is by no means limited to city government. In fact, I propose to show that organized crime has been and continues to be inextricably linked to transnational political movements and to that segment of the American political establishment known as the espionage community or perhaps more aptly, the transnational political police. This means, of course, that arguments about the structure of city politics and the competency of city officials are quite beside the point in accounting for these relationships. My intent then is to develop the history of the relationship between organized crime and the American espionage community whose genesis is found in the mutuality of anti-left interests characteristic of the intelligence services and segments of organized crime. Moreover, I argue that the crucial period for forging the relationships was the early part of World War II and, therefore, the relationship was not simply the product of the Cold War brought about by Soviet imperialism *following* the war.

Collaboration in Perspective

In one important sense the historical question of collaboration is easily and quickly answered: collaboration between professional criminals and espionage agencies has without doubt occurred throughout this century. The foundation upon which collaboration was built is the common ground of anti-left activities that are at the core of the phenomenon unfortunately called labor racketeering (Block and Chambliss, 1979), and as well the most consistent policy objective of the American espionage community. Moreover, the meeting of professional criminals and espionage agents in the various radical and trade union struggles of this century was mediated by a growing industry known as the private detective trade. It is indisputable that private detective agencies in serving the needs of both industrial employers and espionage agencies were major employers of professional criminals (Jeffreys-Jones, 1974). Indeed, some private detective businesses were little more than criminal syndicates themselves. As employers of criminals and employees of espionage agencies, a reasonable inference is that elements of the underworld and the intelligence community worked together. But this is not the whole story. There were also links between the underworld and espionage that were unmediated by private detectives (what we now call the private security industry). Because they were forged directly they are even more revealing of shared interests than is otherwise the case. For these more straightforward connections, the critical period is World War II, not the postwar period, as anti-Communist historiography claims (see Senate Select Committee 1975, xiii). Sometime in the winter of 1942, the Office of Naval Intelligence (ONI) concocted a plan to use professional criminals from the New York metropolitan area in a special and highly secret project. The full details of this collaboration were not known until 1977.

The Herlands Report of 1954

The story of this collaborative effort was pieced together in 1954 by New York State Commissioner of Investigation William B. Herlands in response to a request from New York State Governor Thomas E. Dewey. The reason for Dewey's request was the speculation, rumor and innuendo surrounding his commutation of the sentence of Charles Luciano (better known as Lucky Luciano) on January 4, 1946. What set off the rumors was that "It was generally understood, though not officially confirmed, that Lucky's contacts were valuable in the invasion of Italy and that his rumored assistance to the Allied forces figured in his early release from prison." In fact, Governor Dewey did state on the day before Luciano's commutation that "Upon entry of the United States into the war, Luciano's aid was sought by the armed services in inducing others to provide information concerning possible enemy attack. It appears that he cooperated in such effort, though the actual value of the information procured is not clear" (Wallace in the *Havana Post,* February 25, 1947). Without anything more definite, there were those who believed that Dewey had been bribed in the Luciano case as well as those who claimed that Luciano was responsible for the success of the Allied invasion of Sicily. It was Herlands' task, therefore, to conduct as full an investigation as possible and to prepare a report on his findings. The report was transmitted to Governor Dewey on September 17, 1954. It was not released though, because the Navy was more than reluctant to have its "underworld project" revealed.

Contacting the Underworld

According to Herlands, what lay behind the contact of ONI with professional criminals was the concern with the "problems of sabotage and espionage" especially in and around the Third Naval District, which included "the harbors and waterfront area" of New York and New Jersey. Naval Intelligence was suspicious that information dealing with "convoy movements" was being leaked, and that commercial fishing fleets might be providing "fuel and supplies for enemy submarines." Herlands noted that the main concern was "sympathizers of Mussolini and pro-fascists" and not "suspected pro-Nazis" who were already known. In the light of these problems, Captain Roscoe C. MacFall, who was then district intelligence officer, and his assistants conceived and sponsored a plan to use, among others, persons with underworld associations, their underworld associates and their contacts as instrumentalities of Naval Intelligence.

   The first step in the project was a meeting on March 7, 1942, with Captain MacFall, Lieutenant James O'Malley, Jr. (ONI), New York County District Attorney Frank Hogan, and Assistant District Attorney Murray I. Gurfein, who was then in charge of the district attorney's Rackets Bureau. At that meeting the Navy asked Hogan "for such assistance as he felt he could give in providing the Navy with any sources of information developed in the course of his waterfront investigation which might be of assistance in determining whether and how information or fuel was being supplied to the enemy."[2] It was agreed that Hogan's office would help in making underworld contacts available to the Navy. It was also determined at this meeting that Gurfein would be the district attorney's representative in the project, and that Lieutenant Commander Charles Radcliffe Haffenden would run the project for the Navy.

Haffenden was in charge of "B-3," the "investigative section" of the Third Naval District Intelligence Office. Commissioned a naval officer in World War I, Haffenden after the war worked in advertising, started his own small and unsuccessful manufacturing business, was "vice-president and general manager" of a pump company, and "between 1937 annd 1939 served as president of the Wiley-Moore Corporation, a firm of building contractors, which prepared exhibits for organizations wishing to display their products at the New York World's Fair" (Campbell 1977, 40). In addition, he was the "coordinator of the Executives Association of Greater New York" which was a group said to be "similar to the Rotary Club." The president of the Executives Association was Raymond C. Schindler, "one of the most celebrated private investigators in the country" (Campbell, 40).

It was in the summer of 1940 that Haffenden joined the Intelligence Office, and soon after was "appointed to command the B-3." Interestingly, it appears that Haffenden "continued to maintain his office as coordinator of the Executives Association" located at the Astor Hotel, which also functioned as his headquarters for B-3's new operation. Indeed, so close was Haffenden's Executives Assocation post merged with his running of B-3, at least in the early days, that his executive secretary, Elizabeth Schwerin, "had naval security clearance, and she used to type reports of Haffenden's peacetime investigations for Naval Intelligence and send them to Washington." At least once, Schwerin was instructed to attend "a public meeting" paying particular attention to any "possible communist subversive activity" (Campbell, 41–41). Schwerin's notes were reported to the ONI by Haffenden.

A second meeting was held at the district attorney's office on March 25, 1942, with Hogan, Gurfein, O'Malley of ONI, Haffenden and "possibly Lieutenant (j.g.) Anthony J. Marzullo (now Marsloe) who had been before the War a special investigator for the District Attorney's Office" (Herlands 1954, 27). It was apparently at this meeting that the name of Joe "Socks" Lanza, a notorious waterfront racketeer was first mentioned as a possible contact for B-3. Concerning this meeting, Herlands noted:

> In one of his talks with Colonel Gurfein — probably on March 25 — Commander Haffenden told Colonel Gurfein that he wanted Naval Intelligence to be placed in touch with the underworld, particularly with the Italian underworld, so as to set up a network of informants for counter-espionage. Colonel Gurfein suggested that Joe "Socks" Lanza, then under indictment, might be helpful. Colonel Gurfein offered to contact Mr. Joseph K. Guerin, attorney of record for Lanza, which he did, and arranged for a conference with Mr. Guerin for March 26, 1942. [Herlands 1954, 28]

"Socks" Lanza Enters the Plot

Lanza's official position at this time was business agent for the United Seafood Workers Union, but he was "actually the rackets boss of the Fulton Fish Market enclave in downtown New York City" (Campbell, 33). In addition, Lanza had recently been indicted for racketeering by the district attorney's staff. There were a number of arrests on Lanza's record for such things as juvenile delinquency, breaking and entering, homicide, possession of a pistol, coercion and conspiracy, none of which (without convictions) added up to much. In 1934, however, he was convicted for "violation of the federal anti-trust laws and was sentenced" to two years in prison and fined. He served his time at the Federal Prison at Milan, Michigan (Campbell, 47–48).

Lanza first came to public attention in the summer of 1931 when Samuel Seabury, who was investigating corruption in the district attorney's office, selected Lanza's activities as a labor racketeer to show what the district attorney was neglecting. In Seabury's report, his first example dealt with racketeering in the Fulton Market. The crux of racketeering in this enormous fish market lay in the relations between wholesale fish distributors and the representative of the workers' union local. The employers' representative was J. W. Walker, a director of Middleton Carman & Company, which distributed fish to restaurants, hotels, and steamships. The workers were members of the United Seafood Workers' Union, Local 16975, which was led by Lanza. Every two years, at the end of November, the union contract expired. A short time prior, Lanza and Walker began their negotiations with Lanza demanding higher wages and Walker arguing that it could not be done. This ritual was followed by a deal between Lanza and Walker in which Lanza would be paid a negotiated amount of money for returning a contract with no wage increase. In this particular case, reported on by Seabury, Lanza received $5,000. In order to raise the money, Walker assessed the other distributors $82 for each of their employees. The deal meant that labor costs would be raised only 78 cents a week per man for two years. There is no doubt that the employers found it financially beneficial to deal with Lanza rather than a bona fide trade unionist (Block 1983; 42–43).

Murray Gurfein called Lanza's attorney on March 26th and told him that Naval Intelligence "had been in touch with the District Attorney's office; that the Navy was of the opinion that the many sinkings of ships along the Atlantic Coast by U-boats indicated that the submarines were probably being refueled and getting fresh supplies off our coast; and that fishing smacks were a suspected source of such refueling and resupplying" (Herlands 30). He then suggested to Guerin that Lanza "might be in a position, personally or through his contacts, to find out how and where the submarines were being refueled and resupplied" (Herlands, 30). Guerin called Lanza and a meeting between Gurfein, Lanza and Guerin was set for that night. It was held on a park bench in the middle of the night.

Subsequent to the park bench meeting, Gurfein organized a meeting between Guerin, Lanza and Commander Haffenden at the Astor Hotel. Before the conference began, Gurfein "made a brief preliminary statement to the effect that Lanza understood that he was volunteering to help the Navy; that the District Attorney's Office had made no promise to him in exchange for such cooperation, and that he hoped Lanza would be useful" (Herlands, 32).

There is a slight discrepancy in accounts of this meeting and one other that apparently took place just a few days later. According to the Herlands report and Rodney Campbell's research, there was a second meeting, this time held at Haffenden's "official Church Street office," where he was told that " 'Agent X' (a Naval civilian agent whose name cannot be disclosed; but who testified before us) was to be his contact man" (Herlands, 33). Agent X, Campbell writes, "was an Italian-American who had been a private investigator for the famous detective Ray Schindler, the president of Haffenden's Executives Association" (Campbell, 55). Besides being the "direct liaison with Lanza," Agent X worked under or with Lieutenant Joseph Treglia, who had "once been a rumrunner." Treglia, along with Lieutenant Maurice Kelly, commanded "specialist squads in Commander Haffenden's B-3 investigative section" (Campbell, 54). Their duties were to construct an "anti-sabotage watch" in certain industries, and to organize "the surreptitious breaking and entering of suspect foreign and domestic officers for counter-intelligence purposes" (Campbell, 54).

The discrepancy is found in the report titled "Re: Conference with Dominick Saco and Felix Saco on Friday, April 9, 1954," which is in the Dewey papers at the University of Rochester. Dominick Saco was Agent X and he reported a slightly different version than the other sources. First of all, Saco stated that it was Lieutenant Treglia, the ex-rumrunner, who "suggested that underworld characters who were formerly bootleggers or rumrunners be approached with a view of obtaining information from them." Second, Saco claimed that he first met with Haffenden, Gurfein and Lanza at the Hotel Astor, not at the Church Street office.

It is also instructive that ex-private detective Saco was interested in "anything of a suspicious nature on the waterfront" including "any anticipated labor trouble" and the "activities of the radio and telegraph operators on the various ships who were then members of an alleged communist union." There is an obviously strong and significant line of continuity in the anti-communist spying of Haffenden, Saco, and Elizabeth Schwerin, all working for Ray Schindler, the president of Executives Association.

Lanza's Contribution

In discussing the initial phase of project "underworld," the Herlands report identifies four primary areas in which Lanza and the Navy labored together. The first "related to the use of commercial fishing fleets as an aid to the obtaining of information about possible enemy submarines" (Herlands, 35). Those ships without telephonic equipment were supplied by the Navy, which developed a special secret code for them to report any submarine sightings. The next area of cooperative work called for Lanza to use his influence and contacts "to place civilian agents of the Intelligence office on trucks that were operating in and around the Long Island ports" (Herlands, 35). In order for the agents to work they needed union cards and Lanza arranged for them to receive "Fishworker's Union books." Third, Lanza was able to place a number of Haffenden's civilian agents on fishing boats that sailed from the Fulton Market, New Jersey, Long Island, Maine, North Carolina, and Virginia. The fourth area enumerated by Herlands is the general one of "obtaining information about the waterfront, possible sabotage, and leaks concerning convoy movements." In this section of the report, Herlands noted that in the summer of 1942 Lanza went from North Carolina to Maine setting up contacts for Haffenden. Working with Lanza on this trip was Benjamin A. Espy, a former "rumrunner" and ex-convict who had served time on conspiracy charges and for violations the Volstead Act. In fact, Espy had been contacted by Lanza right after his meeting with Haffenden at the Astor. Lanza asked Espy to work with him on the project; Espy agreed and soon was independently contacting Haffenden as well as working jointly with Lanza.

Was It Necessary?

It is worth pondering that in the listing of Lanza's accomplishments in the Herlands report, the issue of whether or not segments of the fishing fleet were re-fueling and provisioning German submarines has become transformed to using the fishing fleet as a kind of early warning station. This not so subtle transformation may have occurred because Commander Haffenden had another way of determining the answer and knew early on that re-fueling of submarines was out of the question. Working for Haffenden in Naval Intelligence was Lieutenant Herbert F. Kemp, who was "a customs inspector in the port of New York since 1935," and a marine engineer. Kemp worked out a method for calculating "if any of the fishing boats could possibly be refueling U-boats from their own tanks" (Campbell, 56). He concluded that it was not possible. Rodney Campbell suggests that Haffenden put Kemp to work on this issue as "a sensible double-check" on Lanza's information. But one wonders why Kemp's rather straightforward mathematical methodology based on such things as engine horsepower, fuel capacity and consumption of the fishing boats was employed as a double-check, especially as it was vastly more economical and efficient than the underworld operation. Moreover, it also turns out that at the highest levels of military intelligence it was already known that Nazi submarines needed no help from the fishing fleet. Concerning this, Rodney Campbell writes:

> Actually, the combined Chiefs of Staff, which included the chief of Naval Operations, U.S. Navy, must have known even then from their Ultra transcripts of secret German codes what was happening along the Eastern Sea Frontier. The German *Kriegsmarine* was operating brand-new type IX-CU-boats which could

range from Lorient and St. Nazaire on the French Biscay coast to the Caribbean without refueling. Supplies were being ferried to the U-boats at long ranges aboard "milch-cow" U-boats, stripped of all armament except for two machine-guns. Also, American supplies had been available in Europe before the United States entered the war and might easily have been issued to U-boat crews and seen aboard the U-boats by American survivors. [Campbell 1977, 28]

Campbell notes that Ultra transcripts "never" went to "operational personnel at the level of the Third Naval District." The simple fact is that German subversion in the fishing fleet was unnecessary and did not happen. It nevertheless appears that the Third Naval District was unaware of the range and capabilities of the German U-boats and went ahead with their operation. In any case, the fishing fleet went from suspect to watchdog, and if nothing else this transformation of function contributed to the continuing justification of the overall project.

From Lanza to Luciano

Of all Lanza's accomplishments during the initial phase of the operation, nothing was quite so important as his realization that his influence was vastly limited. It was this recognition which led to his most significant contribution. Lanza was instrumental in bringing Lucky Luciano into the operation, an event which materially changed the collaboration between Intelligence and organized crime.

Within about three weeks of the time that Lanza went to work for B-3, he reported to his attorney "that he was having difficulty in getting information from and in making contacts with persons who had been born in Italy; and that 'Luciano could be of great assistance' " (Herlands, 38). His attorney advised him to bring this up with Haffenden. Dominick Saco (Agent X) stated that he had requested information from Lanza that came from "sources" who were a bit outside of Lanza's sphere of immediate influence. The information was not forthcoming because the individuals "approached felt that Lanza was going to use the information as an informer for the District Attorney's office in order to get consideration on his then pending indictment" (see Dewey Papers).[1] Lanza then told Saco that he needed someone to assure these people that he was not an informer. The best person for this, Lanza stated, was Luciano. Saco then brought the Luciano matter up with Haffenden who agreed that it was a fine idea that he would carry out. (In fact, Haffenden may have already started the process of contacting Luciano before Saco mentioned it.)

At this time Lucky Luciano was sitting in Clinton prison, Dannemora, New York, not very far from the Canadian border. He had been convicted of heading a vice syndicate in 1936, and was sentenced to the rather incredible term of 30 to 50 years. The individual responsible for the Luciano investigation and conviction was Thomas E. Dewey, who, later as governor, would commute Luciano's sentence on the condition of his deportation. And as noted earlier, the commutation would raise endless questions about Dewey's probity and Luciano's influence especially because it was Dewey who had put Luciano in prison in the first place.

Past History: Luciano and Dewey

Dewey's prosecution of Luciano was almost as important a stepping-stone in Dewey's career as it was a mill-stone in Luciano's. Back in 1935, Dewey had been appointed as a special prosecutor after a long series of scandals had publicized corruption in the New York County District Attorney's Office. As special prosecutor Dewey and his marvelous staff, which included Murray Gurfein and Frank Hogan, pursued three major and extraordinarily complex longterm investigations. They centered on the activities and associates of Lucky Luciano (real name Salvatore Lucania), Dutch Schultz (real name, Arthur Flegenheimer), and Louis Buchalter. Without doubt the Luciano case was the most spectacular single accomplishment during Dewey's tenure as special prosecutor. According to Dewey's memoirs the investigation began in January, 1936, when rumors reached him that a "single combination" was running prostitution in Manhattan and Brooklyn. Evidence was gathered which indicated that the head of the combination was Luciano, who was arrested on April 1, 1936, in Hot Springs, Arkansas. By the summer of 1936 the trial was over and all the defendants were judged guilty. Luciano received 30 to 50 years; codefendants Betillo 25 to 40, Frederico and Pennochio 25 years, Wahrman 15 to 30, Liguori 7½ to 15, and the rest anywhere from 2 to 8 years. It was a sensational victory for Dewey, justifying the need and worth of a special prosecutor (Block 1983).

Luciano Comes Out of the Cold

The manner in which Haffenden secured the cooperation of Luciano was reminiscent of the origins of project "underworld." Haffenden contacted Assistant District Attorney Gurfein and told him that Lanza needed Luciano's help in continuing and expanding his work. Gurfein then discussed Haffenden's request with District Attorney Hogan, who gave his assent. Both Hogan and Gurfein decided that the proper way to establish contact with Luciano was through Moses Polakoff, who had been Luciano's attorney in the prostitution case. Although reticent at first, Polakoff agreed, and when he arrived, Gurfein recounted what had been going on, and told him that Lanza strongly felt the need for Luciano's aid. In addition, Gurfein stated that "Navy Intelligence desired to enlist the aid of Luciano to establish a source of information concerning the docks," presumably more reliable or more extensive than could be accomplished by Lanza. Polakoff's reply deserves to be quoted in full:

> On an occasion like this, if I could be of any service to him or the Navy, I would
> be glad to do so. I told him that I did not know Luciano well enough to broach

this subject to him on my own but I knew the person whom I had confidence in and whose patriotism, or affection for our country, irrespective of his reputation, was of the highest; and I would like to discuss the matter with this person first before I committed myself [Herlands, 44]

The indispensable patriot, Polakoff revealed, was Meyer Lansky. Following Polakoff's suggestion, Luciano was transferred to Great Meadow Prison at Comstock, New York. What Luciano did, the Herlands report claims, was to discuss matters with friends and associates who visited him at Great Meadow Prison, and presumably enlist them in the burgeoning activities of B-3. The only individals who were at Great Meadow for every visit were Polakoff and Lansky. Overall there appear to have been 20 meetings with Luciano between May 15, 1942 and August 21, 1945; six in the remainder of 1942, four in 1943, six in 1944, and four in 1945. The racketeers who met with Luciano in prison besides Lansky were Lanza, who visited him several times, Mike Lascari, Frank Costello, Willie Moretti, Michael Mirandi(a), and Benjamin ("Bugsy") Siegel. During Prohibition, Lascari had been in the "beer business," and among his criminal associates were Lansky, Abner Zwillman, Joe Stacher, and Jerry Catena. The last three were apparently involved at various times with Lascari in a company called the Public Service Tobacco Company (see note 1). Lascari also owned a machine shop during the war that handled subcontracts for Western Electric Company, General Motors, Curtiss Wright, Firestone Tire and Rubbber, and other major companies (*Dewey Papers,* Digest, 2).

As Haffenden never met with Luciano, and as no one ever visited Luciano without Lansky, it was Lansky who came to be Haffenden's most important underworld contact, intermediary, and organizer. It was Lansky's function (as Herlands put it) to get Haffenden in touch with individuals outside the ken of Lanza's influence, but not outside that of either Luciano or Lansky. And although Lanza stated that doors opened by merely mentioning that Luciano had given his "okay," it seems clear that it was Lansky who actually engineered the meeting of Lanza with more powerful racketeers.

Securing the Waterfront

With the backing of Luciano and the active cooperation of Lansky, what Haffenden next wanted was contact with the most important waterfront racketeers in New York: Johnny Dunn in Manhattan, Joe Adonis, and the Camardas in Brooklyn. (It is a curious fact that in the Herlands report and Rodney Campbell's research, both discuss the Camardas without noting that Emil Camarda, the leader of his family and a principal waterfront racketeer, was murdered in October, 1941. There were still Camardas enough on the Brooklyn waterfront, but despite what Herlands and Campbell state or imply, Emil was long gone. See Block, 1982.) Although Lanza stated that Luciano gave him the "go-ahead" to contact Dunn and Adonis, it was not Lanza but Meyer Lansky who brought Dunn and Adonis to Haffenden.

Securing their assistance, Haffenden subsequently had both men working in-dependently with him.

By the summer of 1942, Haffenden had established an expanding network of underworld informants and managers that included many of New York's most important organized crime figures, especially those who controlled the waterfront. The construction of the network and Lansky's central role are shown in Figure 4.1.

What is notable in the structure of the network is that Lanza became ex-pendable as soon as the network was constructed, and that Lansky domi-nated or coordinated almost the entire network. The expendability of Lanza was crucial because of his prior indictment for extortion and conspiracy. On January 12, 1943 Lanza pled guilty to the charges and several weeks later, was sentenced to prison. Ben Espy took over for Lanza, but he apparently had nothing to do or report; and shortly after, Espy "abandoned his brief ca-reer as a Naval Intelligence contact and went to work gainfully and full-time in Meyer Lansky's jukebox organization, the Emby Distribution Company" (Campbell, 151). The Lanza fishing fleet operation was no longer important — emphasis had shifted (in fact much earlier than Lanza's confinement) to that much greater segment of the waterfront world controlled by the Interna-tional Longshoremen's Association (ILA). It was Haffenden's felt need to contact, penetrate, and use the ILA and its criminal supporters and repre-sentatives that revealed Lanza's inadequacy and thus led to the involvement of Lansky and Luciano. That the ILA was a racketeer-dominated organiza-tion, if not simply a linked congeries of criminal syndicates posing as a labor

FIGURE 4.1
The Network of Underworld Figures and Government Officials

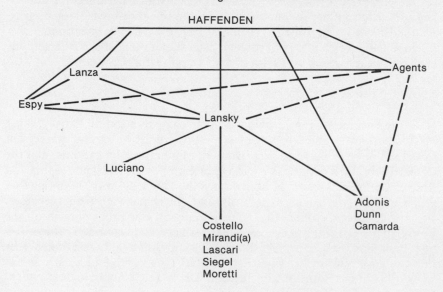

union, was hardly a secret. But just how this world was constructed, and indeed protected, was somewhat less obvious. In fact, it wasn't until the early 1950s that the full extent of waterfront organized crime was revealed in a series of investigations that together exposed its history and sociology (see Block, 1982).

Waterfront Racketeers and Naval Intelligence

New York's most vicious waterfront organized criminals were now linked to Naval Intelligence through the hard work of Commander Haffenden. Being tied to this world meant for B-3 that the waterfront was being patrolled, as it was rather endlessly stated "for sabotage and espionage." Also, Intelligence agents were given ILA union cards and were thus "able to conduct discreet operations on the waterfront and 'do anything they wanted without anybody asking them questions.' " Part of these discreet operations involved "surveillance of suspicious persons" (Herlands, 70).

With certain exceptions there is throughout the Herlands report, a disturbing lack of specificity when it comes to exactly what B-3 and organized crime were involved in and what they really accomplished. The vagueness of statements such as "patrolling for espionage and sabotage," "surveillance of suspicious persons," "a source of information concerning the docks," and so on, convey little beyond the oft expressed need for any and all waterfront information. Originally the desire behind the whole project was to infiltrate the fishing fleet suspected of nourishing U-boats; and ultimately the project would take on a new task, the collecting of information about Sicily and mainland Italy as the American military prepared and carried out its first European invasion. Part of the reason for the vagueness found in the report probably stemmed from Herlands mission, which was to document the fact of Luciano working for Naval Intelligence and not to uncover all that was done; another part from the Navy's reluctance to divulge anything beyond the barest facts. The few instances in which details of activities were given stand out. The major example reported was the Harry Bridges affair.

The Harry Bridges Affair

To put it most succinctly, B-3 and their organized crime collaborators terrorized Harry Bridges (Code name: Brooklyn Bridge), the President of the International Longshoremen's and Warehousemen's Union, when he came to New York in the late fall of 1942. Australian-born Harry Bridges arrived in the United States in 1920 when he "jumped ship in San Francisco" after fighting with his ship's captain "over an order to work on Easter Monday, a recognized Australian holiday" (Bernstein 1971, 253). He joined the Sailors Union of the Pacific and the IWW for a short time in 1931. For over a decade Bridges worked as a longshoreman in San Francisco, and in 1932 was a member of the Marine Workers Industrial Union, which was, according to Irving

Bernstein, a "Communist organization" (Bernstein, 259). In the labor struggles of the mid-1930s, the Marine Workers Industrial Union fell by the wayside, and Bridges and other radical longshoremen (known for a while as the Albion Group) moved to take over the leadership of the major ILA local in San Francisco. In 1934 Bridges played a key role in the complex and violent longshoremen's strike in San Francisco that culminated in a general strike in the city. It was during this strike that Bridges and Joseph Ryan, President of the ILA, became bitter enemies. Three years later after the formation of the Congress of Industrial Organizations (CIO), "Bridges converted his ILA district into the International Longshoremen's and Warehousemen's Union (ILWU) and received a CIO charter" (Bernstein, 587).

The conventional wisdom concerning the attack on Bridges in New York masterminded by Haffenden, Lansky and Lanza holds that Bridges was "coming to the bigger ports and the more heavily populated waterfronts of the eastern states to proclaim" that the ILA "was not properly representing the interests of its membership" (Campbell, 121). Given his extremely radical, if not communist, stance, Bridges' presence guaranteed strife on the waterfront: "And it was precisely the labor unrest Bridges was agitating that the Navy did not want in the midst of the heavy convoy shipments to Great Britain and North Africa" (Campbell, 121). There is some truth in the foregoing, but a very important issue is missing that undermines the conventional interpretation. Of course, Bridges proclaimed that the ILA in New York represented gangsters and not the rank and file; and, of course, Bridges was a radical extremely close to the Communist party. But beginning with the German attack on the Soviet Union on June 22, 1941, Bridges became an advocate of an all-out Allied victory. He proposed before the attack on Pearl Harbor and more vigorously after, a "tripartite board" or "union-employer-council" that

> could speed up cargo handling by finding ways to use more labor-saving machinery, providing central planning in each port to avoid congestion in loading the ships, making better use of small ports, studying the cost of longshore operations, insuring that enough reliable longshoremen would be constantly available, helping to settle disputes, and recommending the most economical methods, even if that meant changes in working rules. He added that the council could also explore ways to work ships during blackouts and guard against accidents and deliberate sabotage. [Larrowe 1972, 251–52]

Within a few days of his announcement an "employer spokesman" stated that what the Bridges plan " 'means is that men who have no financial investment in or responsibilities for an enterprise and who in some case have never worked in the industry are to join in the control of it' " (Larrowe, 252).

Agitation for Bridges' plan got nowhere until February 9, 1942, when the liner Normandie, which was beng refitted as a troop and cargo carrier, exploded and burned at her New York dock. Admiral Emory S. Land, the head of the War Shipping Board, told Sam Kagel, Bridges' representative in Washington, that he was ready to talk with Bridges about his production plan. Less than a month later, "the Bridges plan, officially known as the Pacific Coast Maritime Industry Board, was in operation as an agency of the U.S. War Shipping Administration" (Larrowe, 254). During the war Bridges stood squarely against strikes and other forms of labor unrest that threatened in any way American military efficiency, going so far as to brand John L. Lewis who called the mine workers out on strike in 1943 "the single most effective agent of the Fascist powers within the ranks of labor" (Larrowe, 255).

The point is, Bridges was a threat to Ryan, the ILA racketeers and their business partners, not to the war effort. In addition, his radicalism undoubtedly cast him in the enemy camp as far as Haffenden was concerned. This explains the following conversation on November 24, 1942:

Haffenden: I don't want any trouble on the waterfront during the crucial times.

Lanza: You won't have any. I'll see to that. I'll give you a ring. We'll get together.

Haffenden: O.K., Socks.

What followed from this can be seen in Lanza's testimony before Herlands.

Q. In other words, Haffenden suspected that Bridges was trying to organize the waterfront with what Haffenden thought was a Communist-dominated union?

A. That's right.

Q. And he was afraid of trouble and strikes on the waterfront if Bridges got a foothold here.

A. That's right.

Q. Haffenden asked you to do your best to put a stop to that?

A. That's right.

Q. As a matter of fact, did you actually do something about that?

A. We stopped him from coming in here.

Q. How did that happen?

A. He tried to call meetings, and when he called a meeting up in Webster Hall, I had a fight with him. I belted him and that was that.

A. When you say "he," you mean Harry Bridges?

A. Yes. Joe Ryan had a lot do do with a situation of that kind.

Waterfront labor-relations through this period of collaboration between Naval Intelligence and organized crime were confined to the parameters thought acceptable by such as Adonis, Lanza, and Ryan on the one hand, and Haffenden on the other. And it was also well known that the leaders of the most infamous "pistol locals" in the port were cooperating with the Navy; thus their own actions taken in their own interests were covered by whatever cloak of legitimacy emanated from their military sponsor. That knowledge of the operation was common was mentioned by Dominick Saco: "Well, I do know that practically the entire city of New York knew that the underworld was cooperating with the District Intelligence office, and this I got particularly in person from Albert Marinelli, who was a very influential political leader in New York City at one time, and whenever I used Albert Marinelli as an informer, he would tell me" (Campbell, 126–27).

The Navy, Organized Crime, and Harlem

Subversion did not come only in the form of Harry Bridges, nor was it found and worried-about only on the waterfront. In the same conversation where he expressed concern about Bridges, Haffenden asked Lanza whether or not Meyer Lansky knows anything about "that Harlem thing." What this was about, Lanza said, was "an organization in Harlem that was printing subversive literature." Neither the Herlands report nor the testimony of Lanza give any indication of what subversion meant in this case. What they do tell is that the organization was a "Negro" one, and that Wille McCabe, a policy gambler operating in Harlem, was able to assist B-3 in placing an agent into the "subversive" printing plant. McCabe went on from there to cooperate in a number of ways with Haffenden. There is one clue to the meaning of subversion, however, and it was furnished by Dominick Saco. Working on a "project being supervised" by Paul A. Alfieri, who worked first as a civilian agent (he received his commission as a lieutenant in the summer of 1942) for B-3, Saco wanted "information on activities of the Spanish Falangists" (Fascists), who were stirring up "trouble among the Negroes" in Harlem (Dewey Papers, Re: Conference, 3). Saco stated that he asked Lanza to find Willie McCabe. This was done and in the end, through the help of McCabe, "O.N.I. located the headquarters of the Spanish Falangists at the El Chico restaurant in Greenwich Village and at Waldo's Hotel, Ramapo, N.Y." (Re: Conference, 3). There is no telling, of course, whether what bothered B-3 in this instance was Fascism (and Spanish Fascism at that) or that Harlem's "Negro" population was being stirred-up.

One reason why B-3's interest in matters racial may have been stronger than in Falangist activities was that Haffenden was clearly interested in other individuals and places in Harlem and used Lanza and especially McCabe in securing informants and placing agents in cabarets in that neighborhood. It is also the case that beginning in January 1943, the first stirrings of black protest concerning the Navy were heard in Harlem. What lay behind this was a request from the Navy in December 1942 "to use Hunter College and Walton High School, both in the Bronx, as part of a training center for enlisted women" (Capeci 1977, 136–37). Blacks were angry because of the "racial segregation policy of the Women's Reserve of the United States Naval Reserve (Waves)," coupled with the use of municipal property for training (Capeci, 137). The culmination of black grievances, which were many, came in the summer when it seemed as if all of Harlem erupted in riot.

The Nature of Collaboration

The meeting of intelligence and organized crime took place in the immediate aftermath of America's involvement in World War II. Within three months of the Pearl Harbor attack, the proposal to employ professional criminals in intelligence operations was made, adopted, and implemented. Collaboration between intelligence and organized crime clearly then was not forced upon America by the exigencies of the post-War world. This is not to suggest that the Cold War had little impact on collaboration, but rather that it shaped already extant reltionships. Concerning this first collaborative effort, it is also significant to note the scale of operation. This was no discrete, short term operation involving a limited number of individuals. Instead, this operation called for the almost exponential growth of participants. What Haffenden wanted was a kind of total underworld collaboration on all his intelligence problems for the duration. These problems included all his suspicions and fears of sabotage and espionage possibly carried out or, more importantly, planned by enemy agents and sympathizers. And as we have seen the enemy for Haffenden was more than Germany and Italy, more than Naziism and Fascism; the enemy embraced any and all subversions, especially Communism. In fact, Haffenden's residual pre-war, anti-Communism was apparently neither tempered by the war in general, nor the Soviet Union's struggle with Hitler in particular, nor the fact that radicals like Harry Bridges were totally committed to the war effort. Haffenden could not abide what he perceived as the Communist threat and thus acted in ways consistent with his pre-war position. And to recall again, his past included service with the private detective industry in what were anti-Communist snooping activities. Not only Haffenden, but secret agent Saco and Elizabeth Schwerin shared the same history, in working together for Ray Schindler.

It may seem that the collaboration between organized crime and intelligence in this first major example is being primarily scrutinized to locate anti-Communist or anti-radical activities. One might argue, I suppose, that the Harry Bridges affair was hardly typical of the operation overall. What typified the entire project, to continue this line, was that intelligence would go to any lengths during wartime to protect domestic security including working with professional criminals to prevent any possible disruptions in the war effort. The operation had to be primarily a defensive one characterized by the ceaseless gathering of information about potential saboteurs and fifth columnists, through infiltrating trade unions, cabarets, saloons, hotels, fishing boats, and so on. And it remained primarily defensive because there simply weren't many Nazi and Fascist fifth columnists. Assumed, if not buried, in this type of critique is something one might call the "good faith argument"; to wit, that intelligence was really doing all it could to ferret out Nazis and Fascists and their fellow travellers. The atypicality of the Bridges escapade depends to an extent on accepting the good faith argument.

It is a claim or argument impossible to accept, however. The most compelling reason to reject it is that certain organized crime figures had been allied with the Italian Fascist party for years. In some American communities there was a deeply-embedded infrastructure of Fascist clubs and other organizations riddled with professional criminals, among whom were Frank Garofolo, Joe and Peter Di Palermo, Joseph Bonanno, Tony Bender, John

Dioquardi, Carmine Galante, Joseph Profaci, and Vincenzo Martinez. In fact, so clear were the connections between Italian (and Italian-American) Fascism and organized crime that a fair number of both Fascist organizations and racketeering ones had located their offices in the same building in Manhattan. In addition to working out of the same address, a number of key Fascists and organized crime figures were tied together by Generoso Pope, the publisher of the Nation's largest Italian-language newspaper (*Il Progresso Italo-Americano*), who was a rabid Fascist spokesman as well as organized crime intimate (see Block and Block 1982). Finally, one of the racketeering associations alluded to above, was the Albert Marinelli Association, a political clubhouse. Marinelli was a very influential politician in New York who also was a "member of one of New York's most powerful criminal combinations, which included Lucky Luciano, Vito Genovese, John Torrio, Vincent Mangano." (Block 1983, 73). Marinelli is mentioned specifically because he was another bridge linking both the Fascist and criminal world; he was closely associated with Luciano, known and important Fascists, and was a regular informant for Dominick Saco (Agent X).

To put it briefly, there is not one shred of evidence indicating that B-3 tried to find out anything at all about the pre-war world of Italian-American Fascism, which itself was so deeply intertwined with organized crime. B-3's inescapable preoccupation was subversion and certinly not Italian-American Fascism. In fact, those waterfront racketeers so eager to be enlisted in the intelligence operation with B-3 and later with the Sicilian campaign were amongst the more visible pre-war Fascists. There is then a decidedly misleading element in the interpretive and documentary material dealing with Project Underworld. Both Herlands and Campbell accept (perhaps indeed, embellish) the good faith argument, which then proceeds to structure their work. As long as the Navy claimed that its clandestine efforts were devoted to fighting sabotage and espionage on the part of America's declared enemies, that was good enough. No need to question their dearth of anti-Fascist activities.

The Future of Collaboration

Project Underworld did not depend upon intelligence officers necessarily approving the actions and activities of professional criminals in the abstract (although those with criminal backgrounds might very well have). Instead, it was the product of the merging of the former's ideology with the latter's self-interest. What that merger meant in the postwar world can be briefly mentioned.

In Italian politics two examples come immediately to mind. The first concerns the rapid elevation of Bernardo Matterella, who, Justin Vitiello writes, "was a hack lawyer from Castellamare del Golfo (Western Sicily)" who had performed a number of unspecified acts for the Allies, especially the intelligence services. Vitiello adds

> After the war, as a reward, American and Mafia interests put him into power as a regional deputee (the equivalent of a representative to our Congress). Matarella, who later became a Minister in the Aldo Moro governments of the 1960s, maintained good relationships with Joey Bananas (i.e., Giuseppe Bonanno, scion of an illustrious Mafia family transplanted to Brooklyn) and engineered, in collusion with Salvatore Giuliano, the most infamous of Sicilian bandits, the Massacre of Broom Flower Gate, where scores of trade-unionists and peasant organizers were gunned down May 1, 1947, while they were picnicking to celebrate their Labor Day. [Vitiello 1981, 2]

A much more contemporary example is the still mysterious case of Michele Sindona, convicted in 1980 of "looting $45 million from the Franklin National Bank." Sindona, it has been claimed, was involved in a series of conspiracies with "powerful Italian industrialists, politicians, and Vatican officials who had often used Sindona's numerous banks to sneak fortunes in cash out of Italy"; "members of the dominant Christian Democratic party who had accepted millions of dollars in bribes from Sindona"; "clandestine anti-Communist" organizations and the "Central Intelligence Agency"; and one of the most powerful transnational organized crime syndicates active today (Pileggi 1980).

Italy, of course, is not the only country whose politics has been structured at least partially by organized crime and American intelligence services working together to further anti-Communism on the one hand, and illegal businesses on the other. In fact, many countries that became or were part of the American Imperium following World War II were (and continue to be) subject to similar conspiracies. The list of penetrated and brutalized countries in the Mediterranean area, Southeast Asia, and Latin America is appallingly long; and so too are the innumerable Mattarellas serving in high government posts around the globe — clients all to racketeers and the anti-Communist intelligence services. In addition, clandestine anti-Communist work has been merged for over four decades with clandestine enterprises in narcotics, munitions, counterfeiting, and gambling among others, and both together often submerge into or are expressed through a variety of Fascist, Neo-Fascist, and "Fascistoid" (see Nolte 1966) organizations and regimes. (There has been a mimetic process at work for quite some time making it increasingly difficult to distinguish between the KGB with its organized crime partners in Central and Eastern Europe [see Senate Internal Security Subcommittee 1965] and the CIA.)

For organized crime researchers, the major point to reflect upon is the indisputable fact that certain organized crime figures and syndicates are deeply embedded in transnational political movements and the transnational political police. And the recognition noted at the beginning of this chapter that organized crime and municipal governments are inextricably linked must not obscure the profound impact of organized crime on foreign affairs, the world of "high" politics. It may very well be the case that certain political assassinations or other intelligence moves may be done not in the interests of foreign policy carried out by hired goons and thugs, but rather in the interest of drug smugglers and international gamblers carried out by their clients in the intelligence services. And in this world it appears that the terms "good and evil" are "no more than baroque abstractions" replaced by a "new theology" of "good business and bad business" as the novelist Eric Ambler reflected long ago.[3]

Notes

1. The documents on the Luciano case are located in the *Dewey Papers* held in the Rare Books and Manuscripts Division of the University of Rochester Library. The major document is State of New York, Executive Department, Office of the Commissioner of Investigation, William B. Herlands Commissioner (September 17, 1954) *Report* (cited in the text as Herlands, 1954). Supplementary documents are usually cited *Dewey Papers* . . . All the material is part of the copious Thomas E. Dewey Papers held by the University of Rochester Library.

2. Frank Hogan, perhaps New York's outstanding district attorney of this century, kept careful tabs on the Navy's operation primarily by wiretapping Haffenden's headquarters.

3. Eric Ambler, *A Coffin For Dimitrious*.

References

Ambler, Eric. 1939. *A Coffin for Dimitrious*. New York: Knopf.

Bernstein, Irving. 1971. *Turbulent Years: A History of the American Worker, 1933–1941*. Boston: Houghton Mifflin.

Block, Alan A. 1982. " 'On the Waterfront' Revisited: The Criminology of Waterfront Organized Crime." *Contemporary Crises* 6:373–96.

_____. 1983. *East Side—West Side: Organizing Crime in New York, 1930–1950*. New Brunswick, N.J.: Transaction Books.

Block, Alan A. and Block, Marcia J. 1982. "Fascism, Organized Crime and Foreign Policy: An Inquiry Based on the Assassination of Carlo Tresca." In S. Spitzer and R. Simon, eds., *Research Annual in Law, Deviance and Social Control*. Greenwich, Conn.: JAI Press.

Block, Alan A. and Chambliss, William J. 1979. "Miners, Tailors and Teamsters: Business Racketeering and Trade Unionism." *Crime and Social Justice* 11:14–27.

Campbell, Rodney. 1977. *The Luciano Project: The Secret Wartime Collaboration of the Mafia and the U.S. Navy*. New York: McGraw-Hill.

Capeci, Dominick J., Jr. 1977. *The Harlem Riot of 1943*. Philadelphia: Temple University Press.

Dewey, Thomas E. *Dewey Papers*. University of Rochester Library, Rochester, N.Y.

Gardiner, John A. 1970. *The Politics of Corruption: Organized Crime in an American City*. New York: Russell Sage Foundation.

Herlands, William B. 1954. Report of the Commissioner of Investigation. In *Dewey Papers*, University of Rochester Library, Rochester, N.Y.

Jeffreys-Jones, G. R. 1974. "Plug-Uglies in the Progressive Era," in D. Fleming and B. Bailyn, eds., *Perspectives in American History*. Cambridge, Mass.: Charles Warren Center for Studies in American History.

Larrowe, Charles P. 1972. *Harry Bridges: The Rise and Fall of Radical Labor in the United States*. New York: Lawrence Hill & Co.

Nolte, Ernest. 1966. *Three Faces of Fascism: Action Francaise, Italian Fascism, National Socialism*. New York: Holt, Rinehart & Winston.

Pileggi, Nicholas. 1980. "Sindona: A Little Help from His Friends," *New York Magazine,* April 7.
U.S. Senate Select Committee to Study Governmental Operations with Respect to Intelligence Activities. 1975. *Alleged Assassination Plots Involving Foreign Leaders: An Interim Report.* Washington, D.C.: U.S. Government Printing Office.
U.S. Senate Subcommittee to Investigate the Administration of the Internal Security Act and Other Internal Security Laws of the Committee on the Judiciary. 1965. *Murder International, Inc.: Murder and Kidnapping as an Instrument of Soviet Policy.* Washington, D.C.: U.S. Government Printing Office.
Vitiello, Justin. 1981. "The Client Relationship between the U.S. and Italy." Testimony for the Mass Proletarian War Crimes Tribunal of U.S. Imperialism. Presented at New York City, December 6, 1981. Unpublished.

5

Analyzing the Organization of Crime in Montreal, 1920–80: A Canadian Test Case

Pierre Tremblay
University of Montreal

Richard Kedzior
University of Montreal

In Canada, the simultaneous disappearance during the early 1960s of a patronage system as a way of governing and of corruption practices as an essential element in the organization of criminal practices is very significant in the development of working hypotheses that are essentially heuristic. This leads directly to the study of crime and the degree to which it is organized. Thus, an analysis of the structure of opportunities and black markets should logically and empirically precede a description of the size or complexity of the internal organization of criminal groups.

Political Bosses, "Low" Police, and Corruption

What documentary sources are pertinent for the analysis of the organization of crime? It is generally agreed that police statistics, while now standardized and fairly reliable, tell us more about the organizational qualities of the police than about crime as such. Their principal use is to provide police administrators with information on police bureaucratic performance, and crime is thus recorded merely as a caseload. The investigation files and complaint reports summarized in these statistics, on the other hand, are used exclusively to establish the individual guilt of suspects in accordance with the rules of judicial proof and the general conduct of the criminal courts. Nothing pertinent to the actual police investigation, but that seems of little use to the judicial personnel, is recorded. This lack of documentation serves to keep alive the oral tradition of the police. (The maintenance and development of this oral tradition is so important, incidentally, that a survey would no doubt show that a policeman may be a mediocre writer but often an excellent raconteur.) If the criminal statistics are subject to the organizational norms of a government bureaucracy, the investigation files, on the other hand, are subject to the legal norms that govern the proof of a criminal act. In a democratic regime, the latter is limited, as a matter of principle, to proof of particular, discrete criminal transactions that must be attributed to individuals, who are considered, in fact, to be "isolates" (although they may be working in concert, in dyads or small or large groups, whether as a conspiracy or in the perpetration of their acts). The investigation files are written accordingly and their use for an analysis of concrete criminal practices is fairly negligible.

The best sources of information on the organization of these practices are the Commissions of Public Inquiry. In exploring these sources, we are limiting ourselves here to the case of one city, Montreal. The public inquiries we are relying on cover the period of approximately the first sixty years of the twentieth century. The Inquiry Commissions, during this entire time and at relatively regular intervals, were authorized to uncover corruption in the police forces and in public administration. Their studies and reports confirmed the opinion, fairly general today, that political corruption is a decisive factor in the organization of crime. This warrants careful examination. The literature in this area is sparse, but a detailed analysis of patronage as a way of governing (Lemieux 1975), a methodological description of the workings of these commissions over a long period (Brodeur 1979), and the zealous publications of moral entrepreneurs (Plante 1950; Plante et al. 1972) make a preliminary assessment possible.

1. It is not very difficult to show that these inquiry commissions had a direct political function. Not only did they make it possible to "bring about or prevent a change in the party in power," but they also gave "the illusion of political change by alternating the parties at the head of the various levels of government." (Brodeur 1979).
2. Patronage as a function of democratic government disappeared at the beginning of the 1960s (Lemieux 1975). The quiet revolution in the political economy of Quebec Province marked the simultaneous disappearance of what seemed to be an inevitable characteristic of the social order: corruption among civil servants (especially those in criminal justice), and the payoffs and toleration of the red light district where criminal practices were rife.
3. The patronage denounced by this battery of inquiry commissions is of a specific nature. A plausible hypothesis would maintain that the denunciation did not, in fact, refer to bribery, nepotism or favoritism but only to "corruption," a term that should be limited to relationships of clientele where the client offers or gives the patron so many things or of such great value that the gap between the position of the client and the patron

is largely reduced (Lemieux 1975). A second and complementary hypothesis would point out that such corruption was to be the special attribute or the stigma of "rackets" patronage, more unstable and less lucrative than the higher patronage of city refinancing or the lower patronage of public works, zoning, or permits (Plante et al. 1972, 233).

4. Patronage operates differently in dissimilar political systems. In a liberal democracy, it is the electoral process itself that is vital, with each election involving a redistribution of a large variety of services, goods, and capital. The direct manipulation of an election is, therefore, a crucial element, and this need was usually entrusted to illicit "telegraphers" — "persons previously informed of the names on voter lists who are absent, dead or not voting, and on the basis of this information, vote several times in polls located in different neighbourhoods" (Plante et al. 1972, 211). To date, no detailed analysis has been made of the various political services rendered in this way by criminal entrepreneurs.[1]

5. Constantly at stake during this entire period was the existence of the red light district where criminal practices were concentrated. This type of ghetto had at least three functions. First, it was patrolled by the type of police best suited to a democratic patronage system — one that confined itself to "public order." In this perspective, a red light district made it possible to "reduce the number of illegal houses elsewhere and put them in places where they would be the least likely to cause a public outcry" (Plante et al. 1972, 216). This tolerance would ensure the civil servants involved, whose salaries were purposely made insufficient, an additional off-the-record income. The second function was to make a monopoly of criminal practices possible, a notable advantage for criminal entrepreneurs, but also a process compatible with maintaining public order: "if monopoly in the supply of goods is socially undesirable, monopoly in the supply of bads should be socially desirable, precisely because of the output restriction" (Buchanan 1973). The third function was directly political and derives from the second: a disreputable "milieu," unified and territorially concentrated, facilitated the work of political patrons in recruiting disciplined manpower for certain specialized jobs, the most important, it would seem, being the manipulation of the electoral process.

In short, the organization of crime in a democratic patronage regime can be characterized as follows: political corruption is an essential prerequisite and those in control play a decisive role; the existence of fairly large well-structured organizations enables a small number to actively control the underworld. It is a social structure where close and distant relatives as well as ethnic affiliations shape the criminal transactions — a general characteristic of the political economy of patronage in general.

A democratic patronage system presupposes a supporting police organization. It implies that the government is subject to the particular interests of the civil society. In a regime of this type, the function of the police is not to "reinforce" the state. On the contrary, it appears to be subordinate to the personal interests of the political personnel and their clients. The massive dismissals of policemen following elections and a deliberately low salary level are evidence of this dependency. Limited to passively keeping this peace, the men in uniform and their administrative superiors can best be described as a kind of "low policing" (Brodeur 1983).

The problem for contemporary analysis is, of course, that none of this exists any more. Patronage as a type of democracy ceased to exist at the beginning of the sixties. First, the electoral process is no longer manipulated directly. By the 1980s, there was no longer a "low police"; political corruption was no longer an essential component of organized crime; and the red light district is just a memory.[2] Since the political conditions making a large, well-structured criminal organization possible no longer exist, it seems rather doubtful to suppose that the realm of criminal practices is actually unified today by a small number of semi-esoteric "syndicates."

Welfare State, Surveillance and "High" Police

Since the middle sixties, crime control operates differently. "Police forces are presently operating under the high policing paradigm, or will be increasingly, the long arm of the law being, so to speak, curtailed in favor of the wide eyes of the police" writes (Brodeur 1983). Three major features of high policing are: comprehensive surveillance over civil society, control through storing of intelligence data, and fusion of police and judicial functions:

1. In the first place, surveillance tends to be extensively used in the regulatory activities of the state in a civil society. The target of inquiry commissions is significant in this regard. It is no longer the political institutions that are investigated but civil society itself: complete industries are under special investigation, especially those involved in construction, meat, or clothing.[3] Under attack are the manipulations of labor relations, various forms of economic patronage, and extensive tax evasion. Crime no longer seems to be subversion escaping political control but evasion escaping fiscal control. Notice the recent increase in research lately on the criminogenic market structure (Crooks 1983 in Canada; Denzin 1977, Faberman 1975, Leonard and Weber 1970, in the United States).

We often judge police performance by the number of arrests and criminal convictions they bring about. However, police investigations do not provide information for the criminal justice system alone, but also for a great number of regulatory, licensing and welfare agencies with which they maintain a close working relationship that has just begun to be studied (McIntyre and Henderson 1980, 51; Rico et al. 1981, 189ff). "These agencies control, disapprove of, and punish troublesome people. They need not be charged with crimes and given trials when their moral character can be examined administratively and where their punishment will be the denial of a license or permit to earn a living, or a declaration that they are ineligible to receive certain compensations, benefits or social insurance" (Spector 1981, 144).

When a democratic patronage system is changed into a "public interest state"—a welfare state—police surveillance is no longer limited to maintaining public order but becomes widely used for the general inspection activities exercised by regulatory agencies. This general surveillance in turn makes it possible to give criminal law a new and chilling finality. For example, consider the following project, in effect since 1973, in which the Federal Police and Revenue Department collaborate.

> The program works two ways. The first involves a complete investigation of the financial affairs of individual criminals to determine the location and worth of all assets owned by them. The criminal's net worth in turn forms the basis of an income tax assessment issued by Revenue Canada Taxation. The second way the program works is through jeopardy assessments. A jeopardy assessment is issued when an accused is arrested in possession of a large amount of cash that cannot be linked to the criminal transaction with which he is or will be charged. In these cases it is possible to freeze the cash, and issue a tax assessment for its amount. All assessments are appealable. However, a reverse onus situation applies. [McIntyre and Henderson 1980, 52–53]

Hence the central crime policy statement of the Model Criminal Enterprise Act (inspired by the Racketeer Influenced and Corrupt Organizations Statute enacted in the United States in 1970): "the income tax program attempts to do by indirect means what the law should in our opinion permit to be done directly: confiscate the profits of crime" (McIntyre and Henderson, 54). This confiscation strategy would require an analysis of criminal markets and an exact inventory of victimization costs. It appears that, in a public interest state, the victimological research that has developed since the beginning of the 1960s is the complement of a penal policy resorting to confiscation. Thus, one would expect that criminology will develop a serious research interest in the analysis of criminal practices and that penology will consider studying closely patrimonial penalties limited, up to now, to being substitutes for short prison sentences: "It is (still not) usual for the Crown to tender evidence at sentencing concerning the amount of profit involved in the crime because such evidence is rarely available. The result is that judges, lacking any direct means of assessing the profit involved, decline to guess at it and refrain from imposing a fine" (McIntyre and Henderson, 37).

2. "In January 1966, at the urging of the RCMP [Royal Canadian Mounted Police] the Federal Government convened a Federal Provincial Conference of Attorneys General to establish new methods of national police cooperation and coordination to fight organized crime" (Kelly and Kelly 1976, 458). It was decided to create a crime data computer service, which became operational in July 1972. Kelly and Kelly call it the "greatest technical development in law enforcement since fingerprints were accepted as a means of criminal identification more than fifty years ago" (412). This meeting was

indeed a significant event because it highlights a distinctive feature of high policing which "is first of all absorbent policing. It aims to control by means of storing intelligence, which is in no way restricted to physical behaviour (actual deeds). High policing also makes extensive use of undercover agents and paid informers" (Brodeur 1983). Historians should carefully reconstruct this event and discover the process by which the "construction" of organized crime as a social problem can be linked to the emergence of a new welfare state police paradigm. For the first time in the late 1960s and early 1970s there appeared a specific "police literature" that was not exclusively subject to political needs (inquiry commissions on political corruption), judicial needs (individual investigation files), or administrative needs (criminal statistics).

A survey would probably establish that there has been a proliferation of the number of medium or long term inquiries that are not limited to the production of investigation files but reconstitute the specific conditions under which a particular variety of criminal practices operate. Such surveys often make use, on a routine basis, of preemptive methods (tailing and electronic surveillance). The judicial norms that govern this anticipatory action of the police have become extremely complex (see Bellemare 1981). The proliferation of inquiries, the recent pro-activity of police surveillance and its extension to all the regulatory activities of the state, have very quickly produced an important mass of documents. In turn, this has meant the simultaneous creation of specialized intelligence services at various government levels as well as a data processing system relative to criminal activities.

Sentencing itself contributes to this police literature. The hypothesis of the "fix," so well described by Sutherland, reduced the amount of information useful to an analysis of criminal practices, whereas contemporary plea bargaining has the opposite effect:

> When corruption is a normal practice (in a democratic patronage system), giving information is dangerous and strongly prohibited. Since plea bargaining has become current practice, informing becomes an integral part of the negotiation and its frequency is increasing. At the same time the quality of this collaboration can deteriorate. Hence the problem of a profusion of information sources combined with an increasing difficulty in selecting and evaluating their veracity and tactical pertinence. [Tremblay and St-Pierre 1983, 157]

It is possible that this police literature will eventually become a special statistic, rivalling the present criminal statistics and complementing the new measurements of crime (surveys on victimization, scales of criminal seriousness). On the whole, our knowledge of crime is dependent on crime control. It is far from certain that a systematic analysis of criminal practices could be achieved without crime control operating under a high policing paradigm.

3. The inquiry commissions of the mid-1960s were very different from the traditional commissions on political corruption, typical of a democratic patronage system. They were set up in a context that no longer depended on electoral contingencies. They can function on a close-to-permanent basis

(this has been the case in the province of Quebec since 1972). They are no longer the politico-judicial scene where the "lowness" of the police is exposed. For the first time there is a direct interest in the operation of criminal practices and in the various degrees of their organization. These new inquiries show a "fusion of judicial and police functions"—the third characteristic of a high policing system, according to Brodeur (1983)—whose components, traditionally held to be separate, are hard to distinguish one from the other.

A commissioner differs from a judge and the hearings of an inquiry commission are not those of a court: "The judge is an impartial arbitrator in a contradictory procedure engaged in between the parties in litigation. The commissioner presides at an inquisitorial procedure" (Bisaillon v. Keable 1980). Since the commission is not a "court," the rule of impartiality is expressly dispensed with in the legislation; without this dispensation, it would be impossible to understand how these commissions operate (Keyserlingk, 1983). On the other hand, it is not merely an investigation but an inquiry pursued by "quasi-judicial body" (Saulnier v. The Quebec Police Commission 1976), having special powers, particularly those of search and forcing witnesses to answer on pain of being held in contempt of court.

With regard to these powers, it is generally agreed that "the criminal process is notoriously deficient in 'discovery' procedures. The civil process, on the other hand, coerces such full disclosure not only from parties, but from witnesses, and punishes by committal for contempt . . . the inclination of a defendant or a witness to remain silent in the face of accusation" (Horn in McIntyre and Henderson 1980, Appendix B, p. 2). Jurisprudence being firmly opposed to punishing by civil procedures ("milder" and more "prying") what cannot be punished by criminal procedures, one can easily understand police interest in these commissions, which also have the function of publicizing the findings of what we formerly called the "police literature."

An account of the evolution of the repressive measures taken against organized crime in Quebec, even when limited to a short period of time, may not be indicative of what was occurring in other parts of Canada. Aside from the most obvious differences between Quebec and all of the other provinces, not all of the major cities outside of Quebec may have experienced a democratic regime operating a patronage system on the level described here. This analysis is also limited to variations within the democratic system. A study of variations in the nature of provincial and urban political regimes would no doubt bring forth a plethora of detail on a variety of low and high policing different from that in Quebec and specifically Montreal. With this background and these caveats, one turns specifically to organized crime.

"Organized crime" is an expression most often used in the presence of a political audience. An admission that organized crime exists is an admission that political corruption exists and that power is exercised through patronage. On the other hand, the denial that organized crime exists may emanate from a conviction that patronage is no longer a part of the political process or that it would be harmful to admit that this is so. Another area of controversy is that the admission that organized crime exists forces the concession that crime control is accomplished through a system of "high policing." Again, the denial may be made either because one believes that the police do not operate according to this "paradigm," or because it is too risky to acknowledge.

In spite of all this, the term "organized crime" can be used in a relatively neutral fashion. It would refer only to the knowledge available in the matter of criminal practices, involving coordination among the perpetrators. This is relative neutrality, in that the condition that would make such knowledge possible resides in a democratic system of high policing. This being granted, the analysis of criminal practices consists in finding out what constitutes criminal opportunities: in describing the functioning of black markets; and in discovering the conditions that determine the degree of stability and variable size of the groups that rely on them.

Delinquency and Opportunity Revisited

Criminal statistics present crimes as isolated events, as though the various kinds of criminal practices were completely independent of one another, and as though their geographical distribution were a fact of nature. It is possible, however, to detect even schematically the empirical structure of the criminal opportunities and black markets that sociologists and economists often refer to, albeit vaguely (Cloward and Ohlin 1966). Any thorough analysis of the contemporary organization of crime cannot be undertaken without extensive, in-depth empirical research. The theses presented here stem from a preliminary stratified sample of relevant police archives, which cover the city of Montreal over a recent 15-year period.

1. Tie-ins between criminal practices are numerous and lead, without much difficulty, to the identification of functional concatenations linking crimes together, with such sequences being of variable length and complexity. The frequency of burglary, for instance, depends to a very great extent on the organization of receiving stolen goods by fences. There are garages that will dismantle stolen vehicles and sell the parts on the market. A significant portion of these avowed thefts, are, in fact, "disappearances" arranged to defraud insurance companies. In addition to this fraud, other kinds of related swindles abound, such as the production of false witnesses in automobile accidents, whether "arranged" or not.[4] Receiving and insurance fraud are in themselves part of other chains of criminal practices predominant in the business world (Faberman 1975). One crime can be the starting point of different chains of criminal activity. Thus, car thefts are the preliminary phase for a large number of bank robberies, which, in turn, require obtaining firearms, registration and identificaton papers, license plates, either stolen or counterfeit, on the black markets. Depending on the security measures expected, a bank robbery often entails an extortion operation directed against privileged victims — the bank manager or his family, for example. The fencing of the

loot itself presents problems when the bills are numbered or bonds or other securities must be disposed of.[5]

Fraud involving falsification of exchange forms similar chains. It cannot operate without a stable supply of stolen or counterfeit credit cards, checks or identification papers, and can often be linked with other criminal practices as well (prostitution, for example). Opening bank accounts under false pretenses leads the way to other types of fraud, such as "kiting," but it also constitutes an important step in the deceptive use of payment methods, because it provides a quick supply of personalized checks. Since the final targets of these frauds are retail stores, such places may directly supply the black markets of goods with criminally obtained merchandise.[6]

2. Another way of analyzing the interdependence of criminal practices is to determine the black markets in which they occur. There are at least four. The black markets of goods (for example, the hijacking of vans, trafficking of narcotics or pornographic material, as well as the sale of rotten meat or cheese, and so on); the black market of capital (loansharking, gambling — representing two kinds of financial institutions, as suggested by Light, 1981 — but also "kiting"[7] or organized tax evasion[8]; the black market of means of exchange (fraud by means of credit cards, checks and stolen or counterfeit identification papers); and finally the black market in labor (prostitution and illegel cottage labor). An estimate of the relative size and importance of these black markets is difficult to make, even approximately, and it is, therefore, rarely done.[9] Even when an estimate is offered, it is generally impossible to know how it was arrived at. It would be interesting to evaluate, even partially and superficially, the role of black markets in the general economy and to construct a typology of societies classified according to the differential importance given to each of them. Note that none of these black markets seems to be monopolized by what is conveniently called "organized crime." The latter would seem to be restricted to the exploitation of only a fraction of the black markets.

Two kinds of criminality can actually be distinguished. One is termed "productive criminality," which consists of those criminal practices devoted to the manufacturing and marketing of illicit goods and services. It includes the illegal production of capital (loansharking); of goods (heroin, bootleg liquor); of payment means (counterfeit money or company checks); or services (prostitution). The second kind of criminality is one of predatory appropriation and reallocation of legitimate commodities ("kiting," hijacking and other varieties of thefts, credit card frauds — including a goodly portion of white-collar crime). The term "organized crime" mainly refers to productive crime, although both kinds are highly structured.

Identifying the chains or concatenations of criminal practices will not suffice to round out the picture: two more precise parameters must be taken into consideration. The first concerns the distinction that has just been made between crimes of predation and those of production: does the crime supply the black market or not? The second parameter refers to the idea of "quantity theft" formulated by Walsh (1977). A crime operates in volume or does not. In the first case it is a matter of carrying out a large number of minor illicit transactions rather than succeeding in one major venture. The presence or absence of one or the other of these conditions reveals four possible types of criminal practice in each black market. Thus loansharking[10] or illegal gambling[11] operate in volume and directly supply the black market with capital, whereas securities theft and fencing[12] supply the black market but do not operate in volume; neither automobile insurance fraud nor "kiting," which operate in volume, flow into the black market. A similar analysis can be made for the criminal practices relating to the market of goods, and an analogous typology has already been developed to distinguish different kinds of fraud (Tremblay and St-Pierre 1983). The analysis of functional chains strongly suggests links of *causality* between different crimes. Furthermore, the chronological reconstitution of the events plays an important role in understanding them. The analysis of classes of crime into "families" is satisfied with a more or less close *correlation,* and concentrates more on finding contextual similarities between criminal practices. The concept of "families" of crime has certain advantages: it may afford a better understanding of the logic underlying criminal careers or "phases." Furthermore, the criteria used to construct such families are indicators of crime organization level. Criminal practices will tend to show maximum structure when both criteria are present, that is when they operate in volume-quantity crime — and when they supply black markets directly. This is perhaps the conceptual core of what is meant by "organized crime." Finally, the analysis of functional concatenations and crime families emerges as an empirical method of establishing to what extent — and this is the decisive question — crime occurring in a metropolis or in a given territory is either organized or not, and controlled — or not — by the underworld. Based on the evidence, it would seem then that crime is either organized and/or controlled by the underworld.

3. Thus, there is evidence of certain forms of interdependence between criminal practices. With each of them operating within a specific range or radius of action, it is worth the effort to analyze the quasi-geographic relationship between isolated transactions within the same criminal practice.

There is a long tradition of criminological research devoted to the geography of crime. This "ecological" tradition, however, tells us more about the public reaction to crime than about the criminal practices themselves. These studies are based on official statistics and the findings most often end up in a geography of poverty or of urban fear. There are several varieties of fields of action proper to criminal practices. Thus, a *connection* (as in "The French Connection") refers to criminal practices operating across borders. Narcotics smuggling rings are perhaps the best known connections today.[13] Their range or field of action is made up of all the conveyance points through which goods are funneled to specific black markets. Connections are typical of productive crime. A circuit, on the other hand, refers to the routine path of networks of shoplifters, burglars, or groups of check forgers. A circuit is the structured geographical distribution of a set of victimization points. Circuits are typical of appropriation crimes. When the analysis of circuits and connections is sufficiently advanced, it will be possible to understand more clearly how the radius of action of a criminal practice is established, its more or less optimal range and the basic principles for territorial expansion of given varieties of crime.

The notion of *territory* is fairly complex and constantly used throughout the literature devoted to "organized crime." In a general way, it can be defined as a specific set of sales outlets or business façades of a criminal practice. "Business façade" must be understood in its strict sense. It does not refer to places frequented by the underworld — "hang-outs" — or to legitimate firms involved in crime (for example, fraudulent bankruptcies).[14] Nor are they companies that belong to criminal entrepreneurs or businessmen who are their occasional associates; they are only those businesses that serve as black market suppliers. However, neither the metropolitan networks of massage parlors and prostitution, nor the outlets for the sale of capital or stolen goods, necessarily constitute territories. A territory is created when black market sales outlets are geographically concentrated in a limited section of a city neighborhood and when the organization of this black market has to be restricted either to direct sales — on the street — or to business fronts that are "facilitating" rather than "integrated" (Walsh 1977). The reinsertion of stolen merchandise (as clothing or vehicles) on the market is often channeled through business façades where the product legitimately sold is closely "integrated" with what is exchanged on the black market. The retail distribution of narcotics, on the other hand, is most often done through business façades where the commodities openly offered for sale have nothing to do intrinsically with the goods sold covertly, but where the operations of the front facilitate the organization of illegal exchanges. The evolution of a criminal practice, incidentally, often consists in successive reconversions of its range and façades. Thus prostitution was formerly carried out in a "red light district" through brothels or directly on the street (no business fronts); today prostitution is carried out through integrated façades, territorially dispersed — massage parlors — or through "dissonant façades" as call girls networks.[15]

The development of a territory also requires the establishment of an extortion system called "protection."[16] Two factors are propitious for such organized authority and violence. The first one stems from an inefficiently organized black market: an insufficient number of sales outlets — facilitating façades — given the volume of illicit exchanges carried out in the particular territory. Thus, it is not the trafficking of heroin (a hard drug for a restricted clientele) but rather the trafficking of pleasant, soft drugs that first engendered a territorial protection system. The second factor concerns law enforcement behavior. The relative incorruptibility of the police forces seems to have forced the entrepreneurs of production criminality to modify their strategy: they can no longer buy the tolerance of local public administrations and attendant political services; instead they require, through threat when necessary, a "cut" from those retailers who benefit directly or indirectly, willingly more often than not, from the black markets.

From Crime to Criminal

Traditional analysis of the organization of crime has examined the ethnic composition of numerous criminal groups and has explored the hierarchical relationships of their members, speculating with varying degrees of success on the interaction between groups operating in different cities or countries. The first studies had the polemic virtue of showing that crime could be a collective activity, rationally organized, well-adjusted to social conditions, and subject to specific cultural norms. It refuted the then-current theory that crime is an expression of individual pathologies and the result of social disorganization. Today, the debate has lost much of its intensity. The problem is perhaps no longer to describe and differentiate between types of criminals, but to change the approach and base the categorization of "criminals" on a preliminary analysis of the criminal practices themselves.

1. The idea of the criminal career depends on a conceptual structure more fragile than expected and, curiously enough, is rarely based on a concrete analysis of crime. This idea assumes that crime is a factor of upward social mobility; that criminal practices are restricted to a fraction of the lower social classes; that there is actually a choice "between" two very separate worlds, that of legitimate opportunities and that of criminal opportunities; and that the latter are able to provide on their own for a sufficient number of thriving and lasting careers.

But Glaser (1974) was one of the first to observe that a criminal career was very rare. The career expectation of a "chronic" delinquent is most often very short and the "abandonment of careers" much more frequent than was generally believed (Cusson, 1983). The concept of the "criminal career" thus became problematic and was replaced by that of the "criminal phase."

An empirical and systematic analysis of police archives would perhaps enable one to go further. The least prosperous criminals would not be able to survive without their occasional jobs, unemployment insurance, or social welfare. The prosperous ones would be far less so if they did not have legitimate incomes. Black markets are so closely linked with the official markets that it seems that criminal opportunities and legitimate opportunities should not be considered two sides of a dichotomous choice. Virtue may well decide, for its part, that a normative decision is to be made here. But those who participate in criminal practices abstain from making these choices. A criminal is not a person who lives solely on the proceeds of crime, but one whose income derives from both legitimate and illegitimate sources. "Habitual" criminals are most often part-time adult delinquents. Therefore, the concept of a "criminal career" in the strict sense is not very useful, because criminal opportunities do not coexist "side by side" with legitimate opportunities.

The study of black markets, chains, and families of crime regularly shows that all social classes participate with equal enthusiasm in criminal practices, a theory expounded by Sutherland. A person's social status explains only the type of black markets in which he is likely to participate, the class of crimes he commits or the position he occupies in the chain and division of labor characteristic of criminal practices. It is true that inmate populations are chiefly composed of persons coming from the lower stratum of society. This in no way indicates that there is a "dangerous class" below and on the fringe of other social strata, but only that social stratification is *inherent* in the functioning of criminal practices and in their control. Also, incarceration is not the only form of punishment inflicted by criminal justice. The theory of crime as a factor of social mobility should then be reformulated within a more restricted framework: the social stratification in the realm of criminal practices would be less pronounced than that which prevails in other social spheres: an appealing and romantic hypothesis. But perhaps it would be more realistic to adopt a null or even an opposite hypothesis in this regard?

2. It is hard to conceive of cohorts of criminal careers without the existence of well-structured organizations in which they can function. Since the notion of a "criminal career" does not seem to be very adequate, it is to be expected that the complementary concept of a "criminal organization" will also be troublesome. A criminal practice can be structured without being "controlled" by a "criminal organization" — a view that can be developed either by reading criminal autobiographies or by careful analysis of specific criminal practices, such as fencing (Walsh 1977).

Detailed study of the various sizes of criminal groups should be very instructive in this regard. A criminal group can be defined more easily than a "criminal organization": a person belongs to a group if both members and others recognize him as being one of them. To estimate the average size of criminal groups is risky without a complete analysis of the criminal practices operating in a given territory. However, it is known that Canadian criminal groups reputed to be the largest rarely exceed twenty members. This applies equally to "Italian crime families"[17] and motorcycle gangs.[18] Even the "Montreal decina" can be properly described as a more or less fragile association of at least two criminal groups (Sicilians and Calabrians).

Criminal groups may have a distinctive life style. Much has been said of these subcultural particularities. But cultural differences do not contribute much to the understanding of crime (Cusson 1983). Criminal groups are primarily work groups. Depending on the kind of criminal practice and the organization it requires, a specific life style might or might not be an asset. When police archives refer to gangs, it is quite often a matter of small criminal groups associated on a limited and irregular basis but operating within the same crime families or within the same black market.[19] Check forgery work-groups rarely exceed four persons, and the largest theft operations involve no more than dozen individuals. Criminal "cells" might be a better word than criminal organizations to describe the structure of organized crime groups.

Any number of interlinked criminal cells do not constitute, however, an organization but only a class of criminal activists. Set theory and network analysis are more appropriate here than corporate-like diagrams.

These cells do not encompass all those who engage in criminal practices. On the contrary. Many fences, check forgers, drug couriers or even cannabis pushers are not "members" of criminal groups but operate with them on an occasional and irregular basis. Many business crimes involve participants who do not acknowledge, and rightly so, being members of criminal groups or cells. Nonetheless, without this population of occasional delinquents, the organization of criminal practices would be paralyzed. Thus, the notion of criminal organization should be used carefully. It might be limited to a particular subset of practitioners of criminal activities — those that operate in volume and directly supply the black market. The criminal group would then tend to be larger, the division of labor more impersonal, and authority relations more clearly specified.

Two notable examples of this are bootlegging during Prohibition and today's trafficking in narcotics, particularly that of cannabis. In both cases, however, one sees that the polarization of the activities of criminal cell-groups into more structured hierarchical organizations depends not only on the existence of mass markets, but also on a high level of social tolerance, the probability being that the crime will cease to be, for all intents and purposes, an act carrying the onus that, for large numbers of people, separate criminality from lawbreaking. In the case of crimes involving goods widely used by the public, an organization of criminals appears at best to be a borderline case, unsuitable for the analysis of criminal practices as a whole.

Criminology still dwells largely in the prison world. One can understand why it has, to a greater extent than would be justified, neglected to inquire into what criminals do, in favor of studying the psychological and even the physiological nature of the criminals themselves, or their familial, educational, and socioeconomic backgrounds. The analysis of crime has in part been limited to the nineteenth-century invention of "criminalistics" (a remarkable contribution of criminal anthropology often forgotten) and to the development, during the twentieth century, of more precise measures of the criminal acts (uniform and standardized statistics, victimization surveys, scales of crime seriousness). Relatively little has been accomplished in the development of a cumulative tradition of empirical research devoted to the concrete structure of criminal practices, whose objective would be to empirically verify or falsify the explanations and interpretations advanced by sociologists and economists concerning such linked phenomena as delinquency and opportunity, on the one hand, and the functioning of black markets, on the other. Cross-correlation studies between types of criminal practices and ethnicity may prove the two phenomena more closely related than hitherto suspected. Strict ethnicity membership is a rather rare occurrence for criminal groups, although they may exist in specific parts of the world, or even of a nation, for a limited period of time. A minute analysis of the workings of transnational smuggling practices may well lead to an understanding of why such "connections" required for each part of the world the equivalent of some kind of "mafia" type of criminal group that has nothing to do with Italian or Sicilian culture. Business facades may provide the link between chains of criminal practices and their corresponding black markets, and national and international banking practices, particularly in money laundering, a third link in a criminal triangle. When the triangle has been completed, criminology may be able to grasp the nature and meaning of organized crime, learn the kinds of working partnerships entailed, and the extent to which the perpetrators thrive as a result of an atmosphere of differential law enforcement, social tolerance, and social respectability.

Notes

1. Quebec Research Bureau on Organized Crime (hereafter cited as QRBOC), 306–11 (1973-09-21); C. Jodoin and C. Dubois, *Les frères Dubois: l'enverse de la médaille. Claude Dubois se raconte; propos recueillis par Claude Jodoin.* Montréal, 1976, no publisher given.

2. Quebec Police Commission. 1974. "Rapport d'enquête sur l'étude des liens possibles entre Nicolas Dilorio et Frank Dasti, membres du crime organisé, Pierre Laporte, ministre, René Gagnon, chef du cabinet et Jean-Jacques Côté, organisateur politique." Québec: Ministère de la Justice; Quebec Police Commission, *Inquiry on Organized Crime* (further cited as QPC-IOC), 1975, unpublished report on the Quebec Liquor Board; QPC-IOC, 1977, *Organized Crime and the World of Business: Interim report on corruption*: QRBOC, 330-Q-1-Supp. 48, October 1974.

3. Ontario, 1974, Royal Commission on Certain Sectors of the Building Industry: *Report*. Queen's Printer. QPC-IOC, 1975, Interim report: Fraudulent Marketing of Meat Unfit for Human Consumption and Fraud in Connection with Horsemeat; since November 1980, the QPC-IOC is actively investigating the Quebec garment industry; Quebec, 1975, *Rapport de la commission d'enquête sur l'exercice de la liberté syndicale dans l'industrie de la construction.* Editeur officiel du Québec.

4. QRBOC, 330-1 (1980-03-28); QPC-IOC (1978): unpublished report, File No. P-72-400.

5. B. Provençal and B. Boutot (1983), *Big Ben.* Montréal: Editions Domino, QRBOC, 306-21; QRBOC-NIS: S2641; QPC-IOC (1980) *Rapport de deux enquêtes publiques tenues à Québec et à Montréal en 1979,* pp. 57–118; B. Desnoyers (1968), *Les réseaux de voleurs d'autos.* Troisième journée d'études de l'Association des Chefs de Police et de Pompiers du Québec.

6. Quebec Police Force, 073-791206-21; QRBOC, 340-Q 1 (1978-02-28).

7. QPC-IOC (1977) "Organized Crime and the World of Business." Unpublished Accountants' Report, No. B-75-1006 (1974-11-29); QRBOC, 340-Q-1 (1978-11-24).

8. Quebec Police Force, 073-780315-002.

9. Royal Canadian Mounted Police (1982), *National Drug Intelligence Estimate-1981,* Ottawa: Minister of Supply and Services, Canada; QPC-IOC (1975), see note 3, supra.

10. QPC-IOC (1977), "Organized Crime and the World of Business," pp. 115–30; QRBOC, 342-Q-1: Accountants' Report: An analysis of shylocking (1977); QRBOC, 342-Q-1 (305-Q-1-630) (1974-05-31); QPC-IOC (1974): File No. (UCM-74-061).

11. QPC-IOC (1973), Project A, File No. A-73-1344; QPC-IOC (1971). Preliminary report on a large-scale junket operation (1971-04-06) (Archives).

12. QRBOC, 334-Q-1-Supp. 5 (1975-02-18); QPC-IOC (1977). "Organized Crime and the World of Business," p. 148–224.

13. J. P. Charbonneau (1976), *The Canadian Connection* (Ottawa: Optimum Publishing); M. Mastantuano and M. Auger (1976). *Mastantuano* (Montréal: Les Editions de l'Homme); QRBOC, 330-1 (February 1981); QRBOC, 306–11 (1981-08-21).

14. Anonymous (1968), untitled conference, Troisième journée d'études de l'Association des Chefs de Police et de Pompiers du Québec (1968-11-30); QRBOC, 341-Q-1 (1972-03-02).

15. P. Boisvert (1968), untitled conference, Troisième journée d'études de l'Association des Chefs de Police et de Pompiers du Quebec (1968-11-30); QRBOC, 336-Q-1-Supp. 5; QPC-IOC (1977), "Organized Crime and the World of Business," pp. 93–114; "Prostitution Moves out to Suburbs after Montreal Outlaws 'Massages,' " *The Gazette,* July 23, 1983.

16. QPC-IOC (1977), "The Fight Against Organized Crime in Quebec," pp. 117–118; QPC-IOC (1978); unpublished report, File No. P-72-400.

17. Quebec (1967), Commission of Inquiry into the Administration of Justice, 48 (October 1974); QRBOC, 305-Q-1-702 (UKO 120-121) (1975-07-25).

18. QPC-IOC (1978; 1980), "Motorcycle Gangs in Quebec"; QRBOC, 77-QRBOC-330-Q-2 (February 1983; March 1983).

19. QRBOC, 330-1 (February 1981).

References

Bellemare, D. 1981. *L'écoute électronique au Canada.* Montréal: Editions Y. Blais.

Bisaillon v. Keable, 1980, S.C. 13.

Brodeur, J. P. 1979. "L'ordre délinquant." *Déviance et Société* 3, 1: 1–22.

_____. 1983. "High Policing and Low Policing: Remarks About the Policing of Political Activities." *Social Problems* 30, 5: 507–20.

Buchanan, J. 1973. "A Defense of Organized Crime?" In S. Rottenberg, ed. *The Economics of Crime and Punishment.* Washington, D.C.: American Enterprise Institute for Public Policy Research.

Cloward, R. A., and Ohlin, L. E. 1966. *Delinquency and Opportunity: A Theory of Delinquent Gangs.* New York: The Free Press.

Crooks, J. 1983. *Dirty Business: The Inside Story of the New Garbage Agglomerates.* Toronto: Lorimer.

Cusson, M. 1983. *Le contrôle social du crime.* Paris: Presses Universitaires de France.

Denzin, N. 1977. "Notes on the Criminogenic Hypothesis: A Case Study of the American Liquor Industry." *American Sociological Review* 42: 905–20.

Faberman, H. 1975. "A Criminogenic Market Structure: The Automobile Industry." *The Sociological Quarterly* 16, 3: 438–57.

Glaser, D. 1974. "The Classification of Offences and Offenders." In D. Glaser, ed., *Handbook of Criminology.* pp. 45–85. Chicago: Rand McNally.

Kelly, W., and Kelly, N. 1976. *Policing in Canada.* Toronto: Macmillan.

Keyserlingk, H. 1983. "La Commission d'enquête sur le crime organisé: Ses enquêtes et ses enquêteurs." Unpublished manuscript.

Lemieux, V. 1975. *Patronage et politique au Québec, 1944–1972.* Québec: Boréal Express.

Leonard, W., and Weber, M. 1970. "Automakers and Dealers: A Study of Criminogenic Market Forces." *Law and Society Review* 4: 407–24.

Light, I. 1977. "Numbers Gambling Among Blacks: A Financial Institution." *American Sociological Review* 42: 892–904.

McIntyre, J., and Henderson, A. G. 1980. *The Business of Crime: An Evaluation of the American R.I.C.O. Statute From a Canadian Perspective.* Victoria: B.C.: Ministry of Attorney General.

Morissette, D. 1980. "Les ouvrières à domicile et l'industrie de la robe à Montréal." Mémoire de maîtrise ès sciences, Département d'Anthropologie, Université de Montréal.

Plante, P. 1950. *Montréal sous le règne de la pègre.* Montreal: Editions de l'Action Nationale.

Plante, P., Stanké, A., and Morgan, J. L. 1972. *Pax: lutte à finir avec la pègre.* Montréal: Editions La Presse.

Provençal, B., and Boutot, B. 1983. *Big Ben.* Montréal: Edition Domino.

Rico, J., Kedzior, R., Acosta, F., and Parent, C. 1981. *La criminalité d'affaires au Québec.* Ecole de Criminologie, Université de Montréal.

Saulnier, V. The Quebec Police Commission, 1976, 1 S. C. 572.

Spector, M. 1981. "Beyond Crime: Seven Methods to Control Troublesome Rascals." In H. L. Ross, ed. *Law and Deviance,* pp. 127–57. Annual Review of Studies in Deviance, vol. 5., Beverly Hills, Cal.: Sage Publications.

Tremblay, P., and St-Pierre, A. 1983. "Une criminalité organisée ordinaire: les fraudes opérant au volume." *Revue Canadienne de Criminologie,* 25, 2: 141–58.

Walsh, M. 1977. *The Fence: A New Outlook on Property Theft.* Westport, Conn.: Greenwood Press.

6

Organized Crime in Great Britain and the Caribbean

Joseph L. Albini
Wayne State University

This work presents a description and analysis of the structure and enterprises of organized crime in Great Britain. The basis for the information concerning organized crime in Great Britain is drawn from data collected in a study which I conducted during the period of September 1972 until August 1973.[1]

To note immediately the basic nature of organized crime in Great Britain, I wish to quote a phrase that was heard repeatedly in interviews both with Procurators-Fiscal, solicitors, and with criminal informants—"There is nothing big here, nothing the likes of what you have in America"—"big" referring to the phenomenon of syndicated crime on a large scale.

My research confirmed this observation: it was true that syndicated crime did not exist in Great Britain in any proportion equivalent to the situation existing in the United States. Indeed the most prevalent form of organized crime that was found was that which comes under the category of mercenary crime. I will not go into detail about the distinctions between these two types of crime, since this was treated at length in my book, *The American Mafia* (1971). For our purposes, let us note that syndicated crime refers to that form of criminality in which illicit goods and services are offered to the public; where violence or the threat of it is employed in the enterprise when necessary; and where political immunity from the law is procured by criminals to insure the continuous operation of the enterprise. Mercenary crime is that form of organized crime in which money or goods are taken by stealth, in which force or the potential use of force is involved, or where these goods or money are obtained through the use of fraud.

As noted, the primary form of organized crime found in Great Britain was that of the mercenary type. Here, the majority of enterprises were of the type that employed stealth, especially burglary of either homes or business establishments. The other categories that made up the bulk of mercenary crimes were those of robbery and theft of physicians' medical prescription pads. On a lesser scale I found cases of hijacking and, on an even smaller scale still, I found cases of extortion. Enterprises that employed fraud composed the remainder of the various mercenary-type crimes. These took the form of confidence games played by Bar-Girls, the playing of Three-Card Monte on the streets, the passing of counterfeit money, and the procurement of drugs through the falsification of medical prescriptions. Although the research data produced only one informant involved with the long-firm fraud scheme, some interesting information was obtained regarding this crime from official sources at Scotland Yard.

The cases of extortion and violence—those of the Krays and the Richardsons that are probably the most celebrated—are known to have been covered in the literature in the work of Lucas (1969), Pearson (1972), Payne (1973) and others. I mention these cases, which are not part of this study, to emphasize the fact that since cases involving violence tend to receive much attention by the press and media, the general public often comes to remember and view them as representing the most typical forms of crime. This is true, generally, of crimes attributed to adolescent gangs.[2] The gang problem in Great Britain, like its counterpart in the United States, is one that must be understood within its proper perspective; that is, typically there is more talk of violence than there is actual violence and indeed where violence occurs the combatants are often the opposing gang members themselves.

The question of violence is germane to a discussion of organized crime in Great Britain, as shall become evident in our discussion of mercenary crime.

Mercenary Forms of Organized Crime

One of the forms of mercenary crime found was the organized robbery ring. Here the typical size of the ring was two to three people. There seems to be a practical reason for keeping the size of such groups small: a smaller group reduces visibility and diminishes the suspicion of potential victims on the street. The research does contain data, however, concerning cases where gangs of 15 youths standing on a street corner supposedly would stop a victim at knife-point and demand his wallet. If such occurrences took place it seems that they were the exception rather than the rule. The typical robbery was accomplished by rings of two to three lads who, as part of a modus operandi that was meant to reduce suspicion on the part of their potential victim, would simply casually stroll down the street. Once they were near the victim they would then surround him, execute the robbery, and quickly leave the area.

In contrast to robbery rings, the analysis of the composition of burglary rings revealed a number of different structures as well as differences in the methods employed by these criminals in accomplishing their thefts.

A very common type was the small or *petit* type ring consisting of two or three people who were generally very good friends or relatives. The types of burglaries committed by such groups typically did not net them large quantities of goods or money. Usually they would steal items that could be easily carried and fenced — small radios, silverware, china and other such goods. Occasionally they would hit upon a large sum of money but typically their "take" was small. The structure of this type of ring consists of each person having a designated role or roles which he performs in each burglary. One person, for example, may specialize in breaking and entering while the other serves as a safe-breaker, while a third may simply serve as a "look-out" man. When we use the term "specialize" here we do not mean to imply that these are highly trained or skilled individuals; rather, we refer to the fact that they have their specialized, designated roles in the team effort. Indeed, these types of burglars did not engage in the types of burglaries requiring a great deal of skill. However, this is not to say that within their limited range of activity they were not creative — they were. One informant, for example, described how he entered certain homes by employing the help of a small boy. He would force open the transom at the top of the door and, while holding the boy by his feet, would lower him through the transom, thus allowing the boy to open the lock from the inside. So, too, many of these rings would circulate from town to town in a purposefully unpredictable pattern in order to avert any police and/or community anticipation of them.

These *petit* burglary rings receive information concerning potential victims from a variety of sources. In some cases relatives or acquaintances of the victim, who also were acquainted with the burglar, would steer the burglar to the loot; that is, they would provide information as to the location of safes or other hiding places where money is kept. One informant was told of the location of a safe by the victim's brother-in-law and informed of the exact date when the victim would be on holiday so that no one would be on the premises. As payment for his services, the brother-in-law received a share of the profits after the burglary.

In another case, a cleaning woman who worked for several wealthy families informed burglars of the location of valuables in the homes where she worked. She too received a fee for her services.

A rather interesting system of the burglars' information network involved certain jewelers who, after having appraised the jewelry brought to them by customers, would request the customer's address and pass this information on to the burglars.

Although it was not a common practice, several informants stated that they received, also for a fee, information from police. Since police by the nature of their work have numerous occasions to enter premises, they are often told by trusting citizens the location of special hiding places for money and valuables. The police themselves, while on the premises, can observe and report to burglars the amount and location of valuable items such as china and jewelry. Two criminal informants who were burglars indicated that they received their information in this manner.

As a note to describing their modus operandi, we should emphasize that these *petit* burglars took caution to plan the burlary so that no one would be on the premises when it occurred. Obviously, the reason was to reduce the risk of being apprehended. One informant added that he did not wish to run the risk of causing someone, especially an older person, to have a heart attack from a sudden unexpected break in.

Here the question of violence, as I indicated earlier, comes to the fore-ground. Several criminal informants in this study emphasized the caution of avoiding violence whenever possible since it would only serve to increase public demands for police action. Burglars, then, seemed to purposefully avoid breaking and entering a premise while the inhabitants were at home. This was done not only to avoid being seen by the victim but also to avoid the possibility of violent confrontation.

Although these burglars are not specialized and the amount taken in each theft tends to be small, they are, nonetheless, very active so that the total amount of stolen goods at the end of the year may add up to a large sum.

In contrast to this type of ring that works on a daily or weekly basis, we have another type where the word specialized becomes very meaningful.

Specialized Burglary Rings

The size of these specialized rings depends upon the number of specialists required to do a particular job. Hence, in some cases only three are required, while in others as many as eight or nine may be needed. The type of specialist required will also vary with the nature of the task; thus the burglary of a store or a robbery of a bank equipped with an alarm system may require an alarm expert. Also, if a quick escape is necessary, someone who can skillfully drive at high speeds may be added to the team. In any case, unlike the *petit* bur-glary ring type just described, these specialists do not work together daily; in-stead, they come together for the completion of a specific job. A distinguish-ing feature here is that the amount taken is quite large. The operation is often planned and organized by one person who generally selects the other special-ists. If necessary, rehearsals are staged in order to insure the effective func-tioning of everyone involved. The amount received by each specialist is agreed upon before the job takes place. In some cases each specialist is paid a fee based upon the demand and need for his particular skill. Fees can and are arbitrated. Needless to say, the specialist with the skills most in demand is in the best position to dictate terms.

In both the petit and specialized burglary rings we find that the major fac-tor in selecting and working with personnel in criminal enterprises is that of trust. There is indeed a realistic reason for this. Data obtained both from the criminal informants and from solicitors and Procurators-Fiscal indicated that police receive much valuable information from criminals who engage in "grassing," the slang term for the process in which criminals give police infor-mation about other criminals.

"Grassing"

There is a generally accepted mythology concerning criminals that has been captured in the phrase — "There is honor among thieves." The data obtained in this study revealed that indeed this belief is mythological. Most of my criminal informants were concerned with and cited cases of other criminals "grassing" to the police. Among these criminals there is a constant concern or fear about "grassing."

Is this fear warranted? The data indicates that it is. Police, it seems, under certain circumstances pay certain informants for valuable information. However, this does not appear to be the major form of "grassing." Most "grassing" takes place as a result of revenge of one criminal toward another, or as a technique for eliminating existing or potential criminal competitors.

In any event, the data indicates that, whatever the motive, "grassing" was effective and a constant source of anxiety among criminals. Numerous cases were cited both by criminal informants and by solicitors to illustrate this point. Typically, such cases involved a scene in which the criminal would break and enter a warehouse or other form of business establishment only to find seven or eight police officers waiting for him inside. Similarly, police, in several cases, by being present at the scene, were able to stop a potential homicide and several serious fights simply because they had advance knowledge of the threats and persons involved. There is no doubt that the police in Great Britain do seem to have an effective network for acquiring information. However, not all information obtained by the police is gathered through this network. The police themselves have some rather interesting techniques of their own. Several criminal informants told of how the innocent senile-acting little old lady sitting next to them in the pub while they were talking about their latest criminal venture turned out to be a very healthy and agile police officer in disguise. One officer evidently had turned his disguises into an artform; that is, despite the fact that this technique and the officer were known to the criminals, he repeatedly managed to use it effectively in obtaining information.

Many criminal informants themselves described a typical pattern of behavior on the part of the small-time thieves in which, after committing a theft, they would immediately go to the pub, spend the money they just made on drink, and "tell the whole world about what they had just done." Despite the mythical belief of "Silence among criminals," it is indeed amazing how much information is spoken about quite openly in such criminal hangouts.

It is the question of trust, then, that serves as a barometer for gauging the selection of one's partners in a criminal enterprise. For the *petit* type burglar this problem was solved by their working with and trusting only those people whom one had known for some time. Hence, these individuals tended to work primarily with friends and relatives. So too, the information culled from criminal informants indicated that they worked only with those criminals who lived in the same geographical area in which the informant resided.

In the case of *specialized* burglary rings, the question of trust is not as readily resolved. Here, by the very nature of the enterprise, specialists must come together from different geographical areas. They are not as likely to know one another. But despite this, trust in one's associates becomes a major criterion for selection. Usually one criminal will recommend another. The trust, of course, comes from faith in the judgment of the original contact person who makes the recommendation; that is, it is assumed that before suggesting a person for a particular job, the person who recommends has already "cleared" the participant on the basis of having a practical knowledge of his personal characteristics and abilities. Interestingly, the underworld, like the legitimate world, has its network of contacts in which recommendations lead one source to trust another. However, like members of the legitimate world, not all members of the underworld rely solely upon referrals. Usually these people have had some negative results from operatives who had been given very positive recommendations. In one case, the youth and inexperience of one participant who had been accepted for participation in a burglary resulted in the arrest of all involved. One criminal informant who had never been arrested in any organized criminal venture attributed this fact to his sophisticated form of caution in selecting the personnel with whom he worked. In every case he would insist upon personally observing the person who had been recommended. He would watch for such factors as punctuality, temper, drinking habits and, above all, the ability "to keep his mouth shut." These observations, coupled with further approvals received from those who had worked with the person under question, went into the final decision whether to use him or not. This informant indeed appeared to approach crime and its execution with an appreciation and understanding of its complexities. Much like a scientist, he tried to account for all possible variables that could influence the outcome of a given event. Having an appreciation and respect for the sophistication of police methods as well he tried to control for as many factors as possible. It seems that since he had not been arrested his methods were indeed quite functional and successful.

Hijacking of lorries constituted another area of mercenary criminality in Great Britain. In no way, however, is it proportional to the amount that exists in the United States. An informant explained the difference by citing an obvious fact — "We don't have guns here. Without guns, how can you stop a lorry? Are you going to jump on it while it's coming down the road?" When it was pointed out that in the United States hijackers frequently buy information from dispatchers regarding the content of the trucks and their scheduled routes, this informant stated that such was not the case in Great Britain. Instead, unlike the United States where trucks are stopped at gunpoint along the road, theft from lorries in Great Britain typically takes place only when the lorry is parked. It seems that one method these hijackers employ is that of using a sophisticated system of "tailing" or following the lorry until the driver has parked the lorry and leaves it for one reason or another, whereupon the hijackers break into the cab of the lorry and drive it away to a secluded spot where its contents can later be removed. The more common method of hijacking, however, is for criminals to "case" lorry stops and other places frequented by lorry drivers and wait for a lorry whose driver has taken a room to sleep for the night.

Before ending our discussion of burglary rings and hijacking, we should note another criminal enterprise that is symbiotically connected with the functioning of such enterprises — fencing. An important aspect of successful burglary is that of having a skillful "fence" or person who, for a price, will dispose of stolen goods.

Fencing

In Great Britain, fencing is accomplished in a number of ways. In some cases a pub owner would buy small goods such as gloves, small radios, wristwatches, and other such articles from shoplifters who had stolen them. He, in turn, sells them for a profit. Some criminals consistently use only one outlet — the appliance store of a friend or associate living nearby.

In cases of valuable jewelry, some jewelers themselves served as fences. Having knowledge of the value of the goods, and having a legitimate outlet for the sale of used jewelry, such persons could be very effective in this role.

In those cases where large volumes of goods are involved, such as a hijacked load of liquor or cigarettes, a rather sophisticated method of fencing was employed. Here, typically, the services of a person who himself had numerous business outlets as well as numerous contacts in both legitimate and illegitimate social circles was employed. Informants consistently mentioned one criminal who was in a position to provide this sophisticated form of fencing. For many he represented a kind of patron within a system of patron-client relationships; that is, as a patron he was able to do favors for clients. Since he knew the owners of many business outlets he could easily and smoothly fence goods. Also, he was known for his ability and willingness to use force and intimidation. Hence, many owners of these outlets, through which the patron fenced illegal goods, would comply with his request not for direct payment but as a favor to him in hopes of winning his good graces; thus, they felt they could call for his help in the event that they or their premises were threatened. There was a belief in the criminal community that this person, in order to get revenge on his enemies or competitors, often engaged in very efficient forms of "grassing" to the police. This belief no doubt only served to increase his power and status.

In contrast to robbery and burglary, the passing of counterfeit money did not appear to be a large enterprise in Great Britain. As informants described it, the process consisted of paying a certain amount per bill to a person who provided them with the counterfeited money. Then they would move from city to city disguising themselves as travelers and "pass" the money in shops or market places where their identity would not be readily questioned.

The theft of medical prescription pads is another criminal enterprise. It appears not to be a vastly lucrative business but, for those seeking illegal channels to addictive drugs, it represented a service for which they were willing to pay a sizeable amount of money. In some cases, the blank prescription pads were sold to others who were specialists in forging the Latin symbols for the prescription as well as a psychiatrist's name. In other cases, the thieves themselves would forge the prescription and psychiatrist's name and sell it directly to the drug addict.

It may seem odd that such a demand would exist in Great Britain where drug addicts have legal channels through which they can attain drugs. It seems that the market for these forged prescriptions has to do with the fact that most psychiatrists who are entrusted with legally dispensing addictive drugs are reluctant to increase dosages for addicts. Instead they attempt to maintain addicts at that level where withdrawal is avoided but pleasurable "highs" are no longer experienced. For most addicts, the "kick" comes from increasing the dosage. Hence, if the psychiatrist refuses to increase the dosage, some addicts turn to illicit sources such as those peddling forged prescriptions.

Along with the selling of forged prescriptions, we find a variety of other criminal enterprises in Great Britain which employ the use of fraud and deception.

Confidence Games and Rackets

Because it is a city that appeals to tourists from all countries, London has its share of confidence games that are geared toward unsuspecting tourists. Needless to say, it is frequently the naive person that becomes the victim. Yet in all fairness to the victims, some of the games would not be readily detectable to even an alert and discerning tourist. This is particularly true of a clever game which might be called the sisters game.[3]

One of the most cleverly executed scams on the streets of London is that of Three Card Monte. As John Scarne (1961) notes, this game has been around since the early nineteenth century. Yet daily, victims fall prey to its deceptive simplicity.

The game is a simple one. Three cards are turned, face-down, on a flat board that serves as a table top. The dealer then turns the cards over so that it can be seen that two of the cards are red kings and one is a black ace of spades. The point is that the player must guess, while the cards are face-down, which one is the ace. The victim is persuaded or roped into the game by accomplices who themselves pretend that they are players and by the fact that the corner of the ace is purposefully slightly bent so that the ace can be readily detected.

In London the teams who played this scam generally included two "lookout" men stationed several yards away on opposite sides from where the game was being played. Although they would whistle or call out a code signal if they saw a uniformed officer, their real purpose was to help "blow off" or get rid of the victim quickly.[4]

Another area in which fraud is perpetuated is that of the manufacture and sale of counterfeited war medals. Evidently, there is a sufficiently large enough demand for these medals from amateur collectors to make this a somewhat lucrative enterprise. The process simply consisted of forging a variety of war medals such as the Victoria Cross, the Knight of the Thistle, and others and then selling them as authentic. Cleverly, to protect the forger and the person selling the medal, the forgers will often etch, in a very inconspicuous place, such as the rim or edge of the medal, the phrase — "This is a copy." Usually a magnifying glass is necessary to see this print, but if caught in the act, the forger or the seller, who never said he could vouch for the medal's authenticity, merely concedes that it is a copy.

One of the most lucrative and prevalent forms of fraud in England is that of the long firm fraud. The basic format of this scam is clearly described by Leslie Payne (1973).

"Long Firm" Frauds

First the criminals organize a business firm that serves as a front. A person is selected as a "front man" or "face." This individual is given a rather small but sufficient sum of money to deposit in a bank in order to establish a credit rating for the new business firm that he now supposedly heads. Usually an inconspicuous warehouse will be selected. An accountant and clerks are hired. Now the fraud begins. Using a trade-directory, inquiries are sent to various companies regarding price lists for goods. At this point the company looks good and has a bank reference. The company now begins placing orders, usually for small amounts of those kinds of goods that are popular and can be sold quickly — fabrics, soap, sunglasses, and other such miscellaneous items. In ordering these goods the company requests that they be sent on a one-month credit basis of payment. This is important, since the basis of the fraud is to establish credit for the firm. The first order is paid for before the credit deadline. The money for this payment is obtained by immediately selling the goods when received in the warehouse. These are sold at approximately half the retail price to merchants of legitimate businesses. Merchants pay cash for the goods and are given a receipt that shows that they paid about 4½ percent over the wholesale price instead of the 25 percent they actually paid. This procedure protects the merchant in case any legal problems arise.

By paying the first bill on time, the company now begins establishing credit. Carrying out this procedure with several companies, it can soon begin turning over enough goods so that it can skim profits for itself. Orders are now sent for larger quantities of goods. The money is banked and the cash flow looks impressive. As the company grows, the the other "long firm" companies themselves are used as fronts to write letters of reference for this new company. The orders become increasingly larger as more credit is established and care is taken to keep each new company paid within the required credit time-period. The fraud scheme necessitates a monthly doubling of the volume of business in order to cover-up the 25 percent undersell to merchants and the skimmed profits.

This system of continuously ordering from new companies and increasing orders from the ones for which credit has already been established continues for a period of about six months. Typically, many fraud firms begin in July so that the six month period will fall in December; because Christmas normally is a time of accelerated customer shopping, an unusually large order for goods would not draw suspicion. This becomes the final score of the long firm company. It makes its last order from all the companies. Orders are made for large quantities of goods. They are sold quickly but this time the supplier companies receive no payment. The "long firm" company closes its doors, having made its profit. If inquiries are made, no one can really give any information of any value to the police or creditors.

In an effort to control long firm schemes, Scotland Yard is developing methods of tracing the format of reference letters and keeping vigilance over companies whose origins are suspicious.

Along with the "long firm" fraud is another mail fraud technique in which a person working in the shipping department of a business firm is paid a percentage to simply change the address labels on rather expensive items transported through the mails. By doing so these items are sent to criminal sources who fence them through various outlets.

These, then, are examples of the types of mercenary crime—predatory and fraudulent—that are prevalent in Great Britain.

Syndicated Crime in England and Scotland

As noted above, there is no evidence indicating the existence of syndicated crime in Great Britain that is comparable in any way with that found in the United States. There are several reasons for this. It seems that for syndicated crime to exist anywhere on a grand scale there must be a great demand for illegal services and goods with an equally strong legal mechanism that attempts to seriously block or hamper the acquisition of such goods.

In Great Britain at least two factors appear to explain the lack of development of large scale criminal syndicates. First, the demand for those goods and services that serve as catalysts for the development of criminal syndicates within a social order that defines them as illegal does not exist in any great measure in Great Britain. Secondly, it seems that the British legal structure, recognizing the public demand for certain goods and services, has had, for the most part, the wisdom to make such goods and services available through legal channels.

Great Britain has legalized, among other things, gambling, and it has established a system of legally dispensing addictive drugs to registered addicts. Here we should emphasize a point made by Jerome H. Skolnick, as to the motivation of the British government. Making such goods and services available through legal channels "is not intended to imply approval" (Skolnick 1978, 338). It seems that England and Europe, unlike the United States, have learned that in the long run the consequences of tolerating certain evils is far better than trying to simply legislate them out of existence. As John A. Mack (1975, 40) observes, the British government, like other European governments, do not pass laws prohibiting goods and services unless they are prepared to enforce such laws.[5] Although Mack's observation holds true in general it must be qualified by another observation, a caveat based on empirical evidence that emerged in this study; that is, that the degree to which the law is enforced in reference to the use and sale of illegal goods is largely proportional to the number of problems that are created by those who violate such laws. For example, findings regarding the use of marijuana in Scotland and England indicate that marijuana in Great Britain is illegal and, unlike addictive drugs, there is no legal channel for obtaining it such as that provided for registered addicts. Yet, field work in which attempts were made to obtain marijuana met with no difficulty, particularly in the Soho area of London, in finding people willing to sell marijuana. Interestingly, it was found that neither the police, Procurators-Fiscal, solicitors nor criminal informants seemed to feel that there was a serious marijuana problem either in Glasgow or London. Upon reflection the reason for this soon becomes obvious: despite the fact that there is a law against marijuana use, the demand for it is small; hence, there is no need for any serious legal action to control it. In Glasgow, marijuana use seemed to be confined to a few small areas of the city. Here police, using decoys posing as buyers, would make an occasional arrest. Both the legal and criminal sources of information in Scotland seemed to think that for young people in Great Britain the drinking of alcoholic beverages was a sufficient source for getting one's "kicks." As one informant stated, "We have our drink here. That is all we need." Another felt that most heavy marijuana users were lower class youths who simply did not have adequate resources to buy it in large quantities. In London it was found that the Soho area was the major area of concentration for drug sale. Rumors of various Chinese groups that were smuggling not only marijuana but addictive drugs as well were everywhere. Still, the use and demand did not seem to be prevalent; moreover, there seemed to be no severe police action taken against violators.

We should add, however, that although police tolerance prevailed at the time of data collection for this study, should marijuana use increase significantly in Great Britain, the government undoubtedly would take steps to either legally control the problem or to increase police action against violators.

The reasons, then, why criminal syndicates have never made such headway in Great Britain lies in the fact that the legal checks have, for the most part, kept pace and balance over the demands for those goods which are inherently viewed as evil or undesirable. Even criminal informants concur with this hypothesis.

There is no doubt that some American syndicate members during the 1960s tried to move into the gambling scene in Scotland and England. It is also fairly certain that the efficiency of the gaming boards was largely instrumental in curtailing them. The members of these boards have the power to thoroughly investigate the background of any applicant and, holding hearings behind closed doors, can deny a license to anyone without having to justify their reasons. As Skolnick notes, "the board is all powerful, its position is unchallengeable" (1978, 339).

It is not then for lack of sophistication, ingenuity, or initiative that criminal syndicates in Scotland and England have not emerged; rather the inhibiting factor seems to be the structure of the society in which these criminals live and the effectiveness of social control mechanisms.

However, there have been several enterprises in Scotland and England that have approached levels of structuring and functioning that closely resemble those of syndicated crime. What was missing in these enterprises (according to our definition of syndicated crime) was either the absence of violence or intimidation and/or the inability to obtain immunity from the law.

One of these enterprises was a money-lending or "loan shark" group that operated in Glasgow during the 1960s. It consisted of the illegal lending of money by a group of criminals who used violence and intimidation to collect their loans. The amount of money earned from this enterprise was small. In fact, the participants had to engage in other illicit enterprises in order to subsist. It also seems that the press overreacted and exaggerated the amount of violence actually used. Research conducted among those close to the usury racket indicated that violence was used in some cases but this was the exception rather than the rule. Further, the amounts of the loans were generally nominal and the major problem was locating debtors who owed payments since borrowers generally tried to avoid face-to-face contact with the moneylenders. Because of the public attention given to this enterprise and because of the belief that violence was employed, police action was taken and the enterprise was terminated. Here again, gratuitous violence does not pay.

Another enterprise that resembled but was not a form of syndicated crime in Glasgow was that of the illegal sale of liquor. Here a group of individuals would buy cheap wine that they would sell to customers who wanted to purchase liquor after the pubs closed. Working out of vans, these individuals would locate themselves at a specific street corner so that customers would readily be able to find them. They only operated on Friday and Saturday nights. The profit was made by buying the wine at regular market prices and selling it at about three times that price. Again this enterprise, although illegal, was small and no violence was involved; hence there were no serious police reactions.

Parenthetically we should note that the lack of immunity from arrest in these two enterprises seemed to stem from the fact that the amounts of money made were small. Corruption, as we have learned from American criminal syndicates, is worthwhile only when large profits are realizable. When such is the case, both those who corrupt and those who are corrupted find the rewards lucrative and worth the risk.

Corruption of the police in Scotland does not seem to be as serious a problem as it is in the United States. There was mention of some police taking a "backhander" — a small amount of money or a bottle of whiskey received from a pub owner in return for the officer's keeping an attentive eye on the pub when it was closed. Likewise, if a pub was being frequented by ruffians or troublemakers, a proprietor would offer a "backhander" amounting to a few pounds to the officers patrolling the area. This would suffice usually to rid the pub of its troublemakers. (It will be recalled that burglars sometimes paid a fee to the police for information regarding the location of money and valuables.)

Pornography

There is only one form of syndicated crime which resembles in its general contours that of the United States: the pornography business in London. Pornography exhibits three criteria that qualify it as a form of syndicated crime. First, there is the open and visible offering of an illicit service — the sale of pornographic material that is illegal; secondly, there is evidence of the use of violence and murder among those engaged in the enterprise; thirdly, according to several informants, there are payoffs to police in order to obtain legal immunity for the operation.

Interestingly, when these findings were presented in a paper delivered at a conference at Cambridge University (Albini 1973), the reaction from an official at Scotland Yard who was present at the conference was swift and critical. This official argued that such police corruption was doubtful and noted that Scotland Yard had its own squads that kept surveillance over the department's activities. Surely, it was contended, these internal surveillance squads would have detected such corruption. Four years later a book appeared entitled *The Fall of Scotland Yard*. In the introduction it states, "The 'fall' of Scotland Yard took place between 1969 and 1972. As a result of what happened in those years, a score of London detectives went to gaol, hundreds more left the force in disgrace and the old CID hierarchy was savagely restructured" (Cox et al. 1977, 9). In 1976 this book had been preceded by a host of articles in *The Times of London, The Daily Telegraph,* and other British newspapers telling of the arrest and conviction of several detectives from Scotland Yard's "Obscence Publications Squad."[6]

In the pornography enterprise, the amount of money and the high visibility of the enterprise was obviously sufficient to create the climate for corruption. However, we should also note that with the discovery of the corruption the British legal system and Scotland Yard itself were quick and firm in bringing action against the police and criminal offenders. This action evidently has resulted in reducing profits made from the illegal sale of pornography to the point where it would not pay to corrupt or to be corrupted.

We can conclude our discussion of Great Britain by pointing out that a variety of criminal structures and enterprises exist and have existed at various times. It is important to note the existence and importance of these networks of criminals as well as the patron/client system that interlaces the legitimate and illegitimate parts of society. Although our data showed that most organized criminals tended to work in small groups and trusted only their friends and relatives, a network of contacts between specialists exists which allows for the development and execution of various types of criminal enterprises. Within this network we find gradations of status, with the highest status going to those who make the largest amount of money and have a low number of arrests as well as short terms of imprisonment. These indeed are what John A. Mack calls "The Able Criminals" (Mack, 1972).

Patrons and Clients in Criminal Syndicates in Great Britain

The class of "Able Criminals" with their access to capital are in a position to serve as patrons to participants in various criminal enterprises. They can provide for the manufacture of counterfeit money; they can arrange for the smuggling of goods to and from other countries; and they can help fence goods. Those who aspire to the status of "able criminal" seek to ingratiate themselves with the patron in hopes of gaining, for themselves, access to more lucrative enterprises. Those lacking guile, skill or determination serve the patron out of fear and intimidation. These networks are not bureaucratic in nature with clearly defined ranks, status, and roles. Instead, the importance of the individual participant emerges and changes with his ability to provide those services for which there is a need within the criminal community at a specific time or over an extended period of time.

There is no doubt that the network of organized criminals in Great Britain is such that it can and does operate effectively and creatively. It operates, however, within a societal setting in which the law, the police, and the public place limitations (described above) upon the development and continuation of certain types of criminal enterprises.

Syndicated Crime in Trinidad

The syndicate that Mieczkowski (1976) studied emerged largely because of the myriad political and social functions it performed within the social structure of Trinidad. The syndicate, which Mieczkowski named the "Ras Boys," consisted of a group of males of varying ages who were born and raised in a particular section of the city of Port O'Spain known as the Bridge District.

This district is economically poor but rich in terms of the social cohesion of its inhabitants. Most residents born in this community remain there throughout their entire lives, and friendships that begin early in life serve to later develop bonds of interaction grounded in trust. The Ras Boys exhibited these social and cultural traits and shared, with the other members of the community, a rich tradition which was an extremely vital part of Trinidad's history — the struggle against and liberation from colonialism. This struggle had only served to increase and strengthen the cohesion that already existed. In Trinidad there is a yearly event that ties the entire island together in national sentiment—the celebration of Carnival. This occurs on "Mardi Gras" or the Tuesday before the beginning of Lent. Although it has religious origins, the social meaning of Carnival is one that represents a binding of Trinidad's colonial past and liberated future. The people manifest this meaning by celebrating Carnival with joy and jest. To understand the importance and various forms of social expression manifested in Carnival is to understand Trinidadian society itself. Carnival is also important in understanding the importance of the Ras Boys and the role they continue to play during this festival.[7]

The Ras Boys play a major role as organizers and planners for Carnival in the Bridge District. Although it is a happy time, Carnival also becomes a time of violence as groups of youth from the various districts clash with one another, often very heatedly. The groups of youth who fight the most fiercely are given the honor of being referred to as "jamettes." The Ras Boys were the "jamettes" of the Bridge District, seen both as the warriors and the protectors of the community. This status, coupled with their role as organizers for Carnival, observed Mieczkowski, placed them into a position of power and respect that allowed them to perform syndicate criminal functions as well. They offered illegal goods for sale—cocaine, marijuana, and illegally distilled liquor known as "bush" rum (white lightning). They fenced stolen goods, and when required, would provide protection, which often included the use of physical force. Mieczkowski emphasizes that these two roles performed by the Ras Boys—the legitimate and the illegal—were intertwined both in their eyes and the eyes of the community.

As often happens in syndicate enterprises, when there is money to be made, color barriers and social class differences quickly vanish. And with the Ras Boys we find that whites and blacks, two groups that rarely worked together within the general population, indeed worked together in a tightly bound syndicate network. The union of whites and blacks worked to the Ras Boys' advantage, since neither the local police nor the general population—given the accepted racial divisions and prejudicial beliefs—would suspect that whites and blacks, along with a Trinidad-born ethnic Chinese person, would be part of the same syndicate. Not only was there racial variation in the composition of the group, there were various differences in the social status and class levels of its membership. This difference becomes significant in the vital roles played by the various members. Since the sale of marijuana was the syndicate's major enterprise, describing this enterprise will suffice to clarify these role differences and the nature of the functions and functionaries.

Marijuana was obtained from two sources—that grown locally and that imported from South America. Irrespective of its origin, the marijuana distribution procedure was the same. The Ras Boys would sell a certain portion of the stock directly to wholesalers; the remainder they kept for their own distribution, which took the form of rolled cigarettes sold on consignment by street vendors.

These street vendors were kept immune from arrest by the cooperation of a person to whom Mieczkowski has given the fictitious name of Randolph. Randolph was a police officer. He offered immunity in return for a payoff that consisted of receiving some quantities of drugs for his personal use and for underworld information that he would need at various times in order to perform competently as a law enforcement official.

When the marijuana stock was imported, this necessitated the help of another man who was white and the son of a diplomat. Being able to travel in various social circles not open to blacks, he was made responsible for the foreign contacts necessary to arrange for the syndicate's smuggling of marijuana from South America. Since he spoke Spanish, he was able to communicate with South American contacts from Colombia and Venezuela.

Wing, the Chinese member of the syndicate, served as the "bank" or provider of capital for the drug enterprises. In return for providing the capital used to purchase the drugs, Wing received a part of the contraband. He operated a bar-restaurant and a brothel, which served both as a source of capital and as fronts for the sale of contraband. Wing also operated illegal gambling games in his business enterprises and the Ras Boys served as protectors of these premises. Another member, "Larry," held a position with the customs and immigration service. In return for a supply of marijuana for personal use, he provided valuable information to the drug smuggling process.

Of special interest is a member called the "Secretary." This person held a position within the national government. He had access to many government officials including the Prime Minister. He assured immunity to Mansah, the head of the Ras Boys. The reason why immunity was granted serves as an interesting illustration of the respect and power the Ras Boys possessed in the Bridge District. It seems that in the 1970s during the "black power revolution," in an aborted attempt to seize power by a faction of the national defense force of Trinidad, the national government sought the help of Mansah. He was recruited to maintain order, with the help of the Ras Boys, among the citizens of the Bridge District and kept them from looting and engaging in street riots. In return for this, and through the intervention of the Secretary, Mansah remained immune from arrest.

These functionaries, then, along with three other members, compose the syndicate. As a syndicate, the Ras Boys make available illicit goods and services; they employ violence to assure their functioning; and they enjoy political immunity from the law.

Typical of many criminal syndicates, we find that the Ras Boys network is based on friendship and trust and that membership transcended social class, ethnic, and racial lines. Although the instability or weakness of the central government during the "black power revolution" was an important factor in achieving immunity from the law, we must note that the Ras Boys generated their own potential power for immunity by virtue of the high esteem (and fear) in which they were held by their community. With such social standing, their ability to serve as patrons and clients placed them into the position of serving as brokers for both the legitimate and extra-legal sectors of society.

In conclusion, I should like to note that organized crime, whatever form it takes, must be examined and can be understood only be viewing it as a part of the history and social structure of the society within which it is operating at any given time.

Notes

1. This study, conducted while I held the position of Visiting Senior Researcher in Criminology at the University of Glasgow, Scotland, includes data obtained from interviews with criminal informants, solicitors, and from Scotland Yard, from contact with police and prison officials, and from direct observation (in the case of confidence games, played on the street).

In addition to my own data, where appropriate, I will draw from the literature to further illustrate the nature and types of organized criminality in Great Britain.

Since, both politically and historically, the Caribbean has been associated with Great Britain, I shall give a description of the nature of a criminal syndicate on the island of Trinidad. The data for this study is drawn entirely from the work of Tom Mieczkowski (1976).

2. During my Glasgow research I was repeatedly warned by a number of shopkeepers and other Glaswegians not to go into certain areas of the city because of the menacing threat of the adolescent gangs located in these areas. Typically, none of these people who warned me had ever seen a gang member but they were certain of the fact that gang members had committed numerous foul deeds. I had no doubt that these adolescent gangs did exist but because of my previous research in the United States, I had learned about their major type of crime, a type which I classified as *in-group* organized crime (Albini 1971). Here crimes are committed as part of the gang's engaging in what its members define as fun, as a means of showing their courage or as a result of protecting their turf. The important factor, however, which speaks to our point is that the victims are typically other gang members, not private citizens.

The typical public concern about gangs, indeed, seems to be generated, as Stanley Cohen (1966) notes, by the media which creates stereotypes of gang characteristics and activities. These in turn become the basis upon which the public can and often does become very alarmed to the point of mass hysteria concerning an imagined personal threat from a stereotyped enemy.

3. I became acquainted with this game after meeting two victims, both of whom were middle-aged American males. They had been picked up by two seductive women, dressed alike, who described themselves as sisters whose husbands were out of town. The scam of these b-girls, as they are referred to in the trade, was to lure the victims into eating and drinking at a certain establishment, for which they later (after giving the victims "the slip") receive a percentage of all the food and drink sold.

4. In order to describe the scam, let us take a victim through the steps of the game as it is played.

At the sound of a whistle from one of the "lookout men" men, one of these men puts a small board on top of two milk crates. The dealer then appears and places three cards with their faces up on the board. The game now begins. One of the accomplices, who pretends to be drunk, displays a large roll of bills and approaches the dealer. The dealer explains the game to him and then turns the cards over. The drunk bets a certain amount of money. Quickly, the dealer moves the three cards into different positions. The victim is now nearby, watching the drunk and notices that the corner of the ace is bent. But, much to the victim's dismay, the drunk continuously selects the king and loses. "It must be because he is drunk," reasons the victim. Soon a second accomplice appears and begins an argument with the dealer, accusing him of taking advantage of the drunk. Now this second accomplice begins playing, supposedly out of revenge for the drunk. At first he loses. Soon he is joined by a third accomplice. Within a short period of playing, they pretend to become friends and dedicate themselves to discovering the dealer's secret. Suddenly, they do. Shaking hands with one another and speaking broken English, they do give the impression that they are naive tourists. But now they have found the secret. They begin accurately selecting the ace every time. The victim thinks that the reason for this is the fact that the corner of the ace is bent. He now becomes really interested and approaches the table. The dealer pretends as though he now wants to stop playing because he is losing. The accomplices begin yelling, "No. You son-o-bitch, you play. Me find secret. Me win now. You play." The dealer pretends to be intimidated and continues to play and lose. After each win the accomplices yell with joy. They now pretend to notice the victim for the first time. "You my friend. You make money too," says one of the accomplices as he puts his arm around the victim. Convinced that the men know the secret, the victim pulls out his wallet. The appeal of winning is so infectious and fatal that not only will victims play all the money in their wallets, but they will ask their wives or friends to lend them more. Suddenly all the bets are down. One of the accomplices, who knows that through a slight of hand the dealer has replaced the bent ace with a bent king, picks up the card that has the bent corner. It is a king. Immediately, the accomplice begins apologizing, and tells the victim that he found his mistake and this time he definitely will not lose. This is done in an effort to encourage the victim to play even more money. If he does, he loses again. Sometimes the victim becomes angry. At this point, the whistle or code of the "lookout" man sounds. The victim thinks the police are coming since the dealer disappears and the accomplices look around suspiciously and lose themselves in the crowd. Not wanting to be involved with the police, the victim also hurries away. The game is over.

5. Chapter three of Mack's book contains an interesting discussion as to why syndicated crime has not made a foothold in England and continental Europe.

6. I wish to thank Karen Sandiford, Reference Library, British Information Services, New York, and Janice Dean, Wayne State University, Detroit, for their help in providing me with the material from various newspapers.

7. The inhabitants of the Bridge District, like those of all the other districts of Port O'Spain, prepare for Carnival by constructing a float, designing costumes, organizing a steel-drum band, and obtaining rum, ganja (marijuana) and other forms of intoxicants desired by the people.

References

Albini, Joseph L. 1971. *The American Mafia: Genesis of a Legend*. New York: Appleton Century Crofts, chap. 2. Currently being distributed by Irvington Publications, New York.
_____. 1973. "Structures and types of organized crime: A comparison between Great Britain and the U.S.A." Fifth National Conference on Teaching and Research in Criminology, University of Cambridge, Institute of Criminology, Cambridge, England, July 4–6, 1973.
Boyle, Jimmy. 1977. *A Sense of Freedom*. Edinburgh: Conongate Publishing Ltd.
Cohen, Stanley. 1966. "Mods, Rockers and the Rest: Community Reactions to Juvenile Delinquency." Lecture delivered to Howard League, December 6.
Cox, Barry; John Shirley; and Martin Short. 1977. *The Fall of Scotland Yard*. New York: Penguin Books.
Levi, Michael. 1981. *The Phantom Capitalists: The Organization and Control of Long Firm Fraud*. London: W. S. Heinemann Publishers.
Lucas, Norman. 1969. *Britain's Gangland*. London: W. H. Allen.
Mack, John A. 1972. "The Able Criminal." *British Journal of Criminology* 12, No. 1.
_____. 1975. *The Crime Industry*. Lexington, Mass.: Lexington Books.
Mieczkowski, Thomas. 1976. *Syndicated Crime in the Caribbean: A Cast Study*. Unpublished Master of Arts Thesis, Wayne State University, 1976.
Payne, Leslie. 1973. *The Brotherhood*. London: Michael Joseph.
Pearson, J. 1972. *The Profession of Violence*. London: Weidenfeld & Nicolson.
Scarne, John. 1961. *Scarne's Complete Guide to Gambling*. New York: Simon & Schuster.
Skolnick, Jerome H. 1978. *House of Cards*. Boston: Little, Brown & Co.

7

The Traditional Sicilian Mafia: Organized Crime and Repressive Crime

Henner Hess
Johann Wolfgang Goethe University

> The President: Have you been a member of mafia?
> The accused Mimi: I do not know what it means.
>
> (Trial transcript in the case of Amoroso)

The word "mafia" describes a phenomenon far more complex, it may be assumed, than headlines about a vaunted, secret criminal association suggest.[1] A more realistic definition than those implied in newspaper headlines, popular crime stories, and some books of seemingly scientific status might — though still greatly simplified — be the following: Mafia is not an organization but behavior, a method for achieving certain ends and goals used by those who are called "mafiosi." It is private power employed, exercised and exploited by strong-arm men utilized in a threatening manner in all kinds of social conflicts: in the struggle for land and crops; in the contention for the best pitches and bootlegs for market-place locales and black market goods; over the building-trades, the drug business, tobacco-smuggling; over the control of votes in election campaigns, and in the manipulation and domination of offices in bureaucratic institutions.

It is implicit in this description of the phenomenon of mafia that not only are we dealing with a specific form of crime, but also with important aspects of Italian politics — at least, the politics of certain regions of the mezzogiorno (Southern Italy) that are touched by mafia activities.

Origins of the Term Mafia

The etymological speculations on the origin of the word "mafia" are legend. Even though most of them may be laid aside as folklore, they cannot, by the same token, be challenged by an empirically grounded theory of impeccable scientific validity. Possibly the word "mafia" derives from the dialect of Palermo, Sicily, where it connotes pride, self-confidence and vainglorious behavior as well. A mafioso is a man *che non porta mosca sul naso* — one, that is, who will not allow a fly to dance on his nose, as it were, and who, it is said, at any moment is ready to defend his honor to the utmost.

About the middle of the nineteenth century, the term "mafioso" became linked with crime, marking a certain type of criminal behavior and attitude. A Sicilian, however, will refer to such a person not as a mafioso but euphemistically as a *un uomo d'onore* ("a man of honor"), or *un uomo di rispetto* ("a man of respect") or, secretively, *uno di quelli* ("one of those"). And by so doing, he will not only refer to the criminal, but to the other roles inhabited simultaneously by such a person: that of the village strong-arm man, the boss, and the mediator in many social conflicts. No one speaks of the "Mafia" or of "Onorata Società" (the Honorable Society), but less pretentiously and vaguely of the *amici degli amici* ("the friends of the friends"). This is the way in which groups organized in client-patron relationships around a mafioso are characterized.

In an official report, the word "mafia" is used as early as 1838; and in the second half of the nineteenth century the phenomenon represented by the word became widespread, though its roots can be traced back to the sixteenth century (Llaryora forthcoming).

The Origin of Mafia

For many centuries, Sicily was merely part of one European empire after another. The central governments were in Madrid, Naples, and Rome. The real masters on the island had been landowning barons, especially in the interior and western zones of the island, in the area of large, landed property called *latifundia*. On their farms the landed gentry ruled with unlimited power and authority buttressed by their armed, and very often, ruthless field guards. In the late eighteenth century, many of those barons preferred to live in the cosmopolitan centers of Palermo or Naples than in the countryside. They leased their property to super-tenants (*gabellotti*), who paid them an annual rent and, in turn, these leaseholders sublet the fields in smaller sections to others. When feudalism was abolished in 1812, landed property could be sold and at auction sales the gabellotti, having threatened others through fear and violence, obtained the estates. These new men formed the beginnings of an agricultural or rural bourgeoisie replacing the old feudal masters. In 1860, after the unification of Italy, the landed property of the church was also sold, and it, too, was available to the gabellotti. The traditional rights of way and access that had been held by the peasants to pastures and forests now were withheld from them. The community fields were transformed by the gabellotti into private property. The economic situation of the peasants, which had never been especially good, deteriorated even more during the nineteenth century. Consequently, highway robberies and thefts, which had been sporadic, now became chronic (D'Allessandro 1959).

Through private violence landlords and gabellotti protected themselves against an aroused peasantry, disgruntled farm workers, and bandits. The pressures that demanded self-defense included the fact that the legal authorities were not able or would not provide protection. The power of constituted authority to enforce the law was hindered by the weakness of the state and by the physical conditions in the rural countryside of Sicily: the very primitive modes of communication that existed kept the villages in isolation. In these circumstances, the landowners and gabellotti could use their power to also influence the distribution of crops in their favor. Thus, the class struggle in the countryside was very violent, directly pitting different social strata against each other without the mitigating interventions of the state. The hired hands of the landlords took advantage of the legal vacuum and exploited the peasantry for themselves. The heavily armed guards (*campieri*) — known for their brutality — urged the peasants to pay them a part of the crop as a so-called "protection fee." This tribute exacted from the peasants is known as *u pizzu* (*fari vagnari u pizzu* — "to wet one's beak"). Thus, on the Sicilian landed properties forms of crime arose that later came to be known as racketeering.

In a time of transition, when the feudal ruling order was in a state of decay and collapse and the modern bureaucratic state was not able to assume authority and its legitimate monopoly on physical coercion, mafia violence — from the point of view of the affluent classes — was a necessary force needed to quell disturbances and fill the gap of power in order to maintain estate property. This force, which backed specific economic interests, was illegal because it violated the laws of the state. But on the other hand, the customs and mores of the people themselves legitimated it in some ways. For instance, the subcultural obligation of honor and of silence (*omertà*) forbade collaboration with the insutitutions of the state. Those who sought out the law enforcement authorities in order to redress grievances violated deeply entrenched values. The mafioso fed upon these cultural traditions and fulfilled the ideal image of the Sicilian: he is, at once, independent, mysterious, and capable of imposing personal respect *un uomo d'onore* (a man of honor) who does not work in the fields with a pick and shovel (an image, by the way, that has its roots in the classical Roman *civis* and the Spanish *gentilhombre*).

The mafioso was a complex social type. He was a criminal, but a respected man, nevertheless, who performed some useful functions in village society. As noted above, he would mediate in cases of theft and the robbery of cattle; his help was solicited in abductions and kidnappings; and he arranged employment for the relatives of his clients. The modern state eventually took over his indispensable functions so that little but the criminal dimension of mafia activity was left. The state and mafia, which may, thus, be seen as competing and antagonistic forces in the struggle for power, in reality meet in various cooperative alliances. The very extension of state power ironically provided mafiosi with some new opportunities to enhance their prestige and agrandize their economic position. With the establishment of the right to vote, which was authorized for all males by 1911, and included all females by 1946, a new function arose for the strong-arm men of the villages. The candidates for Parliament needed the mafiosi as campaign assistants. Mafiosi guaranteed the candidates the necessary votes through their client and retainer networks, by the threat of violence, and by fraudulently manipulating the vote when verbal persuasion failed. The politicians who benefited from mafia support acknowledged it by affording protection—that is, they shielded mafiosi against arrest and prosecution by law enforcement authorities. This very personal, client-oriented politics persists today, even though it is greatly dimiinished.[2]

The Mafioso: Stations in His Career

In order to describe the etiology of a criminal life, and in order to explain how it evolves, the concept of a "career" (a succession of progressive, clearly delineated stages in an occupation) will prove useful.[3] And the notion of a career may be applied to the situation of the individual mafioso. The career of a "normal" criminal consists of a series of degradation processes, driving him more deeply into stigmatized, discrediting roles. For the mafioso, however, although in general he, too, experiences many of the same stresses, strains and enticements, the societal reaction is not wholly negative and punitive.

Social Antecedents

In contrast to popular opinion, the mafiosi typically emerge out of very poor social and economic conditions. Initially, many were the sons of shepherds and small tenant farmers. Crime for almost every mafioso was an attractive vehicle for social advancement and economic mobility.

Act of Violence

The essential element in social power is the capacity to use physical violence. As far as the power of a formal government and its agents are concerned, the subordinates may forget this; but for the mafioso, everybody is continually aware of it. In performing his first acts of violence—purely criminal (a robbery, a killing) or criminal only according to codified law but conforming to subcultural norms (a crime of honor)[4] a previously quite ordinary youngster accomplishes two things. First, he proves that he is a man one has to reckon with (*c'avi sangu 'ntra li vini, c'avi ficatu, ch'è omu*—"that blood runs in his veins, that he is a man"). Secondly, he discovers power: for the first time, he has the thrilling experience of being able to manipulate people.

Successful Outcome of the Collision with the Law

Not everybody who uses violence will become a mafioso. Some take to the hills and become bandits, which is quite a different, even contrary, social role. The bandit lives in open conflict with the law and the police and is hunted down after some months or years; the mafioso is stronger than the law; or is rather someone who can "get away with it," which in itself proves in the eyes of many that he is of the stuff mafiosi are made of. To prove himself, he must, if indicted at all, be acquitted, usually for lack of evidence. There are two possible explanations for such an acquittal: either there really is no proof, or someone influential has put a word in for him. In any case, and the first explanation is the more probable in the case of his first trial, the people in his village will think that he successfully intimidated the witnesses and that he has connections with some influential person.

Acceptance by Mafiosi

As a next step in his career, the aspirant must be accepted by older "uomini d'onore" ("men of honor"), as a *picciotto* (a "young man"). He may be mentioned as a friend; the job of *campiere* or *guardiano* (a guard in the fields or on the plantations) may be offered to him; he may be asked to render a special service in exchange for the promise of protection—and thus gradually and in an informal way enter into the *cosca* ("family") of an established leader.

Being Cast and Identified as a Mafioso

Neither his capacities, nor his deeds alone make a mafioso. A mafioso is not somebody who feels like one or acts like one, but somebody who is regarded as such by the public. It would be impracticable and impossible for him to use violence all the time. The respect he commands depends on the village people's complementary action, their fear, and their conviction that he is ready to use violence without hesitation. To achieve this, the mafiosi have perfected the method of terror, which will be dealt with later on.

Furthermore, once people regard him as competent to exercise a special function (the role of protector, broker, corruptor, enforcer), this acknowledgment reinforces his capacity to do so. The more people turn to him, the stronger his position becomes. There is a relation of interdependence between achievement and ascription. It is at this stage of his career, that the authority, respect, and fear surrounding the social role of mafioso become transferred to him as an individual. His career to this point is a rather uncommon variation of the labelling process.

Monopolization

Few of the newcomers go beyond this point. Henceforth they remain in the *clientela* and at the command of a mafioso leader. Some make it to the top and replace the established *capo-mafia* of their community, either by being designated as successor, by killing the older one off, or by being the toughest competitor after the capo has died a peaceful death. The next three steps in the mafioso's career—monopolization, legalization, and legitimization—point up his new problems in consolidating and defending the position he has achieved. He tries to monopolize power, to be the only one who can success-fully fulfill the mafia functions, to hold down competitors and newcomers. At the same time he acquires a monopoly on the profits of certain economic activities. The mafioso is not a parasite simply feeding on the victims of crime. He is a landlord or a leaseholder or has a job or runs a business. but he differs from ordinary leaseholders or businessmen in his characteristic use of violence to frighten off competition.

Legalization

The mafioso also strengthens his position by avoiding too much open con-flict with the law. He tries to come to terms with it, or rather, with the men staffing the law enforcement agencies. By now, he has the members of his cosca to do the dirty jobs for him; and, on the other hand, since he is an estab-lished *uomo d'onore* now, violence becomes less necessary. The mere hint of dissatisfaction may persuade others of his intentions. Nevertheless, he is not a law-abiding citizen and he needs connections with office-holders to cover up his crimes and those of his *picciotti*.

Some older mafiosi even held offices themselves, though usually in the lo-cal community only (a striking example were the many mafia mayors in-stalled by the United States Army in 1943 because they had apparently been enemies of the Fascist government). Quite a few could boast titles bestowed upon them for services rendered to a candidate or a party in an election. Since the mafiosi support the existing social order—though it may be through committing crimes—reaching an arrangement with the official representa-tives of this order has never beeen too difficult.

Legitimization

Legalization is the mafioso's attempt to take measures against the actions of the law enforcement agencies. As I have tried to show, it includes more than just corruption. Even more essential to his position, though, is legitimiza-tion, the act that his behavior, though perhaps illegal, is regarded as legiti-mate according to subcultural values. There are two sources of legitimiza-tion: the subcultural concept of the ideal man and the functional necessity of his actions. The concept of *uomo di rispetto* or *galantuomo* differs substantially from the reality of most Sicilian men. Most of them work in the fields (and regard manual labor as degrading), are powerless and completely dependent on some patron. Little wonder that they are fascinated by the image of the indepedent, powerful, and influential gentleman. Exemption from manual labor and power over other people are the only true criteria of distinction. The ruling ideal is — to vary one of Marx's remarks — the ideal of the ruling class, in pre-industrial society is represented by the aristocrat, the *gabellotto* (leaseholder), the *civile* (professional), and the priest. Sicilian society has produced two self-made variations of this gentleman-ideal: the mafioso and the bandit. Of the two, the mafioso is more in accordance with the ideal, especially with its darker and more mysterious nuances. The bandit's conspicuous consumption of power and his ostentatious display of captured riches (fanciful costumes, horses, weapons, etc.) is less impressive than veiled power that can be expressed in a hint, a gesture, a look only; power that has become natural to the person exercising it.

Secondly, the functions of the local strong-arm man are, at least to some extent, considered necessary and useful by the population. There has to be someone "to sort things out," if they become too complicated. To the mafioso himself such a function may sometimes even seem to be a sacrifice and hard work barely justified by the financial and emotional rewards. It is not easy to distinguish between conscious deceit and unconscious rationalization, when we try to understand the people involved on their own terms. Especially for the persons marginal to the criminal organization (corruptees, for instance), such a rationalization is probably an indispensable defense against norm conflicts: they keep things going, they maintain order, they help a friend. To himself, to his high-ranking friends, to his clients, and in part also, to the public in his sphere of influence, the mafioso is not "mafioso" but something less ambiguous: *uomo d'onore* or *uomo di rispetto*.[5] *(This does not exclude the perception by other people that the mafiosi have always been hated as oppressors and infamous criminals — much like the barons, the gabellotti, the tax-collectors, and the bandits.)*

The Structure of Mafia Groupings

The accused Mimi (cited in the previous epigraph), in answering the question as to whether he was a member of Mafia, claimed he did not know the meaning of that term. He may not necessarily have been lying. A hidden society with criminal ends — which is centralized, efficiently led, having rites of initiation and membership, having statutes and even branch offices in New York and Frankfurt — this society, that is often called the "real" mafia, does not exist and never did. Rather, there were and there are loose, steadily changing textures of relations that are in each case offered around a successful mafioso, a capo-mafia. The Sicilian term for the core of those textures of relations is *cosca* (a local clique).

Cosca

The structure of role relationships that is called *cosca* seems to possess the defining features of an organization: "(1) It has a division of labor (occupational specialization). (2) The members' activities are coordinated by rules, agreements, and understandings which support the structure. (3) The entire enterprise is rationally designed to achieve announced objectives." (Udy, 1965). Nevertheless, the mafia grouping is not to be mistaken for a corporate social unit comparable to a business firm, a political party, or a real secret society.

First, the set of roles that may be mobilized to commit a crime may serve other purposes as well. In fact, it is the same occupational specialization pre-existing in the economic and political structure that is sometimes activated to achieve illegal ends. The organization layout given in Figure 7.1 is, therefore, at the same time a model of social and occupational stratification in Sicilian society. The positions I to IV in the diagram indicate levels in the social hierarchy. Secondly, the rules determining the members' activities have not been especially designed for a criminal group; they are, rather, a stricter application of general subcultural norms. Likewise, the ties binding members to each other draw their strength from the general importance of such personal relationships as kinship, friendship, and patronage (Muehlmann and Llaryora 1968). Thirdly, although the enterprise is set up to achieve certain objectives, those objectives are usually announced only vaguely even to the lower members, so that mostly only the upper echelons are aware of them. Those qualifications have to be kept in mind when the arrangement focussing on a capo-mafia is discussed in terms of criminal organization (Cressey 1972).

The word *cosca* is etymologically related to artichoke and compares the leader to the trunk and the subordinates to the leaves. A number of other terms are in use: *paracu, sodalizio, fratellanza, famiglia, compagnia, associazione, aggregato, cerchio*. These refer to the nucleus composed of the positions that in Figure 7.1 are connected by unbroken lines. The leader and his career have been discussed above. Compared to present-day developments in criminal organizations, specialization in the Sicilian cosca is less elaborate. The position of capo-mafia, for instance, integrates not only the roles of strategic and tactical planner and corrupter, but more executive roles as well, like that of enforcer and sometimes even that of executioner.

The positions under III are usually held by all kinds of the leader's clients — *campieri,* tenants, herdsmen, and they may also be the leader's relatives. This brings us to the binding ties, of which the first and strongest is kinship, consanguineal and affinal. The core of the cosca consists often of brothers, brothers-in-law, or a father and his sons. In this case the positions in III are very close to or even on the same level with II. The second is patronage, common in the relationship between II and III and typical for the relationship between II and IV or III and IV. It develops step by step, beginning with the exchange of services, which takes on the character of favors, partly because

FIGURE 7.1
The Structure of Mafia Groupings

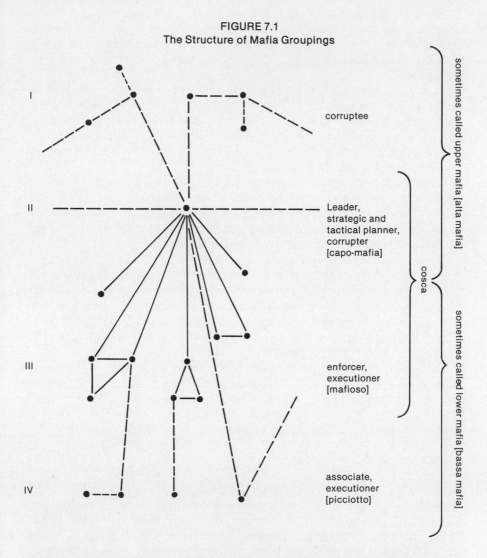

some time usually elapses between service and reciprocal return-service, thus blurring the causal connection, and partly because, to some extent, the personalization of objective relations is general in Sicilian pre-industrial society. Thus, a *gabellotto* may provide seed for a peasant or take the wool of the peasant's 20 sheep to the market along with the wool of his own 500; and, instead of charging him money, the peasant later may be asked to cut a troublesome person's vines. Characteristically, the peasant is asked to do the gabelletto a favor. If the exchange continues, the asymmetry of the relation becomes more and more evident; if the client is an employee, it is asymmetrical from the beginning. But, since the secrecy of the enterprise demands confidence and intimacy, the ties of mafia patronage are sometimes reinforced by intermarriage, or, more often, by the establishment of ritual kinship. Addressing each other as *cumpa* anticipates or expresses the relation of god-parenthood.

Very often the cosca is not a cluster of interrelated positions but rather a network of dyads emanating from the leader. It is for this reason that the cosca ought not to be called a group, since it, then, lacks the sense of belonging, group interaction, and goals common to all members. The dyadic structure, though, gives the leader more power over his subordinates and renders penetration from outside more difficult.

Initiation into the cosca is a gradual process. There is no single instant or rite establishing membership. The dividing line between the men at the lower fringe of the network and those outside it (IV) is blurred; the rank-and-file fluctuate. Being considered a member depends mostly on the number of occasions one is mobilized to carry out certain tasks.

The norms governing the relations described are not different from general social norms, only more explicit. A patron has to protect his clients; a client must be devoted and obedient to his patron. A kinsman does not deceive his relative; it is for this reason that ritual kinship is so important, since it sets up strong kinship obligations between people who have no actual kinship relations. God-parenthood as the customary form of ritual kinship combines the features of kinship and patronage.

Taciturnity is a virtue that is valued highly in the larger society. The sanctions against deviance from cosca protocols, though, are much stronger. Whereas violation of informal social norms is generally punished with derision, contempt, or expulsion from the group, treason within the mafia network is dealt with by violent attacks on the life or body of the traitor.

Corrupters and Corruptees

Besides his use of violence, the essential characteristic of the mafioso is the capacity to cover his crime and to achieve immunity from the law by corrupting influential persons. The corruptee's crime is, legally speaking, something other than the crime he is covering up; but criminologically his cover-up action is part of the whole, especially if the cooperation between corrupter and corruptee is a continuing business with initiatives emanating from both sides, which it usually is. The problem has to be tackled by looking at the structure, not at the individual offender. And the corruptee holds quite an important position in the structural network (and, by the way, might profit more from it than anybody else), even if he is not a member of the cosca and in no way considers himself a mafioso.

As a rule, the mafioso does not directly approach district attorneys, judges, policemen or *pretori* (the lower judges who are situated in the smaller towns, in whose position police and court functions are combined and who can impose *ammonizione*, "police supervision," and *domicilio coatto*, "compulsory residence," two of the more efficient weapons the state has against mafia). He reaches them through a chain of dyadic contacts. The first link connects him to an upper-class person, usually the owner of the estate the mafioso holds as gabellotto; or a deputy. This relation is conceived as a relation of patronage, the mafioso playing the role of client, although it is more of an instrumental friendship, and in this relationship to speak of each other as friends is common. Frequently, a mafioso has several such connections and a landlord or a deputy is connected to several mafiosi. The mafioso's support is valuable or actually indispensable to someone running for election. The mafioso controls the votes in his area, since almost everybody is dependent on him economically, or has moral obligations to him or simply does not dare refuse his "advice." The mafioso might also be useful in intimidating or doing away with a high-ranking person's competitors or critics, with non-corruptable officials, and, above all, dangerous peasant leaders. The corrupted estate owner or politician, then, in his turn becomes a corrupter and influences public officials who depend on him, thus guaranteeing the mafioso immunity from prosecution.

It is noteworthy that, besides the leader, no other member of the cosca has access to this chain of infuence. The capo-mafia dominates his men because he commands the necessary influence to protect them; and he is able to put pressure on the corruptees or be useful to them because he has the men of his cosca at his disposal. Thus, leadership cannot be explained by personal strength, ruthlessness, or wealth alone, but must be understood in organizational terms. Also from the political and economic points of view we can now understand the power of the mafioso: he is the broker between the local and the regional or national levels of politics and benefits from his position at the link between local production and the supra-local economic circuit.[6]

Further Ramifications

It has been argued that there has never been a centralized criminal organization called "Mafia." Mafiosi, politicians, and a number of other associated persons formed a loose alliance to gain political power in the communal court house or the regional or national parliaments, an alliance that may be called a "faction." But then they had to fight other factions, including other mafiosi. Two or more cosche often competed for the control of a certain business. There sometimes occurred (and occurs in present-day Palermo) bloody warfare. On the other hand, the cosche also cooperated. They knew each other as people of the same status know each other. They certainly had a feeling of sharing the same profession and the same problems. They could turn to each other as to colleagues for help, if they had matters to settle in another area. They would come to terms in the case of a cattle-rustling expedition or any other trade that had to be conducted over large distances. After World War II, an astonishing agreement was reached between mafiosi, politicians, and others, to kill off the bandits, threaten and kill peasants in revolt, and support first the policy of Sicilian separatism and later the Christian Democratic party (Pantaleone 1962). It was easy to misinterpret these events as actions planned and supervised by a single command group. But it seems to be closer to the facts to speak only of a consonance of interests. After all, the mafiosi, all of them, in the same historical situation had the same economic and political interests leading to the same actions and to cooperation, but without subordination to a central criminal government.[7] Sicilians call the mafiosi, *gli amici degli amici* ("the friends of friends"), and there is probably no better term to characterize their relationships, at least at this upper level.

The Functions of Mafia

For the individual mafioso his acts are motivated toward one goal: social advancement in the form of economic advancement and upward movement on the ladder of social prestige. At the end of a successful career, a poor shepherd, tenant or peasant may be transformed into a rich and mighty man.

Mediation

The traditional mafioso as local strong-arm man had a number of meditative functions that were always emphasized beyond their actual common usefulness by the mafiosi themselves as a form of legitimization of their position. If two persons or two groups of persons cannot reach an agreement over some business, the mafioso may be asked by one or both of the parties in conflict to step in and help settle the problem. The mafioso decides the conflict to the satisfaction of both parties, in the interest of the party closer to him or paying most or in his own interest, but usually according to subcultural norms. Sometimes he has to put pressure on one party to accept his decision. For this purpose the mafiosi have developed an elaborate language of threat reaching from friendly but firm advice to verbal threats, anonymous letters, symbolic signs like a cross of stones laid on a field, to cutting olive trees or vines, burning a barn, breaking a donkey's leg, or killing some sheep. In the case of cattle-rustling the police, on the average, could only detect 15 percent of the thieves and recover 10 percent of the prey. If the victim turned to a mafioso, however, he got his cattle back in 95 percent of the cases (Mori 1933). However, he would lose a quarter or a third of his stolen property, which went as a "gift" to the mafioso (the thief was also allowed to keep a part), but he saved himself the trouble of travelling to identify his animals, of giving evidence in court, and had no need to fear the thief's revenge. In the case of an abduction, the mediation of the mafioso, sought by the kidnapper as well as by the family of the victim, could save the victim's life, which through police prosecution would always be endangered. The mafioso could force a debtor to pay back his debt or a youngster to marry a seduced girl.

Repression

But far more important situationally for the social system were those actions of mafiosi that could be labelled as "repressive crimes." By these I mean illegal acts, especially violent acts, which are carried out in order to maintain the privileged position of a social class.

Thus the mafiosi — even though they often hired bandits or employed them for political reasons — were principally the counterparts of bandits, who everywhere represented the most original form of agrarian rebellion (Hobsbawm 1969). The owner of landed property and cattle, of plantations and vineyards, always felt compelled to employ men able to deter thieves and bandits by brutality or by the dissemination of fear. Thus the armed *campiere* roaming the estate on horseback and the *guardiano*, rifle over his shoulder, walking the paths of the orange plantation, were common figures in the Sicilian countryside. Usually, when it became well known that someone reputed to be *un uomo di rispetto, un amico degli amici,* had lent his protection to an estate or taken over a latifundium as *gabellotto*, the announcement of this fact alone ensured protection. The mafiosi could achieve this kind of power because they were able to multiply their actually small forces in carrying out occasional sanctions as acts of terrorism. Terror hits suddenly and unexpectedly, hence its blows always have to be expected and cannot be prepared for. The attack has to have publicity, and the public must know the victim was hit, because its main purpose is not the punishment of an individual but the preventive warning to other potential offenders. At the same time, the mechanism must be inscrutable; thus, one never knows for sure whether a mafioso killed someone, but it is always suspected (Hess 1981).

Even more consequential and uncompromising, and characterized by the same terroristic tactics, is the reaction of mafiosi to another kind of threat: the revolutionary strivings of the peasants for change (Blok 1969). These challenges to the extant economic order were aimed not only at the amelioration of economically depressed individuals in the system but at fundamental, radical change of the whole political economy, which were more dangerous and ominous for the principal beneficiaries of latifundia — the owners of estates and the gabellotti/mafiosi. Thus, for example, between 1892 and 1894, the Fasci,[8] a coalition of peasants and craftsmen, sought changes in land-leasing procedures. By means of direct contracts between proprietors and large leasing syndicates, they attempted to circumvent the gabellotti and commission-tenants. Further, the dependency of the peasants on the proprietors would have been diminished since they would have been able to bargain and negotiate with the landlords as joint parties. The Fasci dramatized their demands and claims with strikes and demonstrations that often resulted in tumultuous, bloody confrontations involving the police and armed forces. Many instances of violence were provoked by mafiosi elements who fired on the peasants before the carabinieri arrived.

After 1918, the same claims were pressed with even stronger determination by the peasants. In 1894, the government had acted sharply against the peasants but now had to relax its repression and make concessions to the leagues of veterans returning from the war. Now, more than before, the proprietors were forced to defend their privileges without the open aid of the police and did so illegally as the government, as a matter of policy, had to appear sympathetic to peasant goals and social objectives. In 1920, for example, four officials and organizers of the peasant cooperatives were murdered.

By 1922, the landed classes had the fascist government behind them and it repressed the peasant movement for reform. But after World War II, not only did the landless peasants demand major reforms in landleasing, but succeeded in obaining partitioning of farm land and effected a fundamental change in land distribution and ownership policies. The agrarian reform movement gained great support with peasants acting spontaneously in many places, taking over fallow grounds and distributing them amongst themselves. In the midst of reform fever, the mafia rose again. It participated on the side of conservative landed groups and openly fought against peasant organizations, labor unions and left-wing political parties using menace and terror and murder. Between 1945 and 1965, 41 leaders and supporters of peasant movements for land reform were assassinated — 30 of those in the critical years between 1946 and 1947. On a greater scale, however, mere symbolic acts of violence were sufficient to thwart peasant opposition and the demand that their rights be implemented. The appointment of a known mafioso as an estate administrator would be sufficient to declare the attitudes of land owners towards peasant reform programs (Pantaleone 1962, 117–54; Blok 1974, 190–210).

The Myth of Mafia

In Mario Puzo's novel *The Godfather*, the mafioso is presented as a man of honor caring about the problems of his clients and performing useful functions as a mediator in disputes. As stressed above, these facets belonged to the role of the traditional mafioso, although they were never central to it (and are romantically exaggerated in the novel). In modern times, the godfather-mafioso has finally vanished altogether and has been replaced by the modern gangster who works in secrecy if possible, who merely maintains the semblance of public prestige but does not strive to legitimate his position, and whose only goal is financial profit.

The emergence of this new type of gangster may be attributable to several factors the most prominent of which seem to be significant changes in the economic and social structure of Sicily and increased cultural contact with the United States. No longer operating in a completely agrarian society in which the mafioso did control the fields and the factors affecting farm production, the "new" gangster functions in a metropolis in which the consumption of goods and services constitutes his criminal milieu. In spite of these profound changes in the social worlds in which mafiosi operate, one thing has remained: the myth of the secret society.

The popular myth of a super-government of crime that not only dominates Sicily but has spread its sinister tentacles into the United States and other countries as a multifaceted criminal cartel persists because such a conspiracy theory of crime fulfills very useful political and social functions. As it did (and does) for Northern Italians, today the theory of mafia conspiracy conveniently serves Americans as an explanation of social problems by reducing them to purely criminal problems. Thus, public responsibility for the persistence of a social problem is diminished and relegated to the category of a criminal justice or law enforcement issue. Psychologically, there are benefits as well. Assertions about a "super-government of crime which has its capital in Sicily" (Reid 1964, 28–34), offer satisfying explanations of problems and allay much public anxiety and concern over these questions. Since a problem stems from a conspiracy of aliens, since it is not endemic to the social structure of the United States but an import, the solution is relatively clear-cut and logistically fairly simple. The mafia conspiracy enables Americans to embrace a self-satisfying illusion that their problems are not the manifestations of deep-seated structural stresses within the polity itself.

The power and influence of the criminal syndicates, the mysterious, unsolved murders, the astonishing dominance and vivid toughness of the so-called Cosa Nostra, the curious paralysis of police and the criminal justice system in general — all this becomes understandable once one knows that the nerve-center of the American underworld has its center of gravity in far-off Sicily. Clearly, then, the blame for all of this must be squarely placed in the lap of the Italians whose duty it is to cut off the head of the dragon and destroy these insidious clandestine organizations that are undermining both Italy and America.

The critique of this myth of the super-government of crime is nothing new (Albini 1971; Smith 1975; Morris and Hawkins 1970). One aspect of it, though, is often neglected: the fact that the myth conceals the many important roles organized crime performs for the ruling strata in society. In fact, it may be argued that there is not much of a struggle between the underworld and the upperworld. The view of powerful persons or groups in the political economy as victims of organized crime, and as yielding to rackets and the enticements of corruption, obscures the fact the certain alleged victims purposely make use of organized crime, sponsor it, and even create it where none had existed (Pearce 1976, 131–146; Chambliss 1978).

A New Frame of Reference for the Phenomenon of Mafia: Repressive Crime

The phenomenon of the traditional Sicilian mafia has combined in itself the characteristics of two types of crime: that of organized crime with those of repressive crime. In other words, those of an illegal enterprise for financial gain and profit with those of an illegal defense of economic and political privilege.

Thus, in order to account for all facets of the phenomenon mafia, along with the conventional forms of organized crime, repressive crime as a property of the phenomenon must be included as well. In addition to exploitative crime, mafia represents a political reality, a reactionary force that is employed to resist change, to maintain privilege, and to suppress attempts to redefine property relations and political rights.[9]

Very similar to mafia as it is being defined here are other types of illegal or extra-legal power and violence which serve pre-industrial upper-classes such as, for example, the *zu'ama*, or *qabadayat* of Lebanon (Johnson 1977); the *futuwwa* of Egypt (El-Messiri 1977); the *jagunços* in Brazil (Pereira de Queiroz 1968); and the *goondas* of India (Myrdal 1968). Also, the Ku Klux Klan and similar "protective associations" in the United States could be thought of as kindred organizations (Myrdal 1944; Randel 1965; and Mouledous 1967). Mainly in the service of powerful landlords are also the "death squads" of Brazil, Argentina, El Salvador, and Guatemala as well as those in Spain (*Guerilleros de Cristo Rey*) and Turkey (the Grey Wolves).[10] These vigilante groups everywhere serve economic privilege whose interests require political repression. And, like mafiosi, the members of these *réseaux parallèles* also engage in the exploitation of their relationships with elite ruling factions in order to conduct other illegal activities and enterprises such as drug-trafficking from which they tend to elude arrest and punishment. In underdeveloped societies, and in the more developed ones as well, many examples may be found of repressive crime in connection with the conflicts between political parties. Since the right to vote when it is acquired by the less privileged is apt to threaten established prerogatives, elites in power will not hesitate to apply illegal tactics ranging from deception through intimidation to murder in order to falsify election results in their favor.[11]

In an agrarian society with considerable feudal relics and residual institutions tied to the social structure, the extant elites can utilize extra-economic coercion as well as a host of both legal and illegal practices to crush and discourage opposition. But in industrial societies as well, extra-economic coercion is not entirely missing as a deviant element in the dynamics of politics. The more powerful workers' unions and left-wing political parties become, the more they participate in the formulation and determination of the content of the laws, the more frequent the repressive apparatus of the state must be supplemented by illegal violence on behalf of the privileged class. The murder of strike leaders, unionists and leftist politicans, and the use of "goon squads" to inject fear into the lives of the opponents of established privilege is not an uncommon feature of everyday life in such societies. The squadron of Mussolini in Italy, the radical rightist bands in pre-Nazi Germany, the infiltration of some United States labor unions by gangsters, and the French *milices patronales* are just some of the more glaring examples of this practice of intimidation and class war.[12] The police and other legitimate groups in society that are authorized to employ force are often used illegitimately to serve the purposes of one class pitted against another. It is not unusual to find the police infringing on the rights of political radicals, searching private homes with dubious search warrants if at all, or using excessive force against demonstrators and political dissidents. An interesting social-psychological dynamic becomes apparent in the roles and attitudes of police formations that are regularly employed in extra-legal and blatantly illegal operations against dissident elements in a society that seek to dress grievances or work for the reorganization of the social and political structure. As third parties in disputes, police and law enforcement agencies are used by political leaderships for purposes that have nothing to do, at first, with the subjectively held meanings of the situations by policemen who, however, may come to feel in time, because of their repeated exposure to the seamy underside of politics, personally threatened by those they are instructed to oppress and begin to act out their frustrations against those defined for them as enemies. As long as the police act to destroy political opposition, they may behave illegally with impunity. If, however, their infringement of the rights of others is conducted for private and personal gain, the police may be punished very severely.[13]

Further, whole systems of government may be classified as repressive-criminal. Italian Fascism, for example, was a complex phenomenon that arose from multiple causes, but it now seems clear that it was primarily a defense of the economic and political privileges of a particular stratum of Italian society. The expansion of the right to vote in the beginning of the twentieth century and promises of agrarian reform made to the peasants during World War I in order to motivate them and sustain their commitment to the war were never carried out. Consequently these broken promises created a serious threat to the vitality of the extant system. Only dictatorship could deter evolution. Hence, the rise of fascism. It could be argued that similar circumstances in Germany led to National Socialism and the Nazi dictatorship. Both regimes, even though they had come to power legally, and acted for the most part in their early phases in accordance with the law, did, nevertheless, commit crimes even according to their own laws (Alatri 1963; Santarelli 1967; Kühnl 1971; and Jaeger 1967).

Stalinist repression is yet another example of crimes by government on behalf of a privileged power elite.[14] And illegal measures by western democratic governments may be less spectacular, but no less real (Lieberman 1973). Finally, the brutalities of colonialism, the repressions accompanying neo-colonial policies in Hungary, Czechoslovakia, Poland, Chile, El Salvador and Vietnam, among others, are also forms of repressive crime directed to protect the elites and curb all attempts to seek change (Paczensky 1979).

The cases provided above suggest the following general delineations characterizing repressive crime:

1. Repressive crimes are those violations of existing laws that serve the interests of privileged groups who engage in crime in order to defend the prerogatives of their particular class at the expense of other strata within society.

2. The incidence and frequency of repressive crime occurs with sufficient regularity so that it can be described as follows:
   a. as counterstrikes against rebels and revolutionaries whose "crimes" may be seen as a reaction to legal repression;
   b. as occurring when conventional methods of legal repression fail or are largely constrained by constitutional laws, police law, and court law;
   c. when privileges are legally curbed, as, for example, by reforms (especially agrarian reforms), but coalition rights of the non-privileged, by the right to strike, by extension of universal suffrage, and by the electoral successes of reform parties. In these circumstances, the outbreak of repressive crime increases in scope and violence.
3. Sometimes those elements in a population that are immediately and materially threatened by change in a society act personally and carry out criminal acts. More typically, however, they tend to stay in the background and employ others to do their dirty work. Ordinarily déclassé types (shepherds, small landowners, petits bourgeois, lumpen proletarians) are recruited for the purposes of illegal actions against those elements that pose a serious challenge to wealth and status. The motives of these marginals are mixed: some believe that social advancement and material profit will be achieved through a close association with the privileged; others work from the delusion that they are striking out against their real victimizers—the reformers and rebels.
4. Repressive crime that tends to exhibit more brutality than rebellious criminal acts is designed to instill terror into the oppressed. And as such it tends to release in its practitioners psychopathological traits that engender even more gratuitous violence.
5. Finally, it must be noted that repressive crimes are hardly ever prosecuted or punished compared with rebellious crime, which, in contrast, is vigorously confronted by the organs of state power and authority. The explanation is not difficult to discover: the interests of those engaging in repressive criminality and those of their powerful comrades located in the state and justice apparatus often are concurrent. Thus, they often act conjointly in terms of self-interest and ignore the law.

Conclusion

A major concern of this essay was to demonstrate that the definition of crime as a violation of law as well as the notion of a clearcut confrontation between underworld and upperworld are concepts too simple and too isolated to be illuminating in coming to grips with complicated social phenomena such as mafia and repressive crime as these are found in various societies. Our theme has led us to considerations transcending the Sicilian mafia as well as the sphere of organized crime. But without these considerations neither mafia nor organized crime in general can be really understood.

Notes

1. For the following, refer to Hess 1973. This book is based on material from the Archivio di Stato in Palermo. It contains broad references to sources; here I may limit myself to a few references.

2. Concerning the history of mafia, cf. Llaryora forthcoming, and Romano 1966; as to the social-structural background, cf. Blok 1974, 36–57, as well as Schneider and Schneider (1976).

3. Cf. Becker 1963, 19–39, Box 1981, 121–156 and 208–243, as well as Hess 1973.

4. Initially a man may not be motivated to start a criminal career, much less to become a mafioso. In the course of events which simply unfold, he may develop motives and interests (see Note 5). The story of a mafioso, though, is more complicated than that of an ordinary criminal, since his role is never exclusively criminal; see the steps of legalization and legitimation.

5. Good examples are given in Dolci 1960, 68ff., as well as Montanelli 1950, 282ff. Don Calogero Sedara, the figure of Lampedusa's novel, *The Leopard*, probably is known to many readers. The meaning of those rationalizations by common criminals is theoretically elaborated by Sykes and Matz 1957, in their concept of techniques of neutralization. Examples of comparable ideological cover-ups, through which politicians mystify their everyday frauds, one finds in every newspaper. The mafioso ranges between a common criminal and a politician, and as an ideologist, he equals both.

6. There is also the basic thesis of Blok 1974; the social type of the broker is generally developed by Boissevain 1974, 147–169. In order to understand the structure of cosa, see the chapter "Coalitions" in Boissevain 1974, 170–205.

7. Therefore I do not use the capital "M." Writing of "the Mafia" suggests the idea of such a centralized organization.

8. These "Fasci Siciliani" had nothing in common with the later "fasci" of Mussolini and with the "fascismo"; as to the Fasci Siciliani, cf. Romano 1959.

9. For more details cf. Hess 1973, 9–44 and Hess 1977. Similar questions are dealt by Petras (1977) and Schwendinger and Schwendinger (1977). I agree with these authors on many points. However, I consider the question of whether an act is illegal to be more important for political conflicts; cf. Hess 1977, 101–104. The use here of the category of "repressive crime" is thus similar in intention to Edwin Sutherland's use of the category of "white-collar crime."

10. On the death squadrons, cf. as an exemplary case Lopes 1973; for the American tradition of vigilantism, cf. Brown 1975; for the French *barbouzes*, cf. Jaubert 1973, 399–414 and Chairoff 1975; for the Italian vilenza nera, cf. *La Strage di stato* 1971 and Stajano and Fini 1977.

11. On the United States, cf. Myrdal 1944, 479–486; as to the case of South Italy, cf. Pantaleone 1962, 155–165 and 231–65, Dolci 1966, 241–74, Hess 1973, 145–151 and Walston 1981.

12. On the United States, cf. Kennedy 1960 and Pearce 1976, 111–156; as to France, Angeli and Brimo 1975, Stoerzer 1976, Caille 1977, 1978.

13. Cf. Chambliss and Seidman 1971, 349–67, Cray, 1972, Langlois 1971, *La Strage di stato* 1971, 82–133, Cederna 1975, Tarantini 1975.

14. Cf. Solzhenitsyn 1973. The inclusion of Stalinism in the category of repressive crime, however, does not mean that Stalinism and Fascism are intertwined or interchangeable. As to the sociohistorical unique characteristics of Stalinism (in spite of all superficial similarities) cf. Deutscher 1962, 368–410 and Hofmann 1967, 9–127.

References

Alatri, P. 1963. *Le origini del fascismo*. Roma: Editori Riuniti.

Albini, J. L. 1971. *the American Mafia: Genesis of a Legend*. New York: Appleton-Century-Crofts.

Angeli, C., and Brimo, N. 1975. *Une milice patronale: Peugeot*. Paris: Maspero.

Becker, H. S. 1963. *Outsiders: Studies in the Sociology of Deviance*. New York: The Free Press.

Blok, A. 1969. "Mafia and peasant rebellion as contrasting factors in Sicilian latifundism." *European Journal of Sociology* 10:95–116.

_____. 1974. *The Mafia of a Sicilian Village 1860–1960: A Study of Violent Peasant Entrepreneurs.* Oxford: Basil Blackwell.

Boissevain, J. 1974. *Friends of Friends: Networks, Manipulators and Coalitions.* Oxford: Basil Blackwell.

Box, S. 1981. *Deviance, Reality and Society,* 2d ed. New York: Holt, Rinehart & Winston.

Brown, R. M. 1975. *Strain of Violence: Historical Studies of American Violence and Vigilantism.* Oxford/New York: Oxford University Press.

Caille, M. 1977. *Les truands du patronat.* Paris: Editions sociales.

_____. 1978. *L'assassin était chez Citroën.* Paris: Editions sociales.

Cederna, C. 1975. *Sparare a vista: Come la polizia del regime DC mantiene l'ordine pubblico.* Milano: Feltrinelli.

Chairoff, P. 1975. *Dossier b . . . comme barbouzes: Une France paralleèle, celle des basses-oeuvres du pouvoir.* Paris: Alain Moreau.

Chambliss, W. J. 1978. *On the Take: From Petty Crooks to Presidents.* Bloomington: Indiana University Press.

Chambliss, W. J., and Seidman, R. B. 1971. *Law, Order, and Power.* Reading, Mass.: Addison Wesley.

Cray, E. 1972. *The Enemy in the Streets: Police Malpractice in America.* Garden City: Anchor Books.

Cressey, D. R. 1972. *Criminal Organization: Its Elementary Forms.* London: Heinemann.

D'Alessandro, E. 1959. *Brigantaggio e mafia in Sicilia.* Messina-Firenze: D'Anna.

Deutscher, I. 1962. *Stalin: Eine politische biographie.* Stüttgart: Kohlhammer.

Dolci, D. 1960. *Spreco: Documenti e inchieste su alcuni aspetti dello preco nella Sicilia occidentale.* Torino: Einaudi.

Dolci, D. 1966. *Chi gioca solo.* Torino: Einaudi.

El-Messiri, S. 1977. "The changing role of the futuwwa in the social structure of Cairo." In E. Gellner and J. Waterbury, eds. *Patrons and Clients in Mediterranean Societies,* pp. 239–53. London: Duckworth.

Hess, H. 1973. *Mafia and Mafiosi: The Structure of Power.* Farnborough, Engl./Lexington, Mass.: D. C. Heath (German ed. 1970).

_____. 1976. *Mafia y crimen represivo.* Madrid: Akal.

_____. 1977. "Repressive crime and criminal typologies: Some neglected types," *Contemporary Crises* 1:91–108.

_____. 1978. "Das Karriere-Modell und die Karriere von Modellen." In H. Hess, H. U. Störzer, and F. Streng, eds., *Sexualität und soziale Kontrolle,* pp. 1–30. Heidelberg: Kriminalistik Verlag.

_____. 1981. "Terrorismus und Terrorismus-Diskurs," *Tijdschsrift voor criminologie* 23:171–88.

Hobsbawm, E. J. 1969. *Bandits.* London: Weidenfeld & Nicolson.

Hofmann, W. 1967. *Stalinismus und Antikommunismus: Zur Soziologie des Ost-West-Konflikts.* Frankfurt: Suhrkamp.

Jaeger, H. 1967. *Verbrechen unter totalitärer Herrschaft. Studien zur nationalsozialistischen Gewaltkriminalität.* Olten-Freiburg: Walter.

Jaubert, A. 1973. *Dossier d . . . comme drogue.* Paris: Alain Moreau.

Johnson, M. 1977. "Political bosses and their gangs: zu'ama and qabadayat in the Sunni Muslim quarters of Beirut." In E. Gellner and J. Waterbury, eds., *Patrons and Clients in Mediterranean Societies,* pp. 207–224. London: Duckworth.

Kennedy, R. 1960. *The Enemy Within.* New York: Harper & Brothers.

Kühnl, R. 1971. *Formen bürgerlicher Herrschaft. Liberalismus–Faschismus.* Reinbek: Rowohlt.

Langlois, D. 1971. *Les dossiers noirs de la police française.* Paris: Seuil.

La Strage di stato. 1971. *Dal golpe di Borghese all'incriminazione di Calabresi: Contro-inchiesta.* Roma: Samonà e Savelli.

Lieberman, J. K. 1973. *How the Government Breaks the Law.* Baltimore: Penguin Books.

Llaryora, R. (Forthcoming). *Die sizilianische mafia: Frühe Strukturen und soziale Dynamik in der Epoche der spanischen Herrschaft* (16. and 17. Jahrhundert).

Lopes, A. 1973. *L'escadron de la mort São Paulo 1968–1971.* Paris: Casterman.

Montanelli, I. 1950. *Pantheon minore.* Milano: Longanasi.

Mori, C. 1933. *The Last Struggle with the Mafia*. London: Putnam.

Morris, N. and Hawkins, G. 1970. *The Honest Politician's Guide to Crime Control*. Chicago-London: University of Chicago Press.

Mouledous, J. C. 1967. "Political Crime and the Negro Revolution." In M. B. Clinard and R. Quinney, eds., *Criminal Behavior Systems: A Typology,* pp. 217–31. New York: Holt, Rinehart & Winston.

Muehlmann, W. E., and Llaryora, R. 1968. *Klientschaft, Klientel und Klientelsystem in einer sizilianischen Agrostadt*. Tübingen: Mohr.

Myrdal, G. 1944. *An American Dilemma: The Negro Problem and Modern Democracy*. 2 vols. New York: Harper & Row.

_____. 1968. *Asian Drama: An Inquiry into the Poverty of Nations*. 3 vols. Harmondsorth: Penguin.

Paczensky, G. von 1979. *Weiße Herrschaft. Eine Gerschichte des Kolonialismus*. 2.Aufl. Frankfurt: Fischer.

Pantaleone, M. 1962. *Mafia e politica 1943–1962*. Torino: Einaudi.

Pearce, F. 1976. *Crimes of the Powerful: Marxism, Crime and Deviance*. London: Pluto Press.

Pereira de Queiroz, M. I. 1968. *Os cangaceiros: Les bandits d'honneur brésiliens*. Paris: Plon.

Petras, J. F. 1977. "Chile: Crime, Class Consciousness and the Bourgeoisie." *Crime and Social Justice* 7:14–22.

Randel, W. P. 1965. *The Ku Klux Klan: A Century of Infamy*. Philadelphia: Chilton Books.

Reid, E. 1964. *Mafia*. New York: New American Library.

Romano, S. F. 1959. *Storia dei Fasci Siciliani*. Bari: Laterza.

_____. 1966. *Storia della Mafia*. 2d ed. Verona: Mondadori.

Santarelli, E. 1967. *Storia del fascismo*. vol. I: "La crisi liberale." Roma: Editori Riuniti.

Schneider, J., and Schneider, P. 1976. *Culture and Political Economy in Western Sicily*. New York: Academic Press.

Schwendinger, H. and Schwendinger, J. R. 1977. "Social Class and the Definition of Crime," *Crime and Social Justice* 7:4–13.

Smith, D. C., Jr. 1975. *The Mafia Mystique*. New York: Basic Books.

Solzhenitsyn, A 1973. *The Gulag Archipelago 1918–1956*. New York: Harper & Row.

Stajano, C., and Fini, M. 1977. *La forza della democrazia: La strategia della tensione in Italia 1969–1976*. Torino: Einaudi.

Stoerzer, H. U. 1976. "Selbstschutz und der Weg zur Betriebsmiliz," *Kriminologisches Journal* 8:33–45.

Sykes, G., and Matza, D. 1957. "Techniques of Neutralization: A Theory of Delinquency," *American Sociological Review* 22:664–670.

Tarantini, D. 1975. *La maniera forte: elogio della polizia: Storia del potere politico in Italia 1860–197*. Verona: Bertani.

Tomasi di Lampedusa, G. 1958. *Il Gattopardo*. Milano: Feltrinelli.

Udy, S. J., Jr. 1965. "The Comparative Analysis of Organizations," chap. 16 in J. G. March (ed.) *Handbook of Organizations*. Chicago: Rand McNally.

Walston, J. 1981. "Electoral Politics in Southern Calabria," *Contemporary Crises* 5:417–445.

Walter, E. V. 1969. *Terror and Resistance. A Study of Political Violence*. London-Oxford-New York: Oxford University Press.

8

See Naples and Die: Organized Crime in Campania

James Walston
University of Maryland

"The Camorra . . . that most powerful and sinister of secret societies"
— E. W. Hornung, *Raffles* (1901)

Powerful perhaps, but hardly secret: travellers, politicians and positivist criminologists had been observing camorra in Naples for more than 50 years before Hornung's intrepid "gentleman cracksman" foiled the dastardly Neapolitans' attempt to kill him in Bloomsbury.

The word itself introduces an element of confusion in any consideration of organized crime in Naples. "Camorra" is associated with mafia, brigands, and carbonari, or was, at least, in the nineteenth century. That train of thought goes on to produce images of *Tarantelle* danced on the slopes of Vesuvius or duels with daggers in Pozzuoli, and honor among prisoners in Neapolitan jails.

In the first section of this chapter, I will try to disentangle local color from reality and give a description of organized crime in Naples up until the supposed defeat of the camorra in 1912. We will then look at subsequent events, whether these have been attributed to "camorra," "the new camorra" or most recently, "the New Organized Camorra." I will continue with a description of the changing structures of camorra, the protagonists themselves and their activities. The official response to the phenomenon will be considered as will the reactions of the surrounding society. I will conclude with an overview of organized crime in Naples as it has developed up to the present.

A word about sources: camorra in the nineteenth century was the subject of a number of works by criminologists and observers of Naples. I have used these extensively. After a major trial in 1912, there was a presumption that camorra was dead,[1] and since World War II, until the early 1980s there has been relatively little published at any level on organized crime in Naples. I have therefore used unpublished sources such as court proceedings, police archives and my own interview material as well as newspaper sources.

Nature and Evolution of Organized Crime in Naples

There has been organized crime in Naples since the beginning of the nineteenth century. If we use the distinction made by Alan Block (1983) between *enterprise syndicates* and *power syndicates*,[2] then I would hope to show that camorra in its historical form was largely the latter and that in more recent times there has been and is a mixture of both.

It is important to establish at the outset that at no stage has organized crime in Naples reached the all-embracing cultural control that did mafia in Southern Calabria and Western Sicily. Mafia has a near monopoly of violence and therefore social control in those areas. The mafioso is not merely one who survives largely or wholly on illegal activities, but is an integral part of the social system. Since he has a major hand in the nomination and election of political representatives, in economic affairs, legal and illegal, and has control over the levers of economic and political power, he is therefore not part of a subculture but is part of the dominant culture of his region. His social control is based on fear, to be sure, but also to a large extent on a very broad consensus.

Organized crime on the other hand, when it is manifested as a *power syndicate*, is founded entirely on fear: its function is to provide protection, occasionally genuine but more usually spurious protection from itself. It produces neither goods nor services and may milk legal and illegal businesses equally. As it is based on violence, it is highly unstable. Individual bosses may come and go, but the system itself may continue with very little basic change over long periods.

The simplest form of organized crime to describe, and in a sense the most organized, is the *enterprise* syndicate. This is none other than the more or less effective imitation of any legal capitalist business. The syndicate provides a service such as drugs, prostitution, or contraband tobacco. There is a clear division of labor between the various members of the groups and there is a hierarchy based on that division rather than on the use or threat of brute force. Capital is required to start the business, and particular skills are often needed in general management as well as particular abilities like being able to handle a motor launch or produce false wool or silk.

Until the end of World War II, although there are some examples of camorra enterprises, the main thrust was towards a series of power syndicates.

Etymology, Folklore and Rituals

As with mafia, there are a number of different derivations of the word *camorra*. A carabiniere witness at the Cuocolo trial in March 1911 declared that the camorra was founded in 1654 by a certain Raimondo Gamur, a Spanish adventurer who had fled from Saragossa.[3] The Italo-Swiss scholar Marc Monnier gives a number of less colorful and more plausible origins for the word; a *camorra* is a short coat or jacket mentioned in eighteenth century dialect plays. It is a corrruption of *gamurra,* a garment similar to the Spanish *chamarra.* Another Spanish derivation is that *camorra* means dispute or fight — *hacer camorra,* "to look for a fight." Further afield is the Arabic *Kumar,* a gambling game played with dice and prohibited by the Koran. The least probable of Monnier's suggested etymologies is that of an association of merchants from Pisa which was present in Cagliari in Sardinia in the thirteenth century: *quae facta fint in Kallari dicta de Gamurra.*[4] A Spanish origin is possible given the long Spanish domination of Southern Italy.

Whatever the meaning of the word, camorra is presented as an organic society that started in the prisons and then spread outside. This society is referred to interchangeably as the *societa' dell'umirta'* ("humble society") or *bella societa' rifurmata* ("beautiful reformed society");[5] sometimes and in common with mafia and Calabrian *ndrangheta,* it is called the *onorata societa'* or *annorata soggieta'*[6] ("honored society").

There were, apparently, complex initiation rituals and a variety of ranks with ordeals to go through in order to pass from one rank to another. The "Founder and Director of the Anthropometric Office" of the Naples police, De Blasio, gives three separate rituals for election to the three "ranks" of the *societa' minore dell'umirta': giovinotto onorato* ("honored lad"), *picciuotto* ("henchman") and *camorrista.* For the first step the prospective member appears before a tribunal composed of the chief, the *contajuoli* ("accountants"), of the camorristi and *picciuotti,* and six *picciuotti.* He comes in "with head bowed and arms crossed on his chest" and after going through a catechism correctly, he swears to obey the rules:

1. to love each other;
2. to be humble and respectful to the elders and superiors;
3. to play the peacemaker in any fights which might occur between your *comrades*;
4. to collect without *cheating,* the *levy* for the *camorristi*;
5. not to reveal to anyone what takes place in the *society.*

Whoever *disobeys this code* will not only be expelled from the *beautiful society,* but according to the seriousness of the transgression, may also be condemned to death. [Italics in the original.]

If the new recruit is successful, he may rise in the heirarchy to become a *picciotto,* which means "a man with sangfroid, servant of the camorristi and who has honey in his mouth and vigor in his heart," and then to the final rank, camorrista, which means "a man of fire who runs the *societa' minore* and who has one foot on earth and the other in the grave."[7] The oath and the ritual emphasize obedience and the hierarchical nature of the society. All protection money collected has to be given to the head of the *paranza* or group, of which there were supposed to have been 12 in Naples. De Blasio also prints "The Code of the Society of Humility," which reads more like the articles of a sporting club than a band of gangsters, such is the bureaucratic language used. Other sources talk of a court known as "La Gran Mamma" which met in a cave at Capodimonte (a Neapolitan quarter) and which dissolved itself and the "society" on 25 March 1915.[8]

It has not been possible to establish how much truth there is in these accounts of an apparently strictly ordered secret society, almost masonic in its rituals, but one or two comments can be made. The first is the doubt, expressed by Monnier in 1863, that people of the social and educational provenance of the camorristi would be sufficiently literate to draw up such documents or that the rest would be able to read them.[9] It should be added that even after 120 years of united Italy, 50 years of radio and 25 of television there is still a proportion of the population (small by now) that does not speak Italian but only Neapolitan.

Other arguments against a too-trusting acceptance of codes, laws, and courts is that once the secret is out the "society" would become vulnerable to police action, which it clearly did not. Also, the supposed submissiveness of members would have precluded the internal conflict within "the society" that did periodically occur. Organized crime and, far less, whole subcultures cannot survive solely on a few ritual formulae.[10]

On the other hand the idea of formalized constitutions lingers on. In 1980 a follower of Raffaele Cutolo, one of the present bosses of organized crime in Naples, drew up something similar to the nineteenth-century codes.

It is 24 handwritten pages; the author left school in the tenth grade and there are some (but not many) grammatical and orthographic curiosities. For the most part it has an almost religious air of ritual to it with repetitions as in a litany and arcane replies to curious questions. Apart from a single reference to the "New Organized Camorra," a term coined by the Naples daily *Il Mattino,* there is nothing which suggests that the "constitution is of recent origin." Three mythical knights of Spanish flavor who are credited with the foundation of the Calabrian *ndrangheta* are also mentioned, as is the island of Favignana, close to all mafia, *ndrangheta* and camorra legends.

There is a combination of apparently down-to-earth buraucratic regulations and almost poetic descriptions, lacking punctuation:

Question: When do the picciotti meet after the society is formed
Answer: Every 28 days
Question: When do the cammoristi [sic] meet after the society is formed
Answer: Every 7 days
Question: How much does a picciotto weigh
Answer: As much as a feather thrown to the wind
Question: How much does a cammorista weigh
Answer: As much as a peacock's plume thrown to the wind and he disappears like lightning

[pp. 6–7]

And so on.

As for personal identification, the author is more precise and accurate than some folk chroniclers who identify mafiosi by the long nail on the little finger or the nineteenth-century camorrista by the knot on his kerchief:

> *Question:* What distinguishing signs does a *sgarrista* [hoodlum] carry
> *Answer:*   An invisible cross on the left shoulder which corresponds to the thumb of the right hand with an emerald rose on the front of the right foot which illuminates the whole world that is how I who am a sgarrista illuminate

> [p. 11]

The society is compared to a tree with the chief as the trunk, the main branches the *sgarristi*; branches, the *camorristi*; small branches, the *picciotti* and the leaves are the *giovani d'onore* (p. 17).

After commending the society to the protection of Our Lady of the Annunciation and St. Michael the Archangel, the document ends with the elliptical phrase: "He who does not know how to die, does not know how to live" (p. 24). The picture that emerges is more one of Neapolitan folklore and superstitions than a specifically criminal subculture, although it does give some idea of the belief system of the small army that supposedly follows Raffaele Cutolo. This gang is undoubtedly different from the sort of organized groups it is trying to supplant; Cutolo has a considerable flair and distinction that procure him both loyalty and hatred far stronger than are enjoyed by other gang leaders in Naples (see section below titled "Current Situation").

Similar phrases and references to the three knights, Favignana, and the responses to the litany can be found in literature on Calabria. The passage on the tree and leaves is there word for word,[11] the greetings, misspelled in the manuscript as "Buonpespro" is italianized as Buon vespero, and so on. The dialectal idiosyncrasies of the manuscript would suggest that it comes from oral sources rather than written ones.

The "codes," nineteenth century and modern, are social documents rather than maps of organized crime. But whatever the value or applicability of these "constitutions," criminal organization was heavily present in Naples through most of the last century.

It grew from the prisons:

> In jail the camorra is more ferocious because it is more concentrated. In each cell the camorrista is King, absolute and despotic: his every wish is a command; he is dressed and undressed; he gathers his followers in an assembly and sometimes a sort of tribunal; he sends orders to other cells; he rewards and punishes; everyone is as a slave in chains before him; he must get what he wants even if the world should fall in, and even if it is some obscene desire.[12]

Until 1848, the camorra was limited to purely criminal and, in the main, prison activities. After the 1948 revolution there was a certain influence on the part of the liberals who found themselves sharing cells with non-politicals. Some camorristi turned informers for the Bourbon police or else blackmailed the conspirators, while others took part both in the 1848 movements and the final overthrow of the Bourbons in 1860. In June of that year, the new prefect Liborio Romano used the camorristi, who had been freed on the proclamation of the constitution, to keep order in a city in turmoil. It seems to have worked for some months.[13] These, though, are exceptional incidents in exceptional times—the camorra was much less public spirited, for the most part.

It was not until 1912 that the supposed "end of the camorra" was signalled. This was the Cuocolo Case; seven years previously Gennaro Cuocolo, a small-time gangster, and his wife were murdered. With one key witness the carabinieri were able to prosecute not merely the material murderers but also the whole hierarchy of organized crime in Naples. The court accepted the prosecution's case and sent the ringleaders down for 30 years. There is the suggestion though that the main witness perjured himself in order to gain clemency for his own crimes and also as part of a feud between the police (*Pubblica Sicurezza*) and gendarmes (*carabinieri*),[14] a rivalry that is constant in stories of mafia and organized crime.

After the Cuocolo case, there was a presumption that camorra was finished and with it organized crime in Naples. Undoubtedly the case did deal a severe blow to criminal groups in Naples. The combination of wartime social pressures followed by 20 years of fascism meant that crime tended to operate on a small-time modest basis. It was not until after World War II that there was a clear resurgence of more than simple criminal activity.

Personnel

The rise to a position of power and prestige of Neapolitan gangsters has not changed over the period we are looking at. Indeed, it is similar to the path taken by mafiosi or gangsters elsewhere.[15] The strongest, cleverest, and most ruthless individual, who is prepared to use violence and who gets away with it, immediately gains prestige. The difference between mafia and other forms of organized crime is that the prestige of such a person penetrates further into society.

The act of violence, usually homicide, does not have to be linked with criminal activities. Thus one of the present leaders in Naples, Raffaele Cutolo, made a pass at a girl who was out for a stroll with her boyfriend; the boyfriend reacted and Cutolo killed him. Cutolo comes from a poor family in Ottaviano on the slopes of Vesuvius and his legend recounts that he was a gentle child who served at mass and wanted to become a priest.[16]

From the murder in 1963 until 1970 he was in jail awaiting the final outcome of his various appeals. In May 1970, he was released as the terms for preventive detention had run out but instead of returning for the trial, he went on the run. Less than a year later he was recaptured. From March 1971 until February 1978 he was again in jail. He escaped when his followers dynamited a hole in the wall of the criminal asylum in Aversa. This time he was out for more than a year, until May 1979, when he was captured by the carabinieri. Cutolo has pleaded insanity, which at times the court has accepted as a mitigating factor.

The most striking feature of the bare biographical facts is Cutolo's achievements in jail. He built up and ran an organization estimated at 2,000 people; he tried to take over the most lucrative criminal activities in Naples and mediated between the Christian Democratic Party (DC) and the Red Brigades (BR) during the Cirillo kidnapping in spring 1981.

And yet there are parallels with the last century: the prison structure is such that not only can an established boss maintain control of his affairs from inside, but on occasion, as in the case of Cutolo, he can actually build up his following from inside.

Salvatore De Crescenzo, a boss in the middle of the last century, spent hardly any less time on the outside. This is his police file as copied by Monnier:

> He is the King of the band, the Lacenaire of the camorristi. He comes to the fore in February 1849 with 3 crimes; illegal possession of weapons, obstruction of the police, serious injury against a certain Bornei, navy corporal.
>
> Imprisoned for these facts he continues his career. He wounds an inmate and kills another because the latter would not accept De Crescenzo's authority. Despite these crimes, he is only given a 5 year sentence.
>
> Freed in 1855, he once again starts with the camorra in the city. He is caught again; the police are frightened of locking him up in Castel Capuano [in Naples] so he is sent to the Central Prison in Molise.
>
> The police having given up the struggle against the camorra, De Crescenzo returns to Naples where he is free but under surveillance. Instead of keeping calm, he allows himself to insult a certain De Mata and is convicted to another six months.
>
> He is freed under Don Liborio and becomes head of the City Guard. He exercises his new career with such violence that the City Guard is disarmed and suppressed by Silvio Spaventa.
>
> So the camorra, moved on by the police, goes back to its old job. De Crescenzo is more dangerous than all his comrades and is first locked up in Castel Capuano and then sent to the island of Ponza.
>
> There the fierce fight between him and Antonio Lubrano began. Lubrano was condemned to death through De Crescenzo's influence and was murdered at the entrance to Castel Capuano prison.
>
> That is the last crime of the great man up to now. He has been sent to the Murate Gaol in Florence. One last detail; he is pro-Bourbon.[17]

A more recent gangster leader, Antonio Spavone,[18] known as *'O Malommo* ("the Bad Man") also passed some of his time in the Murate prison in Florence, but Spavone earned himself a pardon by rescuing two wardens and the governor's daughter when the River Arno flooded in 1966. Apart from this episode, his "curriculum vitae" reads very similarly to others both before and after him.

During and after the war, he was part of a gang dealing with black market goods and petty thieving. His elder brother was killed in a fight with a rival gang leader, who then tried to disrupt the wedding of one of Spavone's sisters. Spavone was able to kill the other and then go on the run. He was 19. A month after the murder he was arrested and sent down for 12 years. This first conviction earned him considerable "respect" inside and out of the prison. Inside, he built up his reputation even more with a combination of violence (another prison boss sent an inmate to beat up Spavone; Spavone stabbed the man in the stomach), and Robin Hood style public relations (new inmates, if they were unprotected, were given a "gift package of cigarettes and treats" when they arrived). Like Cutolo after him, Spavone made his name in prison. When he came out, he was accepted as an underworld boss.

The 1970s saw a furious fight between rival gangs, mainly Neapolitan, against the Marseilles underworld for the control of the cigarette and drug smuggling businesses. There were episodes apparently full of local color but in fact tied securely to illicit traffic. In 1971, Spavone killed his old friend Gennaro Ferrigno, supposedly because of a quarrel over Ferrigno's wife but in fact for a disagreement between Neapolitans and Frenchmen.

'O Malommo's reputation continued to grow until April 1976 when he was shot in the face and almost killed. He fled to Chicago where his brother has a restaurant. After much plastic surgery he came back to Naples and lives in heavily guarded houses, a flat in the center and a villa on Ischia. His reputation is still there, especially after his acquittal for Ferrigno's murder (for self-defense), but since Cutolo's rise, Spavone's power is limited.

Politics

We have suggested that camorra has a function of social control, albeit less than mafia in Sicily or Calabria. It is therefore reasonable to suspect that criminal organizations take an active part in politics.

According to Monnier, the camorra was involved in no political activities before 1848.[19] This is hardly surprising given the nature of the state. As mentioned above, the revolution brought liberals and camorristi into contact with each other in the prisons. As in 1799, the vast majority of the people were partisans of the king, with only small areas of the city on the side of the revolutionaries. In the reaction that followed in 1849, the liberals were obliged to turn to the camorristi in order to gain proletarian support. This support was promised but on condition that each *capocamorrista* be paid 10,000 ducats. The money was paid, but the only result was conspiracy without action. On the one hand, the camorristi were bleeding the conspirators dry; and on the other, the Bourbon police thought they were on the side of the liberals and exiled many of them in 1859–60.[20] Thus organized crime took on a liberal political coloration for a time.

For the rest of the liberal period, camorristi played the "grand electors" along with other classes of people. Every now and again there were complaints about the practice of criminals gathering votes for politicians. There were three parliamentary inquiries, in 1880, 1888 and in 1901.

The 1901 inquiry had this to say about organized crime and politics:

> The new, regenerated organism [of the camorra] has managed to reproduce many of the old evils which were almost disappearing and to produce new and worse qualities; it spreads corruption in the electorate by making it work on the basis of *clientele* and interests, it grows alongside the administration's policies; the camorra exercises a strong electoral force and indirectly it becomes the arbiter of public life by putting that same public life at the service of the elections.
>
> In our opinion, the worst fact is that the liberal institutions have made the camorra grow and allowed it to infiltrate all levels of public life and the social texture, instead of destroying it or at least limiting it to the lowest parts of society. There is now an *alta camorra* made up of the most daring and unprejudiced middle classes which corresponds with the original *bassa camorra* which acts on the poor in hard times with a ruthless power. These people take advantage of the ignorance of their class and the lack of any reaction largely due to economic hardship and manage to profit from commerce and contracts, political meetings, with the civil service, clubs and press.
>
> With the development of the camorra, the new electoral organization based on *clientele* services rendered and returned for the vote obtained in the form of protection, assistance, advice, recommendations, allowed the growth of a class of middlemen or intermediaries.[21]

This bears out the accusations made by the Neapolitan deputy Giacomo De Martino when he introduced the idea of a Parliamentary Commission: "One government after another has come to terms in these [camorra] *clientele* in order to achieve electoral victory at any cost."[22] Since then there have been no other parliamentary commissions. In 1959, a deputy suggested that one should be held, but the bill was never discussed.[23]

In political terms, the gangster has always exchanged political protection for electoral support; in general terms: "Racketeers and other outlaws are well aware that their freedom from law-enforcing agencies depends on how useful they can make themselves to politicians."[24] And again: "it is without doubt that part of the extreme right and some parts of the majority party [DC] . . . have used the camorra's electoral weight."[25]

But it should be emphasized that camorra is only one of the elements in the formation of Neapolitan clientele. As Allum points out:

> The most obvious, and the most readily to hand, [means of extending political support] is the winning of the support of the so-called *grand-elettori* and *capi-elettori*. The men are strategically located in the social structure: the former are the local "big-shots," the local mayors and councillors, the local priest and local landowners in rural areas; the latter are the leaders of the group networks, either formal ones like the *circoli,* confraternities, UOC, etc., or informal ones like the *quartieri* and *rioni* networks, occupational ones, like the *edili* (building workers), *communali* (municipal workers), and even the Camorra (criminal syndicate).[26]

Ten years later it is still impossible to attribute a monopoly of political power to the camorristi. In the villages around Naples, gangsters may control the local council; an obvious example is Ottaviano, Cutolo's home town on the northern slopes of Vesuvius. But in the city and region as a whole there is too great a heterogenity for one social group to gain control. Since the war Naples has had Monarchist, Christian Democrat and Communist city councils; the presence of the PCI since 1975 is enough to show that organized crime cannot control local government, at least in the city.

Activities of Organized Crime

Following the distinction between *enterprise* and *power* syndicates, we can divide the activities of camorra into two segments: genuine services and extortion. In 1863 Monnier defined camorra as "organized extortion,"[27] and in terms of power syndicates, the definition still holds. As with all power syndicates, camorra groups are dependent on the financial gain that protection rackets provide as well as on the control that the racket necessarily entails. Payoffs from legal and illegal businesses are taken in a variety of ways; in some circumstances the racket will be tolerated and even approved of when it provides some sort of protection against real dangers or when it guarantees order in a potentially chaotic situation. In other circumstances it is suffered simply because the victims are too frightened to resist and because the institutional authorities are too weak to insure real protection.

Over the past 150 years or so, organized crime has been perceived by the population in both ways. During this period, protection has been paid by large sections of the population inside and outside the prisons, by professionals and shopkeepers, legal and illegal businesses, the living and the dead. Even saints have not been immune from the ten percent rake-off.

In *enterprise* syndicate terms, there are examples of illegal gambling, horse sales and prostitution. With the development of technology and modern tastes, activities have expanded to include gasoline fraud, making false wool, silk and whiskey, and above all, until the early 1980s, the smuggling of mainly American brand cigarettes for which there is a very sizeable market. Forms of extortion, however, remain the base line of organized crime.

Gambling

More than any other Italian city, Naples is a gambler's paradise. Apart from the government-controlled lottery, an institution that pre-dates unification, there are legal and illegal horse races to bet on, card games (gambling is illegal except in the four licensed casinos, at Venice, San Remo, Campione and Saint Vincent), bingo and of course illegal lotteries. Superstition influences heavily the choice of numbers in the lotteries, and tipsters of various shades of honesty flourish, but they contribute to the city's folklore rather than its organized crime.

In the pre-1860 days the Bourbon lottery only sold expensive tickets in the morning before the draw. This meant that the poorer members of the community could not participate. In order to fill the gap the camorristi of each quarter would organize a parallel lottery in which the stakes were as low as the gambler wished to go instead of being the official 1.68 lire. The winning number was the same as in the official lottery and the guarantees of payment equal.[28] Given the local nature of this primitive and only partially illegal numbers racket, there was no need for the elaborate structure that U.S. rackets have evolved.

De Blasio gives a description of the 1890s Neapolitan numbers game. It is called *giuoco piccolo* and is not very different from the North American version. There are those who keep an eye out for policemen and especially plainclothesmen (*pali*); the collectors (*ruofoli*) have to pass an exam before being given the job: being able to write the numbers from 1 to 90. From Thursday to Saturday, they take bets and give out betting slips. The money is passed on to the banks who then use the same personnel to distribute winnings.[29] The winning number is the same as the state lottery.

Seventy years later, the situation has not changed: the *giuoco piccolo* or *riffa* is still active. Campaigns to eradicate it are periodically announced: "Wide ranging actions planned to clamp down on the underground lottery — police mobilized for a war against the 'riffa.' "[30] In addition to the lottery there is illegal gambling on horses, and even on cars. There are at least a thousand unlicensed casinos, all controlled by the camorra, as well as alternative football pools to play.[31]

In November 1984 a bank run by the Giuliano family of Forcella was raided by the Finance Guards. The annual turnover was estimated at lit. 78 billion ($42m at 1984 exchange rates). The bank operated mainly in Campania but also had nationwide connections as well as links with legal bookmakers in London.

Prostitution

Recruitment was traditionally carried out by women who travelled the countryside, *mezzane,* apparently selling haberdashery. Girls were induced to flee to the city with promises of a new and exciting life. Once in the city, the girl was handed over to the brothelkeeper, the *comare* (a word usually signifying artificial kinship).[32] In a later book De Blasio describes how the camorra organization controls each of the houses not only as "protectors" (of illegal services) but also as managers providing a real service.[33] The camorra did not limit itself to heterosexual prostitution but also organized homosexual prostitution and marriages.[34] (This custom is described by Curzio Malaparte during World War II but there is no suggestion that it was organized by criminal elements.)[35]

Illegal prostitution revived after a break of some decades when the trade was state controlled: "'those ladies' . . . have organized themselves industriously with a network of luxury apartments and 'rooms with families,' where a good, dear old aunt receives the lodger's many friends."[36] Recently police sources have pointed out that prostitution is no longer organized by the camorra. It is managed on a smaller scale, and though pimp and whore pay protection money to gangsters, they are, as it were, independent operators.

Tobacco

In the 1960s and 1970s this has become the biggest money earner and employer in Neapolitan organized crime. And it is of recent origin. In his excellent survey of camorra at the end of the 1950s, Guarino lists cigarette smuggling as a "minor activity."

The smuggling business is also important because it was Cutolo's demand for 30,000 lire per case of cigarettes from the principal smuggler, Michele Zaza in the late 1970s that sparked off the war that has ravaged the city in the 1980s (see below, Current Situation).

The cigarette *paranze* show the highest degree of organization in order to deliver the goods from the high seas to the city streets. There is a division of labor, a welfare system for those who are (occasionally) locked up and of course a huge distribution network.

The Neapolitan journalist Jouakin, during an interview with a *capoparanza,* was given details of the cigarette trade. There are around 200 *paranze* operating out of Naples. Competition is fierce, but between launch skippers, who are united against the excise men, there is seldom any violence. A skipper (in 1979) received $500 per trip, his lieutenant $250, and the two crew members $125.[37]

The cigarette trade is conducted on a large scale, despite efforts to contain it. Excise men confiscated 111 tons of cigarettes in 1974, 528 tons in 1975 and 562 tons in 1977.[38]

Drugs

The connections between Neapolitan gangsters and their Sicilian, Calabrian, Northern Italian, French and American counterparts have all been based on the drug traffic. Over the last decade or so the port of Naples has become an import center for heroin on a par with Palermo or Marseilles.

Already in 1976, the Parliamentary Antimafia Commission pointed out that:

> As far as the drug traffic is concerned, Naples has become one of the most important transit and wholesale distribution centers. It is the point of departure for the USA and Canada. It is also the point of arrival for cocaine from Peru which then goes to Northern Italy and Central Europe (Parliamentary Antimafia Commission VI Legislative Doc. xxiii No. 2, Vol. 1:415).

Protection Rackets

The other type of camorra activity is purely extortionary and makes no pretense of producing goods or service apart from protection. Here influence and penetration within society has been and is almost total.

There is an example of a shoot-out in the 1890s between camorristi over the division of money given to Our Lady of Pignasecca; a percentage was due to them and there was a disagreement between the gangsters.[39] Another episode of the 1890s was during the colonial campaigns in East Africa when camorristi conscripts apparently took their percentage from comrades and officers both on the troopships and once they had arrived.[40]

But the main protection racket is and was in the prisons. Every form of economic activity is covered. Gambling in jail and out was charged 10 percent according to Monnier while De Blasio 55 years later quotes the figure of 20 percent. Other covered activities including auctions, even of state-owned horses, were the occasion of extortion, while more recently wholesale markets have become the most favored hunting ground.

Crime in the World of Legitimate Business

Since the decline of cigarette smuggling, the illegal gambling rackets have taken over as the large-scale criminal employer, especially as little social damage is perceived in the activity. The tomato racket on the other hand not only defrauds the European Community but also the peasant producer. The PCI has tried to mobilize support around this issue but so far without success.

In the 1950s there were attempts to discredit the local public administration's dairy operations (mice in milk bottles) and thus return the market to private ownership.[41] And more recently there have been frauds on the tomato market in which the gangster as middleman buys low through intimidation from the peasant and then declares a higher yield in order to claim more European Community subsidies then he is entitled to.[42]

In contrast to the situation involving Mafia in Calabria and Sicily, organized crime does not yet have a real monopoly of the building and transport business. Since the 1980 earthquake there has been a move in that direction and even before that the Giuliano boss had a building firm. However, organized crime's penetration of legal businesses is minimal compared with mafia areas.

Public Tolerance

The activities that provide a desired service or product have a very high level of acceptance in society. In addition to filling the desire for contraband, these activities provide employment on a significant scale. "Stopping the smuggling in Naples would be like closing the Pirelli works in Milan" is a remark heard in the Santa Lucia quarter. There have been leaflets claiming that 50,000 families survive on the cigarette business.[43]

As far as the extortion rackets are concerned, there was little evidence of popular reaction until 1980, when the combination of Cutolo's expansion and the war which that brought has produced a number of demonstrations as well as initiatives from political parties and carabinieri.

In a recent episode in Secondiglano, a suburb of Naples, the carabinieri moved in with force to allow shopkeepers to open up: they had been forced to close in "mourning" for the local boss, and only the presence of more than 100 carabinieri allowed them to reopen.[44] The lockout had been forced, and there was no sign of tolerance on the part of local businessmen.

Structure

Crime can be compared with legitimate businesses in terms of size and scope. In the same way as legal business can evolve from the artisan who works by himself to the vast multinational with thousands of employees, hierarchy and organization, so also can professional crime go from the individual pickpocket to international drug rings.

In this article I have been considering "organized crime" in Naples as criminal activity carried out by professionals in groups of more than a certain size (the number is not and cannot be specified exactly, but a rough criterion would be a situation in which there is the existence of a division of labor and the involvement, with a chain of command, of more than 50 people) with a degree of permanence (again unspecifiable but as an arbitrary figure, a year is suggested) with specific illegal aims in mind. Thus, for example, I have not considered petty thieving or the pimp with his one or two prostitutes.

Apart from Cutolo's gang, which is reputed to consist of about 2,000 men, camorra groupings rarely exceed 300 participants. Some are enterprise syndicates pure and simple, like the smuggling *paranze,* and fit Block's definition.

> Enterprise syndicates as the term suggests take their structure from the necessities of participating in particular illegal enterprises.[45] . . . [They] operate exclusively in the arena of illicit enterprises such as prostitution, gambling, bootlegging and narcotics.[46]

Others combine enterprises with features of power syndicates as defined by Block:

> Power syndicates . . . are loosely structured, extraordinarily flexible associations centered around violence and deeply involved in the production and distribution of informal power.[47] [The power syndicate's] forte is extortion not enterprise. [It] operates both in the arena of illicit enterprises and in the industrial world specifically in labor-management disputes and relations.[48]

One can imagine camorra crime groups that mix the provision of illegal services and goods with the selling and the guarantee of the basic conditions for doing illicit business. Further, such groups may in time come to resemble U.S. crime "families" that do not limit their activities to illegitimate enterprises but actively engage in upperworld businesses as well.

International links change over time. During Salvatore Lucania's (Lucky Luciano's) stay in Naples there were transactions with organized crime in the United States, with the Neapolitans always playing the inferior role. In the 1970s Spavone also used the transatlantic connection, while in the 1980s there have been shifting alliances between Neapolitan groups and Calabrian, Sicilian and North Italian groups. The predominance of the so called *Banda dei Marsigliesi* (the Marseilles group) in the drug traffic ended in the mid-1970s after considerable strife.

Since the rise of Cutolo, organized crime has become polarized, with don Raffaele on one side and all the other groups together in an informal alliance known by the press and themselves as the Nuova Famiglia. Cutolo's "empire" is mainly a power syndicate that feeds on licit and illicit activities throughout the area. The other groupings include both extortion rackets and enterprise syndicates that are territorial and organized according to sectors and to some extent by type of racket or enterprise.

Official Responses to Organized Crime

For the most part, control and prevention of camorra in Naples has been left to police and magistrates, who, as a declared aim would like to see the total repression of the phenomenon or at least to maintain it within "acceptable" limits.

These limits have been exceeded on various occasions over the last 120 years: the various parliamentary commissions in the last century provoked by particularly sensational crimes; the Cuocolo murder and trial, which dragged on for almost seven years; the Pascalone 'e Nola affair in the 1950s; and since 1980, the activities of Cutolo. When this happens, press and politicians call for reform. In Sicily, the Ciaculli massacre in 1962, when seven policemen, carabinieri, and bomb disposal men were killed, spawned the Anti-mafia Commission. So in Naples the present conflict for control of the city and province has brought demands that the anti-mafia laws (emphasizing stringent forms of preventive detention) be applied to the area and that a Parliamentary Anti-camorra Commission be set up. And again, in April 1982, a conference held by the PCI to discuss Neapolitan problems, including camorra, called for massive state intervention. The following month General Carlo Alberto Dalla Chiesa, the carabiniere who had carried out various successful anti-terrorism campaigns, was sent to Palermo as a prefect with special powers and with the specific aim of defeating organized crime in Sicily and Campania. (He was assassinated there in September, 1982.)

There is a realization on all sides that repression will not put an end to ca-

morra in Naples. It is clear enough, given the limitations of men and resources, that neither politicians, policemen nor magistrates expect to eliminate organized crime completely but share the aim of containing it within
reasonable limits. The problems of Naples—its urban decay and social
deterioration—go far beyond the activities of the various camorra groups,
and it is admitted by police, at least in private, that they cannot and do
not want to destroy certain *paranze* of the type we have called *enterprise
syndicates*.

Apart from the facetious observation that one seldom sees a pack of
Marlboro cigarettes with the state monopoly seal on it in a police station or
law court in Naples, there is the more serious aspect of cigarette smuggling.
On the occasions that the excise guards (*Guardie di Finanza*) have clamped
down on the smuggling, there have been demonstrations in the streets. Given
the number of people involved and the high rate of unemployment in Naples
and its surrounding towns, a real and sudden interdictum of the contraband
racket would be socially disastrous.

The political left, however, takes a different line. The PCI, in opposition
with the regional government but in power in the city since 1975, has declared
its intention of fighting camorra on all fronts. A number of Communist mili-
tants have been killed or injured in this struggle. Other parties have been
more equivocal since in some areas they profit electorally from gangster help.
There are exceptions like Marcello Torre, the DC Mayor of Pagani who was
killed in 1980. As a general rule, however, politics are conducted on a
clientelistic basis and camorra is one of the elements in vote gathering.

The DC went to Raffaele Cutolo to seek mediation in the release of the provincial councillor Ciro Cirillo when he was kidnapped by the Red Brigades in
1981. The facts of this case, which will be dealt with in the next section, show
how the parties in power can and do live with organized crime though not as
intimately and completely as in the case of mafia in Western Sicily and Southern Calabria.

In any case, the presumption on the part of the population that gangsters
have political protection is very strong. In an extensive survey carried out by
the Naples desk of the newspaper *'Unita'* in May 1982, almost 84% of re-
spondents thought that "Camorra bosses have protection and links with the
State and political power." The results of the poll suggest a strong lack of
confidence in the State.

In the eighties, greater steps have been taken to combat organized crime in
the area. The arrest of more than 800 people in June '83 (and subsequent
committal of 640 of them) including lawyers, nuns and teachers was an
example of the Neapolitan judiciary's counterattack. The passage of the
Rognoni-La Torre law (no. 646 of September 13th. 1982) after the murder of
General Dalla Chiesa has meant that police and magistrates have been able to
examine the financial affairs of gangsters. They have done so with some success and the '83 arrests and '84 committal were a result of the law.

Current Situation

No account of organized crime in the Campania can ignore the turmoil in and around Naples since 1980. Although the situation changes constantly in terms of its actors and incidents, major trends have been established firmly enough to make clear the basic structure and importance of "The New Organized Camorra."

This period has been characterized by an enormous increase in the competition between groups; a gradual adoption of terrorist methods and language by the camorristi, and to a limited degree overlap between terrorists and gangsters. The November 1980 earthquake, which devastated mountain areas in the region of Campania and caused great disruption in the city of Naples, did not give an immediate acceleration to the growth of organized crime in the city, contrary to general expectation. However, a year after the earthquake, it became clear that camorra had adapted itself to post-earthquake conditions and was profiting from local efforts at reconstruction as well as exploiting the homeless.

The degree of conflict may be measured by the number of murders: in Table 8.1, there were 148 in 1980; 235 in 1981; and in 1982 the figure rose to 265. This gives homicide rates of 4 to about 7 per 100,000 for those years. Though low by the standards of some North American cities, these figures are immense when compared with the rest of Italy. The average rate for the whole country from 1970–75 was 1.0 per hundred thousand; Calabria and Sicily had the highest rates (not surprisingly, given the growth of mafia in Calabria over those years and its continuing presence in Sicily)—3.2 and 1.8, while Campania had an average of 1.6; the province of Naples was somewhat higher.[49]

The Neapolitan figures obviously include a number of murders which have nothing to do with organized crime, such as intra-family killings and purely culture-related violence. (In 1981, eleven people were killed in arguments arising from traffic jams.) On the other hand, the figures do not include

---

TABLE 8.1   Homicides in Naples City and Province, 1975–1984

1975	49
1976	56
1977	52
1978	62
1979	82
1980	148
1981	235
1982	265
1983	205
1984	139 (to September 30th)

---

deaths directly related to the conduct of organized crime, some of which are not classified as murder (for instance, the killing of criminals during attempted robbery).

There has been then, an enormous increase in criminal violence in the city since 1979. This is not due to any brusque change in activities nor is it attributable to the introduction of "foreign" elements. Cigarette smuggling goes on as before and the most widespread crime is still extortion with new *mazzetta,* or payoff, opportunities being continuously exploited. (One new area is housing for those left homeless by the earthquake. In 1981, knowledge of an empty house cost 50,000 lire [$52] and "rent" for those already housed was 120,000 lire [$100] per month.)[50] Current alliances with Sicilian, Calabrian, Northern Italian and Marseilles gangsters present the same kaleidescopic image as ever. Nor has there been any great influx of public money coinciding with this chain of violence, as was the case in Calabria over the 1970s.

The most important single reason for the recent outbreak of violence is the rise to power of Raffaele Cutolo, known popularly as "Il Professore" (because he finished primary schooling), don Raffaele, or *"numero uno nella Nuova Camorra organizzata."*

His righthand man, Antonio Cuomo, organized an escape from Aversa in which a hole was dynamited in the asylum wall and Cutolo walked out. The struggle for supremacy with the older bosses in Naples began then. Although his support and power is greatest in Ottaviano and around the volcano, his control extends over the southern and eastern part of the city and periphery. At least in that area he is respected and honored to the extent that some women wear a medallion with his image instead of a cross or the madonna. Cutolo has even written a book of homilies, popular wisdom, and poems. (Typical examples from it are: "Sometimes a movement, a glance, says more than words" [p. 142]; and "After so many disappointments/from friends/ who I held sacred/I don't believe in anything anymore . . ./And sometimes I'm afraid/to lose my only/Friend:/Myself."[51]

Until Cutolo's entry onto the Neapolitan scene, organized crime had been relatively tranquil. A number of geographically well-defined enterprise syndicates dealt with traditional and modern activities; cigarette smuggling, drug trafficking, and protection rackets. The fact that Cutolo reappeared from jail as an already established figure upset the delicate equilibrium of organized crime in the city. Under normal circumstances, a nascent boss has to prove himself over a long period within a limited area. In his rise, many potential rivals give way without violence or at least without death. If, on the other hand, a new figure appears with the manpower and the will to face all the established bosses in a large city, then there is no possibility of retiring gracefully. At the same time, the increase in violence between power syndicate leaders encourages violence within the ranks, so that a local disagreement that previously might have been resolved with a beating is now resolved with guns or bombs. There is an imitation factor in the growth of the murder rate in Naples since only a relatively small proportion of the killings can be directly attributed to Cutolo's rise to power. The use of homicide to settle disputes becomes a way of proving one's manhood and courage.

"Don Raffaele" was imprisoned in November 1980, convicted of extortion. Since then, though, his influence has not waned. Through his son Roberto and wife in Ottaviano as well as his various lieutenants, he has managed to retain his control over large areas of the province and city of Naples. Between bribery of guards, the use of prisoners on parole, and visiting relations, it is not difficult for a "man of respect" to maintain contact with the outside.

Cutolo was taken from prison in Novara in Piedmont to answer charges of further crimes committed while he was out. When interviewed at one of these trials, he declared that he was a local protector of the poor in Ottaviano,[52] a cross between Hobsbawn's social bandit[53] and the old-fashioned capomafia.[54] Others interviewed confirmed the gangster's self-proclaimed image; however, it was notable that only citizens of Ottaviano came forward to declare their support for Cutolo. As Percy Allum noted with reference to nineteenth century camorra: "The tendency of the urban poor [was] to idealize gangsters in the same way as the rural poor did social bandits."[55] It does not mean, however, that Cutolo and his peers in the contemporary Neapolitan underworld fulfill the same function as a capomafia.

When he was arrested, Cutolo had a note from a local parliamentary deputy saying that he had seen to the transfer of a prisoner from one jail to another. Along with this was a card from an ex-minister of defense. During his trial he was presented with a gold medal from an Avellinese builder. The same builder, who is also chairman of the first division Avellino football team, came into court with a newly acquired Brazilian star player in order to introduce the footballer to Cutolo. Both gestures contributed enormously to Cutolo's standing if not to his defense.

But although these incidents show that a gangster may have close links with businessmen and politicians (and this is nothing new), it does not mean that the camorrista is on the same level as either businessman or politician — let alone that he is a businessman or politician himself, as is the case with mafiosi in Sicily and Calabria. Cutolo, Zaza or Spavone may be compared with urban gangsters in other countries. Charlie Richardson, for example, a South London gangster who reached the apex of his career in the 1960s, had friends in reasonably high places, dealings with local businessmen, and, in this case, his own businesses as well, but he was still primarily a gangster.[56] Similar contrasts may be made with American mobsters.

Given the electoral system in Italy and the deeprooted clientelism existing in the south, it is not surprising that a person of influence such as a gang boss will be influential in the elections of certain politicians. The primary difference between the Neapolitan gangster and the mafioso is that the former is only one of the constituents of the *grandi elettori*. Mafiosi are professional politicians, who have their own machines,[57] and their own local notables, landowners, businessmen. Neapolitan society is too fragmented, as indeed one would expect a city of two million people to be, to allow a single figure to control the whole or even a fractional part of the whole, as is the case in Palermo or Reggio Calabria.

The obvious conclusion is that camorra in the 1980s is more or less the same beast as ever. Camorra is still a subculture among others, in which there is a high division of labor, at least in the enterprise syndicates, and all that has changed is the increase in violence due to conflicts between the power syndicates. And yet, there are elements suggesting potential changes in the structure of organized crime. These changes may be seen in the methods used and the reaction to organized crime, as well as in contacts between camorra, political terrorists, and politics.

The changes in method deal with the apparent influence of political terrorism on organized crime. In the absence of startling revelations as to the links between organized crime and terrorism, we can safely ignore political rhetoric on this issue. An example is the prime minister's remarks in January 1982: "Terrorism has numerous points of contact with the world of crime organized in bands like the mafia and the camorra. We cannot underestimate the operational links which exist between these criminal organizations starting with the international arms trade."[58] Both left- and right-wing terrorists make use of whatever weapons they can get hold of: arms stolen from NATO or Italian forces in Italy; weapons given by or bought from Libya, the PLO, Eastern bloc countries; or weapons purchased on the clandestine international arms market. The gun that killed Judge Vittorio Occorsio on July 10th, 1976 was part of a consignment that the Reggio Calabria mafioso Giovanni De Stefano had imported. Until the present time, however, there has been no proof that there are "operational links" between political terrorism and organized crime.

The "Armed Proletarian Nuclei" (NAP), largely based on the politicization of the prison population, had strong Neapolitan links. But their members were definitely of the petty criminal type (from both North and South), and no links between them and camorra were even suggested in their trials. In Italy, as elsewhere, organized crime tends towards the conservative end of the political spectrum (but not the far right fascist radical extreme). In any case, the activity of the "politicals" severely cramps the style of all "straight" crime. In the days after the kidnapping of Aldo Moro in March 1978, the rate of burglary, bag-snatching, and car-stealing in Rome dropped to almost nothing. While the provincial councillor Ciro Cirillo was held by the Red Brigades in May 1981, the murder rate in Naples saw its only partial respite in that year.

The intensified police control exercised during the period no doubt introduced incentives in favor of Cutolo's mediation between the Christian Democrats and the Red Brigades for Cirillo's release. This episode was revealed in Spring 1982 by the Communist daily *L'Unita*. The scoop itself turned out to be false, in that the DC politicians named had not been in touch with Cutolo, but the substance was true: secret services and Neapolitan Christian

Democrats had been to see the gangster and many irregularities had been committed.

Although Cutolo has been quoted as saying that members of the Red Brigade are "good guys,"[59] it does not follow that connivance existed between camorra and the terrorists. Cutolo seems simply to have exploited the situation. Part of the ransom paid for Cirillo went to Cutolo. The figure has not been divulged in court but there is the suggestion that the camorrista's share was over a billion lire — more than $800,000.

If camorra can be said to have a political ideology, then it is supportive of the parties and groups in power at the moment. This does not mean that local politicians are immune from attacks from organized crime. The usual targets, however, are on the left, largely because of the Communist Party's traditional anti-mafia stance. In May 1981 the PCI party secretary and local councillor at Ottaviano was severely wounded; the deputy mayor of Avella in Irpinia was shot in the legs in January 1982 after he had reported threats from organized crime concerning the reconstruction programs.

But it is not only communists who have suffered. Early in 1981 a Christian Democrat provincial councillor in Naples was murdered, but since he had been an estate agent, the presumption was that there had been some sort of complicity with the camorra on the part of the victim. The most notable killing of a politician was the murder in December 1980 of the mayor of Pagani, Marcello Torre. Pagani is the center of the tomato racket that takes European Community subsidies on agricultural produce, even when the produce has never been grown. In common with the rest of the area from Salerno to Capua, protection is the rule and some local bosses have tried to expand outside the immediate zone of Pagani-Nocera. The fact that Torre was the defense lawyer of one of these local bosses, Salvatore Serra (known as *Cartuccia* or "cartridge") led to the immediate hypothesis of a gang killing. It was said that Cutolo's men were trying to move into Pagani, and in fact a fortnight later, Cutolo's lawyer Bruno Spiezie was severely wounded in Naples.

However, Torre was more than a gangster's adviser. Earlier that year he had taken up politics again after some years' absence and was elected as an independent in the Christian Democrat lists. Before the election he had left a letter with a local judge in which he made his fears explicit. Torre had been trying to stop petty racketeering with the earthquake relief funds and also declared that only those with genuinely damaged houses would have funds for repairs. Whatever his connections with Serra, which certainly existed, it seems clear that his killing was also related to his intended political reforms.

Although no links have been discovered between terrorism and organized crime, the camorra has adopted terrorist techniques, such as phoning newspapers and leaving communiques for public release. Over 1982 various killings were claimed by a group calling itself "The New Family." Others were unsigned but the language is a clear imitation of the Red Brigades style:

> He was a prison executor. He didn't hesitate to take part in mass beatings or knifings . . . Raffaele Cutolo is a useless fanatic and lunatic. He should be care-

ful not to challenge people because they are just waiting for the moment the worm sticks his head out so that they can squash it . . . where justice doesn't reach, we are there with the massacre.[60]

This referred to a particularly brutal murder in which the victim, who had been accused of killing three people in jail on the night of the earthquake, had been killed, his hands cut off, heart cut out and the various pieces left in a car near the main railway stations. This type of violence is a cross between the ritual mutilations carried out in traditional mafia culture and the sheer aggression of some family killings; the degree of viciousness is exceptional in Neapolitan terms even within a culture that accepts and sometimes admires physical violence and cruelty.

In the face of such widespread and far-reaching criminal activity public reaction has been somewhat apathetic. The violence affects relatively few people directly: even with five murders a week the majority of the two million inhabitants of Naples are unlikely to be involved, although all are informed about the situation through the media. On the other hand, large numbers do take an active part in organized crime as consumers: gamblers and smokers in particular, and more generally as victims because of the higher prices charged in shops paying protection money (although the black market is so vast that despite almost universal payment of protection, many goods are still much cheaper in Naples than in other parts of the country).

In November 1980 while the Cutolo trial was going on, there was a strike by shopkeepers protesting against the protection racket. It seemed to be a turning point in public sentiment, but when the police provided a special telephone line for anyone wishing to report extortionary activities (even anonymously), the service was hardly used.

The murder of Marcello Torre, however, did cause public reaction. A month later, there were demonstrations in Pagani in which anarchists and members of left-wing marxist groups marched alongside Communists (as well as the other parties) — an extraordinary display of unity. The Pagani PCI section issued a document with ten demands. These included requests that the anti-mafia law be applied to the area; that a parliamentary commission look into the situation in and around Naples; that the police force be expanded and incompetent officers replaced; that President Pertini take part in a meeting with all the local councils. Fourteen months later, only the first request has been satisfied.

A third and even less practically effective anti-camorra move came at the beginning of January 1982, following the papal condemnation of mafia in Sicily, repeated by the Archbishop of Palermo, Pappalardo. The Dominican assembly in Naples issued its condemnation of the "deviant phenomenon of different rival groups who work towards the control of the fruit and vegetable markets, building sites, contracts and drug traffic."[61]

Despite the lack of any concerted popular rejection of camorra, there are signs that at least the attitudes of the authorities are changing. The ineffectual chief of police was discharged in 1981: his successor has already shown himself to be more efficient. Parliament and government have taken an interest in the slaughter in the Parthenopaeic capital. Such measures alone cannot destroy organized crime, but when combined with the natural selection resulting from gang violence, there is the presumption that camorra will return to something similar to previous decades when the enterprise syndicates operated in peace, at least with each other.

Notes

1. The article in *Enciclopedia italiana* (1930) uses the past tense throughout. In any case, there was the presumption between 1922 and 1943 that any subculture deviant to the norms of Fascism (linguistic minorities, mafia, etc.) had disappeared or was in the process of disappearing.

2. Alan Block, *East Side West Side* (Transaction Books; 1983). Roughly speaking, he defines *enterprise syndicate* as an organization that provides a real service like prostitution, gambling or drugs and a *power syndicate* as an organization that, as its name suggests, seeks merely control without providing any service; i.e., extortion rackets. For a fuller discussion of the terms, see below on *Structure of organized crime*.

3. Vittorio Paliotti, *La camorra. Storia, personaggi, viti della societa' napoletana dalle origini a oggi* (Milan, Bietti; 1973, p. 16.

4. Marco Monnier, *La Camorra*. First published in 1863. (Naples: Berisio, 1965), pp. 85-89.

5. Abele De Blasio, *Usi e costumi dei camorristi* (Naples: Pierro, 1897), p. 3, and others who use him as a source. I have given the orthography as quoted in the various sources. This is sometimes Neapolitan and sometimes Italian; hence the apparent inconsistency in some of the transcriptions.

6. Enzo Avitabile, *L'onorata societa'* (Naples: Regina, 1972).

7. De Blasio, op. cit., pp. 7-15.

8. Paliotti, op. cit.

9. Monnier, op. cit., pp. 22-23.

10. For the destruction of some of the more fantastical descriptions of mafia, see Henner Hess, *Mafia* (Farnborough, Hants:, Saxon House, 1973), pp. 92-97.

11. Sharo Gambino, *La Mafia in Calabria* (Reggio Calabria: Edizioni Parallelo 38; 1975), pp. 7-21. Gambino himself takes the material from a book by the so-called "Monster of Presinacci," Serafino Castagna, a case of multiple homicide in 1957. See S. Castagnia, *Devi uccidere* Milan, Ed. 11 momento 1967 or *Time Magazine* 29th July 1957.

12. C. L. "Review of Avv. S. Pucci: *Schizzo monografico sulla camorra carceraria nelle Provincie meridionali*" in *Archivio di Psichiatria, Scienze Penali ed Antropologia criminale* Vol. 5 (1884) p. 371.

13. Monnier, op. cit., pp. 117-35.

14. Paliotti, op. cit., pp. 236-45.

15. See Hess, op. cit., pp. 43-73, for the mafioso's rise to power. Also Parker, *Rough Justice*, (London: Fontana, 1981), for the Richardson brothers in London, and Block, op. cit., for 1930s New York City.

16. Sergio De Gregorio, *Camorra* (Naples: SEN, 1981), p. 26.

17. Monnier, op. cit., pp. 153-54.

18. This passage uses Mino Jouakim, *'O Malomo* (Naples: Pironti, 1979), as well as interview and newspaper material.

19. Monnier, op. cit., p. 115.

20. Ibid., pp. 120-22.

21. Quoted in Paliotti, op. cit., pp. 211-12.

22. Atti Parliamentari, Camera dei Deputati 15th December 1899, p. 912.

23. Proposta di legge, n. 1546, 20 August 1959.

24. Percy Allum, *Politics and Society in Post-War Naples,* (Cambridge: University Press, 1973), p. 163.

25. C. Guarino, "La Camorra," in AAVV, *Napoli dopo un secolo* (Naples: ESI, 1961), pp. 505–54.
26. Allum, op. cit., p. 170.
27. Monnier, op. cit., p. 1.
28. Monnier, op. cit., pp. 74–76.
29. De Blasio, 1898 op. cit., pp. 120–25.
30. *Paese Sera*, July 3, 1960.
31. *Corriere della Sera,* January 25, 1982: p. 8.
32. De Blasio, 1898 op. cit., pp. 120–25.
33. De Blasio, *Nel paese della camorra* (Naples, Pierro: 1901).
34. De Blasio, 1898 op. cit., pp. 153–58.
35. Curzio Malaparte, *La Pelle* (Milan: Aria d'Italia, 1949).
36. Guarino, 1961, p. 546.
37. Jouakim, op. cit., pp. 92–93.
38. *La Stampa*, March 29, 1979.
39. *Repubblica*, 11th November 1980, p. 7.
40. De Blasio, 1897, op. cit., pp. 32–35.
41. Palioti, op. cit., pp. 207–08.
42. Guarino, 1961, op. cit., pp. 513–16.
43. Interview with investigating magistrate Enzo Scolastico, January 1981.
44. *La Stampa,* March 22, 1979.
45. *Il Giorno,* May 6, 1982.
46. Block, op. cit., p. 13.
47. Ibid., p. 129.
48. Ibid., p. 13.
49. Ibid., p. 129.
50. Tonio Tucci, "Mafia e omicidi in Calabria negli anni '70," (Cosenza: Department of Sociology, 1981).
51. *Repubblica*, January 20, 1982.
52. Raffaele Cutolo, *Poesie e pensieri* (Naples, Berisio, 1980).
53. Ennio Mastrostefano, RAI-TV T.G., 2 Dossier, June, 1981.
54. Eric Hobsbaum, *Bandits* (Harmondsworth: Penguin, 1969).
55. See, for example, Indo Montanelli, *Pantheon minore*, (Milan: Mondadori, 1958), pp. 279–85, on Calogero Vizzini, or Danilo Dolci, *Waste* (London, MacGibbon & Kee, 1963), ch. V on Giuseppe Genco Russo.
56. Allum, op. cit., p. 62.
57. See Parker op. cit., for a complete description of the Richardson brothers' career.
58. For a description of the two major city bosses in postwar Naples, Lauro and Gava, see Allum, op. cit., ch. 9.
59. *Repubblica*, January 22, 1982.
60. De Gregorio, op. cit., p. 142.
61. *Repubblica,* January 22, 1982.

References

Allum, Percy. 1973. *Politics and Society in Post-War Naples.* Cambridge: Cambridge University Press.
Avitabile, Enzo. 1972. *L'onorata societa'.* Naples: Regina.
Block, Alan. 1983. *East Side-West Side: Organizing Crime in New York, 1930–1950.* New Brunswick, N.J.: Transaction Books.
Castagnia, S. 1967. *Devi uccidere.* Milan.
Cutolo, Raffaele. 1980. *Poesie e pensieri.* Naples: Berisio.
De Blasio, Abele. 1898. *Usi e costumi dei camorristi.* Naples: Pierro.
———. 1901. *Nel paese della camorra.* Naples: Pierro.
De Gregorio, Sergio. 1981. *Camorra.* Naples: SEN.
Dolci, Danilo. 1963. *Waste.* London: MacGibbon & Kee.

Gambino, Sharo. 1975. *La Mafia in Calabria.* Reggio Calabria: Edizioni Parallelo 38.

Guarino, C. (1961) "La Camorra" in AAAV, *Napoli dopo un secolo.* Naples: ESI.

Hess, Henner. 1973. *Mafia.* Farnborough, Hants: Saxon House.

Hobsbawn, Eric. 1969. *Bandits.* Harmondsworth: Penguin.

Jouakim, Mino. 1979. *'O Malommo.* Naples: Pironti.

Malaparte, Curzio. 1949. *La Pelle.* Milan: Aria d'Italia.

Montanelli, Indo. 1958. *Pantheon minore.* Milan: Mondadori.

Paliotti, Vittorio. 1973. *La camorra: Storia, personaggi, viti della bella societa' napoletana dalle origini a oggi.* Milan: Bietti.

Parker, Robert. 1981. *Rough Justice.* London: Fontana.

Tucci, Tonio. 1981. "Mafia e omicidi in Calabria negli anni '70." Cosenza: Department of Sociology.

9

Organized Crime in Poland

Andrzej E. Marek
Nicolas Copernicus University

In recent years there has been a growing interest in international cooperation in the field of criminal investigation and control (United Nations 1980). Though truly comparative studies in this field encounter many difficulties because of a range of factors including different criminal statutes, crime reporting procedures, and cultural differences, the role of this type of research has been largely acknowledged as very valuable by criminologists throughout the world (Radzinowicz and Wolfgang 1971). Until now, in the socialist countries of Eastern Europe major research endeavors were directed towards cross-national analyses of general crime trends and crime prevention strategies, but there has not been any systematic study of organized criminality in the countries concerned (Lernell 1979; Gōdōny 1974; Jasinski 1976; Redo 1980).

The concept of organized crime in the form of a continuing criminal enterprise is basically unknown as an investigative tool among researchers and scholars in Eastern European societies; rather, their attention is focused on so-called "affairs"—activities involving the collective misappropriation of social property, which constitutes a serious problem for those countries with socialist economic systems.

This essay is a first attempt to apply the concept of "organized crime" as it has been developed and used in Western societies to the problems of crime in Poland. It is meant to contribute to cross-national cooperation in the analysis and control of crime in all its varied manifestations.

The Notion of Organized Crime

In 1978 an international conference in Italy entitled, "Organized Criminality," showed that the discussions and debates on the concept of organized crime could produce little consensus among scholars about the precise nature of the phenomenon (Rassegna di Studi Quaderni 1979). Some commentators argued that organized crime exists only under conditions when force or the threat of force is applied to obtain illegal profits in violation of law. Others chose to include in their definition of organized crime the illegal activities of business corporations, while still others insisted that illegal activities of commercial firms constituted economic crime and denied the validity of labelling such crime as "organized," because violence and intimidation were generally absent in such cases. Some participants went so far as to suggest the inclusion of organized immoral activities considered to be against the interest of the people into the category of organized crime (Ibid, 1979: Vol. 1).

Similar ambiguities and confusions prevail with regard to terroristic and politically motivated offenses. According to the *Report on Organized Crime* of the U.S. National Advisory Committee on Criminal Justice Standards and Goals (1976), the notion of organized crime does not include terrorists dedicated to violent political change, because organized crime groups tend to be largely apolitical or politically conservative, seeking to maintain the status quo, in which they succeed in gaining enormous profits. But, contrary to this position, many students of the phenomenon do not hesitate to include terroristic and politically motivated organizations within the frame of organized crime (Bassiouni 1979; Fiorentini and Pisapia 1979; Haussling 1979).

Clearly, the phenomenon referred to by the phrase "organized crime" may in reality be understood quite differently or have different meanings for different scholars, and for criminal justice officials, and the public at large. Lejins seems correct when he suggests that a source of difficulty and confusion is the fact that the subject exhibits a variety of aspects that may properly fit the rubric, "organized crime" (Lejins 1979). In addition, it is the case that organized crime is understood quite differently in different societies and cultures. Thus, the utmost care is required in defining terms and in identifying the problem (Lejins 1979, 70). Bearing in mind all of these qualifications, we shall try to identify the phenomenon of organized crime in its varied aspects and manifestations in Poland.

The characteristics of organized crime as it has been described by American scholars and law enforcement officials are not apparent in countries other than the United States. Probably with the exception of Italy, in which it is alleged there is a nationwide criminal organization comparable to the mafia or Cosa Nostra, no other European nation seems to contain groups dominating whole segments of their economic activity — particularly the supply of illicit drugs, pornographic materials, prostitution, gambling and loansharking. The distinction suggested by Hermann that [there is a difference between] "criminals who operate in an organized group for certain purposes, such as a gang planning a bank robbery, and organized crime which is characterized by exclusivity or monopoly of an area of operations whether it be illicit or legitimate business activity" (Hermann 1979, 135–36) points up an area of disagreement. This distinction would be rejected by many scholars describing the phenomenon in Europe, for whom a well-planned bank rob-

bery committed by an organized group would indeed qualify as a manifestation of "organized crime." In Poland, there has never developed any criminal
organization capable of monopolizing an area of criminal operations, and by
now, given the structure of an economy that is predominantly a monopoly of
the state, such possibilities are remote.

For many scientists, an organized crime is a type of well-planned criminal
act committed by a group of criminals who have conspired together. The
term is used in its generic sense and not limited in its application to a form of
crime, mainly syndicate crime that evolved in Italy and the United States in
the nineteenth and early twentieth centuries. Since economic and business
criminality occur regularly, it is understandable that many writers who focus
on organized crime examine business and economic criminality (Kerner 1973,
243; Schneider 1977, 107–11). Tiedemann, however, raises the objection that
such a generalization is misleading because the criterion of "being organized"
loses its descriptive value, especially when structural aspects are concerned
(Tiedemann, 1979: 187). In this connection, it is interesting to note that
French law excludes from the notion of "criminalité d'affaires" the kinds of
economic and business crimes that other criminologists would consider definitive examples of organized crime (Delmas-Marty 1974).

The problem of organized crime should not be restricted to economic and
business criminal activities alone. The world faces many other problems such
as the terroristic acts of very well-organized groups and organizations,
whether clandestine or operating openly who themselves often engage in robberies and hold-ups. Thus there seems to be no good reason for excluding
such dangerous acts and groups from the notion of organized crime (Bassiouni 1975, 215). In fact, it seems reasonable and appropriate to include the
well-organized immoral activities of power elites who seek to dominate and
exploit large segments of society. *The Report on Crime and the Abuse of
Power* presented to the Sixth United Nations Congress on the Prevention of
Crime and the Treatment of Offenders stressed that "some of the most
damaging antisocial acts were not yet legally defined as crimes in some juris-
dictions . . . and even in the case of acts covered by legal prohibitions, the offenses committed are usually not reflected in crime statistics, because of non-
detection, non-reporting, non-prosecution, or preferential treatment by the
criminal justice process" (United Nations 1980, 5, 42). The report goes on to
say that both political and economic abusers of power negatively affect the
moral climate and endanger the development process, particularly in developing countries.

On the other hand, it would be misleading to confuse the notion of organized crime with any form of criminal organization or conspiracy. Many organizations and conspiracies are simply associations or groups of criminals
with no particular hierarchical structure or division of labor or authority. Organized crime groups, in contrast, have a tight formal structure and a ruling
body governing their operations. The concept of organized crime should be
restricted to this latter type of criminal organization—that is, one in which

there is some kind of discernible formal structure, with hierarchical co-ordination of the participants involved in the planning and executing of illicit or illegal acts (Hawkins 1971, 374–75). A key factor of organized crime groups which distinguishes them from loosely grouped gangs is an arrangement that protects its members from prosecutions for violations of conspiracy statutes.[1]

While contemporary organized crime has economic gain as its primary goal, there are other organized crime groups — as the term has been defined here — which have different goals, such as radical political change through terroristic activities. And, on the other hand, the use of threat or violence may not always be employed in organized crime activities and should not, therefore, constitute a defining feature of such forms of criminality. The use of violence may be seen as instrumental rather than gratuitous. For example, black-market operations of well-organized sellers of scarce goods at excessive prices do not ordinarily resort to violence.

Though organized crime has been a phenomenon more endemic to certain developed countries, especially the United States, it is becoming more prevalent in some developing countries, particularly with regard to the distribution of scarce goods. The scarcity caused by imbalances in supply and demand in the declining economies of many countries makes organized criminal activity plausible and attractive to many (*United Nations Report* No. 15, 1976).

Organized Crime in Poland

In Poland there have been only fragmentary studies on the manifestations of organized crime in its broadest sense (Lernell 1965, Błaszczynski 1965 and 1974, Majchrzak 1964 and 1965, Tyszkiewicz 1963, Majewski 1975, Krasucka 1976, Gornick 1977, Daszkiewicz 1971). The general consensus among scholars is that unreported criminality is much more widespread than official crime statistics indicate.[2] In addition, there are vague and hazy notions of organized crime that confound its systematic study. With few exceptions, writers on the subject confine their investigations to so-called "criminal affairs," that is, crimes involving the misappropriation of social and private property by an organized group of offenders, usually those who are employed by state-owned enterprises. In addition, some research has examined organized smuggling of currency and valuable goods — especially those of historical and cultural value — across national boundaries (Bassiouni 1979, Haussling 1979, Fiorentini and Pisapia 1979). Quite recently, in the face of the economic crisis in Poland, the daily press has called for a rigorous struggle against speculations in scarce and rationed goods. On September 25, 1981, the Polish Parliament (the Sejm) enacted special statutes to control and suppress speculation.[3]

The problem of the misappropriation of social property and the speculation in scarce goods is not limited to Poland but appears to be widespread in other Eastern European countries as well. The problem has aroused serious official concern and authorities have stressed "the necessity of decisive struggle against misappropriations, embezzlements and similar phenomena inherited from the past," which currently rank high among various types of crime (USSR 1976). However, the paucity of systematic study and the lack of reliable quantitative data have seriously impeded the scientific investigation of organized forms of crime against social and private property.

Before examining the structure of crime in Poland some caveats need to be stated. An important factor that must be borne in mind when pursuing the incidence and characteristics of crime is the severe deficiency of official crime statistics. Obviously, a large proportion of crimes go unreported; and other offenses that are reported at first but are not prosecuted for any number of reasons do not get included in the crime statistics. Furthermore, the number of crimes recorded as compared with crime in toto varies with the different categories of offense. The problem is familiar to criminologists and is a topic of intense discussion (Marek 1979, 81–86). While the reliability of crime statistics in Poland and the estimations of "hidden criminality" will not be discussed, it is important that the "dark figures" of crime be kept in mind (Sellin 1971).

In Poland, two categories predominate: crimes against persons and crimes against property. Within the category of crimes against property, the offense of "organized property appropriation" is a type of organized crime. This offense is proscribed explicitly in Article 202 of the Criminal code of 1969; it is also called "economic affair," proscribed in Article 134, Chapter 19 of the Criminal Code, entitled: "Offenses Against Basic Political and Economic Interests of the State." Both ordinary and big "economic affairs" are types of crime involving the complicity of persons who are usually employees of a public enterprise. A "big economic affair" is an offense which, by the legal definition, seriously disturbs the functioning of an important sector of the national economy. In contrast, the "ordinary affair" has milder, less serious national consequences, but still is harmful to the state (Gornick 1976).

Note that the Polish Criminal Code regards a perpetrator not only as a person who has committed an offense, but also as one who has directed the commission of an offense by another (Article 16). It means that he will be liable as a perpetrator or organizer or "brain" of the group committing social property appropriations, even if such a person had not been personally involved in the act. While aiding and instigating constitute separate types of criminal offenses, the aider and instigator is punishable within the same purview of the law. In practice, however, such persons tend to be treated more leniently than actual perpetrators but the legal and societal reaction is dependent on the degree of "social danger" of the crime (Frankowski 1981).

According to studies of the record of organized criminal prosecutions, it is those who occupy positions of trust, who manage public enterprises, who are responsible for the distribution of raw materials, and persons who are storekeepers, wholesalers, and retail shop managers who get involved in social property offenses (Gornick 1976).

The methods of criminal operations range from stealing raw materials and semi-finished products to altering inventory records and "moving" products out of firms for the purpose of illegal sale. Members of organized crime groups set up arrangements with buyers of illicit goods, or sellers operating on the numerous black markets. Many of these criminals hold positions in state-owned enterprises. This is an interesting aspect of the Polish economy and its underside. Many of the organized crime groups are not located outside the economic upperworld as is the case in the United States but are situated within the structure of the public enterprises in which they play double-sided roles, both legal and illegal. In fact, key members of criminal groups often inhabit high-ranking positions in governmental agencies. Their major roles appear to be to cover-up and mask illegal operations, which they direct away from public and law enforcement monitoring and scrutiny. In order to do this, these criminal entrepreneurs have developed elaborate systems of bribery, which they regard as the cost of doing business and through which they corrupt and compromise public officials, the militia, and the armed forces.

Because of their high-ranking positions in official institutions and the prestige attached thereto, key members of organized crime groups often manage to elude investigation and prosecution by developing and utilizing connections with politicans and law enforcement officials. The illegal operations of these "white-collar gangsters" constitute the little known "gilded figure of crime."

Since the Polish working-class protest in August 1980 against abuses of political and economic malfeasance by the elites, many such cases have been disclosed and openly discussed. In the past two years the situation has substantially changed: there have been efforts to prosecute formerly "untouchable" persons who were deeply involved in social property appropriation for illicit profit and for private investments.[4]

Many offenders attempt to explain their conduct as somewhat justifiable because their needs and the frustrations they encounter in trying to legitimately improve their life-styles push them into crime. Moreover, they point out that their crimes are victimless, as they steal from big, state-owned firms that can easily make up losses and compensate for shortages by raising prices and thereby reducing demand. Cressey's theory of embezzlement and the Sykes-Matza theory of neutralization may be usefully applied in explaining the etiology of such forms of criminality as they exist in Poland (Cressey 1971; Sykes and Matza 1957; Marek 1978; Gryniuk 1979).

Reliable figures on the incidence and frequency of property and economic crimes are not available. The number of such offenses is known to be high, however, and only a fraction of all law violations have been reported, prosecuted, and disposed of. While attempts at quantitative estimations would be risky, it is reasonable to assume that property and economic crimes rank high (probably up to 60 or 70 percent of all crimes) and have shown few signs of abating. Needless to say, criminologists, law enforcement officials and the general public are deeply concerned.

Since the 1981 Polish crisis, the most pronounced increase in crime is evident in illegal speculations in scarce goods such as clothing, household articles, and building materials — a mixture of both consumer goods and light industrial products. The methods and networks involved in this form of organized crime are fairly simple to describe but quite difficult to interdict. Basically, manufacturing enterprises and wholesalers buy up scarce goods at low prices and sell them at excessively high prices on the black markets or even in state-owned stores (Lernell 1965, Krasucka 1976).

The extent of such illicit operations and black markets functioning in all strata of Polish society remains virtually unknown. The problem is really quite new and has not been studied in any depth. The daily press is filled with descriptions of particular cases, and sometimes uncovers the existence of a large black market organization. Yet, these revelations do not provide a satisfactory basis for a reliable, scientific assessment of the problem. At best it is possible to characterize the problem in general outline. Ironically, many of the laws designed to safeguard the equitable rationing of scarce goods have themselves become instruments for facilitating enormous speculations and black market activities. The legal sanctions appear to be unenforceable and may be said actually to invite their own violation.

Members of organized crime groups engaged in black market activity diligently avoid violence for good reasons: if arrested, the severity of punishment is considerable. And expansionist tactics among these groups are practically nonexistent since they operate within the confines of the state enterprises in which they are employed.

By 1980, organized social property appropriation amounted to only 1,421 convictions, while speculation offenses amounted to 4,626 convictions. The real extent of the occurrence of these offenses is more likely a multiple of the actual numbers of reported convictions. Concerning property crimes, there is no evidence that suggests the development of criminal organizations that would fit into the definitions of organized crime. Typically, the organizations are small associations of a few professionals who come together in order to execute robberies and conduct fencing operations. Groups of professional thieves, including those specializing in auto theft, are included in these groups (Bozyczko 1970; Chybinski 1972). Most professional criminals prefer to operate alone or in small groups; and with the exception of bank robbers, most of their offenses are not very skillful. Practically none use firearms — probably because of the inaccessibility of weapons and strict state licensing and punishment for illegal possession (Biernaczyk 1977).

Fortunately, Poland has not experienced terroristic acts on a large scale, except for unlawful aircraft seizures (hijackings), which occurred with some frequency after the imposition of martial law on December 13, 1981.

In terms of the commission of criminal acts and in complicity without other participation in them, Polish criminal law makes a clear distinction. For example, membership in an espionage organization aimed at basic state interests (Article 124 of the Criminal Code) is punishable even if an individual never engaged in any espionage activity; membership alone is criminal.

Other statutes that apply to organized criminal activity either directly or indirectly are: participating in a criminal organization whose purpose is the commission of crime (Article 276 of the Criminal Code); membership in an illegal organization whose existence, structure and goals are clandestine (Article 278); organized smuggling of currency and valuable goods across national borders — euphemistically referred to as a "smuggling affair" (Article 135); and organized social property appropriation (Articles 134 and 202). So far it seems that organized social property appropriation and the concomitant speculation in black markets have expanded greatly, causing serious problems for law enforcement agencies. In contrast, the scale of remaining types of organized criminal activity is much smaller. Organized smuggling, for example, has rarely been detected or prosecuted, with only six convictions for this crime in 1979.

Other Types of Crime: Alcohol-Related Offenses

It is a matter of historical fact that the prohibition and proscription of alcohol, narcotics, and pornography in the United States precipitated a tremendous rise in organized criminal activity whose main structures and forms exist even today. In contemporary Poland, on the other hand, there is no prohibition on alcohol. However, the problem of the illegal production and sale of alcohol is immense because excessive prices imposed by the state and the systems of rationing have made it difficult to meet public demand. Alcohol abuse, which affects hundreds of thousands of people from every walk of life, has been and will continue to be the most serious problem of social pathology in Poland. And those engaging in meeting the enormous demand for alcohol have proceeded to corrupt officials and law enforcement authorities in order to carry on their illicit, lucrative business.

Prostitution and Pornography

In 1948 prostitution was banned, but it is not by itself punishable. Most prostitutes operate in clubs, restaurants, and hotels associating mainly with foreign guests. They usually pay a "tax" in order to facilitate their trade in clients (Antoniszyn 1980; Akolinski 1976). Most regular prostitutes consider their activities a "commercial business," and only a fraction of them have developed continuous organizational ties with other criminals.[5] It does not appear that prostitutes are organized in brothels or under the control of racketeers, as they once were in the United States.

Drugs

The scope of the traffic in pornographic materials in Poland is very small and has not in recent years shown any substantial signs of increase (Filar

1977). The problem of illegal trafficking in drugs, however, is growing. Precise quantitative data are not readily available because, among other things, the drug trade is well organized and difficult for law enforcement authorities to penetrate and disband. Some estimations suggest that thousands of people, especially adolescents, use "soft" drugs rather than "hard" drugs like morphine and its derivatives (Marek and Redo 1978). The government believes that from time to time Poland has been a transit country for smuggling hard narcotics from Southeast Asia to Western Europe. International criminal organizations were involved in this trade, but there is no evidence that members of Polish criminal organizations were deeply involved. But, again, not much reliable data are available. The possession of small amounts of drugs and their solitary use is not a criminally punishable offense. But the traffic in drugs and large-scale use constitute criminal offenses that are severely punished. The drug menace affects mostly juveniles in secondary schools, and an alarmed public has demanded several preventive measures to stop the spread of regular use and addiction. These programs have been developed under a special organization called "Monar" to deal with the problem.

Juvenile Delinquency

Research shows that most delinquents mature out of their adolescent deviance, although the problems of youth gangs and teenage violence appear to be on the rise. For purposes of this study, however, the link between youth crime and organized crimes is not well established or significant, as it is said to be in other countries (Kossowska and Misciskier 1978).

Major Factors Contributing to Organized Crime and the Problem of Its Eradication

Lejins has indicated that organized crime thrives in situations produced by criminal legislation in the borderline areas of criminal and immoral conduct. Prohibition and state-imposed rationing or taxation of certain products creates black markets and a base of organizational activities for pursuing illegal profits (Lejins 1979, 73–76). Lejins refers to this process as a "prohibition syndrome," which parallels in many ways the evolution of organized crime in the United States marked by the prohibition of liquor, gambling, prostitution, and the like. Certainly, the United States may be characterized as a country that attempts to legislate morality and proscribe morally undesirable conduct. While this tendency is apparent in modern socialist countries, these nations are more inclined to legislate economic and political activity much more vigorously. (The line between morality and politics, however, is often blurred and it remains to be seen how socialist governments will react if confronted with a crisis they define as purely economic or political, while the masses see it as stricly moral and, therefore, out of the orbit of state interest.)

The perspective of the "prohibition syndrome" is a very fruitful conceptual tool in the study of the dynamic processes involved in organized criminal activity. The spectre of a declining economy tends to stimulate temptations to legislate production and market operations, particularly through rationing raw materials and finished products. The imbalances betwen the demand and supply of certain goods creates a base of "secondary distribution" and speculation patterns. Even if illegal prices are much higher than official ones, people in need are willing to pay. As the problem evolves, it creates still further consequences. It seems that anti-speculation laws, even if accompanied by severe punitive sanctions, are not especially acceptable to the public. The result is the non-reporting of offenses to police and the militia and the widespread refusal to appear as witnesses in criminal proceedings. Handicapped by the lack of moral support and noncooperation by large segments of the population, law enforcement officers are subject to demoralization and, ultimately, corruption. In addition, the prosecution process becomes more selective and punishment uncertain. The consequences are unmistakable: severe sanctions imposed occasionally on minor figures in organized criminal groups do not deter those willing to engage in illegal trade. As the risk of arrest and punishment diminish, more persons are attracted into crime. Such a process completes the circle of legal impotence that stultifies the law enforcement community.

One way out of this vicious cycle of crime and ineffectual censure would be an improvement in the economy that would ensure a secure and steady supply of consumer goods most in demand. An economic policy of this kind requires a comprehensive program of change including the encouragment of free investment and trade and the relaxation of excessive state control on all segments of economic production, trade, and consumption.

Economic factors alone, however, cannot fully explain the etiology of economic and property crimes, particularly in their organized forms. Such an explanation does not take into account the complex nature of human motivations. Criminological investigations concerning the role of moral norms in the genesis of such crimes stress the existence of different norms of conduct that are either favorable or unfavorable to legal conformity (Malec 1974). The research reveals that among workers and officials of state enterprises there exist so-called "techniques of neutralization" that mitigate against consciousness of guilt in stealing state property. The most popular rationales for crime include the denial of injury or the existence of legitimate victims, and the appeal to higher loyalties including family needs for survival. It is interesting to note in this connection that workers willing to pilfer state property strongly condemn any similar act aimed against private property (Marek 1978; Gryniuk 1979). The availability of such rationalizations in a situation of acute need may easily lead to criminal behavior. In addition, the extraordinary affluence of some high-ranking officials, obviously acquired through graft and corruption, only serves to weaken collective loyalties and commitments to the law, and at the same time to encourage participation in crimes against state enterprises (Majchrzak 1964). Again, such beliefs are strengthened by the ineptitude of the police in cases of organized and economic crimes.

With the exception of organized property appropriation, the problem of organized crime has not been given the serious attention that it deserves by scholars and the law enforcement community in Poland and in other socialist countries of Eastern Europe. The lack of official data and the presumed low rate of such crime in the official statistics is no excuse, especially since so many of these crimes go unreported. Clearly, systematic studies (and serious efforts at reliable data collection by public officials) are urgently needed. Without such a base of knowledge, effective programs of organized crime control and prevention are not possible.

Notes

1. See "New Perspectives in Crime Prevention and Criminal Justice." Working paper prepared by the Secretariat, Sixth United Nations Congress on the Prevention of Crime and the Treatment of Offenders. Caracas, Venezuela, 25 August to 5 September 1980, A/Conf. 87/10.

2. In Poland, since 1955, two sources of crime statistics have been published: court statistics, and combined militia and public prosecutor statistics.

3. *Journal of Law of the Polish People's Republic*, No. 24, item 124.

4. The concept of conspiracy in the American sense is not known in Polish law. Entering into an agreement with another person for the purpose of committing an offense, and participation in an association having such a purpose, constitute separate offenses punishable only when the law explicitly provides. See Frankowski 1981, 183; also United Nations 1976 and "Conspiracy: Statutory Reforms" 1975.

5. "Circuits" as cooperative working arrangement of brothel-keepers, panderers, and prostitutes are described by Thornton, 1956.

References

Akolinski, S. 1976. "Prostitution." In *Patologia Spoleczna*. Zapobieganie, pp. 104–21.

Antoniszyn, N. 1980. "Prostitution in the Light of Criminological Research." Unpublished doctoral dissertation. Torun: Nicolas Copernicus University Press.

Bassiouni, M. Cherif, ed. 1975. *International Terrorism and Political Crimes. Springfield, Ill.: Charles Thomas.*

_____. 1979. *"Ideologically Motivated Criminality." In Proceedings of the International Seminar on Organized Criminality. International Institute of Higher Studies in Criminal Sciences. Rassegna di Studi, Quaderni* 1:215.

Biernaczyk, Z. 1977. *Robbery in the Criminological and Criminalistic Aspect*. Warsaw: Ossolineum.

Błaszczynski, J. 1965. Organized Criminal Group as a Form of Criminals' Cooperation. *Nowe Prawo* 3.

_____. 1974. *An Affair of Social Property Appropriation*. Warsaw.

Bozyczko, Z. 1970. *The Crime and the Offender*. Warsaw.

Chybinski, O. 1972. *Concealing of Stolen Goods*. Warsaw.

"Conspiracy: Statutory Reforms Since the Model Penal Code." 1975. *Columbia Law Review* 75:1122-88.

Cressey, D. R. 1971. *Other People's Money.* 2nd ed. Belmont, Calif.: Wadsworth.

Daszkiewicz, K. 1971. *Climate of lawlessness.* Warsaw.

Delmas-Marty, M. 1974. "La criminalité d'affaires." *Revue de science criminelle et de droit pénal comparé* 29:45-55.

Filar, M. 1977. *Pornography.* Torun: Nicolas Copernicus University Press.

Fiorentini, P. G. and Pisapia, G. 1979. "Terrorismo e criminalite organizzata: schema per un approccio socio-crimonologico." In Proceedings of the International Seminar on Organized Criminality. International Institute of Higher Studies in Criminal Sciences. *Rassegna di Studi, Quaderni* 1:228.

Frankowski, S. J. 1981. *Major Criminal Justice Systems,* Part III, 8: *Polish Peoples Republic.* Beverly Hills, Calif.: Sage, p. 183.

Godony, J. 1974. "Crime in Industrialized Countries." In *Crime and Industrialization: First Seminar for Criminologists from Socialist and Scandinavian Countries, in Helsinki, Finland,* August 26-29. Stockholm: Scandinavian Research Council for Criminology, pp. 91-128.

Gornick, O. 1976. *Social Property Appropriation.* Warsaw: Prawnicze.

_____. 1977. Problems of Multiple configuration in the Affair of Property and Appropriation. *Nowe Prawo* 1.

Gryniuk, A. 1979. *Legal Consciousness: Theoretical Study.* Torun: Nicolas Copernicus University Press.

Haussling, J. M. 1979. "Criminalité organisée et idéologies." In Proceedings of the International Seminar on Organized Criminality. International Institute of Higher Studies in Criminal Sciences. *Rassegna di Studi, Quaderni* 1:221.

Hawkins, G. 1971. "Organized Crime: Is There a Summit?" In L. Radzinowicz and M. E. Wolfgang, eds. *Crime and Justice.* Vol. 1. *The Criminal in Society.* New York: Basic Books, 374-87.

Hermann, D. J. 1979. "The Nature and Control of the Business and Corporate Activities of Organized Crime in the United States of America." In Proceedings of the International Seminar on Organized Criminality. International Institute of Higher Studies in Criminal Sciences. *Rassegna di Studi, Quaderni* 1:135-26.

Jasinski, J. 1976. "The Punitiveness of the Criminal Justice Systems: A Cross-National Perspective." *Polish Sociological Bulletin* 1.

Kerner, A. 1973. *Professionelles und organisiertes Verbrechen.*

Kossowska, A., and Misciskier, A. 1978. "Peer Groups and Juvenile Delinquency." In J. Jasinski, ed. *Problems of Social Maladjustment and Crime in Poland.* Warsaw: Ossolineum, pp. 367-78.

Krasucka, W. 1976. "Some aspects of the activities of organized crime groups." *Studia Kryminologiczne, Kryminalistyczne i Penitencjarne* 5.

Lejins, P. P. 1979. "Gang and Organized Criminality." In Proceedings of the International Seminar on Organized Criminality. International Institute of Higher Studies in Criminal Sciences. *Rassegna di Studi, Quaderni* 1:69.

Lernell, L. 1979. "Crime Trends and Crime Prevention Strategies." *International Review of Criminal Policy* 35:3-12. New York: United Nations.

_____. 1965. *Economic Crime.* Warsaw: Prawnicze.

Majchrzak, I. 1964. "Criminal Group in Industrial Works." *Studia Socjologiczne* 1.

_____. 1965. *Employee Economic Crime and the Offender.* Warsaw.

Majewski, W. 1975. "Detection of Organized Property Appropriation in Meat Industry." *Sluzba Milicji Obywatelskiej,* 6.

Malec, J. 1974. "A Model of Crime Etiology in Outline." *Studia Kryminologiczne, Kryminalistyczne i Penitancjarne* 1, 141-57.

Marek, A. 1979. "Criminality and Its Control in Poland: The Data, Comments, and International Comparisons." *Acta Universitatis Nicolai Copernici* 106:81-86.

_____. 1978. "Blue-Collar Criminal in the Light of American Criminology." *Nowe Prawo* 2, 301-02.

Marek, A., and Redo, S. 1978. "Drug Abuse in Poland." *Bulletin on Narcotics* 30, 43-53.

Radzinowicz, L., and Wolfgang, M. E. 1971. *Crime and Justice.* Vol. 1. *The Criminal in Society.* New York: Basic Books.

Redo, S. 1980. "Crime Trends and Crime Prevention Strategies in Eastern Europe." Working paper for the United Nations Secretariat, Sixth United Nations Congress on the Prevention of Crime and the Treatment of Offenders. Caracas, Venezuela.

Report on Organized Crime. 1976. U.S. National Advisory Committee on Criminal Justice Standards and Goals. Washington, D.C.: Government Printing Office.

Schneider, H. J. 1977. *Kriminologie.* Berlin: Walter de Gruyter.

Sellin, T. 1971. "The Significance of Records of Crime." In L. Radzinowicz and M. E. Wolfgang, eds. *Crime and Justice.* Vol. 1. *The Criminal in Society.* New York: Basic Books, pp. 121–29.

Sykes, G., and Matza, D. 1957. "Techniques of Neutralization." *American Sociological Review* 22, 664–70.

Thornton, R. Y. 1956. "Organized Crime in the Field of Prostitution." *Journal of Criminal Law, Criminology, and Police Science* 46, 775–79.

Tiedemann, K. 1979. "Is Economic and Business Crime 'Organized Crime'?" Proceedings of the International Seminar on Organized Criminality. International Institute of Higher Studies in Criminal Sciences. *Rassegna di Studi, Quaderni* 1, 187.

Tyszkiewicz L. 1963. "The Notion of Organized Criminal Group." *Ruch Prawniczy, Ekonomiczny i Socjologiczny* 4.

United Nations. 1976. Report No. 15

United Nations. 1980. Sixth Congress on the Prevention of Crime and the Treatment of Offenders. Caracas, Venezuela, August 25 to September 3.

USSR All-Union Institute for Study of the Causes of Crime and Elaboration of Measures for Crime Control. 1976. *Criminology* (Moscow).

10

Organized Crime and Organized Criminality Among Georgian Jews in Israel

Menachem Amir
The Hebrew University of Jerusalem

Organized criminality, and criminal groups with well established divisions of labor and hierarchies, has existed in Israel since the 1960s, mainly in predatory crimes — burglaries, contraband and sometimes even big heists.

Since 1967 a new criminal activity, drug dealing and selling, received the attention of the police and the public. First, hashish and then opium and heroin were introduced into the country from Lebanon, Jordan and from Europe. Criminal groups were formed to bring in and to distribute the drugs and the phenomena of organized crime around the drug activity spread and became firmly rooted in Israel. Conflicts over territories and markets occurred and with them followed death, destruction and corruption. The police organized itself to confront the trafficking in drugs by using undercover agents, special police operatives and other types of police activities.

While the drug scene absorbed most of the attention, the basis of Israeli organized crime — extortion and protection — continued its spread in the various sectors of the economy and business world. The media sporadically dealt with the subject, but the authorities ignored it. A newspaper investigation into this subject led to a report by the Attorney General (1974 — the Shamgar Report) declaring "that there is now organized crime in Israel, but there is no syndicate crime in Israel."

The reaction of the police was to form an internal committee (the Buchner Committee, 1977). This committee confirmed all the newspaper and academic reports and added more information e.g., the prevalence of the "organized imports of 'black money,' " the organized thievery of agriculture, in the existence of organized fencing in the areas of building materials, agricultural products and livestock and machinery, gold, and electrical appliances, the beginning of loansharking, the existence of bombing and fire-setting experts for hire for protection rackets and the attempt to organize prostitution.

Under the pressure of the media, the government decided to form a State Commission, the Shimron Commission (1978). The Commission declared in its report (the Shimron Report, 1978) that "there is an Israeli kind of organized crime," i.e., with no corruption of political figures in the legislature and the judicial branch of the government. The rest of the report confirmed what was already widely known. The report contained certain recommendations, mainly in the form of "strike force" operations against organized crime, more emphasis on intelligence work and the use of income tax as a weapon against known organized figures.

Since the Shimron Report in 1978, the courts have been able to put behind bars some of the major if not the top leaders of organized crime. Some have left the country. This has left the way open for new people and new groups.

Currently, organized criminal activities and organized crime operations (see our following definitions and distinctions) have spread and strengthened their activities in the areas of: protection rackets, drug importation and distribution (mainly heroin); the fencing of gold, agricultural products, which means organized groups who plan and execute the big thefts for Jewish and Arab fences, who then sell the products in the occupied territories, and even smuggling into Jordan. Some groups have entered the building industry, forcing their services upon building contractors. The infiltration of organized crime into legitimate business is now common knowledge, especially with regard to restaurants, bars, boutiques, furniture shops and money lending.

Violence, however, is rampant in the drug scene of wars over territories and of course this attempts to enlarge the area of extortion and the protection of operations already existing. There is no longer any doubt in anybody's mind that organized crime in Israel does exist; it is only the academicians and sometimes the newspapers who keep warning the public about its existence, spread and danger.

The main purpose of this chapter is twofold: to describe and explain the rapid entrance and stabilization of a male ethnic group of Russian-Georgian Jews into the organized crime structure of Israel; and to report on their special criminal activities.

Notwithstanding empirical tests, Daniel Bell (1970), suggested that it takes at least one generation for an ethnic group to enter and sustain itself in organized crime activities. However, the Georgian Jews (GJs) who immigrated to Israel seven to eight years ago, entered quite swiftly into the organized crime scene, and into new types of organized criminal activities.[1]

The Georgian Jews rapidly became a "special police problem," creating a negative image for the whole Georgian group. As a consequence there is a growing prejudice and intolerance against them, although only a minority of them are engaged in crime. They are portrayed as self-isolated and separated, violent, tough, cunning, with a strong penchant toward corruption, and as tending to operate as a tightly cohesive group in legitimate enterprises as well as in crime. They are also known as people who are very ostentatious, gay, and fond of glittery recreation and leisure. The unity of the Georgian Jewish community in Israel is apparent in all aspects of their cultural life. Their life style and social dynamics demonstrate a sense of differentness and insularity from the dominant, institutional structures of Israeli society.

In this chapter I shall not deal with the problem of organized crime in Israel proper, except when it is relevant to the analysis of Georgian Jewish crime. But first, two main terms need to be defined: organized criminality and organized crime.[2] Organized criminality refers to activities carried on by groups (juveniles or adults) of various size and varying degrees of stability, involving division of labor, hierarchy of command, leadership and authority. For example, burglary cliques, robbery groups, smugglers or extortion cliques are typical criminal activities. The term organized crime, however, is used here to suggest a criminal conspiracy of an organized group, which is relatively stable, with a comparatively fixed division of labor, hierarchy of command, and leadership. It is organized for profit mainly gained by the production, distribution and supply of prohibited or scarce goods and services to "black markets" formed in response to government prohibition policies, rationing, and high tariffs; or for profit gained by the mediating power of government (political patronage and bribery, banking services – e.g., loan sharking; or, again by providing security, informal enforcement and justice (underground law enforcement and criminal justice); or by engaging in illegal importing and wholesaling (fencing, smuggling contraband); or through retailing special (often prohibited) goods or services (dope peddling, number running or the sale of pornography). All this is done with, relatively, systematic and structured use of violence and the nullification and neutralization (through bribery, patronage, extortion, and so on) of the various levels of local and national government. These practices aim to protect the organization's activities and its members (especially the leadership), but mainly to advance the quest for monopolizing certain lines of criminal activities, in the criminal or legitimate market in certain geographical areas. Also, organized criminals do not necessarily earn their living from crime.

In Israel, the phenomenon of organized crime was detected in the 1970s, and consisted mainly in extortion, protection rackets, and in the distribution of drugs. The same period witnessed the emergence of various patterns of organized criminality, including burglary and robbery rings, organized theft and the sale of stolen goods, as well as arson and criminal demolition groups. During this time, gangland killings and gang fights[3] frequently occurred. Some cases of law enforcement corruption were also detected during this period, almost exclusively among custom agents and city-market inspectors.[4] Social relationships between organized crime figures and some political and army VIPs were discovered, involving some reciprocal personal indebtedness and obligations.

At first, police publicly played down the phenomenon, interpreting it as "an increase in professional and organized criminality." Media, investigative reports, and studies by criminologists led to the formation of a state commission (the "Shimron Commission"),[5] that confirmed "the existence of organized crime in Israel." It brought about, under the Commission's recommendations, changes in police and prosecutor departments and new policies for handling organized crime that were basically more intensive "attrition" strategies. Lately, these policies have succeeded in bringing to justice some oldtime leaders of organized crime who were mainly situated in drug trafficking and who were able to operate under the cover of legitimate business "fronts."

Methodology

This chapter is derived from two larger studies: one dealing with organized crime in Israel and the other on the Georgian Jews who immigrated to Israel. The study on the Georgian Jews was basically an ethnographic-anthropological investigation of their background — criminal and otherwise — in the Soviet Union, and of their subsequent life in Israel, including the changes that took place in their family, community and economic life in the process of absorption into Israeli society, and what effects these changes had on criminality within their community.

The data in the report are grounded on information gained from the police and the Israeli Ministry of Immigration, as well as on interview with Georgian Jews and other Russian immigrants, with police officials, and prison guards (some of them Georgian). Most of the ethnographic and the anthropological data were taken from the literature, mainly in Hebrew, on the Georgian Jews (Elam 1978, 1980; Nishtat 1970).

The basic argument is that the structure and function (content) of the family, of the ethnic and communal groups of GJs, in Russia and in Israel, prepare some of them for involvement in organized criminality and organized crime enterprises in Israel.

The Ethnography of the Georgian Jews

Georgian Jews began immigrating to Israel about eight years ago, from the Republic of Georgia in the Soviet Union, where they lived for hundreds of years. Most of them lived in small towns surrounded by agricultural communities. A large number also lived in big towns, mainly in Tiflis, the capital of the state.

In Russia they were a marginal group. First, by the very fact of being Jews, especially very Orthodox and observant religiously. Secondly, their religiosity led to isolation, so that they lived in their own neighborhoods in large extended-family households. Thirdly, in terms of Russian standards, they

were often rich. They were engaged in commerce—both legitimate and illegitimate, smuggling goods, such as fruits and vegetables from the rural areas
to towns, even to faraway cities like Moscow. Those who were not merchants, vendor sellers, peddlers (deviant economic roles in Russia) or artisans, and who worked in various government plants, warehouses, and so on
tended, like many Russians, to engage in heavy pilfering or in moonlighting
businesses; in selling raw material or finished products often, again pilfered
from their work site.

The GJs profess a disdain toward physical and manual work. They social-
ize their sons to look on such work as "dishonored." Much preferred and
valued is "brainwork," that is, trading, owning businesses, operated by speculation, scheming, and cunning. The GJs admit that in Russia they formed
corruptive relationships with the authorities: police, licensing boards, plant
and service management; and with whomever they felt such illicit bargaining
was necessary.

When the GJs immigrated to Israel in large groups consisting of extended
families, whole communities were housed by the government in development
towns and in separate neighborhoods in the old towns. This prevented them
from developing contacts with other groups in Israeli society, and enhanced
their already separatist and self-isolated individual and group behaviour.
Their special language, that even Russians could not understand, helped in
maintaining the traditional patterns of ecological closure and social and cultural self-containment.

Georgian Jews immigrated to Israel for messianic religious reasons, and
not because of secular-national ideology. Thus, they see no need to integrate
into the host society. They look down, even angrily, on Israeli society as secular and permissive, especially with regard to attire, female behavior, and
other cultural customs, as well as religious observance. The insularity of the
GJs prevented and hampered those among them who wished to be a part of
Israeli society from assimilating or integrating into it.

Occupationally, in comparison with Jewish immigrants from other parts
of Russia, the GJs are almost all non-professionals, non-academic, with low
levels of educational achievement. They disdain not only physical labor but
academic and professional employment as well.[6] They believe in wealth accumulated through sharp trading and speculation and assume that "dishonesty
in business is natural and normal."

Women in the group are relegated to the role of household caretakers.
Girls aged 14 to 15 are wedded to boys 16 to 17 in prearranged marriages.
Girls are often kidnapped and threatened "to be touched" to enforce marriage on them or their reluctant parents. Thus, most women are uneducated,
and almost all are illiterate. They bear children at an early age. Young fathers
cannot, therefore, study or acquire a profession, but enter into a trade, go
into business with their fathers or close relatives from whom they have acquired experience and training.

Unlike other migrant groups that have exhibited signs of disorganization, or the waning of cultural traditions, and the marked weakening of ethnic co-hesiveness and solidarity, the GJs show the reverse process — a strengthening of their ethnic-community cohesiveness and group consciousness. This can be explained by their social and cultural background, and by their marginal exposure to Israel, their host society.

The cultural dynamics of the GJs will shed some light on their role in or-ganized criminal activities in Israel. We shall treat some of these in detail in order to explicate the motivational subsociety structure and goal orientation of this group. GJs show active loyalty toward religious dictates, which are practiced in group settings and in community gatherings. Religious practices that evolved around the synagogue and in family gatherings surround almost all spheres of life. What characterizes the GJs is that such events become oc-casions for large parties involving the family, the neighbors, and practically the whole community. These meetings become "potlatch" happenings where much food and alcohol is consumed.

Secondly, common to the GJs is supreme loyalty and attachment to the family and strong adherence to the patriarch's leadership. Marriage, as noted before, is prearranged; it is also patrilocal. The children, even when adult, are devoted to the mothers, and to each other. The men, as in many tradi-tional, rural societies, are required to protect the honor of the females in the family. A son, for example, will avenge an insult to his mother or sister with violence, even death. Centering social life around the family means also that newly married young couples, even with children, are expected to live with the husband's parents (patrilocalism). It entails, often, living in one very crowded room.[7] Although the government may have allocated a special apartment to the young newlyweds, they will still dwell with the groom's fa-ther if the apartment is not near to his family's house. Tight familial social life also means that it is relatively easy for the son, who's expected to do so, to go into business with his father.

Not unexpectedly among GJs the supremacy of the family overrides the obligations towards the state, including the army. This cultural feature is en-hanced in Israel by the fact of parents and children living and working to-gether; by the economic dependency of the young on their parents; and by patrilocalism and the general patriarchal culture of the GJs. It creates a well-knit multigenerational extended family with, for the time being, almost no generation gap or rebellion.[8]

The ethnic isolation and self-identity of the GJs enables them to see them-selves as special and superior to other ethnic groups around them. Therefore, except for business contracts, GJs refrain from social relations with other groups. They forbid intermarriage with other groups and any mingling or as-sociation that is not business oriented. Intermarriage between GJs and other ethnic groups is extremely rare and will result in exile from the Georgian community.

Solidarity and cohesiveness are further enhanced by the special language the GJs use and, also, by the self-enforced ecological separation of the GJs as a group. They are concentrated in five or six locales in Israel that are virtual GJ "ghettos." Those who were settled by the government, but not among their people, quickly drifted to one of the GJs' communities where their family or relatives dwell.

GJs' life is permeated by religious and secular ceremonies, which involve lavish parties. These ceremonies commemorate not only special religious events but also family or even daily occasions, such as the arrival of a guest. Through these "feasts," religious and ethnic identities are redefined and confirmed. Social ties and cooperation are formed and fortified, personal prestige and status are displayed, claimed, and confirmed. Other cultural features of GJ society that help to sustain cohesiveness and solidarity are the traditions of mutual aid and economic reciprocity. Georgian Jews are known to rush to the aid of their group members — family friends, or strangers — when one of their members is in trouble with non-Georgians, including the authorities. Aid is given in the form of money, lodging, or participation in the show of force or actual involvement in physical fights. Aid received creates obligations for helping one another when called upon in the future. It should be mentioned that we are speaking here of a "male culture," and one in which an emphasis on alcohol and prodigality clashes with the "Protestant" ethic of Israeli society at large. The spending of money on individual and group "happenings" has earned the GJs a bad reputation, also because they tend to be absent from work on the pretext of a party.

In the Soviet Union, GJs accumulated money and wealth by their involvement in illegal economic activities. This wealth could not be accumulated in banks or invested in business enterprises. Therefore, the money was lent to whoever needed it, or spent on homes, parties, and the "extras" one could buy in the Soviet consumer market. In Israel, too, the money they brought with them (which diminishes very quickly in the inflation-ridden Israeli currency) is lent to those whom one can trust without a formal contract and at almost no interest. But in Israel the needs for resources are even greater. This system of internal money-lending enlarges social ties and increases solidarity in existing relations. Money lenders enjoy influence and some power in the GJs' community, and their aid permits entrepreneurs to start new businesses. Giving money is also a prestige-conferring act and a status symbol. But the "real leaders" are still the traditional (religious) "wise men."

Money is in continuous demand by the GJs, for instrumental-economic and symbolic, individual and group, reasons. From Russia the GJs brought a pattern of acquisition that violates the legal and ethical structure of Israeli society. In the realm of economic activities, the GJs have "normalized" such dishonest business practices as theft, pilfering, burglaries of food stores and food storage house, and "fencing" operations. If bribery is called for, no moral compunction serves as a hindrance. This is what is referred to euphemistically as "brainwork," which can be practiced when one is so unlucky as to get stuck, for a while, in ignominious physical labor.

In Israel, most of the GJs are small merchants owning stores or vending stalls. Many do work in factories, but large numbers work as longshoremen or stevedores. Those who own shops tend to specialize in food, mainly as butchers, and those who have entered factory or service work leave as quickly as possible to become peddlers or shopowners in partnership with relatives.

Trading often requires automobiles, especially moving vans, which are very expensive in Israel. Among the GJs, money is often borrowed for this purpose. There are officially sponsored incentives: the government will reduce the price of the car, because as new immigrants, GJs are entitled to pay less customs and property tax on the vehicles. However, acquiring a license is problematic for GJs as well as any Russian immigrant. Driving licenses are obtained after one can prove about 100 hours of driving lessons in government-approved driving schools. The lessons and the tests are very expensive and the failure rates are very high.[9] Although Israeli law waives the driving test for those who can furnish a license from abroad, very few of the GJs (as is true for the Russian people in general) have driven legally in Russia or had a driver's license. Many of the GJs, not having such a license and with small prospects for acquiring one, resort to counterfeiting driving licenses for themselves and for other Russian immigrants. This has led to the development and expansion of the "industry" of counterfeiting licenses and many other documents, such as engineering diplomas.

The culture of the GJs contrasts sharply with their expectations and experiences in Israeli society, and in fact many of their customs are threatened with extinction if they embrace their new society and its customs. Thus the GJs are alienated and perceive themselves as "outsiders" in Israel. They cannot fulfill traditional social obligations that confer personal familial status and group identity; they abhor and are afraid of the secularism and permissiveness in all aspects of social life. They worry about and are hostile toward the compulsory draft. Entering the army only reluctantly, they develop devious ways to avoid the draft, including bribing of physicians or psychiatrists to issue false certificates of health impairment.[10] Or they simply counterfeit or forge such documents. They object to and are angry about the need for their young housewives to work, mainly doing manual labor in factories. It is an insult and damaging to their pride, and causes them anxiety, since they harshly guard the "chastity and honor" of their women.

Violations of subcultural norms produce severe reactions, including beatings, exile and sometimes even death.[11]

Corruption

Corruption, which is considered an endemic and damaging evil of the Soviet economic political system, is deemed by the GJs as means for the higher attainment of a style of life that they enjoyed in Georgia, but that is denied them in Israel. In Russia, avoidance of "red tape," coupled with the illegal advancement and protection of speculative economic enterprises, was possible through corruption, mainly in the form of money payoffs. An alert and enterprising individual could "move things," "cut corners," humanize a "heartless system." In short, "give and take" was the name of the game. This is not possible in Israel, where the economy is centralized and licenses are needed for almost any kind of enterprise. Red tape is rampant. Being new immigrants put the GJs at the mercy of, and made them dependent on, a highly bureaucratized government and municipal services.[12]

Further, the Israeli bureaucracy is considered almost absolutely clean of corruption. Officials can be swayed by a show of force or threat of violence, but not by bribery. This mixture of centralization, red tape, and incorruptibility led the GJs to view the Israeli state as rigid, heartless, and even "stupid." The GJs are curtailed in the entrepreneurial activities that distinguished them as a people. They feel choked. Thus, they have more reason to practice the old way of doing business, of offering "presents." They do so in the customs, services, in the licensing, housing or welfare bureaus; in any place it seems helpful or necessary. Their attempts to corrupt officials meet with arrest, trials, and imprisonment. In Israel, the law compels mandatory minimum sentences in prison, even for an attempt to corrupt a public official. This is in stark contrast to Russia, where every opportunity could be exploited somehow for profit. Businessmen and public officials are seen as basically corruptible and, at least, dishonest. And if the authorities — both police and bureaucrats — are not overtly dishonest, they are considered hypocrites. Thus, when asked to "wait for a decision," some of the GJs will immediately suggest "a gift" or an outright bribe.[13]

While in business there is much state interference (as in Russia), there is in Israel no such state involvement in the private lives of the citizenry. GJs see this as leading to anarchy and chaos, especially in the light of the leniency of sentences imposed by the court for misdemeanors and more serious offenses. The Israeli state is viewed as a bewildering system that is at once heartless, rigid, and even harsh, but weak in the area of deterrence and law enforcement.

Violence

Someone once said, "in the north part (the wealthy section) of the town they pick up the phone to contact city hall, in the southern (poor) section they pick up chairs" — that is, violence is often a substitute for political influence and corruption. Although they are not mutually exclusive, both have the same purpose — to convince, by "reason," an office holder to act contrary to the rules, and to create preferential results for the corruptor. Violence and corruption appear, also, under similar conditions: lack of resources to attain individual or group goals. Violence may ensue when the legitimate means to realize goals fail, and when the illegitimate but "silent" (corruptive) means fail too. As a group, the GJs are known in Israel for their individual and group violence. But as they testify, they brought this pattern of behavior from Georgia. There, when they could not reason with the authorities, they tried to achieve their demands by a show of force, or the threat of violence. In Russia, the GJs routinely used the threat of violence to change decisions made by officials, or to neutralize red tape, or when they had to react in order to avenge insult or damage to the family honor. Thus, when a GJ was arrested, they would converge around the police station and "negotiate" his release. This threat, together with a bribe, almost always succeeded. Violence among the GJs, compared to other groups in Israel, is often a collective event. "If a Georgian," they say, "is attacked, even his enemies will come to his aid, and his relatives will arrive from all parts of the country." Indeed, when one is attacked by a non-Georgian, or he is set to avenge an indignity he or his family suffered, those who happened to be in the vicinity will intervene on his behalf, and others will be summoned to help. This is why in cases of arrests of Georgian Jews involved in violence, it often is a mass arrest, and in cases of homicide more than one is often made to stand trial.[14] Violence is not only reactive, to real or imagined outrage to oneself or group, but GJs often initiate threats of violence, or engage in it when they think they are cheated in business, or when they come, often in groups, to government bureaus to demand their rights. Thus, symbolically, the group nature and cooperative feature of the threat and use of violence exemplify, redefine and contribute to the GJs' ethnic and communal identity. But it has given the GJs the reputation of being a quarrelsome and violent group, even when they have to face the police, city inspectors, or custom agents. Indeed, in 1974, they converged on the seaport of Ashdod when some of their people were fired for pilfering. The Special Riot Police were sent for. The GJs stood their ground, almost shutting down the whole town. The violence among the GJs is accentuated because of a constant suspicion of their involvement in pilfering and contraband; consequently they are subjected to searches, inspections and interrogations by control agencies.[15]

Their violence is also encouraged because in many service bureaus the threat of violence works. Moreover, they are further stimulated to violence by their perception of the law as "weak and soft." This is because the police and the courts in Israel "understand the plight of new immigrants." Police tend to resort to mediation, and the courts are known to show "special consideration" toward new immigrants.

Now that we have charted what we assume to be the conditions that prepared, contributed, and accelerated the entrance of the GJs into the crime scene of Israel, and those that oriented them toward special types of individual, group, and organized criminal activities, we shall examine their roles and activities in organized crime.

Georgian Jews in Organized Crime in Israel

While only a minority of GJs are officially known offenders, they have acquired a special status in organized criminality and organized crime in Israel. Their offenses are known to be concentrated in organized burglaries, mainly in food supplies and businesses. The amounts are huge and are partly used for private consumption, or to be distributed among family members for their religious and social gatherings. Part of the loot, however, is sold to retailers.

Some burglars are known to establish their own food stores or groceries or, small restaurants where they sell stolen merchandise. Others open catering businesses, supplying food (mainly meat) and alcoholic beverages. Other burglary teams have specialized in stealing from churches and even synagogues (in spite of their strong religiosity).

Engagement in "big heists" has led to the involvement of the GJs in fencing operations. Some became "fences" themselves, especially in stolen jewelry and valuable carpets. Merchants organized themselves and contacted existing organized underworld fences to sell them stolen goods. They were also sought by organized criminals to bring them stolen jewelry. Georgian Jews are trusted by the "native mob," since they quickly acquired a reputation for toughness, loyalty, secrecy, and hostility to the police and, therefore, they have a reputation for maintaining silence under police interrogation.[16]

The burglary rings are organized around a leader, often with criminal experience in the Soviet Union, who may even have spent time in Soviet prisons. The leader will tend to recruit brothers or relatives. The burglaries are well planned. Some of the rings operated for two to three years, and show the signs of professional work — for example transporting loot and stolen goods for fencing in an ambulance, or building hidden compartments in private cars to transport stolen food.

Stolen goods are often sold to Arabs, retailers in legitimate businesses, or to wholesale fences specializing in stolen goods. The Arabs are mainly from the occupied territories, especially the Gaza Strip. The GJs trust them because both groups share common animosity toward the Israeli authorities. Also, the Arabs pay cash on delivery, and they can better hide the stolen merchandise.[17]

Some of the GJs exploited efficiently their status as new immigrants, which allows them to import highly taxable goods to Israel.[18] They organized groups to buy, ship, and smuggle goods in very large quantities. Typically, one will go abroad to buy the merchandise and will arrange the shipment. With the help of some corrupted agents, they will avoid the inspection and taxes at the port of embarkation with the help of false Bills of Lading, issued by custom agents, or Bills printed in press shops specializing in forged documents.

Some groups of GJ criminals consisting, again, of brothers or relatives, burglarized homes of other GJs suspected of having jewelry, carpets and other valuables. Still other groups have specialized in home robberies and forcefully invaded those suspected of having gold or jewelry—they have no hesitation in roughly treating robbery victims.[19]

Some other GJs have entered the counterfeit business and forged document business; involving falsification, sale and distribution of drivers' licenses, professional diplomas, Bills of Lading and other legal documents.

These activities are described as "organized criminal activities" and not as "organized crime" enterprises. The reason for this distinction is that in these criminal activities of the GJs there were no known attempts to monopolize—to exclude other groups from operating in these lines of activities or to fend off other groups (Georgian or otherwise) from operating in the same geographical areas.

We can see, however, in some of these criminal activities certain elements of organized crime—that is organized criminality with attempts to monopolize the market. In the illegal selling of goods, only the "fence" (because of his knowledge of the prospective buyers of the stolen merchandise) can sell. On the other hand, outsiders can conduct business with them. Thus, the GJs can not and do not control the buyers' market. This is why we speak of "attempts"—sometimes successful—to monopolize criminal activities. Real monopoly, in the sellers' and buyers' market, is rarely, if ever, achieved.[20] In other areas, however, the GJs attempted, and for a time gained, exclusiveness and monopoly criteria that permit the label "organized crime" to be used in discussing their activities.

In spite of their disdain of physical labor, and because of what they thought of as immediate economic emergencies, groups of GJs agreed, temporarily, to accept jobs as stevedores in airports and as longshoremen in the seaport of Ashdod. Such employment has allowed them to organize pilfering activities diligently and effectively. From the interiors of the aircraft, they took from passengers' luggage almost anything they could lay their hands on; from airport storage they smuggled electric appliances, gold bullion, diamonds and other stored merchandise. In the passengers' halls and around luggage turnstiles they formed quasi-extortion rings that controlled the movement of personal luggage, for high tips. Any other non-Georgian worker, and even police or undercover agents who tried to interfere, met with violence.

In the seaport, the GJ longshoremen organized stealing and robbery from the ships, from the port storage places and from containers still resting on the ships or awaiting landing. Any attempt to bring in new workers, especially non-Georgians, culminated in violent fights. Efforts to stop these operations by replacing these workers led to a rebellion in which hundreds of GJs converged on the port, shut it down and almost closed the city from the outside. Riot police units had to be called in.[21]

Some, albeit few, of the GJs entered the illegal drug market, as financiers and as carriers, but not distributors—this, despite the fact that GJs completely frown on drugs of any kind. Groups of GJs took up residence in ·

Europe and got involved in robberies (in Holland or Austria) and in smuggling heroin to Israel (from Germany or Holland).

Success in all these operations led to connections with some "big shots" in organized crime in Israel. It is through such connections that the names of GJs appear in the files of "special criminals" under surveillance. After some five years, names of GJs appear also on the list of "big crime" and notorious organized crime persons investigated by the Shimron Organized Crime Commission.

Some Georgian Jews attempted to join the police force and the prison service, but the police weeded out most of them at the end of their basic training. A few remained in the force as auxiliary policemen. One of them organized a group of burglars from different places in the country. The group operated all over the country, burglarizing houses and storage places.

The GJ guards in the prisons are known to accept bribes for smuggling goods to the prisoners, or for delivering illegal services to them. Needless to say, they are very helpful to the GJ prisoners.

The profits from illegal activities are mainly invested in establishing private businesses, for example, small stores, or entering businesses jointly with others, mainly relatives. Investments are also made in enlarging houses, or buying larger houses for the family, so that young couples will be able to live with their parents.

If we remember the alienation of the GJs in Israeli society, and even the hostility towards its authorities, then the tolerance and acceptance of the criminal elements in the GJ community is more understandable.

Structure of Organized Criminal Groups

We have already mentioned some points about the structure of organized criminality and organized crime among the GJs. To recapitulate, we observed a network of social relationships that connect people together, but not only for criminal activities. They are grounded in ethnic affinity, and often family ties, or ecological proximity. This allows basic trust and secures cooperation. The actual criminal action network is based on the same elements as noncriminal activities. In addition, criminal relationships are also formed with outsiders — "fences" or with other criminal networks.

These organizational characteristics of the GJs' criminal networks are different from those of other organized criminal networks in Israel. They originate and operate on ethnic affinities, but accept anyone who has proved himself in crime, even if not of the same ethnic origin or neighborhood. That is, the "recruitment" is more flexible but contains one major criterion: experience in crime, sometimes shared experience in the same neighborhood of the GJs. Those with juvenile institutional or prison experience, and who are proven to be "upright men" are readily accepted in the group (unless they are mentally disturbed or addicted to hard drugs).

While GJ-organized criminal groups tend to consist of brothers, or relatives, leadership is exercised always by a Georgian, but not necessarily a relative or a member of the group. Most often the leader is older, more mature and more experienced in crime. In all the known groups the leader is permanently established in his office, unless he is arrested. In "fencing" operations, it is the leader who will order certain stolen goods, arrange the financing of the operation, and direct the distribution selling operations. He is somewhat like the "Brain" in Cressey's description of organized criminality in fencing enterprises in England (Cressey 1973). He is a mediator between the burglars and the fences, and not necessarily himself a "fence."

GJ criminal group operations are well-planned, with a practical division of labor based on expertise — knowledge of place, of the value of merchandise to be stolen, of "fences," and various skills. The groups also employ or use auxiliary people when necessary with preference, of course, given to Georgians. Corruptive relationships (which are necessary in the conduct of operations and the protection of members) were often formed with non-Georgian public officials.

What impressed police interrogators and prison authorities was the GJs' code of behavior, which is also a code of honor. Among the GJs secrecy is valued. It was always part of the GJs' tradition, for maintaining their religion and the integrity of their business enterprises, and it is enhanced by their inaccessible language. In Israel, their secrecy is further buttressed by their experiences as "strangers" and new immigrants. Criminals have additional reasons to maintain secrecy. Indeed, GJs under interrogation almost never break down. Those who confess, and especially "informers," are severely punished by the group.[22] GJ criminals, as is the case with other criminals in Israel, cannot protect their operations and members merely by corrupting the police. The GJs insure protection of their activities through the code of secrecy.

Some other organized criminal groups secure some protection by social relationships with city politicians, or with political VIPs on the national level. The GJs, and especially the criminal elements among them, are still outsiders to the Israeli patronage system, because they are relatively recent arrivals who are marginal in the political arena and in the economic power domains of Israeli society.

Some General Remarks on the Georgian Jews' Involvement in Organized Crime

Controversies over the concept of "organized crime" take, often, the form of specific debates over isssues concerning its structure, functions, social composition, background and base in the cultural value system of society; the social and political economy environment in which it flourishes; the types of organized relations; the extent of monopolization in the criminal underworld; the extent of infiltration into legitimate enterprises, and so on. Often these controversies focus upon insistence on the *structural* or *process* models of organized crime.[23] This is followed with a description and analysis of particular cases in certain geographical areas or in a certain line of criminal activity, or both.

In the case of the GJs, the structural and process models' descriptive and explanatory components have relevance since the group displays facets of each perspective.

In describing and explaining their criminal activities, structural variables were found to be operating, especially those of particularism and exclusivity (see Table 10.1). For the GJs these normative variables are based on ethnic and class uniformity, on shared value systems grounded on socialization into religious beliefs and practices, ethnic norms, and the fact of social and ecological propinquity. They are further founded on shared and common life experiences in Russia and Israel. In line with the structural model, it was found that within the GJs criminal networks and functions, the dominance of kinship relationships in recruitment and deployment of members was decisive. This explains the rigidity of the organizational networks, and their exclusionary policies, and especially their expedient, instrumental utilitarian relationships with the outside world. In some respects, the "alien conspiracy" theory of organized crime fits the realities of GJ criminality: the GJs are new immigrants and have transposed some of their experiences in crime into their new environments.

The existence of a gray sub-economy and black markets in Israel enable the GJs — together with other groups — to meet illicit demands that governmental policies have inadvertently created. However, the phenomenon of GJ organized crime varies from some of the basic features of the structural model. For instance, their involvement in crime is, indeed, for profit but not, also, for the purposes of assimilation, acceptance and social mobility into the national social status hierarchies. The gains from crime are not employed to broaden their reach within Israeli society but, rather, to foster prosperity within their ethnic social boundaries. Thus, unlike other groups who are involved in organized crime in Israel, the GJs did not develop extortion and protection rackets within their communities, preying on their own people in order to fulfill the larger cultural goal of individual material success. To be sure, they are involved in predatory crimes in the Georgian communities (for example, home robberies and burglaries), but this is very limited and incidental.

The process model emphasizes the economic processes that determine the nature of the criminal organization, and the GJ community exhibits some of these. A key concept in the process model is that of ethnic succession. Ethnic succession is a part of the sociopolitical dynamics by which groups who fail to achieve social and economic advancement legitimately, acquire it illegitimately through crime. However, what the GJs do is neither special nor unique in this regard. Among other groups, GJs operate across the continuum of licit/illicit activities and enterprises. Like other groups, such as the

TABLE 10.1 Georgian Jewish Criminal Structures

Model	Variable	Indicator
Structural	(1) particularism	(1) ethnic cohesiveness, exclusivity and segregation
	(2) acculturation	(2) uniform socialization into shared collective religious, economic and social orientations and acceptability of violence and crime as a legitimate way of life
	(3) authority and power	(3) patriarchalism; male dominance in familial systems, division of labor, and hierarchical leadership in criminal networks
	(4) recruitment and deployment of criminal network members	(4) dominance of kinship links; ecological and marital propinquity.
Processual	(1) ethnic succession	(1) kin relationships of participants in legal and illegal enterprises; degree of cooperation with other criminal groups
	(2) power brokerage and mediation across political domains & economic strata	(2) bribery, loansharking, corruption of public officials

Oriental Jews, they attempt to achieve monopoly in the market and geographical area in which they operate (Shelling 1967; Smith 1978). They are engaged in supplying, or mediating in the supply of what Smith (1978) has termed power brokerage in wholesaling of contraband goods; in product supply of stolen merchandise; and in informal banking (loan sharking). Indeed, the GJs have in the past operated in a rather narrow, circumscribed scope which has continuously enlarged.

Summary

The necessary and sufficient preconditions in the Soviet Union and in Israel that prepared many of the GJs for their immersion in organized crime activities has been described above. Briefly, the conditions favoring the persistence of a criminal orientation among GJs are: (a) various cultural customs and traditions in the GJs social institutional system, including a history of certain forms of economic criminality; (b) discrimination in the host society (Israel) against commercial integration of the GJs; (c) the structure of the Israeli political economy and criminal underworld that encourages relatively easy entry and participation in crime; and (d) closely related, a perception by the GJs of a weak, and therefore inviting, law enforcement and criminal justice administration.

In addition, the social characteristics of the Georgian community itself (the nature of family life and structure; ethnic and communal norms and customs; the emphasis on conspicuous consumption and disdain toward manual and professional work) contribute to their willingness and readiness to pursue criminal careers and lifestyles.

Involvement in organized criminal activities in Israel is fostered by a combination of still other factors. Among these are the political economy of Israel, with its highly centralized and regulated economic infrastructure of prohibitively high taxes and scarcity of goods stimulating the growth of black markets in consumer goods. Further, it cannot be emphasized too strongly that the comparatively benign law enforcement system promotes violence and lawbreaking. Finally, the existence of an organized underworld and a "gray" shadow sub-economy ready to absorb those GJs willing to break away from their collective communal insulation, as well as the existence of an apartheid-type social and economic sector within the Arab community in the occupied territories ready to cooperate with the GJs, function to stimulate participation in organized criminal activities.

The Future of Georgian Jews in Crime

If the socioeconomic forces and conditions noted above persist, it is likely that the GJs will continue, and even expand, their involvement in crime.

Changes in the economic structure and in the policies of law enforcement may significantly reshape the scope of criminal activities but not necessarily reduce them. What will happen will depend in part on the emergence of a new secularly oriented leadership that will urge the younger generation to assimilate into the mainstream of Israeli society.

A "Mertonian" perspective seems applicable to the phenomenon of intergenerational crime among the GJs. While some of the first generation new immigrants overcame the barriers and obstacles of prejudice and discrimination to achieve status, wealth and upward mobility through crime (Merton, 1957), the second generation will choose more normatively acceptable avenues in legitimate enterprises to maintain and achieve mainstream societal goals. The process is underway now to some extent in that those who are now involved in crime tend to invest their money in legitimate businesses from which, in turn, the legitimate business may be used as a front for continued illegitimate criminal enterprises. Or, it may not be so used.

Our discussion, however, provides another, more complex picture of the GJs. They may be perceived as striving for wealth, status and respectability, but not in order to gain acceptance in the national status hierarchy of the bourgeois mainstream of Israeli society. Rather, it seems that the GJs prefer to remain on the sidelines, insisting on a somewhat self-imposed marginality and differentness. In any case, it seems that they may be caught in a "Catch-22" situation where if legitimate opportunity structures do open for them, then both their legitimate and illegitimate behavior will alternatively be construed not as an instance of ethnic-particularistic behavior, but as deviant social behavior functionally rooted in Israeli society. These are speculations based on current social and economic trends whose unfolding will determine the social place and prestige of GJs in Israeli society.

However, some developments in Israel over the past several years portend some potentially grim developments in the near future. The economic recession with its concomitant high unemployment coupled with the policy of "last come, first to go," in hiring and jobs will adversely affect GJs — making it difficult, if not impossible, to start businesses, to move into better housing, and to acquire capital resources. In such circumstances, it would seem that predatory individual crime will continue unabated and many of those already involved in crime will enter into the lucrative illegal drug enterprises.

Notes

1. When the conditions are ripe, other groups have been known to enter organized crime activities in a relatively short time. Examples are, in the U.S. Colombians in drug trafficking and dealing; and Cubans in South Florida engaged in a variety of criminal activities.

2. We shall not dwell in this paper on the controversies regarding the concept of organized crime. Among the main disputants, see Cressey (1969), Albini (1971), or Smith (1978), and Block and Chambliss (1981).

3. Israel does not yet have organized juvenile gangs of the American type. Delinquency as a group phenomenon takes the form of relatively loose-knit "street corner groups."

4. Police in Israel are almost clean of corruption in terms of bribery. Very few cases have been detected. Corruption in the form of bribery and blackmail was discovered in custom, city inspection and some licensing offices. Corruption of city council members, state legislators, prosecutors or judges was unheard of. However, the politics of Israel is marred with patronage. No union and labor racketeering activities were discovered by Israeli authorities in Jewish labor organizations, although in the Arab sector they reported such activities.

5. The author of this chapter helped in writing some of the Commission's investigative reports, pressured politicians and the police to form the Commission, and was its scientific adviser. A sizeable part of the report dealing with the theoretical and "diagnostical" apsects of organized crime in general was written by this author.

6. One can find few academicians and professionals among the GJs. In both Georgia and Israel, professionals and academics are those who studied in Moscow or other centers of academia in Russia. Georgia had few non-Jewish academicians. Because of the "backwardness of the state," professionals and academicians enjoyed high status and special privileges there, and most of the Jewish academicians and professionals chose not to emigrate.

7. It is known that the GJs lived in big houses in the homeland, with sons and their families clustering in or around the father's residence.

8. Rebellion is exemplified by the son or daughter marrying someone from another ethnic group, or willingly accepting housing far from the patriarch household.

9. To fail the driving test twice is seen as normal.

10. Rings of corrupted physicians and psychiatrists were broken by the authorities. Most of the "clients" were GJs who were helped by a go-between GJ soldier. Because most of the young GJ recruits are already married, they serve in units near their home, which again impedes their integration into the Israeli society. Their frequent assignment to "service units" — for example, food storage units and kitchens — led to continual wholesale thefts of food by GJ soldiers. Other non-Georgians were also apprehended but the GJ was involved more blatantly.

11. An unmarried woman who loses her virginity cannot marry within the group. If this is discovered on the wedding night the marriage is annulled. An "unfaithful" wife can expect severe beatings, even death.

12. Israeli economic and social welfare life are very centralized. Immigrants come under the auspices of several government ministries known for their red tape.

13. The GJs have a widespread reputation as corruptors and corruptees in Israel. Many stories of corruption attempted by the GJs have become legend among officials in the custom and civil services.

14. We know of cases of homicide in which the events were like a "ritual murder," each person present knifing the victim with a weapon passed from one to another.

15. Because of dissatisfaction with their public housing apartments, which are indeed much smaller than they occupied in Russia, the GJs often enlarge their dwellings without city permission. They also invade public places such as public shelters or gardens and build on them small stores, destroying all the planting invested in by the state and municipal housing authorities.

16. Police admit that it is almost impossible to make a deal with them. They maintain silence under extreme forms of interrogation. Cases are known in which one group member took the "rap" and a very long prison sentence, while he was only marginally involved, almost an onlooker at the scene of crime.

17. However, it is often through these Arab fences that the burglary rings are detected. This is because Arabs break easily under interrogation.

18. Taxes on electric merchandise are often 70 percent or higher on the retail price; Added Value Tax is about 13 percent; and there are other taxes as well. Contraband is thus a tempting, profit-promising enterprise.

19. Severe beatings were delivered even to old people. Some victims suffered major injuries. In one case, an old woman died after her gold teeth were knocked out.

20. We can see it in Israel in illegal drug operations, in which some groups achieved, for a while, an almost absolute monopoly on selling drugs in certain areas. But continuous "gangland wars" among the drug distributors demonstrate the futility of such ambitions.

21. The government at that time even planned to call the army. Mediation succeeded in calming the situation, and most of the GJ workers were reinstated in their jobs.

22. One type of punishment, probably the most extreme one, is vivisepulture, but with the head out of the ground. Severe beatings, destruction of the "traitor's" property, and ostracism

and expulsion of his family have been known to occur. Examining the various items in the GJ code, one finds it almost identical to that of any "secret society," criminal, political or otherwise, for which it is dangerous to reveal its identity or membership.

23. For the main studies involved in these controversies see: Cressey (1969), Albini (1971), Ianni and Ianni (1976), Smith (1978), Block and Chambliss (1981), Ianni (1972).

References

Albini, J. L. 1971. *American Mafia: Genesis of a Legend*. New York: Appleton Century Croft.
Amir, M. "Crime, Organized Criminality and Organized Crime." Part IV and V. In E. Shimron, *The State of Crime in Israel*.
Bell, D. 1970. "Crime as an American Way of Life: A Queer Ladder of Social Mobility." In Wolfgang et al., eds., *The Sociology of Crime and Delinquency,* 2d ed. pp. 165–79.
Block, A., and Chambliss, W. D. 1981. *The Political Economy of Organizing Crime*. New York: Elsevier.
Cressey, D. R. 1969. *Theft of a Nation*. New York: Harper & Row.
_____. 1973. *Criminal Organization*. New York: Harper & Row.
Elam, Y. 1978. "Use of Force Among Moroccan and Georgian Immigrants to Israel." *Plural Societies* 9, 4 (Winter) 1978:35–54.
_____. 1980. *Georgian Immigrants in Israel*. "Papers in Sociology." The Hebrew University in Jerusalem.
Ianni, F. A. J. 1972. *A Family Business: Kinship and Social Structure in Organized Crime*. New York: Russel Sage Foundation.
Ianni, F. A. J., and Ianni, E. R. 1976. "Organized Crime: A Social and Economic Perspective." In E. R. Ianni and F. Ianni, eds. *The Crime Society*. Meridian, ch. 11.
Maltz, M. 1976. "On Defining Organized Crime." *Crime and Delinquency* 22, 3:338–45.
Merton, R. K. "Social Structure and Anomie." In R. K. Merton, *Social Theory and Social Structure. New York: Free Press, 1957.*
Nishtat, M. 1970. *Georgian Jews.* Tel-Aviv: Am-Oved. In Hebrew.
Shelling, T. 1967. "Economic Analysis of Organized Crime." In *Task Force Report on Organized Crime*. The President's Commission on Law Enforcement and Administration of Justice, Appendix D, 1967.
Shimron, E. "The State of Crime in Israel." Report to Home Office Secretary, Government of Israel, Jerusalem, 1977.
Smith, D. C. 1978. "Organized Crime and Entrepreneurship." *International Journal of Criminology and Penology* 6:161–77.

11

Organized Crime as it Emerges in Sections of Africa

James S. E. Opolot
Atlanta University

Background

Until fairly recently, the crime problem in general — adult crime and juvenile delinquency — was but a faint stirring, and organized crime in particular was unthinkable in what outsiders (European adventurers, traders,missionaries, and colonizers) popularly labeled the "Dark Continent of Africa." However, since the 1960s and early 1970s, both adult crime and juvenile delinquency, as with so much else in the same period, began to undergo profound change. There has been a growing awareness that serious lawlessness, including even organized crime and such related offshoots as professional and white-collar crime are cropping up in much of modern Africa. An important question related to this phenomenon is: if organized crime exists in Africa, does it take on the forms and aspects that characterize it in Western societies, especially in the United States? In other words, in what respects is the African version of organized crime unique and to what extent does it resemble its counterparts in other parts of the world?

The purpose of this chapter is to analyze the emergence of the elements of organized crime within the contexts of the crime problem in general in several new African states. It begins by presenting a definition of organized crime in Africa and moves on to the organizations' structures, the casual conditions, costs, and preventive strategies as a means of shedding more light on the problem.

Definition of Organized Crime in Africa

The African version of organized crime, as it is being manifested in some sections of the continent, may be defined as a criminal conspiracy to make money through the exploitation of business opportunities and through corrupt practices that are evidence of the existence of political instability. Its perpetrators and participants include:

(a) businessmen and well-placed public officials who use their position to criminal advantage, in order to launch into smuggling, poaching, profiteering, racketeering, tax evasion, and illicit extractive industrial operations in search of valuable minerals, using ordinary people as frontmen;

(b) marginal businessmen who are closely connected with criminal activities and well-placed officials;

(c) criminal operators whose activities extend into highway robbery, illegal immigration, smuggling, drug traffic, and poaching.

Kibuka (1974, 20) notes the gradual change toward organization of criminal activities: "Instances of lone operations are giving way to groups and gangs. In most cases, these groups and gangs are still very loosely organized."

Types of Organized Crime Found in Africa

T. R. Pasha (1949) writes that in the old days when contraband hashish came entirely from Greece, Arab caravans smuggled it into Egypt across the Western Desert from Cyrenaican ports. The Arabs in charge were all armed — in fact, better armed than the Coast Guards — and did not hesitate to make use of their weapons. However, there is no longer any evidence of the continued existence of such structures in the new states of Africa.

In 1973, there were reports in West Africa of illicit digging and smuggling of diamonds out of Sierra Leone, an East African country. Also, a year earlier, the same magazine reported that smuggling was abundant on the continent, both from west to east and the reverse direction:"Smuggling of cocoa from Ghana into the Ivory Coast and Togo was a regular occurrence, while most of Nigerian cocoa goes into Dahomey and Nigeria, groundnuts are constantly smuggled into Niger." On the eastern side of Africa, the finance minister of Uganda under Idi Amin estimated that out of 12,600 tons of Arabian coffee produced in the country, only 2,600 tons were officially exported. "It is presumed," he said,"that an estimated 10,000 tons were smuggled out of the country into neighboring countries"(*Africa* 1978). Moreover, there appeared to be significant involvement of well-placed public officials:

The coffee culture has, of course, been most dramatic in its impact upon the elite — the MP's business, administration people — who have been engaged in the illicit trade. Depending on how much of the market they have been able to corner, their lifestyles have changed conspicuously. A number of MP's from western Kenya, who were shrewd enough to go into business before the field got overly crowded, made killings which allowed them to withdraw from the fray and sink their newly-earned wealth into more long-lasting projects far away from the scene of their ill-gotten fortunes. Some have changed cars, going for heavier Mercedes and Volvo models. Others have brought property. [*The Weekly Review* 1978]

A May 1978 report of *Africa* indicates that "recently organized bands of Somali poachers armed with machine guns have been traveling along a broad swathe of Kenya's border with Somalis shooting elephants and other animals, and leaving their carcasses to rot in the scorching sun." Not only Somalis but also people from inside Kenya reduced elephant herds from 25,000 in 1973–74 to an estimated 20,000 in the world famous Tsavo National Park (*Africa* 1978, 52).

Perhaps the best examples of organized criminal groups that are multi-ethnic but in which one nationality dominates were found in the smuggling of cattle in West Africa in the late 1960s and early 1970s. The dominant tribes were the Fulbe of Futa Jallon and North Cameroon, especially in smuggling into neighboring Nigeria. Frechou's research on the destination of cattle sold in North Cameroon showed that when the buyer was Fulbe, its destination was mostly for further commerce, but when the buyer was Kirdi, its destination was mostly dowry or slaughter for ceremonial consumption (Frechou 1969). In both countries, other criminal activities have developed. With the opening of canned meat factories (in Kano and Banchi in Northern Nigeria and Maroua in North Cameroon) and the building of new slaughterhouses with refrigerated storage facilities (in Ngaoundere and Maroua in North Cameroon) came an increased demand for cattle and higher prices, which thereby increased the incentive and the income of Fulbe cattle rustlers and smugglers.

Ad hoc groups, multi-ethnic in composition and chosen for their varied professional criminal skills, are perhaps found most commonly in international smuggling operations. An example of this appeared in *Africa Confidential* where it was reported:

> It has been alleged that at least one of the companies is controlled by people who have long been engaged in illicit diamond transactions. But since Sierra Leone exerts little control over such transactions, it is difficult to see why such a firm should wish to pay for the appearance of legitimacy. Some of the suggested names are unknown in the diamond world; other companies are experienced. In the end, the only reason for a firm to enter the Sierre Leone market may be a desire to bypass the CSD in London and to "cream off" the best stones in Sierra Leone. That could be a dangerous policy. But diamonds also attract gamblers. [*Africa Confidential* 1974, 7]

In the late 1970s, Hong Kong dealers were offering such high prices for ivory that elephants in the Central African Republic were in danger of being wiped out within the next twenty years, delegates were told at a 36-nation International Conference of Hunters. The Central African Republic Minister for Water Resources and Forests warned: "We are going to use military means including a spotter plane to fight this poaching which is carried out by gangs, armed with automatic weapons, from neighboring countries." He continued: "They are killing so many elephants that the Central African Republic will be unable to reach its aim of organizing 500 safaris for 1982" (*Times of Zambia*, 1982). Early in 1983 the Kenya customs authorities foiled tusk-smuggling by seizing a shipment of 56 elephant tusks valued at $37,000. This was just hours before they were to be smuggled to Luxembourg aboard an Air France jetliner.

The concept of "raids" plays a major role in the African version of organized crime. It refers to poaching and smuggling, and while it need not be restricted to poaching across national borders, it is usually a transnational operation. The *Area Handbook* for Kenya (1978, 384) indicates, "Particularly in the regions bordering Somalia, Uganda and Tanzania, where border raids, often marked by the killing of the victims, have long been a serious problem, four-wheel vehicles, submachine guns, and automatic rifles have come into use."

An official of the Bank of Sierra Leone disclosed that diamond output dropped from 307,000 carats in 1981 to 209,000 in 1982. The Alluvial Diamond Mining Scheme fell by 29 percent, while Dominco's output rose by only 16 percent. The official attributed the drop in Alluvial production to the massive rate at which diamonds were being smuggled out of the country. He also called for what he termed "the imperative need to dam this massive outflow of our valuable assets through unofficial channels."

In recent years organized crime in several of the new states of Africa has seen a regrettable and ominous development—the involvement of some young university graduates:

> In some countries young university graduates who are not readily absorbed into legitimate available jobs take advantage of this prevailing socioeconomic situation to engage in illegal activities. Their talents and potentialities are exploited in the furtherance of criminality. The offenses that attract their attention include smuggling, hoarding of commodities, black marketeering, illegal currency transactions and transnational thefts of vehicles. [Kibuka 1974, 18]

Just as in the United States where there have been notorious figures in organized crime, so it is in a few new states in Africa, at least in the recent past. In desert smuggling, for example, the best known and most formidable operator was a Tripolitan Arab, named 'Abd el-Ati-Hassuna. His base was at Benghazi in Cyrenaica, where he made up his caravans, and with his well-armed Arab escorts protecting his convoys, he would dash across the Egyptian desert and fight anyone who opposed him (Pasha 1949).

Conditions That Favor Organized Crime in Africa

Historically, the interpretation of and response to crime have passed through several consecutive but frequently overlapping phases. The first phase was the application, on the popular level, of nonscientific explanations for criminal behavior. An example is the demon theory, or any of its variants. Within this perspective, any person who failed to follow the accustomed ways of the group was assumed to be possessed by demons. Hardly any distinction was made between sin and crime, as in the medieval period in Europe, the theory of possession by the devil tended to merge with the Christian concept of original sin.

This type of interpretation has gradually given way to more modern views. Criminologists have come up with explanations of criminal behavior, resting on various types of theory—biological, psychological, sociological, and combinations thereof.

The available data suggests that a political-economic paradigm best fits the trends and developments occurring in some of the modernizing states on the continent of Africa. The approach taken here focuses on the ramifications of major structural changes that are occurring in the economies of some states, and the political realignments and social differentiations that emerge in their aftermath.

Among the major conditions that have played a decisive role in producing situations favorable to organized criminality are: (1) the introduction of a money economy, (b) the existence of political instability, (c) the expansion of international trade, (d) price fluctuations and variations in the marketplace, (e) urbanization, (f) unemployment. These features of economic change are of course not unique to African states but have appeared in Western and Eastern societies as well—often with similar criminal implications and new forms of crime.

The Introduction of a Money Economy

Long before the introduction of European money, exchange of goods for goods or services and bartering in general dominated economic activity in Africa. With the introduction of money by the Europeans came the ability to acquire what a person wanted and needed without the necessity for a mutuality of wants. The acceptance and willingness to use money as a means of exchange permitted specialization and division of labor throughout a growing and increasingly complex economy. The money economy led almost inevitably to an increase in robbery, burglary, fraud, bribery, and white collar crime.

The introduction of European money has had relatively gradual but far-reaching effects on African values, especially among the educated and entrepreneurial classes. In this respect, what Africa has been going through is reminiscent of Europe in the seventeenth and eighteenth centuries (Hanna and Hanna 1981).

The Existence of Political Instability

Again, as with Europe in the nineteenth century, Africa has been beset by political instability and the breakdown of political and social institutions since the latter part of the 1960s. With the deterioration of political structures, opportunities for both organized and unorganized criminal activities tend to rise in number. Perhaps the consequences of political instability as it relates to criminal behavior will be more readily appreciated if we look at the Uganda situation during Idi Amin's reign.

> The inventories left in the African businesses have been largely sold, and there are few in the shops now — and what goods there are, offered at unheard of prices. This has led to a thriving black market, often supplied by duty-free goods from shops or by goods smuggled from Kenya. [Gannon 1981, 141–42]

What had occurred, and more dramatically in Uganda but not exclusively there, was a panic when Europeans and others, not citizens of Uganda, were expelled. They made up a large part of the smaller traders and shopkeepers, the small manufacturers and retailers, whose exodus left a gap in the structure of the society. In this situation of extreme scarcity, crime thrived.

Expanding International Trade

Along with the introduction of European money came expanded international trade. The word "expanded" is used here because prior to trade with European countries there was international commerce between Africans and others, particularly the Arabs.

As the European — the British, French, Portuguese, Italians, Spanish, Germans, and Belgians — established colonies, they began to introduce their methods of international commodity exchange. They started plantations and opened mines for raw materials; they built roads, railways, waterways, and airports. By no means were all these developments legitimate and legal; they also included illegitimate and illegal activities. In either case, the trade opened up new opportunities for criminal exploitation at all levels, especially where valuable commodities were concerned.

Price Differences and Fluctuations

International trade results in a considerable amount of price differences and fluctuations. For example, a comparison of the official buying prices for cocoa, coffee, and palm kernels during the late 1960s and the early 1970s in West Africa shows the Liberian Produce Marketing Corporation generally offering rather higher prices than its Sierra Leonean equivalent — dramatically higher in 1974. Not surprising, therefore, is the fact that produce flowed illegally over the border from Sierra Leone to Liberia, helping to bring about substantial market increases in Sierra Leone (*West Africa* 1978, 586).

Urbanization

Organized crime activities in the new states of Africa tend to be concentrated not only on borders between two or more countries, but also in the cities and big towns. Kibuka comments on the environment as it relates to the increase in crime:

(a) The cities are characterized by heterogeneity, anonymity, rapid social change, competition, materialism and growing individualism;
(b) there are many opportunities for association among offenders, which can lead to greater criminal sophistication;
(c) there are numerous opportunities for a variety of conventional offenses. Some offenses, such as theft of or from motor vehicles, shoplifting, pocket-picking, certain traffic offenses and bank robberies are mainly committed in cities and towns;
(d) cities offer ready markets for stolen goods, including used household items, such as clothes and domestic utensils. Disposal of stolen property is not a problem within cities and towns;
(e) cities offer protection and facilities for new forms and dimensions of criminality. Thus, crimes like smuggling, black marketeering, printing of forged currency notes, illicit currency and drug transactions, as well as corruption, find their base in cities and towns.
(f) there is usually a concentration of law-enforcement personnel in cities; hence, there are greater chances of crimes being detected and reported to authorities. On the other hand, traditional arrangements for dealing with some offenses through arbitration and councils of elders are lacking. [Kibuka 1974, 19]

The *Area Handbook for Kenya* likewise notes:

Urban crime was becoming increasingly sophisticated, in the form of highly organized gang operations, daylight bank robbery, the use of guns instead of traditional *panga*, or long-bladed bush knife (despite stringent gun control laws), and the use of automobiles for street robbery.

Unemployment

Kibuka documents how unemployment contributes to organized crime activities in the new states of Africa. He notes that the ease with which organized crime and related activities are transacted is facilitated by:

(a) The presence of many young people not gainfully occupied, some of whom are highly educated (some with university education but who are not readily absorbed into available employment avenues). Some of these youths rationalize their criminality on the grounds of their economic survival in situations of uneven distribution of wealth and power;
(b) available modern means of easy transportation by air, sea or on land in and out of countries. The improved physical infrastructures within countries facilitate various modes of transportation. The more the countryside is opened up, the greater the chances for all types of criminality to spread out to every part of the country.
(c) The officially promoted tourist industries which frequently offer easy means of transacting illegal activities. [1974, 19]

Costs of Organized Crime in Africa

In addition to defining the types and scope of organized crime in Africa, analysis must also take into account factors affecting its costs in terms of (a) monetary loss or loss of government revenue, (b) inflationary impact on the economy, (c) loss of human life, (d) disrespect for the law or aggravation of the existing crime problem (both adult crime and juvenile delinquency) and (e) the erosion of personal integrity among the public and among those in positions of national leadership. An example of the severe problems associated with crime is found in the Zambia region, better known as the Copperbelt, which has been inundated with illegal emerald traffickers draining resources. Kibuka (1974, 18) has also noted that in some parts of Africa a thriving smuggling trade involving illegal dealings in currency and black marketeering has had disastrous consequences for the economies of the affected countries.

The preceding sections have attempted to portray the extent to which organized crime, relative to the crime problem in general, has become a growing disease in certain parts of Africa. We have examined its organizations, workings, "causes," and effects. In the following sections we will take a look at what has been done about it.

Numerous efforts have been geared toward arresting the growth and spread of organized crime in the new states of Africa. These efforts can be divided into two major categories: namely, governmental (formal) and nongovernmental (informal) efforts.

Preventive Strategies: Governmental Action

Governmental strategies of interdiction and prevention in the new states of Africa vary from one country to another and from one ethnic group to another even within countries. To illustrate these efforts, we will examine the following: (a) introduction of special law enforcement agencies and control systems, (b) legislation, (c) public denunciation, (d) introduction of stern penal measures, and (e) signing of bilateral agreements.

Introduction of Special Law Enforcement Agencies and Control Systems

As far back as the turn of the century, coast guards were introduced to patrol Egyptian ports in efforts to counteract desert smuggling (Pasha 1949). In order to put an end to profiteering and black market activities in Nigeria during World War II, the British Colonial government decided to introduce a control system known as the "Pullen System," named for Captain A. P. Pullen, Controller of Native Foodstuffs. Control boards were set up through the colony. The system was aimed at protecting the average consumer against exploitation by ensuring that foodstuffs were sold at fixed prices. This was to be achieved by bringing foodstuffs to the markets and distributing them through the headwomen to traders whom they recommended and then ensuring that the sales took place at the controlled prices in special stalls.

In more recent years, the governments of new African nations have introduced various measures to counteract organized crime. In Lagos, centers were established at several places, and in each market the government built a store and about 40 stalls. Similar control was exercised in the provinces although only salt, gari (a local food), and a few other items were under control. This measure would have attracted a great deal of support if the government had been able to ensure a continous flow of supplies and a proper check in profiteering. It was, however, unable to do so, basically because there was a lack of cooperation in reporting known cases of profiteering to the authorities. Thus, profiteering continued unchecked. As one official observed, control only brings one's own administration into disrepute "unless it can be enforced — and we cannot enforce it" (*West Africa* 1978).

Either in response to heightened public outrage or simply out of conscious duty, the Lagos State Police Commissioner announced plans to establish new police posts, several of which were check points in Lagos, as well as to embark upon systematic gathering of intelligence reports on criminals. Many observers viewed this as a move in the right direction, but a mere token step when seen in the light of the severity of the problem.

In the late 1970s, the Nigerian head of state, Lt. General Obasanjo, turned to one of the world's most unusual service companies, the Geneva-based Société Générale de Surveillance (SGS), to help curb short-changing by foreign salesmen. The inspection company, owned by less than 100 stockbrokers, primarily Swiss, contracted with Nigerian authorities to inspect almost all goods exported to Nigeria. Although it is too early to make an assessment of its impact on Nigeria's trade transactions, it was hoped that this plan would turn out to be effective. Nigeria has attempted to deal with the narcotics problem as well, by establishing units in 12 states to enforce drug abuse laws.

In the mid-1970s, Gabon ordered its security forces, police, and customs service to make strict border checks on goods leaving the country in an effort to stamp out alleged trafficking by foreign traders. The Information Secretary of State, Jean Boniface Assele, who also heads the National Security Agency, announced the measures after a cabinet meeting chaired by President Bongo on his return from France. The minister said the frontier checks would be imposed without infringing upon the rules of the Central African Customs and Economics Union (CUDEHC), but were necessary to prevent damage to Gabon's economy.

In Uganda during Idi Amin's reign, the government set up anti-corruption units under the command of the notorious British-born Major Robert Astles. However, the units were said to have met with little success (*Africa* 1978.)

In the late 1970s, in Mozambique, the government appointed an administrative commission to run one of the country's major industrial concerns. This was done following an investigation that revealed serious financial and economic irregularities in the firm's operations. The move was announced by the Minister of Industry and Commerce, Mr. Mario Machungo, at a meeting with workers of the firm Couretal-Mometal, which makes railway wagons, cranes, bridges, and other heavy engineering items. The firm was being run by an agent of the owners who had, themselves, fled to Lisbon from where they continued to make policy decisions for the company (*Africa Research Bulletin* 1978).

In early 1982, special operations were set up along the Ghana-Togo border to combat the smuggling of petrol, where a gallon was selling at far higher prices across the borders in Togo. This operation, organized by Ghana's Volta Region Students and Youth Task Foce, was also set up to check the illegal trafficking of the country's currency (*West Africa* 1982). That same year, on September 12, the Provincial National Defence Council of Lt. Terry Rawlings of Ghana ordered closure of all the country's land borders, to check the drain on the economy. Currency trafficking, smuggling and black marketeering were the major targets (*West Africa* 1982).

Recently, Zambian police mounted Operation Alien Clean-up, an attempt by the Zambian Government to control the increasing numbers of people (aliens and Zambians) with no official permits found in the restricted emerald areas. The exercise resulted in the apprehension of 529 Somalis, 187 Senegalese and 184 Zaireans, with others from Nigeria, Gambia, Angola, Malawi, Tanzania, Upper Volta, and Sierra Leone (*New Africa* 1982).

Not all of these efforts have been successful in curbing organized crime in Africa. For one thing, law enforcement agencies operating within a country or cooperating between two or more countries are in most cases as yet poorly organized to deal with the newly emerging criminal activities (Opolot 1981).

Legislation

Among the new states of Africa, Ghana is the country that probably has legislated the most frequently to curb elements of organized crime. The following are some of the Ghanian measures:

The Criminal Code (Amendment) Act — 1/3/62 (Act 108)
The Criminal Code (Amendment) Act — 3/1/63 (Act 157)
The Criminal Procedure Code (Amendment) Act — 9/2/65 (Act 261)
The Public Property (Prevention) and Corrupt Practices Act — 12/6/62 (Act 121)
The Corrupt Practices (Prevention) Act — 3/3/64 (Act 230)
The Commission of Inquiry Act — 1964 (Act 250)

In early 1978 the head of state, General Acheampong, issued a new Price Control Amendment Decree. This decree made it illegal for anyone to buy goods from an unauthorized source without approval of the Commissioner for Consumer and Cooperative Affairs. Those guilty of such an offense were liable upon summary conviction to between three and five years imprisonment without the option of a fine.

The decree also stipulated that anyone, "manufacturer, importer, merchant, wholesaler, retailer," or any manager or employee of any such firms, including trading companies, who directs goods to places not recognized by the Commissioner of Consumer and Cooperative Affairs, or who sells above the control price, would be guilty of an offense and liable upon summary conviction to between three and five years imprisonment without the option of a fine. The decree went on to say that such a person can, if the court is satisfied that circumstances exist, be sentenced to not less than three months imprisonment and a considerable fine.

According to the decree, an offender who is convicted of charging between 20 and 50 percent in excess of the controlled price shall be sentenced to a term of imprisonment not less than 12 months; and an offender who has charged more than 100 percent in excess of such controlled price shall be sentenced to three years (*West Africa* 1978). Although these decrees are specific to Ghana, analogous legislation exists in many other parts of sub-Saharan Africa.

Public Denunciation

In the early 1970s, the President of Egypt was reported to have declared: "Never shall I allow parasites to indulge in their unwarranted commissions. Adventurous exploits and profiteering and illicit dealings in people's foodstuffs will not be tolerated either." This statement was followed by a high-powered probe that precipitated a major political shake-up and the dismissal of 16 cabinet ministers.

In August 1973, the Sierra Leone minister of state, S. B. Kawusi-Konte, issued a stern warning to unlicensed diamond dealers. He cautioned them to desist from their practices or face prosecution. In an address to diamond dealers at the Kenema Information Center, he said that illicit dealers were not accountable to any authority, and that they consitututed the majority of those smuggling diamonds out of the country. The majority were foreigners and enemies of the state. He declared: "If you don't have licenses, pack up and go immediately" (*West Africa* 1973, 1094).

In 1979, in Kenya, President Moi's most spectacular assault on corruption came with his attack on the police force. His Attorney General, Charles Njonjo, accused senior police officers of being involved in coffee smuggling. As a result, the Commissioner of Police resigned and five provincial assistant police commissioners were retired (*The Weekly Review*, 1979). President Moi's campaign was seen as more than just a cosmetic operation, but how far he intended to go in attacking the establishment remained to be seen and events surrounding the recent coup attempt seem to attest to this skepticism.

Although useful in terms of increasing public awareness, the effectiveness of public denunciations by West African leaders is questionable. William John Hanna writes; "I am unaware of any such campaign which has had any lasting effect, or indeed has even led to many prosecutions. Various remedies from prayer to flogging have been suggested but none has been seriously tried" (Hanna and Hanna 1981).

Introduction of Stern Penal Measures

Many rationales for punishing those who have violated the criminal law have been advanced. The five must commonly cited purposes for such punishment are: (1) retribution, (2) rehabilitation, (3) special deterrence, (4) general deterrence, and (5) public education.

Retribution is the oldest rationale for punishment and is concerned with societal revenge (the notion that society rightfully should punish criminals for the harm caused by them) and with expiation (the idea that through punishment criminals atone for their misdeeds). In restraint (or incapacitation) the focus is on the isolation of offenders from society to prevent their committing other crimes during the period in which they are "dangerous." The implicit premise underlying restraint is that if not incapacitated, the criminal will commit further crimes. The other side of the restraint coin is the *rehabilitation and treatment program,* designed to eliminate the offender's need or desire to commit crimes after release from supervision. In theory, a dangerous offender needs to be restrained until rehabilitated. Once rehabilitated, there is no longer any need for restraint. There are different types of rehabilitation programs—job training, education, farming, shoe repair, animal husbandry, and so on. However, most prison rehabilitation programs leave much to be desired, often because of understaffing or because the theoretical base of the program is unsound, reflecting ignorance as to why people commit crimes.

The rationale behind *special deterrence* is that by exposing a criminal to sufficiently distasteful punishment, that individual will lose the desire to commit crimes. In *general deterrence*, unlike the previous rationales, the concern is not with the individual prisoner, but with the general public. It is hoped that punishment of offenders will deter other would-be criminals. Closely related to general deterrence is another function of punishment—*public education*. Conviction and punishment help inform the public regarding exactly what is deemed to be socially unacceptable. Of course, both general and specific deterrence and public education require public awareness of the sanction being imposed.

In the case of those convicted of engaging in organized crime in the new states of Africa, various combinations of the above rationales have been invoked. In Guinea, for example, general deterrence, public education, and retribution were all being employed when a native was sentenced to death by public hanging for illegally smuggling counterfeit Malian currency. This was part of the introduction of draconian measures (known as the "syli") by President Touré in October 1972, in his effort to reduce counterfeiting by foreigners. Guinean officials appeared to have been satisfied with the actions taken, since there was an apparent reduction of the volume of illicit exchange (*Area Handbook for Guinea* 1975, 325).

A more extreme example occurred during Idi Amin's regime when Ugandan authorities were ordered to shoot smugglers on sight. This order was also intended to affect farmers found engaging in illicit coffee trading. The dispensation of instant justice, without trial, and severe punishment, following trial, was thus widely used in several new African nations to combat organized crime. No such measures are ever completely effective, and the dispute as to their consequences in Africa is strongly paralleled by controversies in the United States and parts of Europe. In Africa, the numerous tribes, languages, nations, traditions, and life styles make even more difficult an evaluation of the effectiveness of severe punishment. As in the United States and elsewhere, crime and punishment thrive, side by side.

Bilateral Agreements

Bilateral agreements have a long history in Africa. In the south, four countries (Swaziland, Botswana, Lesotho and South Africa) have close economic links dating back to 1889. This situation is remarkable, especially in view of the geographical location of the three states in relation to South Africa, notorious for its apartheid or discriminatory policies. Both Swaziland (population around a half a million people) and Lesotho (population of 930,000 in the late 1960s) are entirely encircled by South Africa, while Botswana (population about 630,000 in the 1960s) is surrounded by South Africa and Zimbabwe. All three countries are landlocked and must rely on South African ports for access to the sea. In addition, the three countries are very poor and depend greatly on the South African economy.

Historically, these three countries were under British rule, and it was during this time that the link between them and South Africa was formed. This link was formalized in a treaty between South African and British governments in 1910. Following the independence of these countries, it became necessary to replace the 1910 agreement with a new one. Hence, on December 11, 1969, a new agreement known as the Customs Union Agreement among the governments of Swaziland, Botswana, Lesotho and South Africa was entered into, went into force on March 1, 1970, and replaced the 1910 agreement as of April 1, 1969.

According to the preamble of the 1969 agreement, the objectives of the treaty are to maintain the free interchange of goods between the member countries and to apply the same tariff and trade regultions to goods imported from outside the common customs union, thereby weeding out opportunities for smuggling of goods between borders.

The leaders of other African nations have made some progress in terms of cooperating with neighboring countries or with trade partners outside of Africa in solving the crime problem. For example, in January of 1972, Nigeria was reported to have embarked upon negotiations with her four neighbors to start intensive training of personnel as a step toward the curbing of smuggling (*West Africa* 1972).

On the other hand, some governments, both African and others, have sought to deal with illegal practices without formal understandings. Perhaps the classic example is Hong Kong. In July 1978, it was reported that Hong Kong, by virtue of an informal understanding with Kenya, had tightened restrictions to prevent ivory from legally entering the colony without an export license from its country of origin. About one-half of Hong Kong's supply of ivory was being imported from Kenya. Conservationists concluded that Hong Kong's action could probably save hundreds of elephants from death at the hands of poachers (*Kenya Sunday Nation* 1978). But cooperative measures of this type are rare, difficult to enforce, and often unilaterally abrogated.

Preventive Measures: Nongovernmental Efforts

Informal efforts of a nongovernmental nature range from the subtle to the overt. Whereas the former tend to be those of the average citizen, the latter tend to be those of the social critic who seeks to put into focus those issues that increasingly affect significant numbers of citizens. Such efforts are still in a rudimentary stage, require democratic means of expression, a government not repressive of its critics, in order to be effective. Nigeria, despite its tribal divisions, demonstrated such trends preceding its recent coup, but whether they will continue is unpredictable. Kenya is more advanced in having a society with a structure conducive to informal preventive efforts than many other countries in Africa.

Summary and Conclusions

Organized crime in contemporary Africa is a fledgling phenomenon—a set of criminal undertakings usually by small groups of highly placed public officials and entrepreneurs acting in concert with low-ranking members of society. Further, it tends to occur when certain conditions—such as political instability, the introduction of a money economy, increased international trade, urbanization, unemployment, and price fluctuations—prevail. The effects of organized criminality can be devastating. Attempts to deal with it have not, on the whole, been successful thus far.

In the preceding sections, some illustrations of the main features and developments of organized crime in several of the new states of Africa have been presented. Further study and comparisons are needed to determine the extent to which these developments are unique to Africa and the extent to which the African experience corresponds to that of countries in other parts of the world. In considering, for instance, the theory of ethnic succession, which is applied to organized crime in the United States, there arises the question of whether this phenomenon arises (or will arise) in Africa. To this, it can be said that there is as yet little evidence of ethnic succession, but the groundwork for it is certainly being laid.

Organized crime in Africa has mainly involved smuggling, poaching, profiteering, some forms of racketeering, tax evasion, and the illegal digging and sale of valuable materials. While not as sophisticated or complexly structured as its American counterparts, these forms of organized criminality in Africa are usually directed by marginal businessmen with close connections to criminal activities and highly placed public officials who abuse their positions of trust and authority. At the lower level, and responsible to these officials and businessmen, are people drawn from the urban unemployed, including some college-educated youth. Other criminal activities extend to highway robbery, illegal immigration, and drug trafficking, which in many instances are also organized undertakings.

Compared with American and European criminal syndicates and so-called crime families, African organized crime is characterized by relatively loose groups of the same or mixed nationalities working alone or in concert with public officials and well-established businessmen who primarily smuggle and illegally sell goods and livestock.

Many African nations have taken steps to curb the growth of organized crime in their countries. These measures include: (1) establishing special law enforcement agencies (for example, the Egyptian coastal guards, check point police in Lagos, and governmental units inspecting imports entering Nigeria); (2) enacting legislation to prevent the growth and spread of organized criminal activities (such as Ghana's criminal codes regarding smuggling offenses and Kenya's ban on game trophies); and (3) bilateral agreements among countries operating to stem the flow of illegal international trade.

Much research remains to be done to clarify the underlying issues and processes and to provide a base for developing workable solutions. Criminology—the systematic study of crime and crime promotion—in an African context may provide a means of linking an understanding of both general crime and organized crime with the larger pursuit of nation-building, thus aiding in the struggle to establish viable public institutions and political leadership.

References

Africa. 1978. No. 81 (May; November).
Africa Confidential. 1974. Vol. 15, No. 4 (April 5), p. 7.

Africa Research Bulletin. 1978. (February 15; March).

Area Handbook for Guinea. 1975. "Foreign Areas Study." Washington, D.C.: The American University.

Area Handbook for Kenya. 1978. "Foreign Areas Studies." Washington, D.C.: The American University.

Bell, Daniel. 1960. *The End of Ideology*, rev. ed. New York: The Free Press.

Chambliss, W. J. 1976. "Functional and Conflict Theories of Crime: The Heritage of Emile Durkheim and Karl Marx." In W. J. Chambliss, and Mankoff, eds., *Whose Law? What Order?* New York: John Wiley, pp. 19–27.

Cressey, D. 1969. *Theft of the Nation: The Structure and Operations of Organized Crime in America*. New York: Harper & Row.

Frechou, H. 1969. "L'Elevage el le Commerce du Bedaildans le Nord du Cameroun." Cahiers d' Orstom, *Series Sciences Hamainas, 3 No. 2.*

Galliher, John F., and Cain, James A. 1972. "Citation Support for the Mafia Myth in Criminological Texts." The American Sociologist 9 (May), pp. 68–74.

Gannon, James P. 1981. *Managing Criminal Warrants*. National Institute of Law Enforcement and Criminal Justice. Washington, D.C.: U.S. Government Printing Office.

Hanna, William J. and Hanna, Judith L. 1981. Urban Dynamics in Black Africa. New York: Aldine.

Hawkins, G. "God and the Mafia." 1969. *The Public Interest* 14 (Winter), pp. 24–51.

Kefauver, E. 1951. *Crime in America*. New York: Doubleday.

Kenya Sunday Nation, June 11, 1978.

Kibuka, E. 1974. "Crime in African Countries." *International Review of Criminal Policy* 35:13–23.

The London Sunday Times. July 2, 1978.

New Africa, November, 1982.

New York Times, March 26, 1983.

Opolot, J. S. E. 1981. *Organized Crime in Africa*. Jonesboro, Tennessee: Pilgrimage.

Pasha, T. R. 1949. *Egyptian Service*. London: John Murray.

Salerno, R., and Tompkins, J. S. 1969. *The Crime Confederation*. New York: Doubleday.

Sexton, P. C. 1965. *Spanish Harlem*. New York: Harper & Row.

Sutherland, E. 1961. *Principles of Criminology*. Philadelphia: J. B. Lippincott.

Times of Zambia. June 21, 1982.

The Weekly Review. 1978–1979. (August 22, 1978; January 1979).

U.S. General Accounting Office (GAO). 1977. *War on Organized Crime Faltering*. Washington, D.C.: U.S. Government Printing Office.

United States Senate Special Committee to Investigate Organized Crime in Inter-State Committee (Kefauver Committee). 1951.. Especially *Third Interim Report,* Senate Report No. 207, 82nd Congress, 1st Session.

West Africa, January 28, 1972; August 6, 1973; March 5, 1973; February, 1978; May 16, 1978; September, 1982; November, 1982.

12

Organized Crime in Japan

Hiroaki Iwai
Toyo University Graduate School

Historical Background

The gangster organizations of Japan are composed almost entirely of professional criminals generally known as *yakuza*. They can be classified according to their origin as *bakuto* (gambling gangs), *tekiya* (racketeers, drug dealers, etc., among street stall-keepers), *gurentai* (hoodlums or hooligans), and so on. All these groups share some common traditional features, including a distinctive group structure, behavior patterns, codes, value orientations, and their own jargons.

The history of *yakuza* is very old. The bakuto (gambling gangs), for example, can be traced back as far as the seventh century. Gambling was already prohibited by law by the emperor in the year 689, but according to the book *Azuma-Kagami*, published in the *Kamakura* era, gamblers had already organized themselves. There are some indications that they were a prototype of the *yakuza* organization of today.

Leaving aside early historical origins, we can clearly see the emergence of the Yakuza from the seventeenth century. At that time, they were generally called the *kyokaku*. In the eighteenth century, particularly with the event of the collapse of the *shogunate* regime, the early *yakuza* activities became very conspicuous. Many of the heroic gangsters and bandits in Japanese novels and dramas are based on the lives of well-known underworld figures of that period.

These traditions of the underworld, with well-organized and strong ties, were passed on even after the *Meiji* in the last half of the nineteenth century, restoration. It is especially noteworthy that before World War II, the military authorities had tried to organize these groups into a nationwide organization. The attempt failed, however, because of Yakuza resistance to being controlled by any outside power.

Japan's defeat in World War II destroyed many cities, and urban residents were forced to scrounge on the black market to survive. In these circumstances, to stay within the confines of the law was extremely difficult for most people. Petty legal infractions were everyday events. These conditions provided the most appropriate seedbed for the growth of the yakuza who greatly extended their power and influence during this chaotic period.

Since the 1950s, with Japan's economic and social recovery, the law regained its authority among the people. Despite intensive industrialization and vast increases in urban population, crime rates remained relatively low. The yakuza, however, survived.

Demographic Distribution

In contrast to the closed, secret nature of American gangs, Japanese organized gangs are relatively open and accessible. Consequently, Japanese police have not had great difficulty in producing comparatively reliable data about them. According to police statistics in 1980, the total number of the organized crime groups is 2,487, with a total membership 103,955, with the arrestees among them numbering 52,382. The largest one is the *yamaguchi-gumi*, which has a membership of 10,528. Table 12.1 shows the trends in the

TABLE 12.1 Trends of *Boryokudan* (Organized Violent Groups)

Year	Number of Groups	Total Membership	Arrestees
1960	5,119	124,763	56,780
1961	4,970	162,450	58,924
1962	5,131	172,711	52,429
1963	5,107	184,091	51,065
1964	4,573	177,035	58,687
1965	3,944	156,293	56,704
1966	3,790	147,171	43,303
1967	3,750	142,660	38,573
1968	3,603	138,288	38,808
1969	3,500	139,089	38,180
1970	3,481	138,506	42,815
1971	3,214	129,432	43,527
1972	2,957	123,044	48,177
1973	2,723	114,506	52,877
1974	2,650	110,819	53,277
1975	2,607	110,042	53,053
1976	2,555	109,955	56,423
1977	2,502	108,266	57,351
1978	2,525	108,700	58,750
1979	2,517	106,754	51,462
1980	2,487	103,955	52,247

bōryokudan (organized violent groups, synonym for "yakuza") since 1960. As it indicates, the highest membership was 184,091 in 1963. At present, there is a downward trend, 51 percent in the number of groups and 44 percent in membership.

The ratio of gang members to the total number of arrestees of penal code offenders was 0.9 percent on average from 1976 to 1980. This is relatively high, considering that the number of members of these gangs is only 0.1 percent of the national population.

Offenses and Socioeconomic Characteristics

Of the total offenses committed by gang members, violation of the Stimulant Drugs Control Law was the most numerous, standing at 19.2 percent in 1980. This was followed by bodily injury (18.1 percent), gambling (10.5 percent), assault (9.2 percent), and extortion (7.2 percent). If we add together both bodily injury and assault, however, offenses total 27.3 percent, a figure that indicates the major role of violence in organized crime.

Looking at the percentage of those indicted for criminal offenses, the gangs rank higher than all the other Penal Code offenders, being 64.2 percent of total offenses compared with the latter of 56.2 percent.

In 1979, the first attempt to estimate the income of organized crime members was made by the National Research Institute of Police Science (N.R.I.P.S.). Two methods of statistical inference were used; the results are shown in Table 12.2. The average annual income per capita was 9,789 million yen or about 414 million dollars. This figure is nearly four times that of an av-

---

TABLE 12.2   Income Data on Organized Violent Groups

Source of Income	Amount (million yen)
Sales of stimulant drugs	45,796,100
Bookmaking (including speedboat, bicycle, etc.)	17,536,600
Gambling	6,919,400
Prostitution, pornography, etc.	6,642,900
Racketeering regarding business firms	41,212,000
Bouncer	43,002,400
Forcible collecting of loans	29,805,500
Supplying labor forces in illegal ways	166,400
Extortion	1,215,000
Fraud	538,700
Theft	36,300
Legal businesses	13,205,400
Total	103,761,700

TABLE 12.3   The Income of Major Organized Crime Groups

Yabuza Group	Membership	Total Income (billion yen)	Income Per Capita (million yen)
Yamaguchi-gumi	10,382	5,383 ($215)	17,730,000 ($71,000)
Sumiyoshi-rengo	6,194	5,336 ($215)	29,467,000 ($117,800)
Inagawa-kai	4,475	3,357 ($134)	25,670,000 ($103,000)
Other 7 organizations (including *Kyokuto-gumi Matsuba-kai,* etc.)	11,124	5,798 ($23)	17,825,000 ($71,000)

erage salaried person $40,000 in Japan which is 2,460 million yen $5,200. Needless to say, the real income of each member varies according to the group and his status within the group. Table 12.3 shows incomes of the major crime organizations.

Patterns of illicit income distribution are largely dependent on status within an organization. If we take as an example loan collection, the point will be clearer. Income derived from usurious loans is divided among organization members according to their status as follows: the Boss, 50 percent; *Kanbu* (executive staff) 25 percent; *Kumiin* (ordinary members or "soldiers") 15 percent; and *Jun-kumiin* (quasi-members) 10 percent.

There are, as well, significant differences in income and lifestyle among leaders or bosses. Some live in palatial mansions while others live more modestly in small, unassuming houses in quiet neighborhoods. Legal businesses such as construction firms, harbor works, entertainment, restaurants, taverns, street vending, and money-lending are just some of the enterprises into which illegal income is invested.

Politics and Crime

The involvement of the yakuza with the political system has occurred historically in three stages. The first major penetration took place during the immediate postwar period, between 1945–1950, when Japan was occupied. The leaders of the yakuza themselves sought to enter into politics directly, with some partial successes on the local levels. But as the nation as a whole regained its strength, the yakuza were gradually excluded from the political world by public pressure. In the second phase, organized crime figures turned from the highways to the byways of politics, supporting the revival of the right wing. And even though the resurgent right lacked its previous influence and power, it took on a brokerage function in the interface between the political spheres and the underworld, acting as intermediaries between some of the conservative dietmen and yakuza leaders. However, this honeymoon did not last long. Since the early 1960s, newspapers and other mass media have waged campaigns against these corrupt connections. Intense criticism and protest spread among the public once again. Politicians could not ignore the voice of the people in the new democratic Japan, and with the death of the old conservatives of the prewar type, corrupt liaisons with gangsterism declined noticeably.

In the third contemporary stage, the political environment surrounding the yakuza has changed remarkably: the political connections with the yakuza seemed limited to small sections at local levels, for instance, members of municipal assemblies. Governors and mayors and others prominent in the arena of national politics now have almost no relations with them. As to the police themselves, they have maintained a strong tradition and history of incorruptibility. Policemen, especially experienced detectives, do sometimes utilize gangsters as informants in the search for other criminals, and as a consequence there is a danger — although remote — of going "for wool and coming back shorn," that is to say, of policemen who develop associations with yakuza for purposes of information and intelligence becoming contaminated by contact with them.

Types of Organized Criminal Groups

(1) Gamblers

As has been stated, gambling is illegal, and the men who work as dealers and run gambling houses have solid criminal group affiliations. There is a structure of authority and power within the management body of gambling syndicates. In Tokyo, for example, the gambling syndicates number around 40 including the *Sumiyoshi-rengo*, the *Inagawa-kai*, the *Matsuba-kai*, the *Tampo-ikka*, the *Kohei-ikka*, and the *Koganei-ikka*.

These groups possess a fairly well-defined hierarchical organizational structure and division of labor. There are eleven *kashimoto-oyabun*, or bosses in charge of loans, under the president. In addition, the territories in several areas of Tokyo are divided up among them, and each holds ruling power over the gambling places located therein. Subordinate to each boss in charge of loans — and known as the *kashimoto* — are three classes of proteges referred to as *daigashi* (managers), *dekata* (workers in the gambling establishments), and *sanshita* (general workers). Together these individuals in their positions carry on the operations of the syndicate.

The hierarchy of gamblers, consisting of the *Socho* (the presiding leader) and his subordinates described above, is unique to Japan. The structure derives from that formerly characteristic of the legitimate activities of ordinary merchants and artisans. The president superintends the group as the big boss who represents the whole family; the *kashimoto* is local district manager or boss; the *daigashi* assume responsibility for the operations of one gambling place and function as assistants to the *kashimoto*; *dekata* run the games as dealers; and *sanshita*, those at the bottom of the ladder of authority and power, perform miscellaneous menial chores such as cleaning the house, running errands, and the like.

The president is also called *hon-beya* (literally, the main room) as opposed to *shita-beya* (or inferior room). The president is chosen from among influential *kashimoto* on recommendations from members of the group. When there is no man with sufficient dignity for the presidency, or the position is occupied by several bosses, the whole family is disrupted. If an emergency arises (as for instance, an arrest), one of the *daigashi* takes on the responsibility of the *kashimoto* in an effort to preserve the family. A prominent follower is appointed to this position.

Dekata formerly were divided into *hondekata* and *sukedekata* both working to carry on gambling operations. *Sanshita* have different roles within the status system, which include watchmen, gate keepers, caretakers of footgear, inside servants, and ladder keepers, *teppodama* ("the bullets"), whose job is to protect higher-ups from policemen, or to risk their lives in violent confrontations with other gangs. Within the authority system both *dekata* and *sanshita* are called *wakamono* or *wakaishu* ("young fellows").

(2) Drug Dealers

Tekiya, the drug syndicates, were at one time called *yashi* and prepared and sold incense, drugs, and other pharmaceutical products in the nineteenth century. According to the secret histories of various traders kept by the bosses of the *tekiya*, drug syndicates were first formed during the age of Bunji (the seventeenth century A.D.) by Rokuro Takatomo Nagano, or much earlier by the sons of Prince Shotoku (A.D. 574–622). Whatever the accuracy of these legends as to the genesis of the drug syndicates, today they form a closed society that is well-organized and very powerful.

Various organizations with the family names of *Kyokuto-rengo, Anegasaki-ikka, Koshu-ya, Aizu-ya, Hashi-ya, Kano-ya, Masu-ya*, are some of the tekiya groups making up the 50 that dominate Tokyo.

In the tekiya groups, the *chomoto-oyabun* superintends his family. His assistants are known as *cho-waki* (lower-level bosses), and beneath them are the *yaki* (workers, dealers) who, in turn, supervise the *wakaishu* (the apprentices), or the young group. The first job for a newcomer consists of three years of the lowest apprenticeship, selling his boss's articles and goods for 10 percent of the earnings. In the second stage of his apprenticeship, the wakaishu obtains permission to work independently, buys articles and goods from his boss at near cost with his own capital and retains his total profits from sales. In the final step of his initiation, he may accumulate his own capital and purchase large amounts of goods from special wholesalers. Each stage marks a period of growing independence and responsibility for the initiate and eventual assimilation into the ranks of full-fledged membership.

(3) Violent Entrepreneurs and Power Brokers

The *gurentai*, groups of hoodlums who perhaps come closest to Western conceptions of the gangster, are unlike gamblers and drug dealers in that their product and service is power and violence — illicit violence. The gurentai, although they constitute another organized criminal group, do not have the distinctive structures of gambling and drug organizations. Nevertheless, they are organized and possess structure and approximate to some degree their counterparts in the enterprise syndicates described above.

Recently the enterprise and power syndicates in gambling, drug dealing and those engaging in violence involving extortion and murder have begun to coalesce into new forms somewhat indistinguishable from each other. For example, the *Yamaguchi-gumi*, the largest group in Japan which followed the tradition of tekiya in the past, today includes bakuto (gamblers), gurentai (violent groups) and others who have been subsumed under control of the organization.

Even in the case of nomenclature, the name *kumi* or *gumi* (company) instead of *ikka* (family) is often used today. And titles such as *dai-kanbu* (subleader), *jun-kanbu* (semi-leader) and the like, are employed as referents to status positions. Whatever the names bestowed however, no significant change has been observed in the basic organizational principles which hold these groups together.

Group Structure and Social Relations of the Yakuza

The basic unit of a yakuza organization is the *ikka*, the "family." *Joman-ikka*, for example, means "the family of Joman." This is a "fictive family" — not one bound by blood ties; a crime family in Japan is composed mainly of unrelated individuals, but this fact does not make it any less cohesive. Members of the same ikka are referred to as *miuchi* ("members of the same body"). This reveals the character of the ikka as a closed, organic group that assumes certain special attitudes and pyschological postures toward the outside world. The head of the ikka or gumi is known as the *oyabun* (meaning, "having the status of father or leader"). The members of the ikka are called, in general, *kobun* ("having child status," or subordinates).

The oyabun/kobun role relationships make up the central organizing principle on which the yakuza is based. The relationship constitutes a superior-inferior status difference with the *kobun* owing absolute obedience to the supreme authority of the *oyabun*. Kobun are not an undifferentiated group of individuals beneath the leader of the organization: there are distinctions and rankings within this level of the family.

Recruitment into the Yakuza

Admission into the ranks of the yakuza is symbolized by a pledge given during the "rite of exchanging cups" known as the *sakazuki-shiki* (the cup ceremony). In its formal aspects the initiation ceremony requires that all members of the *ikka* attend, with the *torimochinin* (the go-between; the arranger) or *azukarinin* (sponsor; guarantor of the initiate) present as intermediaries. Rice, fish, salt, and sake are placed in the Shinto shrine alcove when the ceremony begins. The oyabun first drinks and then turns his cup to the kobun. The kobun who is being admitted into the organization drinks from the same cup. The *torimochinin* warns of the solemn duties of the kobun:

> As long as you carry this cup, you must be loyal to the ikka and serve your oyabun with filial piety. Even if your wife and children starve, you must work for the oyabun and the ikka at the risk of your life. Your duty now is to live with this relationship for life. Consider the oyabun as your eternal father. Do not fear water or fire, and volunteer to undertake every difficult task.

Yakuza Organizational Structure

The idea of union, of an unbreakable liaison in these words does not necessarily capture the real relationship of reciprocity in obligations, rights, duties, responsibilities, and mutual loyalty between the oyabun/leader and his kobun/follower. While this alliance is sealed ceremonially and strengthened by the ritual symbolisms of the cup and the pledge, and the words of the binding oath resemble those of a biological son expressing his devotion and commitment to his father, the actual dynamics of the relationship are more rationalistic, prudential, and pragmatic than might appear.

The oyabun assumes the responsibility for the welfare of the kobun, furnishing him with the necessities of life and, if required, even sharing his food with his subordinates. In return, the kobun serves his leader unquestioningly, even at the cost of his life. The subordinate is obliged to follow the pattern of familial paternalism, putting the oyabun in the place of a real father. This relationship is the central organizational axis of the group. A secondary but no less important principle of organization that shapes the structure and identity of the group is the relationship between the ritual "elder" and "younger brothers." This may be described as a horizontal axis, as compared with the vertical axis created by oyabun/kobun relationship. Of the oyabun/kobun role structure, it may be characterized as a hierarchical system, and within the ikka there exists another set of roles in which other relationships of authority prevail. Among gamblers, especially, there has existed a hierarchical system of elder-younger brother kinship (kyodaibun), with elaborately differentiated kinds of relationships within the same family and traditional numerical ratios between membership groups. Today, however, as with many other customs, such divisions among the members of Yakuza organizations are disappearing.

Among the lower ranks of kobun, there are approximately three sets of relationships which govern interaction within a family: the brotherhood "exchanging sake," the "forty-sixty" brotherhood, and the relationship between elders and their younger protegés.

Brothers exchanging sake address each other as equals, whereas in the "forty-sixty" group the upper-status member refers to the lower "brother" as *kyodai*, and the inferior uses the word *aniki* ("elder brother") when deferring to superiors. In the third type of brotherhood, the upper status individuals call their inferiors *shatei or "my brother;" whereas, the inferiors address their superiors with the term aniki*, or "elder brother." These titles establish the status and power hierarchy and the order of authority within the family group.

The relationship between an oyabun and a kobun is expressed in terms of protection and service. The kobun offers absolute obedience, and in return the oyabun grants favors and offers his protection and influence. Kobun subordinate themselves for a variety of reasons. Clearly, the immense influence and power of the oyabun makes the decision to subordinate oneself easier. The boss's sphere of influence, called *nawabari* ("roped-off area"), forms the substantial structure of his power authority. The Japanese word *nawabari* originated in the ancient ethnic custom in which personal territorial property was designated by stretching a rope around a geographical space to establish its boundaries. Three meanings are included in the idea of nawabari: it refers to a specified area of territory, the right of the possessor's dominion over that area, and a boundary separating the territory from those adjacent to it.

At the boundaries of each group may be a confrontation of power. Among gamblers, a geographical circle controlled by a whole family is called *shima* (island) or *hibasho* (place of fire). The boss has general control over the management of gambling places within his territory and lives off the collection of a percentage of the profits, which he imposes as a sort of tax. He distributes his power over gambling places and areas by dividing his sphere among individual bosses — his relatives — and permits them to manage these activities.

A boss in charge of money-lending rackets keeps *bon* (a tray) and collects rents from the gambling houses and tribute from other rackets associated with gambling. The kobun take percentages of this rent money in proportion to their status and importance in the organization. Islands — spheres of influence and control — represent the "property" of the whole family and no infringement by others (outsiders) is tolerated.

Yakuza Succession

Ikka members perceive each other as relatives of sorts. They work together in opposition to other groups, and in so doing are welded into a closed and exclusive family. The name of the ikka becomes a symbol of the power and authority of the group. Since great importance is associated with the family name in Japanese society, the genealogical succession, or the succession of the head of a house (*atome*) is naturally a vitally important issue within the family. Therefore, the succession is announced with some formality in the relevant social segments of the underworld. The more influential the family name, the more circumspectly it is treated, so that other groups may pay it due respect. In the case of the *Sumiyoshi-ikka* in Tokyo, for example, the names of more than two hundred bosses including the presidents of the main families in the whole of Tokyo, in Kanagawa, Chiba, and in other areas, were listed in a leaflet as supporters of the succession to the headship of this ikka.

The succession to the headship of an ikka or crime family generally falls to the most powerful and influential follower who is or was under the direct control and supervision of the retiring or deceased boss. Usually he holds the title of *wakashu-gashira,* or a leader of young fellows. He must be nominated by the oyabun and receive the recognition of the family members. Occasionally, the leadership of an ikka may pass to the real blood brother of an outgoing boss, especially when the follower logically in line for the position is neither powerful enough nor influential to assume this position and maintain the family's prestige among the other groups in the underworld. This happens when there is dissatisfaction among the kobun with a candidate for the position. While a blood brother may become the new oyabun, according to the unwritten code, the boss's real son does not succeed to the family leadership.

When the boss transmits his family name to the family heir, he becomes a retired master, called *inkyo.* He does not concern himself with practical, everyday matters any longer. In some cases he lives on an allowance from the group. But even in retirement, the situation is not quite the same as if he had stepped down from a position, an executive position, in a legitimate business firm. The retired oyabun may enter into business, open a restaurant, or manage an entertainment enterprise, exploiting much of the power and influence he held during his active service and leadership.

The leadership change is accompanied by significant changes in the rank and standing of subordinates. In particular, a novice gets his position under the new boss as a "transferred young fellow," while a follower of the new boss is called "a handmade young fellow." Brothers of the ex-boss become "uncles."

Formation of a New Family

On occasion when a follower reaches a certain status in the hierarchy, he is given permission to train his own followers and become a small boss. He announces the name of his own family and, in accordance with his prestige, he is permitted to call himself either the boss of "a branch family" or the boss of "a whole family."

In some situations he can give his group his own family name, as in the case of the Ozu group, which was formed as a second generation of the Ogura group of the whole family Iijima; and Gijintō, which split from the whole family Kyōwa and formed a separate group, having declared their independence. Since the fundamental principle is "ability first," there is no such thing as dependence of a branch family on the main family based solely on tradition. Independence is a function of the ability and skill of the boss. The Miura group, for example, which is an offshoot of the Kyokutō family, does not necessarily serve under the sixth generation of the Kyokutō main family. However, as mentioned above, even in the case of an uncle, if he does not establish a firm basis for an independent group, he customarily subordinates himself to the control and authority of the stem family.

Intergroup Links Among Yakuza

The criminal syndicates and families have, as we have seen, fairly well-developed relationships organizing activity within their groups. They also extend their connections outward to other criminal associations for support, profit, and in order to present a solid wall of defense against law enforcement groups.

Nevertheless, Yakuza organizations sometimes find themselves in tenuous or difficult relationships with other groups. Then, in order to sustain and gain strength, they must arrange alliances with other Yakuza. To do this, they must develop broadly based acquaintances in the underworld by doing favors and performing services and thus accumulate what is called a "bank of obligations."

Leaders of the various families set up liaisons with others and form a "brotherhood relationship" among the bosses. Favorable relations among groups are based on agreements reached in these brotherhood relationships. Weaker bosses of less powerful families are constantly searching for opportunities to join in alliances with the more powerful bosses in order to secure the safety and raise the status and power of their families. In this way, an intricate and strong network of group relationships — often as elaborate as a spider's web — is formed. The practice of forming alliances among the strong and weak families is roughly comparable to the pledges given by samurai to military overlords in the Middle Ages.

In addition to these broad affiliations, bosses may also seek to build up reciprocal arrangements of aid and loyalty within narrower circles. That is, leaders of geographically neighboring groups may enter into supportive relationships. Moreover, it is not rare to find local confederations emerging for the purpose of generating collective violent power. Gambling, drug, and extortionate gangs may join together for these purposes. These linkages, however, are somewhat different from those among kindred groups of gamblers and drug traffickers, but all types will resort to all possible means to increase their own power.

The Concept of "Face" and Maintaining a Sphere of Influence

A yakuza group attempts to monopolize certain illicit and, where possible, licit activities, accomplishing this through alliances with other groups and through the distribution of power to various members of the organization in accordance with their status. Collectively, when others threaten an activity under the control of a family, all members are obliged to protect the honor and prestige of the organization.

Violent confrontations connected with gambling and other illicit operations are not unusual. When disputes occur, success in violent coercion depends upon mobilizing the whole family. Prestige, the notion of the family's "face," comes into play in maintaining hegemony over its clients and territory. The principal reason that a kobun pledges his obedience to his oyabun is in order to share in the "face" of the family and enjoy the wealth it generates within its spheres of influence.

In the case of the drug syndicates (tekiya), the sphere of influence is called *niwaba*—"a garden." This establishes the right to occupy a certain street or vacant lot and to open a street stall. At fairs and festivals in the past, a stall vendor would bring "greeting money," called "cost of arrival" fees, to the resident boss, who knew the area thoroughly. This sum is also a customary formal mode of deference among the tekiya. When the individual fulfilled his obligations to the local strongman, he would open his stall in his assigned space under the protection and supervision of this local boss. The boss would restrain competition within the trade and guarantee no infringements from others. When the vendor closed his stall, he would pay the boss another fee called "the cost of the place" (*bashodai*) or "the dust cents" (*gomisen*).

A local boss would ensure control over an area by obtaining licenses through negotiations with police authorities, shrines, temples and landowners. Places of operation were distributed on the basis of family names. Usually, those who acquired the more lucrative locations were members of, or associates of, the influential families.

The motives of vendors in paying tribute to local family groups are obvious. First, it provided an opportunity to earn a livelihood; secondly, it enabled a vendor to share in some of the power (or "face") of a local yakuza, which it would be difficult to do otherwise.

The attributes of "face" and sphere of influence are very important for both a boss and his followers, and it is characteristic of the yakuza to enlarge their circle of influence as much as possible. This means that they are expansionist and do not accept a policy of sectionalism—or "live and let live." Naturally, clashes among groups result, often developing into a struggle for supremacy. In fact, as soon as a boss becomes popular, another family boss is bound to challenge and oppose him. For this reason, gambling organizations tend to be relatively short-lived, with disputes over spheres of influence constantly arising. The very involvement of yakuza in these activities sets the stage for competition and struggle; consequently, the rise and fall of yakuza groups is endemic to organized crime in Japan.

Conflict Resolution among the Yakuza

Although struggle among yakuza groups for control—for expanding spheres of influence—is commonplace, the subculture of the ikka also contains mechanisms for compromise. Often, when the danger of a clash is apparent, a "go-between" may emerge from the brotherhood relationship who attempts to arrange a resolution of the problem through non-violent means. During the processes of bargaining and arbitration, the go-between does not settle the issues merely by reason alone, by weighing the claims and grievances of both parties; he usually achieves a solution through personal magnetism as well. Ordinarily, the go-between is a man highly esteemed, of higher status than either of the contending parties, or at least their equal. A meeting is arranged to reconcile the warring factions, in which the go-between brings the opposing leaders together in a room containing a screen separating the two. As the ceremony, called *teuchishiki* (the "clapping ceremony") proceeds, the screen is removed and discussions continue until finally two swords on a wooden stand are tied together with a single cord by the peacemaker. The representatives or leaders of the two sides then drink simultaneously from cups of sacred sake while all participants clap their hands in a special rhythm.

Characteristics and the Cultural Heritage of the Yakuza

The yakuza share many of the cultural folkways and mores of feudal Japanese society. Those characteristics are residues of an older system of social relationships and practices that were embedded in the cultural and social life of villagers, merchants, and craftsmen. The archaic styles of deference, authority, and hierarchy within the yakuza represent a kind of cultural lag. The idea of membership in a family in order to gain a place, participate, and earn a living bears a relationship to the ancient practice of the novice in a village traditionally seeking to place himself under the protection and guidance of a headman; or an apprentice seeking to align himself with powerful individuals outside the sphere of his family or family connections.

The purposes of a criminal group and the manner in which it recruits followers are actually only slightly different from the manner in which feudal lords maintained their power and attracted subordinates. Although there are differences in the ways in which a yakuza leader utilizes his followers, the motives of his kobun are initially no different than those of feudal villagers seeking out the powerful in their communities and locales. As in feudal times, the ambitious seek out the influential—the kobun looks for the patronage of a boss. By joining the retinue of a headman in feudal society or a yakuza leader in the modern era, the individual experiences a sense of power and may confidently take his first steps into society.

In modern times among the bakuto groups of the yakuza there is the practice of "taking off straw sandals," which may be understood as a continuation of some ancient Japanese village customs. Such deferential displays signified that one came under the care and protection of an influential landowner in the village. In the case of the yakuza, the practice symbolizes respect as well. The person who is the object of such deference is called *sewauchi* (one "being served"), and others who engage in these practices signal that they are followers and are forming a master/servant relationship by such behavior.

The process of subordination has some patterned steps culminating when the individual, after some time as a loyally obedient follower, is permitted to assert his independence and individuality. Among the yakuza the apprenticeship and its varied rituals function to school the individual in the basic skills and techniques of gambling, street merchandising, and violent struggle in the streets. Thereafter, the individual is permitted by his boss/patron to announce his acquired family name as a reward for accomplishments during his apprenticeship. After the period of mortification, testing, and tutelage, the candidate for membership is treated as an independent person, as an equal. This newly acquired freedom is the same thing one finds in a commercial house — the process of socialization into the business ends and the trainee enters what is called *noren-wake* or *noren-bekke* ("separation within the shop"). Especially in the case of the tekiya, it is natural to identify each member as a branch family or an independent, affiliate family as they are not unlike petty merchants at the bottom of the social hierarchy of the larger group. The branch family is not based on a blood relationship with the core groups but corresponds, instead, to a subsidiary or satellite family.

When the individual attains stature and acceptance, it means he obtains a "family name" — the name of the boss's family with its tradition and history. To give or confer the family (ikka) name is to permit an individual to also train his own followers and to assume the authority and prestige of a satellite leader within the yakuza.

The feudal custom of land partition among family members in a village or the lending or the division and subletting of a house, house properties, capital stock, and merchandise of a store has its modern equivalent within the yakuza in the partition of areas for illegal activities among groups of gamblers and drug dealers. These represent the spheres of influence of the so-called "island," in the case of the gamblers, and the "garden," of the drug dealers, which are divided up among the crime family members. In the boss-follower relationship within other types of criminal groups, the organization of territory does not apply — rather, members apportion the work of lending and distributing money, instruments and other goods.

These social relationships based on family membership and ties were rather widespread in feudal Japan. However, tracing the cultural and historical origins of the role relationships within the criminal social system is not sufficient to explain recent trends. First, the ancient systems are being gradually and systematically destroyed, or are too archaic to be functional in the modern industrial, urban nation-state that is Japan. Second, there are important differences between criminal groups and the old Japanese social systems. Some of these differences are as follows:

1. Pathological (criminal) groups artificially create combinations of individuals, whereas groups of farmers or merchants in the past were mainly

composed of blood relations — although they sometimes included others. The yakuza groups under consideration are heterogeneous organizations different from kinship and parent-children relationships.

2. In criminal groups, the relationship between the main family and the branch family is not perpetual, but is sustained for only one generation.

3. The solidarity of a yakuza association that includes a whole group of branch families is very weak.

4. Another point that must be made is that the criminal groups are composed of men who live in a rough and tumble violent world, and the spirit of the brotherhood is based primarily on internal and external group confrontations. This is the most important characteristic of the yakuza.

Structurally and dynamically, the yakuza exhibit the following characteristics:

1. A system of regular recruitment and mobilization of members has evolved; and, because of the violence associated with criminal groups, the yakuza have provided for rapid expansion through "cadres" — loosely connected gangs that can, when situations dictate, be incorporated into the main body of families.

2. There exists tight central control and authority by the oyabun over his subordinates, which follows from the oaths of allegiance sworn by both at the time of recruitment into the family. Frequently, this situation gives rise to a strong, usually unspoken, antipathy between the leader and his followers which may threaten the oyabun's authority and the cohesion of the group at large. In spite of the obsequious displays of loyalty and fealty, it is not rare for a kobun to reject his oyabun.

3. Historically in Japanese villages there were two kinds of brotherhoods: (a) the blood brotherhood that succeeded to the headship of a family, and (b) the fictive brotherhood of friends that did not culminate in succession to leadership. There are also two types of brotherhoods in organized crime groups. One consists of the brotherhood within a crime family, and the other is the brotherhood of kindred spirits, the filiation and confraternity with members of other groups. Interestingly, in view of the violence and mayhem that is so common in the underworld of criminal groups, this latter relationship is especially binding and serves several important functions. When the crime family member completes his apprenticeship and achieves full status, a camaraderie with individuals belonging to other families develops that may be more meaningful in yakuza society than the brotherhood relationship that forms within the same crime family group. Generally, excepting the formal relationship with the boss in the family, the brotherhood relationship with members of other groups is most important.

As a whole, despite these outside ties, a yakuza family is enclosed and insulated and made even more impenetrable by its use of a secret language. Within the society, the organization of members is somewhat analogous to a beehive. The complicated and secret rituals carried on among members during the succession to leadership and on other occasions, such as member induction or the settlement of interfamily disputes, strengthen group sentiment and enhance its cohesion.

The yakuza family is always vigilantly cognizant of dangers and attacks from the outside. In order to avert such threats, the members try to work in teams in their enterprises. Confrontations, disputes, dissolutions of partnerships, and other forms of competition characterize the yakuza — in fact the process of competition for supremacy among the groups is one of the most distinguishing features of the ikka making up the criminal societies.

Customs, Values and Personality Characteristics

As has been noted, many of the traditional customs, mores, and institutional forms found among farmers, peasants, merchants and artisans of premodern Japan may still be found among yakuza. This is not to say, however, that the yakuza are merely archaic throwbacks to the past. Their adaptation to the conditions of modern Japan has been successful. Their utilization of ancient custom has a function that is twofold: first, it enables them to develop a distinct identity and character; secondly, it affords some continuity with the culture from which they originate. Some of the customs are worth exploring.

The convention of *jingi,* or the traditional code of conduct, includes two general practices. First are the moralistic norms specific to the internal society of yakuza, and second are the unique forms of greeting and identification. The latter are employed to establish a relationship with members of other yakuza groups. When two yakuza meet for the first time, each of them will take up a pose. Stepping forward, slightly bending his legs, putting his clenched fist on the right femur, and stretching out his left arm each will recite at length his place of origin, present residence, the name of his oyabun, and his own name in stilted archaic language. When he has finished, the same type of greeting is repeated by the other party. Even before the proceedings start, each of them will have yielded precedence several times — at least three times — to the other. This form of greeting was also a characteristic of artisans in feudal Japan, when they travelled to the other parts of the country and met members of the same craft, or master craftsmen from whom they wished to obtain lodging and employment. This custom disappeared long ago among craftsmen, but is still practiced within the antisocial yakuza groups.

Another residue of past customs of the lower classes in society is the cutting off of a little finger to take responsibility or to show repentance for some failing or offense. This custom existed over two hundred years ago among prostitutes, but remains only among professional criminal groups.

The value system which is important for the collective life of yakuza includes *giri-ninjo* (justice and charity), *kao* (face), and *hara* (belly or guts). Some of these cultural values are exaggerated to a pathological degree in the case of yakuza. In actual practice, however, rules of compliance are revised downward in terms of convenience. "Face" is the core of behavior and has a direct relation to status in the yakuza group. The idea of "hara" includes not only guts (courage and bravery) but also readiness for action without relying on logic or theory.

In connection with this, we must look at the character of a yakuza. First, he places the highest value on the idea of manhood (*otoko*). The word "otoko" has various usages, such as "brush up," "raise," and so on, all of which relate to manliness, virility of character.

The second characteristic is aggressive offensiveness. *Uridashi* ("opening sale") means a willingness to attack a powerful counterpart. When an individual gains ascendance, another is expected to exhibit the manly traits by seeking to challenge him. This results in a continuous competition for power and position within the group. Those who succeed are perceived to be the best.

A third characteristic of the yakuza is the importance attached in their thinking to the present moment. For example, a yakuza would rather obtain a million yen a year now than a promise of 1,000 million yen next year. The significance of an orientation fixed on the immediacy of everyday life is also characteristic of the vagabond or those with little hope of a future, of those for whom the future is precarious. The yakuza thinks that life is uncertain and extremely volatile and, therefore, suppresses a future-looking orientation.

Fourth, the psychological makeup of the yakuza influences their view of the concept of "destiny." For many yakuza, individual life is seen as insignificant. Coupled with this is a belief that the self is somehow contemptible, requiring curtailment. The term "yakuza" itself means "a useless person," "human refuse." The yakuza thinks of himself as worthless and incompetent. In the exchange of words in the traditional jingi he deprecates himself and engages in gestures of self-degradation. At the same time, there is a fifth personality characteristic that contradicts the others. Apparently there is a conflict between self-expansiveness and self-denigration which suffuses his personality. The yakuza wishes to confront others and extend his power and influence indefinitely without being vanquished despite his projected low self-esteem and self-contempt. He has a need to succeed and sustain "face." When hurt, even slightly, he will fight no matter how desperate the situation. From a psychoanalytical perspective, the yakuza may be classified as a narcissistic exhibitionist.

Next, the yakuza typically thinks and acts in an extravagant manner. The world as perceived by the yakuza is a hostile world. Thus, his exercise of extremely formal patterns of courtesy and deference towards others is designed to control impulses that may precipitate anger and aggressiveness in inappropriate circumstances. The yakuza strive to maintain a cool, prepossessing posture psychologically. We can conceive of the character of the yakuza from basically two perspectives. On the one hand there are those individuals who prefer the association of what might be called "kindred" personalities, and consequently, actively seek out and enter into outlaw groups. On the other hand, there are men who, having entered into this sort of deviant group for one reason or another, acquire the personality traits needed for participation in the group's collective life. It may be assumed that these two personality types tend to overlap within the pathological groups — within underworld organizations.

Recent Trends

Having described the cultural origins of the yakuza and emphasizing the traditions that molded their society, it must be noted that the current structure of the underworld has drastically changed during the past three decades. These changes are attributable in general to the impacts of the modernization process Japan has experienced and revolutionary developments in the economic infrastructure of the society, including methods of capital accumulation, transportation facilities, and the new modes of thought the development has encouraged. As mentioned above, one of the most notable changes is that the traditional distinctions among individuals based mainly on family origin and social status have largely disappeared in the everyday activities of the yakuza. The strict barriers of birth and class among them have virtually vanished. Even the leader of gambling gangs comes from the leadership of the *gurentai* (hoodlums). Authority and leadership within the yakuza depend more on skill, cunning, brains, and stealth than on origins and privileges.

Another aspect of change that is discernible is the tendency toward centralization and the concentration of power, with large gangster groups absorbing smaller ones — a situation that parallels the legitimate business world in general. A typical example of this process is the Yamaguchi-gumi. Its expansion as a yakuza crime group began in 1960 and by 1976 it dominated 552 small criminal groups. The president, Kazuo Taoka (a third generation master of Yamaguchi) was a charismatic dictator.[1] He created a vast pyramidal power structure, with sub-groups organized down to the fifth level. The primary group members are concurrently leaders of the secondary groups. The secondary level consists of 85 groups; the third, 306 groups; the fourth 67 groups; and the fifth, 4 groups as of 1978. The groups from the second to the fifth level are scattered over 39 prefectures in Japan. While these groups enjoyed relative independence (as a unit) in their activities, they stood under the strong control of the president Taoka in many important respects, together forming a criminal combination of great power.

An example of another type of criminal conglomerate is the *sumiyoshi-rengō*. In this type, the bosses of the large families organize a federation and select the president among them. Although the president has the duty and responsibility to maintain the order of the entire organization, his power is not as absolute as in the case of the Yamaguchi-gumi. Each boss under the president has his own tight organization and branches of groups. The structure of

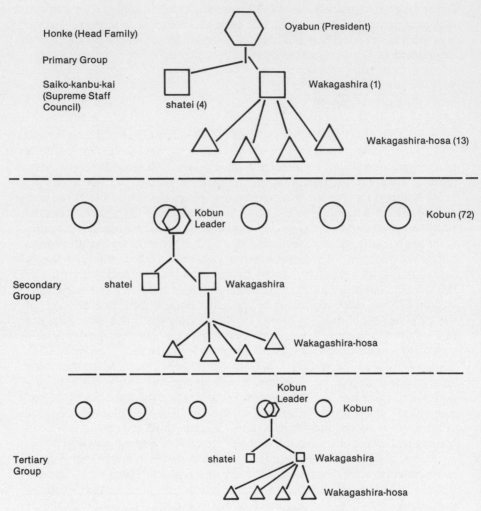

FIGURE 12.1
Structure of the Yamaguchi-gumi Criminal Organization

a unit group, which is more or less the same thoughout Japan, consists of secondary leadership cadres, gang operatives, and at the bottom, apprentices. The pryamidal organizations include Yamaguchi-gumi and Inagawa-gumi, while the federation types are Sumiyoshi-rengō, Kyokutō-rengō, Iijimi-rengō, Matsuba-kai, and others.

There have been many changes in their customs. For instance, the "cup-ceremony" on the occasion of the affiliation of new young members tends to become increasingly simplified year by year, while that of the succession to the leader's position has become increasingly ostentatious. Research on the changing rituals of yakuza was carried out by Fumio Mugishima, Kanehiro Hoshino and Kenji Kiyonaga in 1970. According to their results, those who do not perform jingi in the exchange of formal greetings (particularly the younger generation) have increased to 35 percent. Those who have tattoos on their bodies number 73.3 percent; and those who had cut off fingers amounted to 39 percent of the membership. Though the original meaning of the self-mutilation of the hand was to demonstrate sincerity, it is now usually in the nature of an apology for failure in the performance of a duty toward

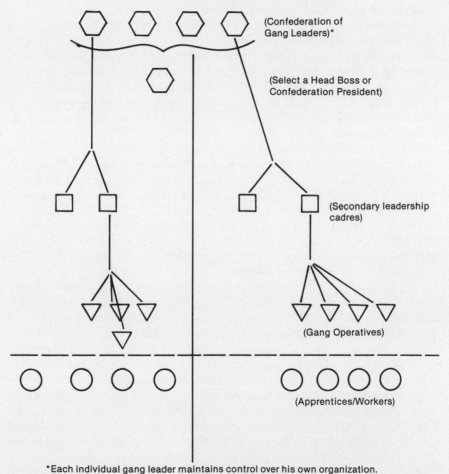

FIGURE 12.2
Structure of Sumiyoshi-rengo Criminal Organization

(Confederation of Gang Leaders)*

(Select a Head Boss or Confederation President)

(Secondary leadership cadres)

(Gang Operatives)

(Apprentices/Workers)

*Each individual gang leader maintains control over his own organization.

members of the group or the leader. There has been a tendency for the leaders to forcibly utilize this custom for the purpose of controlling the organization.

Policies and Implementation Process

The definition given by National Police Agency (N.P.A.) says that the violent group is "an organization or group which commits illicit violent crimes collectively and habitually, or has a tendency to commit such crimes." Almost the same definition is given in the Notification on Gang Control in 1961; that is, the violent group is "a group which threatens the lives of citizens with violent activities to gain money on the basis of organized power."

The police have waged a continuous and widespread battle aimed at their eradication. At the height of their power, wholesale arrests of yakuza were made on four occasions between 1946 and 1950 on a nationwide scale (September 1946, March 1947, June 1948, and January 1950). In an attempt to expand legal sanctions, the Act of Control Associations were enacted by the Diet in 1950. As the result of these efforts, gang activities were slowly reduced for several years. In the course of time, however, they gradually regained their power.

In 1959, one of the leading newspapers (*Mainichi*) began a campaign against organized gangs. This campaign coincided with the implementation of new police initiatives. The National Police Agency set up the Headquarters for Arresting Illicit Violent Offenders and ordered all police stations to appoint full-time investigators for this particular purpose. As the statistics show, the number of gang arrestees reached its maximum at that time. Since then, full-scale and semi-permanent policies towards organized crime have been implemented. A series of laws and regulations were enacted, including Assembling with Dangerous Weapons (1958), Intimidation of a Witness (1958), the Exception for Release on Bail (1958), and an Anti-hooligan Regulation in each prefecture, (1962, 1965). The first "cutting-off summit operation," which means to concentrate police energies on arresting the leaders of the organizations, was set in motion in 1958. To make this operation effective, the National Police Agency established the second Investigation Division in the Criminal Investigation Bureau as a special unit to give full attention to the problem of gangsters. In Tokyo's Metropolitan Police Department, the Fourth Criminal Investigation Section was set up as the unit to cope with the problem in 1959. Other main Prefectural Police Headquarters (for instance, Osaka, Kanagawa, Hyogo, Fukuoka, and Hiroshima) adopted similar measures from 1958 to 1972. In 1960, the Diet adopted a resolution on Elimination of Violence. Another resolution on the Reinforcement of Controls against Violent Groups was also adopted in the Diet in 1976. Wholesale arrests were carried out six times (1959, 1964, 1969, 1970, 1975, 1976), including three roundups of yakuza leaders.

One of the most important police activities is intelligence gathering on the structure, personnel and various activities of organized crime organizations. For this purpose, the Intelligence Center was established in each prefectural police headquarters. In Fukuoka Prefecture in 1976, for example, the Fourth Section in the headquarters division had 44 full-time investigators. In police stations under the headquarters, there were altogether 115 full-time investigators, 59 of whom had other concurrent duties.

As has been mentioned before, it is not difficult to get into direct contact with organized criminals because many violent gangs operate openly in large and small cities. They do not conceal their affiliations, even though they remain silent about their activities. Needless to say, the major intelligence effort of investigators has been to cultivate good informants. The information gathered is analyzed and classified according to the reliability of the informants and the accuracy of the information. Each center has accumulated data concerning the formal structure, informal interpersonal relationships, residences of members, and so on. The N.P.A. has a large body of research files on organized crime and illicit organizations through Japan. In addition to the exchange of information between each of the prefectural police headquarters, the data of the N.P.A. are sent to prefectures through a nationwide network. Broadly speaking, the information is analyzed according to various indices, such as size, hierarchic structure, solidarity and the characteristics of organization; finance, stability of incomes, and the degree of influence and power of the yakuza group. Organized crime groups are ranked in terms of these criteria in order to determine the efficient deployment of law enforcement resources.

The success of this program can be seen in the example of Fukuoka. The arrest rate in 1976 was as follows: bosses, 46.3 percent; executive staff, 52.4 percent; regular members, 44.5 percent; associate members, 56.2 prcent. Nationwide, the total number of arrestees among all gang members accounted for 47 percent per year on an average, for this decade.

The strategy adopted by N.P.A. at present is to insulate the leading members from the outer world by imprisonment, although this is quite a formidable task. Table 12.4 shows the insulation ratio of the leading members in seven major gangster groups in 1978. (The figures include both those who are serving in prison and those who are due to serve in the near future.) The N.P.A. is seeking to achieve a 30 percent arrest and imprisonment rate.

Obstacles in the Battle Against the Yakuza

Although some reduction and decline in the membership and in the number of groups is evident, the yakuza is still a deeply rooted element in the underworld. There are several reasons why total eradication is difficult.

First, crimes reported by victims are well below their actual incidence and frequency. Low reportability may be explained by the fear of reprisal. Witnesses are reluctant to make themselves known or available to the police.

TABLE 12.4   The Insulation Rate in Seven Major Groups

	Number	Percentage
Yamaguchi-gumi	41 (148)*	27.7
Sumiyoshi-rengo	40 (70)	14.3
Matsuba-kai	4 (43)	9.3
Nippon-kokusui-kai	1 (35)	2.9
Inagawa-kai	14 (83)	16.9
Dainippon heiwa-aki	9 (26)	34.6
Kyokuto-gumi	10 (65)	15.4
Others	87 (419)	20.8
Total	176 (889)	19.8

A sampling survey of Koriyama city conducted by the National Research Institute of Political Science in 1970 indicated that the nonreporting rate was 54 percent and the chief reason was "the fear of reprisal." People were worried that there was "no promise of solving the problem;" or, others averred that "the amount of damage is small," or that the cumbersome police procedure discouraged persons from coming forward.

The vulnerability of victims to retaliation was shown as a salient factor in the 1979 research conducted by the Institute. More than half of the victims had one or more vulnerable points. Those susceptibilities included the victims' own illicit activities such as tax evasion, illegal contracts, dealing in forbidden products, price fixing and bid rigging, loansharking, and so on. Such "weaknesses" create a climate for exploitation and victimization which the yakuza seem to have an uncanny ability of undercovering. Yakuza are, so to speak, "nectar-sippers." As long as there are irregularities, they can survive by imposing themselves into illegal activities. The problem, of course, lies to a large degree in the social constitution of Japanese society itself. Blackmail and extortion by yakuza will continue so long as people continue to violate the law themselves.

The second major reason why it is difficult to bring yakuza to justice has to do with their skills in evading the law. Even though in general the rate of prosecution against them is higher than that against other offenders — 64.2 percent as compared with 56 percent for non-yakuza criminals) — one of the problems has to do with gathering sufficient evidence against them to prove their guilt in court. As they are professional criminals, they are familiar with legal loopholes, and through the shrewd use of courtroom tactics when they are prosecuted, they tend to receive short prison sentences, fines, or suspended sentences. Large criminal organizations such as yakuza usually employ able lawyers and often succeed in avoiding convictions. The prolongation of trial proceedings is one of the common tricks employed by yakuza in avoiding imprisonment.

Third, the tight link between leader and follower also tends to subvert police activities. One of the main obstacles in seeking to arrest and obtain a conviction of a leader is the willingness of followers (kobun) to assume the blame and go to prison for crimes committed by their oyabun.

Moreover, the oyabun or leader is seldom directly involved in criminal acts. The loyalty of members and their desire to enhance their prestige among the leadership encourages many of them to do the dirty work for a boss uncomplainingly. In the relationship between an oyabun and a kobun, a verbal, explicit order is rarely needed. It is said that the best kobun should act without missing the slightest gesture or movement of his oyabun's eye. This being the case, the oyabun, and the organization itself, are well protected. For the young member, a term of imprisonment for the sake of the leader or the group is almost synonymous with a decoration of yakuza. When released from prison, he will be welcomed by many members waiting for him outside the main gate of the prison and will have a grand homecoming party at the best restaurant (this ceremony is called *homen-mukae*). By this sort of unquestioning service and obedience he will rise in status slowly but steadily, with a chance to eventually become oyabun himself.

To prison authorities, the treatment of yakuza is one of their most laborious tasks. There is always a danger that conflicts between gangs in the streets will spill over into the prisons. Nowadays the Section of Scientific Classification pays the utmost attention to sorting out the inmates according to their status and gang membership. Even if it is unavoidable that potential rivals or enemies must occupy the same workshop, the prison officers try to separate them physically as much as possible. Sometimes the news of strife among gangs reaches prisoners before the prison officers know it. To prevent this, prison authorities must make every endeavor to get information, constantly maintaining connections with the police and the prosecutor's office.

In order to cope with gangsters, the police have taken three basic steps. The first is the repeated arrest of gang members. As I mentioned, they are apt to receive relatively minor punishments. So the best measure at present is to separate them from citizens by repeated arrests. Secondly, the most important strategy is to cut off their resources and funds. Research on gang resources was carried out precisely for this purpose as a part of the policy. As Table 12.2 shows, the largest source of their funds is the sale of weapons and stimulant drugs. Almost all weapons and illegal drugs are brought into Japan by smuggling.

To prevent smugglings, international cooperation is indispensable. A single country cannot win the battle against smuggling without international cooperation. Japan has had international conferences with its neighboring Asian countries, including the Philippines, Hong Kong, Korea, Thailand, Taiwan. Through these conferences, the exchange of information, knowledge, and experience has been strongly emphasized. In 1978, the first conference with U.S. officials on the problem of narcotics control and gangs was arranged. Hawaii is regarded as one of the most important underworld links between the two countries.

Among their many methods of operation, yakuza tend to recruit new members from delinquent groups. Once a group of young offenders comes into contact with adult groups, their illicit activities increase dramatically. In Japan, the problem of adult gangs cannot be separated from that of delinquency. There are studies on the juvenile pools of reserves for the recruitment of yakuza in which age, family background, school performance, job career, status in a delinquent group, the degree to which yakuza values have been internalized, and overall alienation are taken as indicators of the likelihood of the transformation of youthful offenders into adult yakuza.

Conclusion

Undoubtedly organized gangs in Japan have their own traditional culture. Outside observers might conclude from this that Japanese citizens tend to be tolerant or permissive of the yakuza in their midst. But nothing is farther from the truth. To share common cultural characteristics is one thing, but to destroy peace and social well-being is another.

Some have argued that gangs serve, in a sense, society's needs and that they fill the gaps created by laws and policies that are at odds with the general culture. Gangs perform compensating services in a malfunctioning social system and will be tolerated to the extent that they continue to do so. The yakuza, however, are a cancer in the body of Japanese society; they are parasitic, exploiting inefficiencies and weaknesses in the political economy. By coping with the conditions that give rise to yakuza and sustain them, society can effectively eliminate them or, at least, sharply reduce their role in the nation's life. This means that collective social attitudes within the body politic must change in the direction of supporting police efforts at control and refusing to cooperate with the underworld.

Notes

1. In 1981, Kazuo Taoka, the legendary leader of Japan's largest organized crime group, the Yamaguchi-gumi, died. His organization's 12,000 members have enriched themselves since World War II in rackets ranging from prostitution and drug-dealing to gambling and corporate blackmail. Taoka's friendships and contacts extended to the highest levels of government, with two former prime ministers numbered among his friends. This kind of relationship reflected not only Taoka's personal charisma and success but also existing historic ties between gangsters and government figures. After World War II, Taoka revived the Yamaguchi-gumi and exploited the re-building of Japan in both the construction and entertainment industries. Recently, the Yamaguchi-gumi has been active in the sale of amphetamines smuggled from South Korea. Since 1937, when he was arrested and jailed briefly for a murder which was allegedly committed to avenge the death of another gang leader, Taoka has eluded arrest. The most that prosecutors could pin on Taoka after that were charges of blackmail and other offenses 15 years ago. The case was still in court at the time of his death.

References

Author's Note: Citations have not been used in the body of this chapter. Instead, I have relied on the following sources, a small list, in Japanese and English, that I recommend to those wishing to pursue their study of this subject.

Criminal Investigation Bureau of National Policy Agency. *Bōryokudan Kaimetsu no tameno Shoseisaku no Hiyō-tai-Kōka Bunseki* ("The Analysis of Cost Performance of Policies for the Eradication of Violent Groups"). National Police Agency. March, 1979.

Hiroaki, Iwai. *Byōri-shudan no Kōzō* ("The Structures of Pathological Groups"). Tokyo: Seishin Shobō. 1963.

Hoshino, K., Mugishima, F., and Kiyonaga, K. "Ritual and Discipline Imposed on New Recruits — A Study of the Traditional Subculture in Organized Criminal Gangs (2)" — *Report of the National Research Institute of Political Science* 12, No. 2 (December 1971).

Kanehiro, Hoshino. "Victims of Organized Crime and the Process of Victimization." *Report of the National Research Institute of Political Science* 20, No. 2 (December, 1979).

Mugishina, F., Hoshino, K., and Koyonaga, K. "Tattoo and Cutting off of the Finger Joint by Members of Organized Criminal Gangs — A Study of the Traditional Subculture in Organized Criminal Gangs (1)." *Report of the National Research Institute of Police Science* 12, No. 2 (December, 1971).

Mugishima, F., Takahashi, Y., and Tsurumi, A. "Attitudes of Citizens toward Violent Gang Groups — A Study at Kōriyama City." *Report of the National Research Institute of Political Science* 12, No. 2 (December 1971).

The Research and Training Institute of Ministry of Justice. *The White Paper on Crime*. (Annual Publication.) Government of Japan: Ministry of Finance, Printing Bureau.

Tokyo Hōrei Shuppan. *Bōryokudan Hanzai* ("Organized Crime"). Sosa Kenkyu, Special edition. Vol. 27, No. 92 (September, 1980).

13

Organized Crime in Australia: An Urban History

Alfred W. McCoy
University of New South Wales

Organized crime has recently emerged as a powerful force in Australian society, and syndicated vice now represents a significant share of the nation's consumer economy. Public perception and official recognition have, however, lagged far behind social reality. Although living in the most heavily urbanized of the world's major nations and several generations removed from the frontier, Australians have persisted in the belief that their society is still somehow blessed with a rural innocence and is singularly free from the vice of city life. Through regular exposure to American police dramas, Australians have generally viewed organized crime as a uniquely American or Italian cultural creation that could enter Australia only through alien contact. Charged with investigating his state's drug traffic in 1977, a New South Wales Royal Commissioner completely ignored the Sydney syndicates in control of a nationwide drug distribution network and instead concentrated his resources upon Italian migrant market gardeners involved in cannabis cultivation in a remote country town (N.S.W. Parliament 1979b). Until the late 1970s, it was customary for Australia's state police commissioners to deny the existence of organized crime.

In 1981–82, after a decade of scandals over crime and corruption, the Australian Commonwealth government launched a series of investigations which concluded that organized crime had become a serious national liability. In September 1981 the Commonwealth's Costigan Royal Commission identified a "flourishing" five-tier organized crime syndicate based in Sydney and operating throughout Australia. The Commission found that state and federal police response to organized crime was characterized by "ignorance" and incompetence (*SMH,* 8 September 1982). Awareness of the problem within the autonomous state police forces has also developed only recently. The State of Victoria, for example, established a Bureau of Criminal Intelligence within its police in 1977 and received its first major report on organized crime only in 1980: "The interim report establishes the existence of organized crime in Victoria. It highlights areas never before considered by law enforcement agencies probably because the expertise to conduct an investigation was not available (Victoria Parliament 1982).

Although Australian awareness of the problem only dates from the early 1970s, organized crime syndicates have been developing continuously in the country's major cities, Sydney and Melbourne, since the 1920s. As state parliaments sought to regulate personal behavior by imposing legal constraints upon personal vice — alcohol, narcotics, gambling and prostitution — entrepreneurs in vice and violence emerged in Sydney and Melbourne to exploit the new economic opportunities. Instead of disappearing or diminishing as the laws had intended, the supply of these goods and services simply shifted from the legitimate economy to create a parallel vice sector within the economies of these two cities. In Sydney four powerful new criminal syndicates emerged to dominate the combined cocaine-prostitution trade, but only one survived the razor gang wars of the late 1920s and the police suppression campaign of the early 1930s. Melbourne police were even more successful and all its major syndicates were broken by the late 1920s.

Profiting from blackmarket opportunities during World War II, a second generation of vice entrepreneurs emerged during the postwar period. Although the level of activity within the vice economy was generally high, the level of syndication remained low until 1966–67 when a small group of criminal entrepreneurs reached an understanding with influential elements of the New South Wales (N.S.W.) government and police. Following six months of gang warfare in 1967, the new syndicate took control of much of Sydney's vice economy and initiated a marked expansion. Existing trades, such as off-track betting and casino gaming, were modernized, and new ventures — abortion clinics, slot machine fraud, and drug trafficking — were introduced. By 1977 the estimated turnover in all Syndey's syndicated vice was $2,219 million, an amount approaching Australia's national defense budget (McCoy 1980: ch. 5).

After saturating the city's vice economy, Sydney's syndicates began an interstate and international expansion during the mid-1970s. By the end of the decade Sydney's syndicates had made contact with middle-echelon organized crime figures on the U.S. West Coast, established a working relationship with Southeast Asia's Chinese heroin syndicates, and controlled a significant share of Manila's prostitution industry. In their home city, Sydney's syndicates had, through their corruption of police and politicians, achieved a defacto immunity to investigation and were beginning to penetrate the legitimate economy — through property development, casino license applications and tax evasion schemes. In sum, Sydney's criminal syndicates, now synonymous with Australian organized crime, have achieved a level of influence comparable to the Corsican *milieu* in France or the mafia on the U.S. West Coast.

Analysis of Organized Crime

This half-century gap between the reality and the recognition of organized crime in Australia is due largely to a problem of definition. Instead of analyzing the whole of the vice economy and defining it as organized crime, Australian police have dealt with each of the separate vice trades in isolation. Similarly, the tabloid press have depicted Sydney's vice entrepreneurs as anti-heroic titans and shrouded the vice trades, particularly off-track bookmaking, in a romantic urban mythology. Like their counterparts in Britain and the United States, Australia's state police are organized on nineteenth-century principles of criminal action and police reaction. Once a crime is committed, its victim files a formal complaint and the police investigate. The universal standard of police efficiency is based on the ratio between citizen complaints and criminal charges. Police agencies are rewarded when the ratio of complaints to arrests is high, and individual police officers advance when their contribution to those arrest statistics is exceptional. Leaving aside the question of corruption, a traditional police bureaucracy using action-reaction methods will remain officially ignorant of a well-established vice economy. As provisioners of illegal goods and services — narcotics, gambling or prostitution — vice syndicates create not victims but repeat customers who have, under most circumstances, no reason to complain to police. Since their crimes are victimless, vice syndicates remain outside the knowledge of a traditional police bureaucracy. Hence, Australian police required a new definition of organized crime before they could recognize the existence of Sydney's criminal syndicates. In his 1982 report Commissioner Costigan found that most Australian law enforcement agencies had not identified the nature and extent of organized crime: "Indeed, in some of the agencies there is ignorance as to its existence." (*SMH,* 8 September 1982).

The study of organized crime in any society must begin then with an explicit definition. Most simply, organized crime is commerce by other means. From the Australian experience over the past half-century, we can define organized crime as the vice sector of a large and relatively well developed urban economy. It is a permanent, peacetime black market in goods and services in demand but not available — usually because of legal restrictions — through the normal distribution channels. Organized crime syndicates are coalitions of those entrepreneurs in vice and violence active within a city's vice economy. In analyzing organized crime in Sydney, or any other city, there are then two key factors which must be considered: (1) the overall level of activity within the vice economy; and, (2) the structure of syndicate control within that same vice economy. To determine the level of vice activity, we must examine the demand for all goods and services provided outside the normal distribution channels. It is not enough, for example, to know that alcohol, gambling and narcotics are legally restricted or prohibited. We must somehow establish the actual value of illicit goods and services provided before we can determine the overall scale of the vice economy.

With the economic base established, we can then determine the level of syndication by studying: (1) the hierarchy of control within each illegal enterprise; (2) the evidence for some linkage of syndicate control among the separate vice trades; and, (3) the internal organizatinal structures of the vice syndicates. In using this model to study prostitution, for example, we would ask: (1) the number and average income of a city's prostitutes; (2) the amount each prostitute is or is not paying to a vice trader who lives off the income of one or more prostitutes; and, (3) evidence that a prostitution syndicate is simultaneously involved in other vice trades such as gambling or narcotics.

Once we have established the degree of syndicate control, we can study the internal social organization of a criminal syndicate. Popular terms like "triad," "milieu" or "mafia" carry connotations of both the ethnic origins and internal organizational principles of well-known vice syndicates. The archetypical, quasi-military hierarchy of U.S. mafia syndicates is only one of a wide variety of syndicate structures. It is, then, the level of activity within the vice economy, the degree of syndicate control over the vice trades, and the internal structure of criminal syndicates which, collectively, have determined the patterns of organized crime in Australia or any society.

The Urban Setting

Unlike banditry or peasant mafia activity, organized crime is a distinctly urban phenomenon. To understand the rise of syndicate crime since the 1920s we must then know something of the changes in urban life that facilitated formation of the vice economy. In Europe, the Americas and imperial Asia of the late nineteenth and early twentieth centuries, rapid urbanization produced cities of sufficient size and anonymity to sustain a mass commerce in personal vice—prostitution, alcohol, narcotics and gambling. Initially, most of these trades were legal and largely disorganized. Gathering strength in the late nineteenth century, Western religious movements, largely Protestant, sought through moral and legal reforms to eliminate all forms of commercial vice. In a certain sense, these reform groups were seeking to reimpose—through the power of law and police—the moral consensus and social controls of small-town society upon the impersonal and multi-ethnic metropolis.

The reform movements achieved a string of major political victories during the first two decades of the twentieth century. By the 1920s many Western nations and their Asian colonies had laws restricting or prohibiting alcohol, narcotics, prostitution or gambling. These laws did not eradicate personal vice; they simply forced its transfer from the normal economy to an emerging vice economy. It is, in fact, this delegalization of personal vice which is the essential precondition for the creation of a coherent vice economy and the subsequent growth of organized crime syndicates.

While almost all major metropolitan cities developed something of a vice economy during the 1920s, it is the port cities of Asia and the West which provided the conditions most conducive to the growth of strong criminal syndicates. A hasty global survey indicates a significant coincidence of port cities and powerful criminal syndicates. Marseilles produced the French Corsican *milieu,* pre-1949 Shanghai the Green *Pang,* postwar Saigon the Binh Xuyen, New York and Chicago of the 1920s the major mafia syndicates, and Sydney Australia's most powerful syndicates. Most major ports sustained a waterfront criminal milieu of prostitution, smuggling and cargo theft that predated the rise of the vice economy of the 1920s. In port cities illegality can provide a source of employment — gambling, protection and theft for men; prostitution for women — in weak economies dependent upon the up-and-down cycles in world trade. Lacking stable industrial or commercial employment, en element of the port city working class often finds relief in the vice economy. Moreover, cargo transport and warehousing — the essentials of an entrepôt economy — are by their very nature vulnerable to outlaw expropriation by theft or related protection payments. With their large populations of transient sailors, stevedores and travelers, port cities had a sufficient population base and demand to sustain a loosely structured underworld. When legal prohibitions fostered the growth of large-scale commericalized vice in the early decades of the twentieth century, the established criminal milieu of the port cities spawned the powerful new vice syndicates.

Once established in a port city, vice syndicates often gain an exceptional level of formal and informal political power. In metropolitan cities with a strong industrial and commercial base, established burghers hold firmly to the reins of social control and block the rise of the nouveau. In port cities, however, syndicate leaders can gain political power by default since so much of the legitimate transport activity is controlled by branch managers of foreign firms with little interest in the port's political life beyond the narrow waterfront margin. The absence of industrial captains and the abdication of the port city's foreign merchant princes creates an opportunity for syndicate lieutenants to gain political influence.

Although geogrpahically remote, Australia's organized crime followed the same patterns of development as its counterparts in Europe and North America. After 150 years of European settlement, Australia had, by the early twentieth century, developed sizeable cities and was one of the world's most urbanized nations. In 1911 Sydney had a population of 648,000 — some 47 percent of New South Wales' total — and was comparable in size to San Francisco, whose population of 670,000 represented only 28 percent of the California total (McCarty 1978: 14–15). Founded as capitals for the administration of six separate colonies, Australia's major cities developed during the nineteenth century as junctions of port and rail heads linking world markets to rural hinterlands that produced wool, wheat and minerals. Even after Federation in 1901, the states preserved many of their constitutional prerogatives and their capital cities maintained much of their administrative autonomy. Although over 30 percent of every state's populations resides in the state capital, the continent's dry climate has concentrated settlement in Australia's southeastern corner, leaving Sydney and Melbourne as the only cities of significant size. In 1976, Sydney and Melbourne, with populations of 3.0 and 2.7 million respectively, contained over 40 percent of Australia's total population of 13.4 million (Burnaly 1980: 73). With their size and complexity, nineteenth- and early twentieth-century Sydney and Melbourne were home to an inner-city milieu of petty theft, prostitution and illegal gambling.

Law and Police

Like two other federations of former British colonies, Canada and the United States, Australia has a federal constitutional structure which leaves much of criminal law enforcement in the hands of state agencies. In such federations sovereignty derives, at base, from the royal charters originally granted the separate colonies, and the federal government acquires only such powers as the new states cede to it. In Australia the states have guarded their police prerogatives jealously. As the latest and weakest of the three federations, Australia has still not developed an effective federal police agency to deal with interstate organized crime. The weakness of the Australian Federal Police has left organized crime control to states hampered, in varying degrees, by corruption and inefficiency. Interaction between state police, parliaments and local criminal milieu has thus played a key role in determining the patterns of syndicate crime in Sydney and Melbourne.

While legal and social changes created an economic base for commercial vice in the 1920s, state police played a significant role in determining the patterns of syndicate formation in both Sydney and Melbourne. From the time of their establishment in the nineteenth century, Sydney and Melbourne police were plagued with periodic corruption scandals that sprang from quasi-official interactions with the criminal milieu. The 1880 Victorian State Royal Commission into police, Australia's first major inquiry, found Melbourne's Detective Branch "so iniquitous" that it constituted "little less than a standing menace to the community." Significantly, the Royal Commission discovered that Melbourne police, deviating from the official London metropolitan model, were not using patrols or forensic techniques to control crime but instead relied on a social control system within the criminal milieu. The Commission found the most serious of the branch's many derelictions to be "its manifestly un-English" practice of employing professional criminals, called "phizz gigs," as informants to recover stolen property and make arrests. So important were the "phizz gigs" to police that "the detectives appear even in the most ordinary cases to be comparatively helpless." Subsidized and protected by police, "phizz gigs" organized robberies, reported violators to police—after taking a share of the spoils—and received a share of the reward. "Phizz gigs" who failed to "put up" cases upon police demand were usually "prosecuted on a variety of charges." (Victoria, Royal Commission 1883: v, vii, viii).

Although the Victorian Commission urged an end to such use of informants, it remained a standard police practice in Sydney and Melbourne during much of the succeeding century. Since World War II, work as a police informer has been necessary for any entrepreneur in violence who wishes to dominate his fellows within the milieu. During the quarter century following World War II, Sydney's most notorious criminal and most renowned detective enjoyed a parallel rise from street thug and constable to prominence in their respective fields. Following a pattern described by the Victorian Commission in 1880, the detective rose rapidly through the ranks on his remarkable ability to pluck a convincing accused from the ranks of the underworld and garner sufficient evidence, usually through spurious unsigned confessions called "verbals," to win a conviction. Simultaneously, the young thug won an awesome reputation within the criminal milieu through his ability to eliminate rivals by arranging their arrest or by killing them without facing police charges. Since the late 1970s, this pattern as been repeated and the city's leading "standover merchant" and one of its most decorated detectives are now practicing a similar symbiosis with equal success. During the 1970s two New South Wales Police detective sergeants moved directly from the police into the upper-middle echelon of organized crime, quickly becoming two of the most feared of Sydney's vice entrepreneurs. In cooperation with influential politicians, police thus have the capacity not only to influence individual criminal careers but to shape the overall operations of Sydney's criminal syndicates.

Since the emergence of Sydney's vice syndicates in the late 1920s, one or more senior officers in every police administration has been the object of corruption allegations. Since 1935 three New South Wales Police commissioners and a number of their senior superintendants have been suspected of collusion with organized crime. Until the vice syndicates became involved in drug dealing during the 1970s, such charges were not investigated and relatively open institutional corruption was tolerated. Several years after Police Commissioner Fred Hanson (1972–76) retired, an independent member of the New South Wales Parliament accused him of complicity in the growth of organized crime. In 1979 Police Commissioner Mervyn Wood, Hanson's handpicked successor, resigned after allegations of corrupt dealings with Sydney's illegal casino and off-track betting syndicates, charges that surfaced again in a 1982 libel suit against the leader of the state opposition (*Bulletin,* 19 June 1979). In April 1982 Deputy Police Commissioner William Allen, the government's favored candidate as the next commissioner, was allowed to resign from the force after an administrative tribunal determined that his close associations with Sydney's syndicate leaders and acceptance of their gratuities had "brought discredit upon the police force" (*National Times,* 11 April 1982; *SMH,* 22 April 1982). This continuing corruption of the New South Wales Police command structure has been one of the essential preconditions for the massive expansion of Sydney syndicate activities since the late 1960s.

The organizational structure of the New South Wales Police provides a partial explanation for its senior officers' susceptibility to corruption. As the sole police agency in a constitutionally autonomous state, the New South Wales Police has a virtual monopoly on law enforcement in Sydney and is effectively immune to the threat of any external oversight. The Australian Federal Police has exceptionally limited powers to interfere in state matters, the New South Wales State Parliament is too weak to query all but the most blatant corruption, and there are no city and local police to expose State Police failings. Moreover, the police command and operational structure is exceptionally elitist and hierarchical. Specialist central squads have the sole authority to investigate syndicate vice activities, and the commissioner supervises these squads as commander of a para-military structure. By corrupting the commissioner, his deputy, or the supervisor of a specialist squad, a vice entrepreneur can guarantee his immunity to any police investigation. There are few Western public servants with the effective power of a New South Wales police commissioner and few such offices so perennially plagued with the problem of corruption.

Political Corruption

In the Australian parliamentary system of ministerial responsibility for subordinates, such systematic police corruption could not long continue without the tolerance of a state's premier or his police minister. Although the New South Wales police commissioner is a powerful figure within the force, he and his senior officers are subject to summary dismissal by the state's police minister or premier. Over the past half century, high-level police corruption has been matched by a parallel level of corruption within the government of the day. Such systematic police and political corruption in New South Wales has been a determining factor in the emergence of Sydney's crime syndicates as the most powerful in Australia. In September 1982, the director of the Australian Bureau of Criminal Intelligence told a Victorian State inquiry: "There is far more corruption of public officials in Sydney than in Melbourne we believe" (Victoria Parliament 1982: 2559). Other police observers have noted the contrast between Melbourne's generally honest police and the systematic corruption characteristic of the Sydney force.

As a large port city, Melbourne had the same potential for the development of organized crime syndicates but its police have restrained their growth. During much of this century Melbourne has had a vice economy comparable in size and sophistication to Sydney's. In 1982, for example, police estimated that Melbourne had 190 massage parlors with 5,000 employees, by far the largest number in Australia (Victoria Parliament 1982: 2542). Yet police have managed to confine potential syndicates to the waterfront area, and available evidence indicates that syndicate control over the city's prostitution, gambling and narcotics is less than in Sydney. The South

Melbourne docks have produced an exceptionally violent criminal sub-culture, but local groups have had very little success, until recently, in extending their operations beyond the waterfront. By contrast, criminals from Sydney's Balmain peninsula, a comparable waterfront district, have spread their influence far beyond the docks to become the dominant element in Australian organized crime.

It is, of course, far easier to describe this contrast between the two cities than to explain it. A possible explanation might lie in the differing economic base of the two cities. As the historic home of Australasian finance, commerce and industry, Melbourne has formed a conservative establishment that controls the state government and has historically demonstrated little tolerance for police corruption. Beginning with the 1880 Royal Commission, the Victorian Parliament has purged police corruption about every decade, with a major royal commission inquiry into police affairs. In 1958–59, 1962–63, 1970 and 1976, Victorian Royal Commissions probed police procedures and uncovered relatively low-level corruption in relation to abortion, off-course bookmaking and prostitution. During the same period, New South Wales did not have a single such investigation of its state police. The allegations against Deputy Commissioner Allen in 1982, for example, were the result of a Federal Police initiative (*National Times,* 11 April 1982).

Since World War II, New South Wales's two dominant political parties have displayed different styles of institutional corruption. During its quarter century in control of the state government from 1941 to 1965, the Australian Labor Party (ALP) shared the views of its working class constituency and adopted a tolerant attitude towards the illegal alcohol sales and off-course betting prevalent in Sydney's poorer neighborhoods. Often of Irish-Catholic origins, ALP politicians, regarding drink and gambling as innocent working-man's pleasures, were hostile to the vice laws passed by Protestant, upper-class conservatives. As the only cash-rich entrepreneurs in working class districts, "sly groggers" and "SP ("Starting Price" or off-course) bookmakers" were regular Labor Party contributors and worked without interference from the state police when Labor was in power. When the ALP returned to government in 1975, organized crime was able to use these traditional alliances to once again penetrate the Labor Party's inner-city branch structure and the upper echelons of its right-wing political machine.

In contrast to the Labor Party's system of central bureaucracy and local branch structure, the Liberal-County Party, a conservative coalition, governed through a highly centralized executive during Sir Robert Askin's tenure as New South Wales' premier from 1965 to 1975. After his death in 1981, Australia's leading weekly, the *National Times,* ran a front-page obituary (13 September 1981) with the banner headline, "Askin: Friend to Organized Crime." The accompanying story charged that Askin had been instrumental in his government's tolerance of syndicated vice. Whether through Labor bureaucracy or Liberal executive, Sydney's syndicates have been able to secure a sufficient level of political protection for their operations since the early

1940s. The first official police statement on political corruption in New South Wales came in 1980 when the Victorian Police Bureau of Criminal Intelligence reported: "Up until late 1979 illegal betting operations in Sydney were conducted by known organizations who ran a multi-million dollar business. Corruption in that city is believed to extend as far as parliamentarians" (Victoria Parliament 1982: 2464).

There are some forms of official support for organized crime found in other societies that have not yet been satisfactorily studied in Australia. Corruption of the legal profession is important for the survival of syndicates in a society when there is a possibility, no matter how remote, that some of their operatives may come before the courts. A major controversy erupted in 1978 when the *National Times* revealed that in July 1977 the N.S.W. Chief Stipendiary Magistrate, Murray Farquhar, had been photographed at Sydney's racecourse with George Freeman, a man identified as an "organized crime figure" and the city's leading illegal bookmaker. The chief magistrate had used his member's pass to admit Freeman, who was barred from the course, and sat with him for an hour chatting convivially. Despite photographic evidence, the N.S.W. government found no impropriety in the association and no action was taken.[1]

National Intelligence Agencies

Similarly, we know little about relations between Sydney syndicates and Australia's intelligence organizations. As the two leading practitioners of the clandestine arts, criminal syndicates and intelligence agencies often find themselves natural allies. In France, for example, factions within the Corsican *milieu* were closely allied with SDECE, the Republic's external intelligence agency, under the Gaullist government. Under threat of assassination by the *Organisation de l'Armée Secrète* after his withdrawal from Algeria and unsure of the loyalties of his security agencies, De Gaulle relied on the Corsican *milieu* for much of his presidential security apparatus. So protected, Marseilles' Corsican syndicates were able to expand their heroin exports to the United States in the 1960s (McCoy 1972: 49–52; Kruger 1980: Part 1). Nationalist Chinese intelligence in Taiwan maintains close working relations with both overseas Chinese heroin distributors in Southeast Asia and the Chinese irregular forces that dominate the Golden Triangle heroin trade from bases in northern Thailand. When Hong Kong's leading heroin manufacturer, Ma Sik-yu, was charged with drug trafficking in 1977 he was given refuge in Taiwan since he had used his heroin income to operate a Nationalist China "spy network" in southern China and Southeast Asia (McCoy 1980: 351–58). And in the United States there have been frequent associations between the CIA and various mafia figures, most recently in connection with the agency's terrorist raids against Cuba during the 1960s. There are some indications that both the CIA and the Australian Security Intelligence

Organization (ASIO) may have had contacts with Sydney's syndicates through the Nugan-Hand Bank, a Sydney-based merchant bank that served both the CIA and Australian organized crime (*SMH,* 10 November 1982).

Like ordinary businessmen, vice entrepreneurs require a range of specialist services from legitimate professionals. A limited number of Sydney solicitors have made careers serving a syndicate clientele — incorporating their operating companies, advising them of ways around and through the law, and handling funds through their accounts. As the vice economy expanded after 1967, syndicate entrepreneurs needed banking services geared to their special requirements. In earlier decades SP bookmaking had served as an informal banking service and the racecourse as the vice economy's stock market. By the early 1970s the growing scale and dispersal of syndicate operations required a proper banking service and the Nugan Hand Bank grew in response to this need. When it began to collapse, some syndicate operators transferred their accounts to a more recently formed merchant bank related to the defunct Nugan Hand. (*SMH,* 10 November 1982).

Syndicate Structure

Analysis of a syndicate's internal structure is an important element in the study of organized crime. Influenced by American media images of the quasi-military mafia, Australian police have tried to apply the same hierarchical model to their own society with little success. Sydney's syndicate structure is more comparable to the looser organization of Marseilles' Corsican *milieu.* Looseness should not, however, be misinterpreted as a lack of organization. There are clear principles of organization within this relative decentralization. Sydney's milieu is, in fact, a discrete group whose members know each other personally or by reputation. There is, moreover, a loose hierarchy within the Sydney milieu which has tightened considerably since the imposition of syndicate controls in the late 1960s. When an illegal operation such as a drug shipment or cargo theft is underway, operatives deal exclusively with those inside the milieu. Although there are nuclear syndicates that serve as focal points within the larger milieu, organized crime entrepreneurs demonstrate varied patterns of association as they use several personnel networks to recruit manpower for an operation.

The organization of Murray Riley's $48 million Thai cannabis operation in 1978 provides an apt illustration of the Sydney milieu's operational methods. An ex-detective sergeant who resigned from the New South Wales Police after facing administrative charges in the early 1960s, Riley used his criminal contacts to enter the milieu and soon earned a reputaton as a key figure in slot machine fraud. When exposure before a 1974–75 Royal commission forced him out of the slot machine business, Riley arranged finance of something less than one million dollars through more senior syndicate figures and began travelling to Southeast Asia where, with the assistance of the Nugan

Hand Bank, he organized the shipment. To smuggle the Thai cannabis into Australia, Riley chartered a vessel and recruited a crew through the Sydney milieu. When Riley tried to move the cannabis off a Coral Sea reef into Sydney on a yacht, he and his operational associates were arrested. The evidence presented at his trial reveals a good deal about the structure of the Sydney milieu. First, instead of dealing within an established hierarchy of fixed associations, Riley subcontracted the work through the loose networks of personal contacts within the milieu—traders involved in stolen vehicle sales and his former associates in poker machine fraud. There were, moreover, five identifiable sectors of the milieu involved in the operation: (1) unidentified senior syndicate leaders, who supplied much of the capital; (2) The Nugan Hand Bank, which provided financial services and contacts with drug dealers in Southeast Asia; (3) Murray Riley himself, the project manager; (4) senior figures within the motor trader (car thief rings) and slot machine networks; and, (5) the young motor traders recruited as gunmen and technical personnel (New South Wales District Court, 1978a).

In its development over the past half century the structure of the Sydney milieu has been strongly influenced by its interaction with the police. Instead of eradicating commercialized vice, police sought a mutually advantageous relationship with the syndicate leaders that ensured the survival of the vice trades. Moreover, the patterns of police and political corruption have determined quite directly the scale, scope and structure of Sydney's criminal syndicates. Since the 1920s there has been an ebb and flow in the fortunes of organized crime determined largely by the amount of police pressure placed upon the vice economy and, conversely, the amount of protection police and government have conceded to individual syndicates. The growth of syndicate crime in Sydney is due not to a failing of police and politicians but rather to their active cooperation.

Origins — The 1920s

As the level of syndicate warfare in Sydney's inner Darlinghurst district escalated in 1927–28, the city's mass-circulation tabloid *Truth* editorialized: "Razorhurst, Gunhurst, Bottlehurst, Dopehurst—it used to be Darlinghurst, one of the finest quarters of a rich and beautiful city; today it is a plague spot where the spawn of the gutter grow and fatten on official apathy" (*Truth,* 23 December 1928).

Indeed, the 1920s was a watershed decade in the history of organized crime in Sydney. Responding to the economic opportunities created by legal restraint upon the traffic in alcohol, narcotics and sex, the city's first major criminal syndicates emerged to organize the vice sector of Sydney's economy. The city's thriving tabloid press began a long tradition of entertaining their mass readerships with the simultaneously vilified and romaticized exploits of these local bad men and women. Through hyperbolic headline, the tabloid media invested the city's vice merchants with the aura of the anti-hero and projected a protean image into Sydney's collective consciousness—the gangster as master of the metropolis. Media transformed the mundane reality of commercialized vice in a modern urban mythology.

Media coverage of organized crime reflects Sydney's changing urban character. During the 1920s, Sydney underwent a sudden transformation from a small, compact city into a sprawling metropolis with a decaying inner city surrounded by affluent suburban sprawl. Between 1911 and 1931 Sydney's population doubled—rising from 630,000 to 1.23 million. In an age when mass urbanism reduced the individual to powerless anonymity, the gangster alone retained the power to rule the city. Hence the tabloid fascination. The radiating grids of tram and train drained inner Sydney of its gentility, and the city center suffered a 10 percent population loss during the 1920s. As the garden suburb became the archetype of a life that was both comfortable and moral, the gangster's downtown kingdom of vice—cocaine, prostitution, gambling and "sly grog"—became everything that was neither moral nor comfortable. The gangster's domain was an inner-city demimonde of degradation, the antithesis of surrounding suburban propriety. The sense of separation and opposition was complete. Playing upon the tension between suburb and inner city, the tabloids created a profitable genre of hyperbolic reportage that shrouded organized crime in a romantic haze and has served, over the decades, as a positive barrier to analysis or understanding. Australians are familiar with the careers of the tabloid anti-heroes, but have looked upon them as something apart, not realizing until recently that organized crime was well established within their society.

The formation of the vice economy during the 1920s was a response to the passage of conservative legislation aimed at reforming standards of personal behavior. During the latter decades of the nineteenth century, Sydney was a tawdry colonial port city with inner-city slums and a waterfront district that sustained a loose underworld of prostitutes, petty thieves, opium dealers and illegal gamblers. Inner-city health and social welfare services were minimal and residents suffered from the effects of congestion and from disease. An 1892 Royal Commission into Chinese Gambling conducted a walking survey of inner-Sydney streets and found Chinatown a dismaying density of bed-space, boarding houses, opium dens and gambling houses.[2] A major outbreak of bubonic plague in Sydney's worst slums coincided with federation in 1901 and inspired a civic campaign to transform the tawdry colonial port into a model metropolis for the new Commonwealth.

While planning commissions laid out the transport and service infrastructure for the projected suburbs in the decade following federation, the N.S.W. Parliament, dominated by conservatives, passed new laws that sought to impose social controls upon the city's slums. The first strong anti-gambling measures were contained in the Amended Vagrancy Act of 1905. Passage of the Gaming and Betting Act of 1906 strengthened these provisions and forced closure of Sydney's off-course "tote shops." But it was an omnibus crime bill, the Police Offenses (Amendment) Bill of 1908, that laid the legal foundations for the early growth of Sydney's vice economy. Passed over the strong opposition of the N.S.W. Labor Party, the bill contained the first legal constraints on a number of vice trades. It became illegal for a woman to solicit in the streets, banned off-course horserace betting, and outlawed most forms of gaming, including even the traditional Australian "two-up."

In the debates Labor attacked the bill's class bias and revealed an ideological posture toward legal control of vice that has remained more or less constant throughout this century. "As regards the unfortunate women on the streets," protested one Labor M.P., "I say they are driven there by some of the pillars of the society . . . where any person who wants can come along and make use of them . . . The bill is aimed at the poor unfortunate wives, sisters and daughters of the workers" (N.S.W. Parliament 1908: 1710). Another Labor member predicted, with considerable prescience, that the outcome of the bill would be to force independent street walkers into criminally controlled brothels. Opposing the bill's prohibition of off-course betting, the Labor member for the working-class district of Balmain stated: "Because a man happens to be a worker, and is unable, by reason of unfortunate position, to pay 3s.6d to enter the ledger at Randwick [Racecourse], and makes a bet elsewhere, he is designated a criminal" (N.S.W. Parliament 1908: 1706).

As Labor had predicted, the 1908 Police Offenses Act did force Sydney's prostitutes off the streets into brothels and thereby laid the foundations of the city's vice economy. While the start of radio broadcasting in the early 1920s drastically expanded the scope of off-course betting, the 1906 Gaming Act and the 1908 Police Offenses Act applied to the new system and made it *ab initio* illegal. The N.S.W. Parliament completed the legal basis for the vice economy during the 1920s when it passed new laws restricting alcohol sales after 6:00 PM and prohibiting narcotics. By the mid-1920s, these four vice trades—cocaine, "sly grog," prostitution and off-track bookmaking—had created a sufficient economic base for the formation of a coherent vice sector within Sydney's economy. This concentration of commerce within the vice sector created, for the first time, a sufficient surplus to sustain criminal entrepreneurs who lived, not by committing crimes themselves, but by organizing those who did.

Although Sydney's vice economy expanded markedly during the 1920s, it was still far smaller and less affluent, but the Sydney and Melbourne vice sectors were proportionally smaller than those of New York and Chicago. Unlike the total prohibition of alcohol passed by the U.S. Congress in 1919, Australia's separate state laws restricting liquor sales after 6:00 PM were a modest partial prohibition. Consequently, Australia's illegal liquor traders, called "sly grogers," acquired a far smaller share of the alcohol industry than their American counterparts. In 1922, for example, Melbourne police calculated that the city's 29 sly grog dealers controlled only 20 percent of its *retail* liquor trade, while a comparable statistic for an American city at that time would have been 100 percent (*Herald,* 23 March 1922). Similarly, America banned narcotics in 1922, five years earlier than New South Wales, giving her syndicates a more prolonged market opportunity. Starting then from a much narrower economic base than their New York counterparts, Sydney's syndicates grew slowly from the 1920s and did not achieve significant influence until the late 1960s.

Influenced by the global temperance movement, Sydney's Protestant churches had advocated the prohibition of alcohol for several decades before the imposition of 6:00 PM closing for public hotels in 1919. The movement had gained impetus during World War I, when several thousand Australian Army recruits rioted in downtown Sydney over conditions in their training camps, breaking into hotels and stealing beer. The Commonwealth government banned all liquor sales in Army canteens and imposed 6:00 PM closing on public hotels, the nation's main liquor outlet. When the war ended in 1919, the Protestant churches successfully lobbied the N.S.W. and Victorian State Parliaments for continuation of 6:00 PM closing and it survived in both States until the 1950s (Scott 1937; *Herald,* 28 February 1919). One worker response to the restriction was the legendary "six o'clock swill." Arriving at the hotel after 5:00 PM quitting time, "schools" of male drinkers accumulated three or four glasses of beer as the 6:00 PM closing hour approached and swilled them down in a rush, stumbling home in a stupor. For those who wished alcohol after 6:00 PM, the prime liquor trading time, there were "sly grog shops" located in every residential neighborhood where beer and spirits were sold illegally, usually from 6:00 PM to midnight.

The progressive prohibition of cocaine in New South Wales between 1925 and 1927 produced a similar market response. During and after World War I, cocaine became popular among prostitutes and limited numbers of innercity residents. Narcotics sales were not controlled and habitués could secure unlimited supplies from local pharmacies at low retail prices. Concerned over addiction among war veterans introduced to narcotics in the trenches of the Western Front, Australian state governments began restricting cocaine sales immediately after the war. In Melbourne, pharmacies were barred from unrestricted cocaine sales by the Victorian Dangerous Drugs Regulations of 1922, which required a medical practitioner's prescription for narcotics. Restrained by a politically powerful pharrmacists' lobby, the N.S.W. Parliament did not pass its Police Offenses Drug Bill, which required prescriptions for all narcotic sales, until early 1927 (N.S.W. Parliament, 1923: 1264–66; and 1926: 1144–53). The N.S.W. Police Drug Bureau was formed in 1926, and over the next four years its officers applied sufficient pressure to force Sydney's pharmacies to desist from open cocaine sales.

During the 1920s off-course or SP bookmaking emerged as Sydney's largest and most consistent source of organized crime revenue. Horse-racing, which was well established in Australia by the 1860s, became the country's major spectator sport. A N.S.W. Royal Commission into the racing industry in 1912 discovered that legal betting was a major enterprise. New South Wales had 1,310 licensed bookmakers; the annual attendance at Sydney's six racecourses was 926,000, with an average at Randwick of 35,000 per meeting; and the annual on-course betting turnover of £6.3 million. One of Sydney's legal bookmakers testified that his annual turnover averaged £300,000 with profits of £60,000 (N.S.W. Legislative Assembly 1912: 141–82).

The growth of illegal off-course betting paralleled racing's rising popularity. During the late nineteenth century, off-course betting shops proliferated in Sydney and Melbourne to service those too poor or too distant for regular visits to the racecourse. The most famous of Australia's turn-of-the-century bookmakers was Melbourne's John Wren, a man whose combined career as criminal and political broker is still today the subject of intense controversy. Operating with apparent immunity to police investigation between 1893 and 1906, Wren's Collingwood Tote Shop earned him a profit of £750 per week, or $78,000 per annum, until the scandal of its open operations forced police action (N.S.W. Legislative Assembly 1912: 134). The tote shop was nothing more than a large hall or yard where a Saturday afternoon crowd of males, usually numbering no more than 1,000, or in Wren's case 1,500, gathered to bet on a pari-mutuel system. Race results arrived from the tracks illegally by carrier pigeon, and later telephone, to allow continuous betting as the race program progressed. The need for bettors to actually assemble within the narrow confines of the crowded tote shop reduced the volume of betting and kept even the largest operations — like Wren's — comparatively small.

The new off-course betting business of the 1920s was the illegitimate offspring of a union between two technologies, the radio and the telephone. While limited numbers of telephones had been in operation in Australia's capital cities for several decades, there was a 400 percent increase in the telephones connected in New South Wales during the quarter-century before World War II — from 49,000 sets in 1914, to 71,000 in 1927, to 197,000 in 1940. Commercial radio broadcasting began in the early 1920s, and radio receivers licensed in New South Wales showed an even more spectacular increase — from 25,000 in 1923, to 177,000 in 1933, to 495,000 in 1941[3] (N.S.W. 1920: 247; 1929: 125; 1941: 313).

The growth of this electrical telecommunications grid in the capital cities freed bettors from old tote shops and made every home and hotel a potential SP bookmaking shop. The scale of the new illegal betting industry was revealed in 1938 when a new New South Wales betting act closed the two registered companies that had been providing SP bookmakers with advice of the on-course odds for several decades. Covering the whole of the state, Teleposts Pty. Ltd. operated 100 telephones and paid annual bills of £30,000, while Eatons Pty. Ltd. had 65 telephones and bills of £20,000 (*Smith's Weekly,* 19 October 1938). While most SP bookmakers were specialists removed from the violence of the innercity cocaine trade, their illegality exposed them to demands for protection payments from Sydney's emerging criminal syndicates.

Sydney's first organized criminal syndicates appeared in the late 1920s in the inner-city's combined cocaine-prostitution trade. Unlike the sly grog and SP bookmaking rackets, prostitution and cocaine selling were both concentrated in the center-city vice districts of East Sydney and Kings Cross, the row-house slums of Darlinghurst police division. This concentration made syndication a logistical possibility, and by the late 1920s four syndicates had imposed loose controls over the prostitution and cocaine trafficking in the area. The combination of cocaine and prostitution created exceptional profits and for the first time Sydney's vice economy generated sufficient surplus to sustain entrepreneurs who lived by controlling, not committing, crimes. In the decade before cocaine became popular among Darlinghurst's prostitutes, it was possible for a woman to accumulate savings and quit the trade when she was capable of establishing another livelihood. Cocaine, however, allowed the syndicates a more perfect exploitation. By selling cocaine to the prostitutes under their control, syndicates increased their income from both sources. Sale to prostitutes guaranteed a syndicate's cocaine sales and reduced women to working for subsistence and drugs. As cocaine and heroin addicts, prostitutes had to both intensify and prolong their time in the trade, an effort that the drug itself made more palatable.

These exceptional profits prompted conflict among Sydney's emerging syndicates over market share in 1927–28, a period of violence known locally as the "razor gang wars." Barred from carrying concealed firearms without a police license by the 1927 Pistol Act, the syndicates armed themselves with ordinary straight razors which folded neatly into a jacket pocket and sharpened to a weapon capable of inflicting gruesome scars. Syndicate collectors, called "standover men," found their display a convincing argument for a prostitute with reservations about making her payments.

The gangs that fought these battles were led by four dominant personalities. Eliminated early in the fighting, Norman Bruhn was a Melbourne "standover merchant" who had fled to Sydney to escape arrest in his home city. Using the razor as his weapon of choice, Bruhn made onerous collections from East Sydney's prostitutes (*Truth*, 26 June 1927). The eventual victor was Philip Jeffs, known in the media as "Phil the Jew." Born in the Jewish ghetto of Riga, Latvia in 1896, Jeffs migrated to Sydney via London and by 1925 was established in Kings Cross as proprietor of a sly-grog shop called the 50–50 Club. When he died in 1945 after a quarter century in the Sydney *milieu*, the Sydney tabloid *Truth* published a hyperbolic obituary under the headline "Phil The Jew—King of Thugs." The first line read: "Phil the Jew, Sydney racketeer, gangster, drug peddler, procurer, sly groger, alleged phizz-gig for some detectives, gunman, and wealthy friend of some politicians and many police, died on Tuesday."[3]

Protected by a legal loophole which made it illegal for a man but not a woman to live off a woman's immoral earnings, two of Sydney's syndicate leaders were women. Born in the country town of Dubbo, Kathleen Behan Leigh became a brothel keeper after passage of the 1908 Police Offences Act and used that base to organize armed robberies. Supported by a gang of male standover men, she expanded into cocaine and sly grog selling during the 1920s and soon emerged as one of the city's main syndicate leaders. Her combination of cocaine trafficking and brothel-keeping made her a wealthy woman, influential with inner-city Labor Party politicians.[4] Kate Leigh's perennial rival for control of the Darlinghurst vice trade was Matilda Mary Twiss Devine. Born a London Cockney bricklayer's daughter in 1900, she migrated to Sydney with her Australian soldier husband in 1919.[5]

Lasting just over two years from 1927 to 1929, the razor gang wars produced a lurid violence. As victims with bone-deep slashes on the face, arms and legs began appearing the city's casualty wards for stitching, the tabloid press published hyperbolic accounts of the violence. After the elimination of Bruhn's cocaine-prostitution syndicate in the first round of violence in 1927, fighting remained sporadic for two years. The first round in this new war was fought in May 1919 when rival cocaine dealers assaulted Jeffs' gang in retribution for the sale of cocaine heavily adulterated with boracic acid (*Truth,* 9 June 1919; 4 November 1945). Two months later, Kate Leigh and Tilly Devine began a prolonged struggle for the East Sydney vice rackets that produced several gun and razor battles. Unlike the invisible vice trade, gang violence produced headlines and public concern.

Repression — The 1930s

The razor gang violence prompted a community consensus for the repression of Sydney's syndicates that culminated in passage of the N.S.W. Vagrancy (Amendment) Act of 1929 and its Draconian "Consorting Clause." Specifically targeted at the cocaine syndicates, this clause, one of the most authoritarian ever passed in a Western democracy, made it a felony offense to be a person "who habitually consorts with reputed thieves, or prostitutes or persons who have no visible means of support." Since police testimony was sufficient to establish an individual's "reputed" criminal status and the act of "consorting," the N.S.W. Police were given almost unlimited powers to imprison any citizen deemed criminal (N.S.W. Parliament 1929: 681–96; *Truth* 12 January 1980). To implement the new law, police formed a Consorting Squad which made 116 arrests in 1930 and 149 in 1931 (N.S.W. Legislative Assembly 1932: 10–11).

Infected with the spirit of the new act, the New South Wales courts sentenced Sydney's syndicate leaders according to classical judicial practice — notably rustication, exile and ostracism. Charged in January 1930 with consorting with prostitutes — that is, her employees — Tilly Devine was ostracised to England for a period of two years (*Truth* 9 February 1930). After serving sentences for consorting and cocaine trafficking in 1930 and 1931, Kate Leigh was sentenced to "rustication" in 1933 — that is, she was barred from approaching closer than 200 miles to Sydney for a period of five years.[6]

Similarly charged in 1933, Kate Leigh's daughter Eileen agreed to exile herself from the state for three years in lieu of a prison term (*Truth*, 26 March 1933; 4 June 1933).

By the mid-1930s the syndicates were in disarray and the cocaine traffic had been largely suppressed. Attributing progress to the Consorting Clause, the 1933 N.S.W. Police report claimed that "the drug traffic is being kept in check, and there was a considerable falling off in the illicit traffic in cocaine" (N.S.W. Legislative Assembly 1934:2). In 1936 the police reported, accurately enough, that cocaine trafficking had been almost completely eradicated (N.S.W. Legislative Assembly 1937:5). Judging from these and other reports, the suppression campaign of the early 1930s was an effective exercise in social control. Supported by Parliament, the press and the public, the police applied legislation of Draconian intent and brought a disruptive social element under control. The experience reveals that organized criminal syndicates were still relatively weak and the police were, on balance, generally free from serious corruption.

The failure of a simultaneous suppression campaign against SP bookmaking showed the paramount importance of community consensus in the N.S.W. police success. Unlike the other vice trades, the SP business boomed during the Depression, and racecourse operators lobbied the conservative state government to enforce the betting laws. At Sydney's Kensington racecourse, for example, average race attendance fell from 7,189 in 1929 to 4,064 in 1934 and racecourse tax collections from £14,323 to £4,230 (*Truth* 14 July 1935). The police formed a special SP Squad and made 20,000 arrests for off-track betting between 1930 and 1936, making gambling offenses the largest category in police arrest statistics. Working-class communities bitterly resisted the government's effort to force them back to the racecourse and supported the SP bookmakers, rendering the supression campaign a failure (N.S.W. Legislative Assembly 1936, 116–17). The conservative government passed a stronger Betting Act over an impassioned Labor opposition in 1938, but again the police raids foundered on the rock of community resistance.[7] When Labor returned to power for a quarter-century beginning in 1941, the suppression campaign ended, with SP operators firmly established in their local communities.

The sole survivor of the police campaign against the razor gangs was Philip Jeffs, who became the progenitor of a more modern style of syndicate operation. Unlike his rivals, Jeffs sensed that the cocaine traffic was becoming controversial and shifted his capital, now greatly expanded, back into the sly grog trade. Insulating his business from harassment by regular gifts to police and parliamentarians, Jeffs opened a chain of sly grog shops—the working-class 50-50 Club in Darlinghurst, the society 400 Club in central Sydney, and Oyster Bill's, an exclusive roadhouse in Sydney's southern suburbs. When police responded to public pressure by raiding Jeffs' clubs in mid-1937, a member of parliament spoke on the floor of the Upper House defending his clubs as "most respectable" and excoriating the office responsible for the raids.[8] With a fortune estimated at £250,000, Jeffs began selling off his clubs in the late 1930s and retired to a luxury apartment building he had constructed. He emerged from retirement only briefly before his death in 1945 to open Sydney's first illegal baccarat club (*Truth,* 6 August 1944; *Daily Mirror,* 20 December 1972). His retirement and the earlier eclipse of his rivals marked a turning point in the history of the Sydney *milieu.* While the first generation of syndicate leaders who had emerged in the 1920s had lost their influence by the start of World War II, the war itself produced a second generation who were to play a dominant role in Sydney's postwar vice economy.

Expansion — The 1940s

During World War II Sydney's vice economy experienced a period of unprecedented growth. Australia became the supply base for General Douglas MacArthur's Southwest Pacific Area, and Sydney served as the main leave center for Allied troops. As several hundred thousand American troops passed through the city, Sydney experienced a sudden surge in demand for its traditional vice trades — prostitution and sly grog. War mobilization placed enormous strains upon Australia's consumer economy and the government rationed a wide range of ordinary goods — tires, gasoline, clothing, alcohol, and certain foodstuffs. Bureaucracy's entry into the marketplace created inefficiencies and unnecessary shortages, and the city's vice entrepreneurs exploited the opportunity fully. As vice merchants and blackmarket traders prospered, there was a boom in all forms of illegal gambling that further expanded the scale of the vice economy.

Sydney's wartime brothel trade prospered under the close supervision of Australian and American military police. As leave-time legions crowded into Sydney from troopships and the jungles of the Pacific, military authorities cooperated with Sydney's brothel keepers to provide an orderly and safe sexual service. Brothels in Kings Cross and East Sydney were racially segregated and supervised by U.S. Military Police who kept the queues moving forward in an orderly manner. After suffering a series of reverses during the 1930s, Tilly Devine prospered again with the outbreak of the war. Her brothel in Palmer Street, East Sydney serviced the troops and she finished the war a wealthy woman. She hosted ostentatiously lavish social affairs during the war and on a visit to London in 1948 wore diamonds insured for £10,000. Arriving in London to witness the Coronation in 1953, Mrs. Devine attracted considerable publicity with diamonds worth £20,000 on her hands.[9]

The sly grog trade attracted a class of younger, more dynamic vice entrepreneurs. The State's 6.00 p.m. hotel closing remained law during the war, providing a vast clientele of affluent workers and Allied troops who did most of their drinking in the evening. While alcohol demand increased, beer production remained constant and much of the available supply was allocated to military canteens and troopships. From 1942 to 1951 the government imposed a quota on beer deliveries to public hotels and the amount sold in New South Wales declined steadily—from 38 million gallons in 1942 to 32.9 in 1944. Similarly the Commonwealth government set wartime spirit imports at 40 percent of the 1938-40 figure (N.S.W., Royal Commission on Liquor Laws, 1954: 62-66). The combination of short supplies and 6.00 p.m. closing created ideal conditions for a boom in the sly grog trade. As the 1951 Liquor Royal Commission later discovered, the trade operated by diverting beer from public hotels, where it was sold at low official prices, to nightclubs concentrated in the Kings Cross area where it could be sold at blackmarket prices to U.S. servicemen.

According to the Royal Commission, "the most notorious and disreputable nightclub in the city" was Abraham Gilbert Saffron's Roosevelt Club in Kings Cross. A name that has been cited repeatedly in organized crime investigations over the past 30 years, Saffron is a good example of the type of entrepreneur who emerged in Sydney during the war. Convicted in 1940 for the possession of four stolen automobile radios, Saffron then had identifiable assets of £80. A decade later, the Liquor Royal Commission discovered that he held, among his other assets, seven public hotel licenses worth £4,500. The commissioner attributed Saffron's commercial success to his practice of diverting beer rations from his public hotels, where he was obliged to sell them at the low official price, to his Roosevelt Club where he sold them to American troops at "extortionate prices."[10]

The war greatly expanded Sydney's vice economy by creating a vast blackmarket for a wide range of basic commodities, an opportunity that was fully exploited by Sydney's prewar vice entrepreneurs. In February 1945, for example, police arrested nine people for operating the state's largest illegal trade in clothing ration coupons and charged Richard Gabriel Reilly with being the organizer. Then 35, Reilly had begun his career in the *milieu* during the 1930s as a dance hall bouncer and later shifted to a similar position in Philip Jeffs' exclusive sly grog shop, the 400 Club. Reilly remained an ordinary syndicate gunman and on the eve of war was charged with the murder of another gunman in a hotel shoot-out. With his profits from wartime blackmarket dealings, however, he was able to buy out some of his former employer's business interests—Jeffs' baccarat club and his exclusive roadhouse, Oyster Bill's. During the postwar decades, Reilly who became known as the "King of Baccarat," drove a Masarati sports car, and lived in a $100,000 house in one of Sydney's best suburbs.[11]

The boom in the vice economy was reflected in the wartime rise in all gambling, legal and illegal. Turnover at New South Wales racecourses among licensed bookmakers more than doubled from £13.4 million in 1939 to £28.5 million in 1944 (SMH, 8 June 1945). Australia's wartime government, which regarded gambling as an antisocial vice, estimated that Sydney's wartime SP bookmakers were handling £2 million per annum. In one of their periodic sweeps against the illegal bookmakers, Sydney police arrested James F. Cook near the city's fruit markets and seized betting books that revealed the scale of the wartime boom in illegal gambling. Instead of the typical pre-war bets of 5s. or £1, Cook's books showed a weekly total of 62 bets for £3,221 which ranged from 20s. up to £200 (*Sunday Sun*, 8 July 1945). Reflecting the postwar demand for illegal gambling, Philip Jeffs and a younger criminal named Sidney Kelly opened Sydney's first baccarat club at Kings Cross in 1944. The innovation was an enormous success and soon inspired imitations. The wartime baccarat clubs survived until the late 1960s when the *milieu* transformed them into the present illegal casinos.[12]

Lasting until 1950, the decade of wartime economic controls left an indelible imprint on Sydney's vice economy. The increased scale of the vice economy produced a second generation of vice entrepreneurs. Of equal importance, the requisite wartime tolerance for vice trading fostered institutionalized corruption among the N.S.W. police. The quality of postwar police administration was evident in two public rituals enacted in 1950. Retiring from the N.S.W. police after two-and-a-half years as metropolitan superintendent, Mr. Sweeny was honored with a banquet by 300 vice traders active in gambling, sly grog and prostitution. Attending the fete in person, Superintendent Sweeny accepted a check for £600 from his grateful clientele. Inspector Noonan, retiring after four-and-a-half years as Metropolitan Licensing Inspector with responsibility for liquor law enforcement, was feted in a similar manner at the Australia Hotel and given a check for £1,000. The 1951 Liquor Royal Commission found such practices "indiscreet" but not illegal. Such "indiscretion" has remained a constant feature of organized crime enforcement in Sydney since the war (N.S.W. Parliament, 1954: 98–99).

Postwar Prosperity

During the two decades of Labor Party government in New South Wales from 1945 to 1965, Sydney's vice economy enjoyed a steady but unspectacular period of growth. Labor's ideology of tolerance and its established alliances with local vice traders through its branch structure allowed a considerable number of small- to medium-sized bookmakers, sly grog dealers and brothel keepers to survive and even prosper. While Labor's web of alliances with the *milieu* fostered a steady growth of the vice economy, it simultaneously prevented any one syndicate from taking control. Since all vice entrepreneurs had access to political and police protection, no single syndicate could achieve a sufficient comparative advantage of protection to impose its dominance.

After the end of the war, there was a marked contraction in all the vice trades associated with Sydney's wartime role as a campfollower city. The decline in demand for prostitution was particularly sharp and by the late 1940s many East Sydney brothels had closed. The influx of Mediterranean migrants during the 1950s created a temporary sexual imbalance and demand for sexual services, but the new brothel operators were Maltese migrants out-

side the established Anglo-Irish Australian *milieu*. As waves of Maltese began landing at Sydney in the 1950s, they were attracted to East Sydney by the
low rents, and the old Palmer Street brothel area became engulfed by a Maltese ghetto. With the ghetto providing a natural security network, a Maltese
migrant named Joe Borg emerged as "the King of Palmer Street." Borg, who
arrived in Sydney in 1952, within three years had a police file which described
him as a "gunman, thief, shop-breaker, and pimp." After purchasing his first
East Sydney brothel house for $2,000 in 1962, Borg prospered and by 1967
owned twenty houses worth an estimated $80,000 (*Daily Mirror*, 29 May
1968; *S.M.H.*, 8 November 1969).

The baccarat clubs continued their steady growth after the war. During the
early postwar years there were six clubs in Kings Cross and the largest, the Ex-
citement Club, earned an estimated £250,000 in its two years of operation
(*Sun Herald*, 21 October 1962). The full scale of baccarat gambling was not
known until 1965 when a Sydney solicitor was charged with malversation of
£16,065 and testified about his compulsion in open court. Between 1962 and
1964 he lost some £50,000 at four inner-city baccarat clubs — Percival Galea's
Victoria Club, George Walker's Goulburn Club, Richard Reilly's Kellet
Club, and Eli Rose's International Club.[13] All had sufficient protection to remain open at known locations for many years, but the threat of an occasional
police raid was real enough to keep incriminating assets to a minimum. The
clubs consequently remained austere premises with no formal gaming
equipment.

During its two decades in office until 1965, the N.S.W. Labor government
sought to reduce the vice economy and its attendant police corruption by
legalizing the separate vice trades. The sly grog trade gradually disappeared
as the government extended hotel trading hours during the 1950s to meet consumer demand patterns.

Similarly, Labor tried to end SP bookmaking by legalizing off-course betting. Following the decline of the inner-city syndicates in the 1930s, SP bookmakers had remained largely apart from the violence of the Sydney *milieu*.
Unlike the city's other vice trades, SP bookmaking had expanded steadily
during the 1930s. In 1951 New South Wales racing officials calculated the
state's annual illegal SP betting turnover at £80 million, twice that of Victoria, which was estimated at £90 million divided between 30 to 40 thousand illegal bookmakers (Sun, 16 May 1951). Revelations of systematic police corruption in Victoria before the Royal Commission into Off-the-Course Betting in 1958-59 prompted a similar line of inquiry in New South Wales.[14]
Responding to allegations of police corruption, the New South Wales government formed a Royal Commission in 1962 to investigate current off-
course betting practice and recommend reforms.

The N.S.W. Labor government was known to favor some form of legalization and the Commission consequently investigated two possible reforms:
State licensing of the SP bookmakers then operating illegally or the establishment of a new chain of state-owned, off-course betting shops accepting bets

on a pari-mutuel system. Hoping to win legalization and state licensing, some 600 of Sydney's bookmakers formed the Racing Commission Agents Association to lobby the Royal Commission and the N.S.W. State government. Based on testimony and survey data from the illegal bookmakers, the Commissioner concluded that there were some 6,000 SP bookmakers in the state with a total annual turnover of $550 million and a clientele comprising 28.7 percent of the state's adult population. The Commissioner recommended the establishment of a Totalisator Agency Board (TAB) as the most efficient means of eliminating off-track betting and heavy penalties for illegal SP operators (N.S.W. Parliament 1963: 16–21).

The SP bookmakers responded with full-page advertisements in Sydney's daily newspapers denouncing the recommendations and instead offered the state government a guaranteed annual licensing payment of $20 million.[15] The offer aroused a storm of incredulous protest. The council of churches called it "defiant law breakers offering a most blatant bribe," and the *Sydney Morning Herald*, the city's leading daily, said the government's acceptance would "bring public morality to a new low in a state hardly distinguished for its political standards."[16]

Although half the Labor cabinet was known to favor some concession to the SP bookmakers, the political costs of an open alliance were too high, and the government settled on a compromise — establishment of a TAB system as recommended but deletion of any harsh penalties for SP bookmakers. Nominal fines of $200 per offense were hardly a deterrent to men turning over $100,000 to $3 million per annum. The opening of the first TAB shops in December 1964 was followed by a series of ineffectual police raids against the SP networks. Moreover, the TAB network itself did not compete effectively against the superior service of the illegal operators and attracted only $60 million turnover in 1965 — small compared to the SP total of $550 million three years earlier.[17] Thus, with Labor's reforms, two parallel off-course betting systems were in operation — the massive, illegal SP network rooted in the telephone system and the public hotels; and a smaller, legal system of TAB walk-in shops serving a new clientele of women and middle-class suburbanites uncomfortable in the all-male ambience of the working-class hotel.

The Rise of the Sydney Syndicate

Sydney's vice economy experienced a fundamental transformation during the decade of Liberal-County Party rule from 1965 to 1976. In a period of unparalleled police and political corruption, an alliance of six vice entrepreneurs was able to impose strong syndicate controls upon the city's loosely structured vice economy and then expand both the scale and scope of its operations. After saturating Sydney's vice economy, the city's syndicate expanded interstate across Australia and developed international contacts with organized crime syndicates in Southeast Asia and the United States. By the late 1970s, Sydney's syndicate was a powerful organization that posed a major law enforcement problem for Australian authorities.

As the decade of Liberal Party rule in New South Wales drew to a close, a number of government bodies began damage assessment surveys of the extent of organized crime influence. Appearing before the N.S.W. Parliament's Select Committee on Crime Control in 1978, the State Attorney-General Department's liaison officer, Robert Bottom, gave the most comprehensive survey of the state's organized crime leadership. According to Bottom, "the top six of Sydney's underworld" were well-known criminals who specialized in certain types of criminal activity. Bottom identified George Freeman as "either No. 1 or 2 in the underworld" and stated that he controlled a large SP off-course betting network. Freeman's close associate and alternative for the number one position was Stanley John Smith, known as "Stan the Man," a criminal involved in drug dealing (N.S.W. Legislative Council 1978a: 63–77). A 1974 Commonwealth Police Report had identified both men as associates of an elder criminal, Leonard McPherson, whom they described as "a vicious, powerful criminal who is so well entrenched in organized crime that he is often referred to by the media and his associates as 'Mr. Big' (N.S.W. Legislative Assembly 1974: 1097). In his testimony Bottom identified two other leading organized crime figures — Karl Frederick Bonnette and ex-police detective Murray Riley — and discussed their involvement in drugs (N.S.W. Legislative Council 1978a: 63–77). Another Sydney personality frequently named in organized crime investigations is Abraham Saffron, the city's leading sly grog trader of the 1940s. In 1978 the South Australian State attorney-general described Saffron as "a key figure in organized crime in this country," and N.S.W. police later reported that Saffron "dominated the Kings Cross vice scene" and was known in the media as "Mr. Sin."[18]

Political corruption was the key factor in the emergence of this powerful syndicate. Speaking on the floor of N.S.W. Parliament in 1979, an independent Member of Parliament charged: "Under the Askin government in the 1960s, the real penetration of organized crime . . . took place. Shop front gambling and rackets came of age . . . I have no doubt that ex-Premier Askin and [Police commissioner Fred] Hanson knew and may have encouraged these activities" (*SMH*, 17 August 1979).

After Askin's death in 1981, the *National Times* wrote an obituary of the former New South Wales premier, who also served as his own police minister, which alleged that he had accepted bribes of $700,000 per annum from illegal casinos and lesser amounts from other vice entrepreneurs. Askin's two police commissioners, Norman Allen and Fred Hanson, allegedly received some $100,000 per annum from the casino operators (*National Times*, 13 and 27 September 1981).

This new political alliance became evident in the first half of 1967 as the emerging syndicate systematically eliminated all opposition within the *milieu* through a series of contract killings. The nature of the violence itself was indicative of the change. Over an eighteen-year period from 1944 to 1963 there were only eight murders within the Sydney *milieu*, an average of one killing every 2.25 years. Most sprang from personal conflicts and involved face-to-face combat with knives, chains and revolvers. In contrast, the five 1967 killings occurred at the rate of one every five weeks, and were impersonal liquidations involving machine gun, sniper rifle and dynamite. The victims were major vice entrepreneurs who resisted the new syndicate or hardened independents who refused to recognize any authority.

Significantly, none of Sydney's new syndicate leaders were indicted or even investigated for their role in these killings. Through their alliance with senior police, syndicate leaders were able to ensure that cooperative detectives were assigned to the murder investigations and uncorrupted detectives were given other assignments.[19] When it became apparent to the *milieu* that the new syndicate "powers" had an immunity to police investigation, independent vice entrepreneurs either sold out their business to the syndicate or retired.[20]

With their control over the *milieu* established, the new syndicate leaders were able to expand the city's vice economy. Summing up the 1976 estimates for the State's various vice trades reveals a total turnover of $2,219 million, comparable to Australia's 1978 national defense budget of $2,300 million — SP bookmaking ($1,420 million), illegal casino gambling ($650 million), poker machine fraud ($90 million), and narcotics ($59 million) (McCoy 1980: chs. 3–6).

Illegal Casinos

Perhaps the most convincing evidence of the alliance between the Askin government and the syndicate was the sudden opening of a network of five major and 21 minor London-style gambling clubs across Sydney after 1967 (Victoria Parliament 1982: 10 September, 2506–7).

The illegal casinos constituted an enormously profitable criminal enterprise. A scientific survey of their operations in 1974 calculated their combined annual turnover at $650 million with a profit of $15 million.

Although the Liberal government lost power in 1976, casino operators had parallel alliances with the new Labor government and managed to remain open until mid-1982. The N.S.W. Labor Premier, Neville Wran, simultaneously serving as his own Police Minister, favored eventual legalization and in the interim was apparently unwilling to move against the illegal casinos. In November 1977, however, his new Police Commissioner, Mervyn Wood, told the press that he would not close down the casinos in the coming months since he did not wish to spoil Christmas for their 300 employees. Simultaneously, the Leader of the Opposition in the N.S.W. Parliament charged that Commissioner Wood had met secretly with George Walker, "who runs an illegal gambling casino in Goulburn Street."[21] To avoid embarrassing the government further, the casinos temporarily adopted a lower profile and Commissioner Wood resigned his post after the government received anonymous allegations of his associations with illegal gambling. (*Bulletin*, 19 June 1979; *SMH*, 6 June 1979). Although Premier Wran declared in January 1978 that "all long-established casinos are closed," they were to remain open for another four years until further scandals forced the State government to act (*SMH*, 27 January 1978).

Off-Course Bookmaking

SP bookmaking experienced a parallel expansion during the Askin government's decade in power. The sustained police pressure following the establishment of the state-owned TAB in 1964 created both a temporary recession and conditions conducive to syndicate penetration of the illegal industry. The technical complexities of off-course betting had long protected the SP fraternity from anything but simple "standover" demands by the city's entrepreneurs in violence. After the consolidation of control within the *milieu* in 1967–68, the more sophisticated syndicate that emerged soon gained both the capital and competence to establish its own illegal betting operation. The new syndicate bookmaking operation had a number of advantages that allowed it to displace several thousand of the independent SP bookmakers: a comparative advantage of police protection meant it did not suffer losses from raids; larger operating capital allowed investment in more sophisticated telecommunications and computerized accounting; and violence allowed systematic race fixing, which bankrupted rival bookmakers and increased its own profits.

The character of the new SP syndicate emerged from debates during the 1979 sitting of the N.S.W. Parliament and the subsequent police raids unleashed on the SP bookmakers by the government. The controversy began in March when the Deputy Leader of the Opposition asked Premier Wran: "Is concern now being expressed openly that George David Freeman has unusual and undue influence over the [Police] 21 Division?" (N.S.W. Parliament 1979a: 3302). The following day Freeman himself appeared on the steps of Parliament at the head of camera crew from T.V. Channel 7 and demanded, without success, that the Opposition Leader appear to debate him. A week later independent M.P. John Hatton charged that Freeman had been photographed at Randwick Racecourse with the N.S.W. Chief Stipendiary Magistrate; was "one of the leading criminals in this State"; and was "the Australian contact man for one Danny Stein, an associate of notorious American organized crime figures, including Meyer Lansky" (N.S.W. Parliament 1979a: 3556–61).

To still the storm of controversy, N.S.W. Premier Neville Wran released a comprehensive report on Freeman's operations prepared in March 1977 by the Police Crime Intelligence Unit. Directing his operations from a central office with six employees, Freeman, according to the report, maintained 20 phone betting agencies scattered across central and eastern Sydney, concealed behind real or fictitious commercial facades such as Effective Cleaning Services Limited. Judging from the operations at one of his abandoned suburban agencies, Freeman's network had 200 telephones in operation capable of handling a vast volume of illegal betting. The report further alleged that Freeman was involved in manipulation of the racing industry. In 1975 Freeman had been investigated for his possible involvement in a conspiracy to fix trotting results that included bomb threats, killing of several horses, and manipulation of betting.

The report, moreover, documents in detail Freeman's remarkable rise during the Askin government's decade in power. Born in the waterside suburb of Annandale in 1934, Freeman first came to police notice in 1947 at age 13 and a decade later was described in the State's *Criminal Register* as "an active and persistent criminal" who resided at the Horne Bay Housing Settlement and worked as a casual laborer in the state abattoirs. Later police reports listed him as a "hoodlum type" who had himself tattooed with a "heart dagger, Maria and Mother" motif on his right arm and "T.R.U.E. L.O.V.E." on the backs of his fingers. During the 1960s his fortunes began to improve through his associations with some of Sydney's rising criminals. Apparently specializing in up-market shoplifting, for which he was arrested seven times between 1961 and 1968, Freeman travelled to London in 1967 where his involvement in "an organized campaign of shoplifting" with fellow Australian Arthur "Duke" Delaney attracted the attention of New Scotland Yard. Arriving at Perth in 1968, he was arrested for shop stealing with his close friend, the Sydney criminal Stanley John Smith.

After his release, Freeman returned to Sydney where his associations with the emerging syndicate and his involvement in SP bookmaking resulted in his rapid rise within the *milieu*.

Freeman had developed the most extensive contacts with American organized crime figures of anyone within the Sydney *milieu*. Between 1965 and 1971 Freeman had extensive meetings with a Chicago Mafia figure named Joseph Dan Testa. During this six-year period, Testa made three visits to Sydney where he made several investments, and Freeman and Stanley Smith reciprocated with a six-week visit to Chicago and Las Vegas in 1968. The F.B.I. described Testa as follows:

Testa has been characterized as a member of the Organized Criminal Element in Chicago, Illinois. Testa has been active in Real Estate Development, Cocktail Lounges, Financial Institutions and other enterprises alleged as a front or clearing house for syndicate money. Testa has been associated with a number of notorious hoodlum figures in the Chicago Illinois area including Rocco Pranno, convicted Stone Park Illinois hoodlum who operated the village of Stone Park for Chicago hoodlum leaders Sam Giancana and Sam Battaglia. In addition various sources have alleged that Testa has been an associate of Chicago hoodlums Tony Accardo, Joe Battaglia, Jack Cerone, and the late Felix Alderisio. In 1966 information was received that Testa allowed his fifty-two foot cabin cruiser to be used as a meeting place for top organized crime figures.

When Testa came to N.S.W. police notice in the early 1970s, he suddenly discontinued his Australian associations and liquidated his Sydney investments. Shortly thereafter, Las Vegas syndicate criminal Danny Stein began visiting Sydney as Freeman's guest. The F.B.I. identified Stein as follows:

> Alleged to represent hidden interests in the Flamingo Sands and Caesar's Palace Hotel and has been characterized as a thief who was fired from his job in those establishments because of this trait. He is known and has associated with the most notorious hoodlums to have visited Las Vegas including Meyer Lansky. In 1970–1971 Stein was the hidden owner in the Rosebowl Sports Book which was operating an illegal interstate gambling operation. This Book was ultimately raided by the F.B.I. and closed by the State of Nevada because of its illegal operations.

Between 1972 and 1976 Stein visited Sydney five times, staying from three days to five months on each visit. Like Testa, he purchased a racehorse and made several property investments in partnership with Freeman.

By 1977 Freeman had emerged as one of Sydney's most influential syndicate figures. The Crime Intelligence report stated: "This investigation indicates that Freeman should be considered *the leading criminal figure in this State* at this time, together with Stanley John Smith . . . with whom he is closely associated and in this regard have replaced the so-called 'Mr. Big' Leonard Arthur McPherson." In August 1972 Freeman was one of seven Sydney syndicate figures at a "summit" meeting "called to discuss current activities re organized crime" — including Leonard McPherson, Stanley "The Man" Smith, Karl Bonnette, Frederick "Paddles" Anderson, Milan "Iron Bar" Petricevic and Labor Party M.P. Albie Sloss. Similarly, in June 1976 Freeman participated in a summit of illegal casino operators called to discuss the legalization of casinos then being proposed by the N.S.W. government. The police précis of Stanley Smith's address to the illegal casino operators reads:

> Concern is expressed at attempts by others, such as [Terry] Page (the bookmaker) to interest themselves in the operation of legalized casinos. That the present illegal operators, who expect to be granted licenses, should combine as a team to lobby, otherwise, "[N.S.W. Premier] Wran will turn on you. He's a politician." That they represent a multimillion dollar business and that in dealing with politicians, that means "hard cash." That they must unite to ensure who the (gambling) Board is to be.

The N.S.W. detective-sergeant who compiled this report on Freeman's career concluded with an observation on the overall direction of Sydney's syndicates:

> During my recent overseas study tour it was found that American Organized Crime is extensively involved in illegal gambling and from this area the necessary finance is supplied . . . to operate in areas such as narcotics, the penetration of legitimate business and the corruption of public officials. Our inquiries to date indicate that Organized Crime in this State is developing along the same lines (N.S.W. Police 1977).

Prompted by these revelations, the new Police Commissioner, James Lees, appointed Inspector Mervyn Beck to head the 21 Division gaming squad and ordered an assault on the SP betting industry. Unlike the cosmetic efforts of the previous decade, the new SP suppression campaign attacked the large operators and quickly uncovered major betting operations, some almost as large as Freeman's, equipped with phone banks and computers. Police analysis of confiscated records revealed a turnover far higher than previous estimates. The 21 Division raided an SP center in northern New South Wales with an annual turnover of $100 million and an operating range covering the whole of eastern Australia, Papua-New Guinea and the South Pacific. A raid on an SP center in central Sydney discovered a leased computer carrying 10,000 phone accounts and an illegal direct line to the State TAB.[22] Judging from the scale of these operations, our estimate of $1,420 million as the total turnover in the N.S.W. SP industry—achieved by correcting the 1962 Royal Commission's $550 million estimate for inflation—would appear conservative. Since most illegal bookmakers earn an average 10 percent profit on turnover, the industry yields an annual profittaking of $142 million—a vast uncontrolled capital available to finance a range of organized crime activities. Recalling John Wren's annual profit of $78,000 from his Collingwood Tote in 1906, profits of $10 million for a SP single operation and $142 million for the N.S.W. industry in 1979 indicate the enormous expansion of the vice economy during this century.

Poker Machines and Clubs

Along with casinos and bookmaking, the third major area of syndicate penetration during the 1970s was the N.S.W. poker or slot machine industry. Although New South Wales has refused to legalize casinos, it has allowed private clubs to operate poker machines. Since 1956 when the N.S.W. government decided to license poker machines for revenue, the number of machines has grown from 5,596 providing a tax revenue of $1.5 million to 45,519 machines in 1978 providing $98 million in tax.[23] New South Wales is still the only Australian state that allows poker machines, and its industry is one of the world's largest, comparable to Nevada's 50,000 licensed machines. Poker machine gambling quickly became something of an addiction among segments of Sydney's working class and profits financed an almost explosive expansion in the size and services of the private clubs. The number of registered clubs in New South Wales has increased from 85 in 1946, to 932 by 1956, to 1,507 by 1977 (*Financial Review*, 3 August 1978).

The state's licensed clubs have become a social phenomenon without parallel anywhere else in the world, and are a unique marriage of Australian working-class culture—embodied in mateship, sport, patriotism and beer drinking—and the poker machine. Occupying sprawling premises decorated in a pseudo-Las Vegas style, Sydney's giant Rugby League clubs offer members free live entertainment, moderately priced restaurants, sauna baths, sporting facilities and holiday lodges — all for the price of a $10 annual membership fee. The largest Sydney Rugby League clubs have 30,000 to 50,000 members and regularly sponsor tours by leading American and European entertainers. In 1976 some $4,600 million passed through the state's poker machines, equivalent to 20 percent of its total disposable personal income and over three times the $1,568 million turnover on the Sydney Stock Exchange. The club industry had become the state's largest private employer with 32,000 workers, compared to only 15,000 for its largest industrial concern, the iron and coal conglomerate B.H.P. (*Bulletin*, 22 October 1977; *Financial Review*, 3 August 1978).

There have been two avenues for organized crime exploitation of this vast leisure industry — directly through the manufacture and sale of poker machines and indirectly through penetration of club management. Sydney's first poker machine manufacturing company was established in 1948 and by 1954 competition had produced two bombings. One of the automobiles destroyed in those explosions belonged to poker machine manufacturer Raymond Smith, later described as "a man with a substantial dossier of criminal activity." Constable Murray Stuart Riley was assigned to protect Smith and later joined his company as sales manager after resigning from the N.S.W. police in 1962.[24] When one of Riley's associates, Wally Dean, was elected manager of South Sydney Junior Rugby League Club, the city's largest club, in 1968, the two formed a partnership to sell poker machines and manage clubs. Both men were associates of Leonard McPherson ("Mr. Big"). As the Moffitt Royal Commission into Organized Crime reported in 1975 all three men were key figures in criminal penetration of the poker machine and club industries (N.S.W. Legislative Assembly 1974: transcript 1097, report, 69).

The Moffitt Royal Commission was prompted by a preliminary police investigation of the New South Wales poker machine industry in 1971–72. An anonymous informant had told Commonwealth police that American "organized crime money was being used in the poker machine business in New South Wales," and Leonard McPherson was conspiring with Chicago mafioso Joseph Testa and a poker machine company to corner the market and to "attempt penetration of clubs" (Legislative Assembly: 1974: transcript, 1042–3). After a comprehensive investigation reaching as far as North America, Commonwealth police filed a detailed report that largely confirmed the substance of these allegations. Since 1963 the Bally Manufacturing Company of Chicago had been controlled by New Jersey mafioso Don Gerardo Catena through "dummy investors." Commonwealth police alleged there was a conspiracy between Bally Australia and Leonard McPherson to drive Australian-manufactured machines off the market, secure Bally's monopoly over the $400 million New South Wales industry, and use this "corner" to control a wide range of club supply services, particularly entertainment bookings. The penetration had begun in 1971 when an "American crime organizer," either Testa or one of Bally's Chicago executives, had visited Sydney to "campaign against club managers who have refused to purchase Bally products." The report concluded:

(a) that a direct and deliberate attempt has and is being made to infiltrate an American organized-crime controlled legitimate business concern into Australia;
(b) in the establishment of this company (i.e. Bally) the "classic" American organized crime methods and corrupt tactics are being adopted. [Legislative Assembly 1974: 1132–34]

Released in 1975 after seven months of investigations, the Moffitt Commission's report was Australia's first major inquiry into organized crime and concluded that Commonwealth police had understated the extent of penetration. The Commission found that Bally's American and European operations were completely controlled by organized crime. During the 1950s, Bally's East Coast American distributor was Gerardo Catena, who became surrogate head of Don Vito Genovese's New York Mafia family in 1958 and a controlling stockholder in Bally in 1964. When Bally expanded into the Caribbean and Europe, its distributor was Dino Cellini, the "right hand" of Meyer Lansky in his Cuban casino operations of the 1950s. During the 1960s Bally's European manager, Alex A. Wilms, was a promoter of organized crime enterprises. At a November 1966 London meeting of syndicate figures to discuss control of Spain's first legal casino, Wilms announced that he was representing Marcel Francisi, a Corsican who held government licenses for two French casinos and was identified by the U.S. Congress in 1965 and 1971 as Marseilles' leading heroin manufacturer (Legislative Assembly 1974: report 116–21).

The report did not, however, probe deeply into the antecedents of Bally's Australian manager, Jack Rooklyn. It did condemn Rooklyn's business offers to the three N.S.W. police assigned to investigate Bally Australia and noted that he had approached Abraham Saffron, Sydney's leading sly grog trader of the 1950s, now proprietor of several Kings Cross strip clubs, "to see somebody in authority to take the heat out of the investigation" (Legislative Assembly 1974: report 28, 57–63).

The Commission came to similarly damning conclusions about organized crime penetration of Sydney's clubs. Through Wally Dean's position as manager of South Sydney Junior Rugby League Club, ex-detective Murray Riley had been appointed club poker machine supervisor. The Riley-Dean partnership operated companies that serviced South Sydney, and they simultaneously gained managerial posts in two other Sydney clubs. Together the two men plundered the assets of the three clubs. Commissioner Moffitt concluded that Riley had operated according to "the U.S. gangster patterns in the Las Vegas and London clubs" by "organizing the skimming — by illicit means and shams — of monies from the clubs" (pp. 69–73).

Sydney's syndicate also became involved in two smaller but highly profitable industries during the 1970s — abortion and domestic marijuana distribution. The patterns of police corruption so evident in casino gambling were extended to the abortion business, and Sydney became a major interstate and international center servicing Victoria, Queensland and New Zealand. Following a government inquiry into police protection for illegal abortionists, Melbourne's illegal abortion clinics closed and Victorian women had to travel to Sydney. Queensland and New Zealand had never tolerated illegal clinics, and as sexual mores changed and demand for abortion increased, their women too came to Sydney. Operated by licensed medical practitioners, Sydney's clinics are located in Kings Cross and made regular payments to syndicate agents who in turn paid a share of their income to police.

Australia's domestic marijuana industry began in the early 1970s when Italian migrant market gardeners from Calabria planted extensive cannabis crops in the Griffith area of western New South Wales. The first police raid in February 1974 discovered 10 hectares of cannabis and another in November 1975 found 32 hectares, indications that marijuana cultivation was substantial. According to the 1979 report of the N.S.W. Drugs Royal Commission, cultivation was controlled by a Calabrian-Italian syndicate led by local migrant vintner Antonio Sergi and distributed by a Sydney Calabrian businessman, Robert Trimboli. Despite visible assets of $2.6 million, Sergi was a purely local operator and his involvement in organized crime extended no further than the Calabrian networks of which he was part. (N.S.W. Parliament 1979b: 1908, 2627). Trimboli, however, had developed contacts with the Sydney syndicate who distributed the Griffith cannabis crop across Australia, and later became involved in importation of Southeast Asian heroin with his Australian associates (*SMH*, 1 September 1980).

International Expansion

The election of a N.S.W. Labor government in 1976 coincided with a major transition period in the history of Sydney's syndicates. After a decade of continuous expansion under the benign gaze of the Askin government, many of the city's major vice trades experienced a marked recession. Moreover, the city's vice economy was saturated, and its capacity to absorb further innovations was now limited. Finding expansion in the established vice trades blocked, Sydney's syndicates shifted their energies in three directions: penetration of Australia's legitimate business sector, particularly Sydney property development; a geographical extension, both interstate and international, of their vice trading; and the introduction of a new and controversial commodity into Australia — Southeast Asian heroin.

The contraction in Sydney's vice economy during the mid-1970s was only partly associated with the change in state governments. In 1974 a New South Wales court ruled that a woman could, upon medical advice, have an abortion if she so desired. Within two years, several state-licensed abortion clinics were operating in Sydney and abortion shifted from the vice economy to the legitimate economy. Instead of making regular payments to syndicate agents and corrupt N.S.W. police, the abortion clinics paid N.S.W. state licensing fees and their medical practitioners paid Federal tax on their income. Similarly, the publicity surrounding the hearings and release of the Moffitt Royal Commission report on organized crime in licensed clubs led ultimately to the expulsion of syndicate members from managerial positions. Murray Riley was forced to sever his connections with the South Sydney Club and the poker machine industry. And the State Licensing court cancelled the permit of the Associated Motor Club, a downtown Sydney club systematically plundered by Dean and Riley.[25] The sporadic police pressure on casinos which started in early 1977 prompted a noticeable shift in location from central Sydney to inner-Western suburbs, a change which reduced their visibility and income.

Perhaps the most dramatic development was the near-eradication of Australia's domestic cannabis industry in the latter half of 1977. On July 15, a local Liberal Party politician and anti-cannabis crusader named Donald MacKay disappeared in Griffith, the center of the Calabrian cannabis industry in New South Wales. The disappearance and presumed murder of a well-known politician produced public outrage, and across Australia State and Federal police, using satellite land-sat photos, unleashed a coordinated assault on cannabis cultivation. In the space of a few months, hundreds of hectares of cannabis were uprooted across eastern Australia and the domestic marijuana industry had been destroyed.[26]

The decline in Sydney's vice trades coincided with the syndicate's expansion into the Southeast Asian drug trade. The earliest police intelligence on the syndicates' interest in narcotics came during the last visit of Las Vegas gambler Danny Stein to Sydney in early 1976 as the guest of local SP bookmaker George Freeman. According to the N.S.W. police report titled "Organized Crime—George David Freeman": "Towards the end of Stein's stay on this occasion, information was received that Stein was here for the purpose of organizing a network for the reception of heroin into this country from the Golden Triangle and for subsequent distribution on the local market and in the United States" (N.S.W. Police 1977).

Over the next four years, several groups of smugglers closely connected with Sydney's syndicate were arrested for drug running between Southeast Asia and Australia. Initially, the demand for heroin was low in Australia and smugglers concentrated on cannabis. After mismanagement forced closure of the 33 Club casino in 1974, Michael Moyland, Jr. reorganized his staff for a cannabis smuggling operation between Bangkok and Sydney. With a team of 40 couriers each carrying 10 kilograms of compressed cannabis worth $84,000 retail in Sydney, the Moyland operation prospered for three years and became one of the city's main suppliers. Moyland was exploring the possibilities of the heroin trade in 1976, when his couriers were intercepted by Customs and he was charged with drug smuggling (N.S.W. District Court 1977 and 1978).

Australia's largest drug shipment was organized by ex-detective Murray Riley in 1977–78. After exposure before the Moffitt Royal Commission into Organized Crime forced him out of the poker machine business, Riley began travelling to San Francisco and Las Vegas, where he met with a number of known American mafiosi. In November 1976 Riley was photographed in San Francisco meeting with mafiosi James Fratianno and Salvatore Amarena, an associate of the Santos Trafficante, Jr. family of Tampa, Florida (*Bulletin,* 7 November 1978). After his return to Australia, Riley began travelling regularly to Southeast Asia where, with the assistance of the Nugan Hand Bank, he arranged shipment of 4.1 tons of Thai cannabis worth $46.8 million retail in Sydney. With a crew recruited from the Associated Motor Club and Sydney's network of auto thieves, Riley's shipment left the Gulf of Siam in February 1978 and was intercepted by the Australian Bureau of Narcotics when it landed in northern New South Wales several months later. Riley himself was arrested in the police operation and later sentenced to ten years' hard labor (N.S.W. District Court 1978).

As the Sydney syndicate's Bangkok contacts developed, a number of smuggling groups began moving substantial quantities of heroin into Australia in the late 1970s. The first firm evidence of the traffic's operation emerged in October 1978, when Bangkok police arrrested three Sydney men with a suitcase containing 8.4 kilograms of number four grade heroin. Four days later Sydney police aided an inner-city terrace house and eventually arrested several suspected distributors. According to later N.S.W. police evidence, the ring had operated for over a year moving from Bangkok into Sydney some 11.3 kilograms per month—equivalent to about 15 percent of New South Wales' minimum estimated supply. Later convicted for his role in organizing the shipment was William Sinclair, an elderly ex-Sydney resident who had been associated with the Riley-Dean club fraud schemes of the 1960s and later moved to Bangkok, where he owned a prostitution bar. The couriers were recruited from the lowest echelons of the Sydney *milieu* and included a Rugby League football star. The alleged Sydney distributor was a notorious "standover man" with 25 arrests named Neddy Smith, who was described by police as having "a reputation as an enforcer with the criminal element and is feared among them." Significantly, there were overlapping personal ties between the three drug smuggling groups, indicating that they were all operations based within the Sydney criminal *milieu* (N.S.W. Parliament 1979b: 2405–36).

The most remarkable of the drug smuggling groups detected during the late 1970s was the Terrence Clark organization, known in the press as "the Mr. Asia syndicate." Operating between Sydney and Southeast Asia from 1976 to 1979, the Clark group were all young New Zealanders who had migrated to Sydney and established contacts with the Sydney syndicate. Clark himself had spent most of his working life as a petty criminal in Auckland and served time in New Zealand's prisons. After release, Clark became involved in drug dealing in Auckland and transferred his operations to Sydney in 1976 to escape arrest. Through a resident buyer in Singapore, the group moved regular shipments of Thai heroin into Sydney and distributed it through the networks of New Zealand youth that frequented the city's hotels and moved among the unemployed young who were turning to heroin in growing numbers. Escaping from a declining island economy cut off from its traditional English markets, a flood of New Zealand school-leavers, perhaps numbering 100,000, crossed the Tasman Strait in the 1970s to seek their fortunes in Sydney. Unskilled and unconnected, they formed a youth ghetto in the city's Bondi area and many drifted into prostitution, petty theft and heroin dealing. With his enormous profits and contacts in the Sydney syndicate, Clark was able to purchase protection from the N.S.W. police and retain the services of perhaps two agents in the Australian Bureau of Narcotics. For an annual retainer of $25,000 plus $1,000 for each data search, Clark gained access to the Bureau's centralized computer system and was able to learn if any of his prospective couriers would attract a Customs' search at the airports.

After two years of successful operations, Clark began to encounter discipline problems among the addicts, prostitutes, and petty criminals who comprised his organization. A nearly perfect predator, Clark cultivated a self-image as a sadist to maintain discipline. When several arrested couriers gave information to police, Clark tortured and killed them as an example. During his syndicate's three years of operation, he is known to have murdered at least six people, including his partner and Singapore agent, Martin Johnstone. After two of Clark's operatives made substantial revelations to Queensland police and Federal narcotics agents in June 1978, Clark obtained a tape recording of their confession through his contacts and had them killed. The discovery of their bodies in a shallow grave in Melbourne in May 1979 prompted a Victoria police investigation of Clark's operation which exposed the corruption in the Australian Bureau of Narcotics. The Federal government reacted to the scandal by dissolving the Australian Bureau of Narcotics, transferring its director Harvey Bates to an administrative post in customs, and integrating most of the narcotics agents into an expanded Federal Police. Clark himself, however, had escaped to England where he was later convicted of murder after British police recovered the mutilated body of his partner Martin Johnstone from the waters of an abandoned quarry in October 1979. (McCoy 1980: 320–25; Hall 1981).

The Sydney syndicate's involvement in heroin distribution coincided with a surplus in Southeast Asia's heroin supply. Illicit heroin production began in the Golden Triangle in 1968–69, when Hong Kong's Chiu Chow Chinese syndicates dispatched chemists into the Thai-Burma-Laos border area to open refineries for number four grade heroin. Almost all production was exported to South Vietnam, where the ruling military cliques distributed it to U.S. combat troops. With the heroin sold cheaply and unadulterated, an estimated 100,000 G.I. addicts were consuming enough to sustain some two million users in the United States.

This market collapsed unexpectely in 1972–73 following the rapid withdrawal of U.S. troops from Vietnam. Suddenly awash in surplus heroin, the Chiu Chow syndicates of Southeast Asia found two solutions to their marketing problem — penetration of the vast U.S. domestic market and increased local distribution within Southeast Asian cities. President Nixon's "war on drugs" had effected a temporary suspension of Turkish opium cultivation in 1972, and there was a fortuitous shortage in the American market. Sample street seizures analyzed by the U.S. Drug Enforcement Administration (DEA) showed that Southeast Asia heroin climbed from about 8 to 10 percent of U.S. consumption in 1971 to 30 percent by 1974. However, by increasing its Southeast Asian contingent from two agents in 1972 to 31 by late 1974, the DEA was able to block Southeast Asian heroin exports to the U.S., and by 1974 the region's share of the American market had dropped back down to 9 percent.

Faced with the alternative of closing down their refineries, the Chiu Chow syndicates decided, according to the DEA's intelligence, to develop new markets in Europe and Australia where there were then relatively few addicts. The Chiu Chow leaders calculated, accurately enough, that there were only four societies affluent enough to sustain the high cost of the international heroin traffic — North America (Canada and the U.S.), Japan, Western Europe and Australia. Denied access to the U.S. by the DEA and Japan by strict Custom's controls, the Chiu Chow were left with only two markets. The results of their export efforts were soon evident. Total European seizures of Southeast Asian heroin increased from 22 pounds in 1972 to 1,540 pounds in 1976. There was a parallel increase in Australian drug use. Between 1974 and 1976 narcotics-related deaths in New South Wales increased 300 percent, from 14 to 49. In 1978 the N.S.W. Drugs Royal Commission calculated the State's addict population at 9,250, consuming $59 million worth of heroin annually. (McCoy 1980: ch. 7).

The Philippine Prostitution Industry

The heroin trade was only one aspect of the Sydney syndicate's expansion into Southeast Asia during the 1970s. Exploiting the growing numbers of male Australian tourists visiting Manila, Sydney vice entrepreneurs began buying up prostitute bars and became a major force in the Philippine sex-tourism industry by the end of the decade. Manila now serves Sydney's syndicate in much the same way that Havana did American organized crime in the 1950s. The Philippine prostitution industry is a source of major profits for both Australian and Japanese organized crime, and the scale of the industry is indicated by the exceptionally high percentage of males among both Australian and Japanese tourist arrivals. Of the 50,000 Australian tourists who landed in 1978, 42,000 (84 percent) were males and of the 226,000 Japanese arrivals, males numbered 191,000 (85 percent) — sex ratios which compare rather strikingly to the 65 percent male arrivals among Americans, 61 percent among British, and 55 percent among Canadians (Republic of the Philippines 1980: 100–107).

Concentrated in a square kilometer of Manila's downtown Ermita district, several hundred bars, massage parlors, and discos serve as pick-up points for contracts completed iin the city's tourist hotels. Despite domestic political backlash, the Marcos regime has encouraged the prostitution industry to generate tourist dollars, provide unemployment for the surfeit of young women on the labor market, amortize the international loans that financed a wave of poorly planned hotel construction in 1976, and generate passengers for the country's ailing national carrier Philippine Airlines. Prostitution in Manila is not a mere vice trade but is an integral component of the national economy. Manila itself is a poor and visibly squalid Third World city with few attractions for affluent tourists. Consequently, there are at least six major hotels in the tourist belt that rely upon prostitution to fill their rooms and pay off their substantial debts. Wary of either local or American organized crime, the Marcos regime has instead chosen to let Japanese and Australian syndicates dominate the Manila bar and brothel strip.

The Australian presence became increasingly visible in Manila during the early 1980s. While there are several clubs with obvious Australian names like the "Kings Cross Social Club" and "The Kangaroo Club," some fifteen others are wholly or partly Australian owned. The clubs cater to middle-aged Australian males who spend their annual two- to four-week holidays using two and more women per day. Several Sydney emigré entrepreneurs have organized package tours that include not only Manila clubs but the even more tawdry bars at the outskirts of the U.S. Air Force base at Clark Field and the U.S. Naval Base at Subic Bay north of Manila.

In May 1980 the N.S.W. Drugs Royal Commission presented a second report which incidentally indicated the scope of Sydney syndicate activities in Manila. In essence, the Commission argued that Sydney criminals had purchased bars and were using them as a base for moving narcotics between Bangkok and Sydney. The primary target of the Commission's investigation was a network of heroin, smugglers based in the criminal *milieu* of the Sydney dockside district of Balmain. Until the gentrification of the 1970s, the Balmain peninsula on Sydney's inner harbour was a tough waterfront area that was home to many of the city's leading communists and criminals. Sydney's postwar "Mr. Big," Leonard McPherson, and his protegé Stanley "The Man" Smith, are Balmain natives, and both have maintained their ties to the area. Their close asociate George Freeman, identified as "number one or two" in organized crime, is a native of the neighboring Annandale waterfront district. In his investigation into drug smuggling on the Balmain docks, the Royal Commissioner uncovered a network of suspicious associations among men who traced their roots to the old working class neighborhood — syndicate figures Stanley Smith and Leonard McPherson; Labor Party officials including Balmain Alderman Daniel Casey, proprietor of shipping container repair firm, and Balmain State M.P. Roger Degen: as well as a number of locals with criminal identities who made frequent trips to Manila. Significantly, the district's minor criminals showed an interesting pattern of overlapping interaction with their social superiors that indicates that the criminal *milieu* is closely interwoven into Balmain's social fabric. These criminals participate in McPherson's syndicate operations; some work for Alderman Casey's container firm; and many support the local right-wing Labor Party faction headed by Casey and Degen as branch members and muscle at unruly meetings.

Sydney's criminal contacts with Manila apparently began in the late 1960s when Balmain criminal Leonard McPherson began travelling there, eventually opening a prostitute bar and cane furniture export business. An April 1976 N.S.W. police report claimed that "during 1975 a person 'is alleged to have gone to Manila, at least once a month, to bring back white powder for McPherson (not known whether heroin or cocaine)' and that about the same time McPherson was seeking recruits." After McPherson's deportation from Manila in 1975, a younger Balmain criminal named Martin Olson purchased a "club type bar in Manila" and "was looking after Leonard McPherson's prostitution business in Manila." Simultaneously, Olson managed a company called Filipino Imports which may have been involved in smuggling drugs into Australia (N.S.W. Parliament 1980b: 35–49).

As the Commissioner probed deeper into Manila's role in the smuggling of drugs into Sydney, he discovered a web of complex connections between the two cities. In addition to the resident syndicate members, the commission uncovered the "shadowy figure" of Baron Antony Moynihan, a British peer who had been a drummer in Sydney's Chequers Nightclub in the early 1960s and later migrated to Manila. There he married for a third time, operated several nightclubs and played host to visiting Sydney criminals (pp. 1983–203). Among Baron Moynihan's close associates in the late 1970s was Sydney heroin dealer Robert Rolla Evans, the financier of the three Australians arrested in Bangkok with 8.4 kilograms of heroin in October 1978. Between July 1977 and October 1979, Evans made six trips on a Sydney-Bangkok-Manila-Sydney route to arrange heroin shipments. On one of these trips in September 1978 Evans carried $30,000 cash, which he claimed was to finance investment in a Manila bar with Baron Moynihan. But the Commissioner felt that the money was probably used to finance the purchase of heroin in Bangkok for export to Sydney (145–211).

One of the most controversial of any of these Manila trips involved the Member for Balmain in the N.S.W. Parliament, Mr. Roger Degen. When Degen "deliberately lied" to conceal the circumstances of a 1975 trip to Manila, the Commission investigated him and discovered his associations with a remarkable number of Sydney criminals—Leonard McPherson's apprentice, Stanley Smith; the proprietor of Balmain's illegal casino; and convicted heroin dealer William Sinclair (pp. 83–87). After following the twisted path of these connections, the Commissioner concluded:

The evidence in this re-opened inquiry has drawn attention to Manila in the Philippines. It will be recalled that a number of persons with whom I have dealt in this report have been to the Philippines on a number of occasions, and some have apparently lived there. Many of these people are both criminals and drug traffickers. . . . I am now satisfied that whilst Manila is still not a primary source of heroin, it is a significant point of transshipment of heroin. It is a potential source of supply for Australian traffickers, and, in particular, it may be used as the actual point of origin of the journey . . . [p. 269]

The Nugan Hand Bank

The Sydney syndicate's diversification and dispersion is perhaps most evident in the tangled history of the Nugan Hand Bank. Like an irregularly cut gem that casts a different hue as each of its several faces is held to the light, the Nugan Hand Bank served several constitutencies simultaneously and reveals a good deal about the operations of each. Based in Sydney, the bank was a partnership between an Australian lawyer, Frank Nugan, and an ex-Green Beret businessman, Michael Hand, who worked closely with an American intelligence operative named Maurice Bernard Houghton. Through the three men and their separate, sometimes overlapping networks, the bank served corrupt Labor party politicians, Sydney crime syndicates, Australian tax avoiders, and the U.S. Central Intelligence Agency (CIA).

In less than a decade after its incorporation in 1973, the Nugan Hand Bank went through a complete cycle from modest origins to spectacular global expansion, to precipitous collapse. During its brief life the bank's character was shaped by its three founders. Son of a Spanish migrant fruitgrower, Francis Nugan grew up in Griffith, New South Wales, graduated in law from Sydney University and did advanced legal studies at the University of California. While his brother Ken built the family produce business, the Nugan Group Ltd., into Australia's largest, Frank made a substantial profit—he later claimed $3 million—from Australia's mining boom of the early 1970s (*SMH*, 2 May 1980; *National Times*, 17 August 1980).

The other partner, Michael Jon Hand, was born in New York in 1941 and raised in the Bronx. After finishing a year's course in forestry at Syracuse University, he joined the U.S. Army Green Berets in 1963 and was sent to fight in Vietnam. After finishing his tour, he joined the CIA in 1966 as a contract officer directing Meo hilltribe mercenaries in northern Laos. The CIA was then heavily involved in the Laotian heroin industry through its local mercenaries and its contract airline Air America, and Hand may have acquired the expertise in narcotics that he was to apply with such profit in his later management of the bank. Hand moved to Sydney in 1967 and in September 1969 formed Australasian and Pacific Holdings Ltd., a real estate company whose 71 shareholders included 19 men then employed by the CIA's contract airlines in Indochina, Air America and Continental Air Services.[27]

The key figure in much of the bank's history, Maurice Bernard Houghton, is a mysterious Texan who arrived in Sydney from Saigon in 1967 with an impressive list of references from U.S. military officers and Washington politicians. An older man born in 1929, Houghton soon formed a business association with an Hungarian emigré, Sir Paul Strasser, owner of one of Sydney's leading property companies, Parkes Development Corporation. With the support of Strasser and his associates, Houghton opened the Beefsteak and Burgundy Restaurant in Kings Cross in 1967, the first of three of such clubs catering to American troops on "R & R" leave from the war in South Vietnam. Among his customers were Australia's CIA station chief from 1973 to 1975, John D. Walker; N.W.S. Premier Robert Askin; and the man who "for many years dominated the Kings Cross vice scene," Abraham Saffron. Unlike his younger associates, Houghton maintained excellent contacts with senior U.S. military personnel in the Asia-Pacific region and was a close friend of many CIA agents. Houghton was apparently employed by the CIA throughout his years in Australia and, as the agent of an allied power, was protected by the Australian Security Intelligence Organization.[28]

Combining their assets to form a paid-up capital of $1 million, the three men formed the Nugan Hand Bank and registered it at Sydney in early 1973. Over the next four years the bank grew at a remarkable rate by providing a bridge between legitimate banks and a shadow universe of organized crime, illegal money laundering and intelligence operations. The bank's annual report dated January 1977 showed assets of $21.8 million and a public relations release in August claimed a turnover during the financial year "in excess" of one billion dollars (*SMH*, 2 May 1980). Building upon this success, the bank undertook an ambitious global expansion program and grew at an even more spectacular rate until its collapse in April 1980.

Within Australia, much of Nugan Hand's growth was achieved through close contact with Sydney organized crime and N.S.W. state politics. Through the agency of a former Rugby League star and Labor Party politician, the bank secured deposits of up to $3.8 million from a number of Sydney's municipal councils. Among the bank's clients was Abraham Saffron, the leading sly grog trader of the 1940s, since identified by several government commissions as one of Sydney's main organized crime figures.

The bank, moreover, provided a range of consultancy and financial services for a number of Australia's leading drug traffickers. In 1977–78, for example, Murray Riley is believed to have moved $250,000 to $1 million from Sydney to Southeast Asia to finance his four-ton cannabis shipment. At least two of his operatives also had extensive dealings with Nugan Hand. Terrence Clark's "Mr. Asia syndicate," which may have earned as much as $100 million, is thought to have made extensive use of the bank, as did others involved in Sydney's drug traffic.[29] Through Michael Hand's initiative, the bank opened a branch at Chiangmai in northern Thailand, the financial center of the Golden Triangle heroin trade, with the express purpose of attracting deposits from drug traffickers. In 1976–77 the Chiangmai office in fact collected $3 million in deposits from six known heroin dealers and sent the money to Michael Hand in Hong Kong. There have also been claims that the bank had dealings with the region's leading opium warlord, Chan Shee-fu.[30] There were, moreover, allegations that the Nugan family's produce firm, the Nugan Group Ltd., was involved in Australia's domestic marijuana industry. Responding to such allegations made on the floor of the N.S.W. Parliament, Francis Nugan's brother Ken, the company president, took out full-page advertisements in Sydney's newspapers denying any involvement with the Calabrian cannabis growers in the town of Griffith, also the site of the Nugan group's produce processing plant.

Although the Australian Bureau of Narcotics (ABN) had ample intelligence on the bank's drug dealings, it failed to take action. There were "serious allegations" that Hand and a former Air America pilot named Kermit King were smuggling heroin into Australia after Hand's arrival in 1967. In 1973 the ABN had reports that Hand and King were landing Golden Triangle heroin at abandoned airstrips in northern Australia. After learning of the Bureau's investigations in 1978, however, Frank Nugan met personally with the Bureau's Commissioner Harvey Bates and pressured him to drop the investigation. Finding itself penetrated by a paid informant and its investigation making no progress, the Bureau discontinued its inquiries.[31] In November 1982 a joint commonwealth N.S.W. State Police task force into the bank's operations reported that Nugan Hand had dealt with 26 reputed Australian drug dealers and handled $4.3 million in deposits from suspected drug transactions. Drug importer Murray Riley had formed "a close business and social relationship" with Hand and the two were involved with American mafioso Jimmy Fratianno in a $23 million casino project in Las Vegas.[32]

As it expanded so dramatically in 1977-78, the Nugan-Hand Bank acquired a number of retired senior U.S. Military and CIA personnel as employees or associates. The key figure in making these contacts was Bernie Houghton, who began taking a more active role in the bank after the collapse of Sir Paul Strasser's Parkes Development company in 1976 forced a contraction of his restaurant business. Houghton recruited his old friend Admiral Earl Yates, former chief of staff of the U.S. Pacific command, to serve as president of Nugan Hand in early 1977. A succession of such appointments followed: General Leroy J. Manor, former chief of staff of the U.S. Pacific command, manager of the Manila branch; General Edwin F. Black, former O.S.S. officer and commander of U.S. forces in Thailand, president of Nugan Hand Inc., Hawaii; Walter McDonald, CIA deputy director of economic research 1972-77, bank executive; William Colby, CIA director 1973-76, legal counsel; Dale Holmgren, manager of the CIA airline Civil Air Transport, manager of the bank's Taiwan office; and Robert Jansen, former CIA station chief in Bangkok, representative in Thailand. With its new officers, the bank expanded with a network of 22 branches covering Asia, Europe and the Americas (*Wall Street Journal*, 24 August 1982; *National Times*, 6 June 1982).

The pattern of events surrounding this expansion indicates a possibility that the bank may have become a CIA "proprietary" involved in global money transfers in support of clandestine operations. In 1976 the Nassau-based Castle Bank closed its operations after a U.S. Internal Revenue Service (IRS) investigation showed that it was handling the CIA's clandestine financial services and was laundering money for American organized crime. The Castle Bank's founder Miami lawyer Paul Helliwell, was a former CIA operative who had played a key role in establishing the Nationalist Chinese forces as the Golden Triangle's leading opium merchants during the 1950s. Although the CIA forced the IRS to suspend its investigation on national security grounds, public exposure and Helliwell's death in 1976 ended the Castle Bank's utility for the Agency (*Wall Street Journal*, 18 April 1980). In the same year that the Castle Bank closed its Nassau offices, Nugan Hand launched its formal "banking" operations in the nearby Cayman Islands. The opening of Latin American branches, a new area for Nugan Hand, and recruitment of retired CIA officers gave it a corporate structure quite similar to the collapsed Castle Bank. Indeed, a former CIA agent named Kevin Mulcahy, a key witness in the Edwin Wilson case, gave details to the *National Times* "about the Agency's use of Nugan Hand for shifting money for various covert operations around the globe" (*National Times*, 21 February 1982).

Through Houghton as well, the Nugan Hand Bank developed contacts with the network of ex-CIA mercenaries surrounding Edwin P. Wilson. A man of considerable charisma and cunning, Wilson joined the CIA in 1951 and was involved in maritime intelligence operations until his resignation in 1971. He then joined a special unit in the U.S. Office of Naval Intelligence, Task Force 157, and began setting up small cover firms for the Task Force which he used simultaneously to start his career as a private arms trader. Entrusted with operations deemed too sensitive for the CIA, Task Force 157 was active in Australia and is believed to have employed Wilson's close friend Bernie Houghton as one of its agents. In a 1977 report on the Nugan-Hand Bank, the Australian Bureau of Narcotics described Houghton as "still affiliated with the CIA" (*National Times*, 4 January and 14 June 1981; 5 October 1980).

By 1976 Wilson had resigned from Task Force 157 to devote himself to his arms dealing, a move that was paralleled by Nugan Hand's move into the arms trade. Until his indictment in April 1980 for illegal arms exports, Wilson was Libya's leading supplier of terrorist weapons and was active in other areas of Africa and the Middle East (*National Times*, 14 June 1981). Some of the bank's early arms trading in 1973–74 was done as a cover for CIA operations, but its later deals were often connected with Edwin Wilson. In 1979 Houghton met with Wilson in Switzerland and the bank tried to export howitzers to Libya by shipping them through Brazil (*National Times*, 21 February and 6 June 1982). The bank's close involvement with the Wilson group was indicated by Houghton's dealings with Thomas Clines, former director of training in the CIA's Clandestine Services. After quitting the CIA in 1978,

Clines established A.P.I. Distributors, Inc. for Wilson, a company that later assisted Houghton in negotiating the purchase of an English bank for Nugan Hand. Six weeks after Nugan Hand's collapse in April 1980, Clines flew into Sydney and left two days later on a flight to Manila with Houghton (*National Times*, 12 September 1982).

The Nugan Hand Bank's rush to ruin began on 27 January 1980, when a N.S.W. police patrol discovered Frank Nugan's body, hand clutched about a rifle, lying in his Mercedes on a deserted road west of Sydney. The apparent suicide precipitated a panic among the bank management, and during the following months several key personnel destroyed bank records, closed out branches and stole as much as $50 million in assets and deposits. The bank finally collapsed in April, and two months later Michael Hand, disguised and carrying a false passport, fled Australia and disappeared, followed several days later by Bernie Houghton.

Although the collapse was sudden, the bank had been in deep trouble for almost a year. The Nugan family's produce company was being investigated for fraud, leading commercial banks were warning customers of Nugan Hand's alleged drug dealings, and the bank's Cayman Island branch was facing fraud investigations because the auditors refused to certify the books. In October 1977 the Nugan Group hired one of Sydney's leading organized crime figures, a former detective in the N.S.W. police named Frederick Krahe, to force approval of the company accounts at the annual meeting, but the attempt backfired when N.S.W. Attorney-General Frank Walker announced an investigation. In 1979 Nugan tried to block the investigation by depositing $6,000 in the Union Bank of Switzerland in Attorney-General Walker's name and then using contacts with the state opposition to leak the information to the press. The attempt failed and the local investigations, combined with mounting problems in the Cayman Islands, evidently pushed Nugan to suicide (*Wall Street Journal*, 24 August 1982).

The suicide and the bank's subsequent collapse made the Nugan Hand affair a great Australian *cause célèbre* of this century. For over two years, a steady outpouring of media and government revelations had charted the bank's relations with Australian organized crime and the CIA. With new revelations breaking in the press almost daily at times, the Nugan Hand story stripped Sydney's *milieu* of its romantic, working-class aura and projected an image of the city's syndicates as participants in heroin dealing, political corruption, gun running and CIA espionage. Perhaps more than any other single incident, the Nugan Hand affair has convinced Australia's press and parliamentarians that organized crime is a matter of some seriousness.

Legitimate Business

Simultaneously with syndicate expansion into Southeast Asia, organized crime began penetrating the legitimate sector of the Australian economy. One of the first areas to attract syndicate interest was property development in the Kings Cross area of Sydney. During the spectacular Sydney land boom of 1972–74, several property developers announced plans to transform a row of nineteenth century terrace houses on Victoria Street, Kings Cross, into high-rise buildings. Among the firms participating was Sir Paul Strasser's Parkes Development Corporation, which was then employing CIA operative Bernie Houghton as a company executive (*SMH*, 28 September 1982).

Determined to resist the demolition, local resident groups forged an alliance with the Builder's Labourers Federation and imposed "green bans" which blocked construction for 18 months. To crush the demonstrations, developers hired Joseph Meissner — brothel keeper, karate champion, and Labor Party branch leader — to assault squatters occupying the buildings. The effort failed. On 4 July 1975 the "green leader," Juanita Nielsen, heiress and community newspaper publisher, disappeared never to be found again. Her last known appointment was with pimp and petty criminal Edward Trigg, then manager of the Kings Cross Laramie Restaurant owned by Abraham Saffron, the man who "dominated the Kings Cross vice scene." Trigg was later indicted for the murder and fled to the United States to avoid trial.[33]

Nielsen's disappearance and the collapse of the "green bans" movement came too late for Parkes Development. Pressed by a liquidity squeeze in 1973, Parkes began reducing its Kings Cross investments and sold its long-term government lease to 107/109 Darlinghurst Road to Abraham Saffron's Togima Leasing Pty. Ltd. for $400,000. Parkes Development ultimately went bankrupt in 1977. The following year the owner of 107/109 Darlinghurst Road, the Public Transport Commission, investigated charges that Togima Development was tolerating a brothel on the second floor and paid Saffron $2.6 million to buy out his lease (*SMH*, 28 September 1982). While the full story of the Nielsen murder and the Kings Cross development is far from understood, investigators are convinced that there is ample evidence of organized crime interest in legitimate property development.

The tax avoidance industry was another semi-legitimate enterprise that attracted organized crime interest in the late 1970s. As the only major developed nation without a capital gains tax, Australia witnessed a number of tax avoidance schemes during the 1970s based on the common principle of transforming company profits into capital gains. As administrative action by the Taxation Office outlawed some of the more modest schemes, a small circle of entrepreneurs concocted an ambitious tax fraud known as the "bottom-of-the-harbor" scheme. Like earlier tax avoidance practice, the new scheme operated on the principle of transforming a taxable company profit into a nontaxable capital gain. A businessman with a substantial company profit sold his company through a tax agent or merchant banker to an intermediary, thereby making a non-taxable capital gain on the sale. The intermediary company, in turn, voided its tax liability by selling the company and its still taxable profit to a third firm with fictitious or elusive board of directors. The third party simply destroyed the records, perhaps by dumping them into Sydney harbor, and disappearing.

The most active of these tax avoidance promoters was the Sydney merchant bank Ward, Knight and Dunn, a lineal descendant of the Nugan Hand Bank. Before establishing his own bank in 1977, Francis Ward was a managing director of the Nugan-Hand group and his partner had also been an executive in the same company. In two years Ward, Knight and Dunn arranged the sale of legitimate firms with some $1 billion in taxable income through about 80 companies under their corporate umbrella. It was Ward, Knight and Dunn's genius to make their final sale to spurious third companies whose directors often included members of the Melbourne Ships' Painters and Dockers Union, a waterfront criminal fraternity so violent that no Taxation Office investigator would dare approach them to inquire after the companies sold to them.

Unlike Sydney syndicate members from the city's dockside Balmain district who had expanded into nationwide criminal activities, Melbourne's waterfront criminals had been largely contained inside the docklands of South Melbourne. Many of the most violent were members of the Painters and Dockers Union, and during the 1970s internecine struggles for control had produced a wave of executions.[34] The wave of union violence prompted formation of a Federal Royal Commission into its affairs in 1981. The government appointed an exceptionally intelligent barrister as commissioner, Francis Costigan, and he began an ambitious investigation of the wider ramifications of the union's activities, uncovering their role in the tax avoidance schemes. With a budget of $2 million and a mainframe computer, Costigan followed the threads of organized crime activities from the Melbourne docks; through the corporate accounts of Ward, Knight and Dunn; and into the operations of Sydney's organized crime syndicates. The Commissioner found, for example, that Abraham Saffron had shifted his business to Ward, Knight and Dunn after the collapse of the Nugan-Hand Bank (*National Times*, 19 September 1982). Based on these investigations, Commissioner Costigan issued a landmark report on Australian organized crime.

Released in September 1982, the report described a "flourishing" Sydney-based national criminal organization that operates in every state and controls much of Australia's narcotics, prostitution and illegal gambling. The organization operates through a five-tiered structure: (1) those who supply capital for an organized crime operation; (2) specialists who provide technical services required for gambling and narcotics importation; (3) professionals such as lawyers who operate on the periphery of the legal system to defeat law enforcement; (4) the Sydney syndicate entrepreneurs who market the criminal schemes and supervise their execution; and (5) the lower ranking criminals such as the Painters and Dockers who distribute drugs, carry out executions and handle bribery. The crime structure's operations reached as far as the Philippines, other Southeast Asian nations and the United States. In essence, Costigan found that Australia had a powerful, nationwide organized crime syndicate that had grown beyond the capabilities of any Australian law enforcement organization, state or Federal. Arguing that a standing crime commission with the powers of prosecution was required, Costigan urged the government to appoint him to form such a body. The Federal government released Costigan's report and announced that it was pressing ahead with legislation for a national crimes commission (*SMH*, 8 September and 21 October 1982).

The National Crimes Commission

Between 1979 and 1982 a series of sensational events fostered public concern over organized crime and created a climate conducive to a major Federal intitiative — the National Crimes Commission. During this three-year period, revelations about organized crime came in quick succession. Throughout 1979 police investigations of the "Mr. Asia" heroin syndicate and its corrupt contacts with the Australian Bureau of Narcotics attracted headlines, culminating in the Federal government's dissolution of the Bureau.

In January 1980 Frank Nugan's suicide unleashed a chain of events which ended with the collapse of the Nugan Hand Bank in April, prompting a flood of front-page stories about its dealings with the Sydney syndicate and the CIA. In July, Mr. Peter Baldwin, Labor member of the N.S.W. Parliament's upper house, was savagely beaten about the face by a karate expert to discourage his continuing investigations into organized crime penetration of inner-Sydney Labor Party branches. Sensational tabloid press photos of Baldwin's battered face, scab-covered and eyes swollen closed, shocked public opinion, and the state government's subsequent inaction seemed mute testimony to its complicity.[35] Together with Inspector Mervyn Beck's raids on illegal casinos — part of the continuing investigation into the "Mr. Asia" syndicate — the Nugan Hand Bank and the Baldwin bashing made headlines throughout 1981, maintaining organized crime as a highly visible public issue. But the most convincing evidence of the N.S.W. State government's inability to cope with organized crime came in November 1981 when police began investigating corruption by William Allen, N.S.W. Assistant Commissioner of Police and the state government's favored candidate as the next commissioner.

The Allen investigation began in November 1981 when Prime Minister Malcolm Fraser notified N.S.W. Premier Neville Wran formally that Allen had accepted a free trip to Las Vegas from Jack Rooklyn, poker machine entrepreneur and former owner of Bally Australia. Since Allen was Premier Wran's personal appointment as assistant commissioner, the N.S.W. government was reluctant to act, and several weeks of vitriolic Parliamentary debates were required before Premier Wran finally ordered the N.S.W. Police Tribunal to investigate Allen.

The Tribunal heard evidence that Allen had accepted a free trip to Macao in May 1981 as a guest of Lori Yip, president of the Macao Trotting Club. A month later Allen and members of his family took a free trip to Las Vegas: the complimentary Pan Am tickets were arranged by a N.S.W. Leagues Club that was applying for a casino license. Honolulu accommodation was provided by Macao's Lori Yip; the San Francisco hotel was paid for by Sydney bookmaker Bill Waterhouse; and his room account at Caesar's Palace in Las Vegas was billed to poker machine magnate Jack Rooklyn.

While in Sydney, Allen had often dined with Mr. Lum Wang, operator of an illegal Chinatown casino, and met Rooklyn on a number of occasions (*National Times*, 11 April 1982). The most controversial of such contacts were the seven private meetings between Allen and Abraham Saffron at police headquarters between March and September 1981. Saffron's involvement in prostitution, pornography, homosexual bars and low class nightclubs in the Kings Cross area had earned him the title "Mr. Sin" in the Sydney press (*SMH*, 18 March 1982). Saffron was having some difficulties with the head of the police licensing squad, and Allen subsequently paid the head of that squad, Sgt. Warren Molloy, $2,500 in cash. Sgt. Molloy's counsel told the Tribunal that Allen had intended to run a "corruption protection racket" within the police force, and investigators found a $13,210 discrepancy in Allen's personal accounts for 1981 (*SMH*, 3 and 22 April 1982). The Tribunal finally released its report in April 1982, finding against Mr. Allen on most counts. Rather than bring criminal charges against Mr. Allen, the N.S.W. government allowed him to resign with his pension, a move that raised charges of a cover-up (*SMH*, 22 April 1982).

Following Commissioner Costigan's well-publicized report on organized crime and police inadequacy in September 1982, the Fraser government introduced the National Crimes Commission Bill into Federal Parliament. Arguing that traditional law enforcement techniques were not effective against organized crime, Mr. Fraser announced that he would push ahead with this bill despite the objections from state governments concerned with their police prerogatives. As initially read, the bill provided for an autonomous Federal commission "with the function of investigating organized crime and official corruption."

Balanced by clauses protecting individual rights, the bill armed the Crimes Commission with extensive powers: the right to obtain search warrants, seize passports, compel appearance at its hearings, investigate either state or Federal matters, pursue criminal investigations, and recommend prosecution. Like the other two Federations with similar constitutional protection of states' rights, Australia had reached the point in its history when organized crime and political corruption at the state level required formation of a powerful Federal law enforcement body (*SMH*, 21 and 22 October 1982; Commonwealth Parliament 1982:1–20). The Bill's mere introduction is testimony to Australia's concern over the sudden growth of organized crime.

Conclusion

Over the space of a half century, Sydney's organized crime syndicates have evolved from predatory street gangs battling for the cocaine trade in the

1920s to a powerful national criminal organization with a foothold in Australia's legitimate economy and operations reaching to Southeast Asia and the United States. By the Federal government's own admission, organized crime has become Australia's leading law enforcement problem and major economic liability.

Although Australian police had in the past tended to regard syndicate crime as an American phenomenon, the events of the 1970s demonstrated the power, coherence and political influence of Sydney's criminal syndicate. In all major organized crime operations since 1967 there has been a remarkable continuity of personnel. If we were to draw a management table of each separate criminal operation and then plot the lines of overlapping association, the result would be a web of crossed lines with the density of a village kinship chart from a Third World nation. Although perhaps organized on somewhat less formal procedures, Australia had, by the early 1980s, produced an organized crime syndicate the equal of most found in Europe or North America. Developing in almost complete isolation during most of its history, Sydney's experience with organized crime demonstrates the universality of the phenomenon. Organized crime is not a uniquely Mediterranean cultural trait but is instead of global phenomenon that has developed in response to a certain historical combination of economic, social and legal conditions.

The Australian experience with organized crime during the 1970s points towards an incipient global integration of criminal syndicates. Beginning as a parochial criminal *milieu* in the postwar period, Sydney's criminal syndicate expanded its vice trading into every Australian state during the decade following the 1967 gang war. During that same period, Sydney syndicate leaders developed contacts with a remarkable range of foreign syndicates—the American mafia, Japanese yakuza in Manila, the Chinese gambling and narcotics syndicates of Hong Kong and Southeast Asia, Calabrian-Italian mafias, and the French-Corsican syndicates. All of these syndicates seem to have experienced a parallel transformation, expanding their range from the parochial through the national to the global. Just as criminal syndicates in America used state boundaries to frustrate local enforcement in the 1920s, contemporary syndicates are using international boundaries to defeat national law enforcement agencies. The crime syndicates that first appeared as parochial gangs in the metropolis of the early twentieth century have developed a multinational range which should ensure their survival until well into the twenty-first century.

Notes

1. N.S.W. Legislative Council 1978b:1–8; *Daily Telegraph*, 8 September 1978; *National Times*, 6 March 1978.

2. N.S.W. Legislative Assembly 1892:475–94; Kelly 1978a and 1978b.

3. *Truth*, 3 April 1938, 20 April 1941, 4 November 1945; *Daily Mirror*, 20 December 1972.

4. *Truth*, 30 January 1927, 3 March 1929, 13 and 30 March 1930, 19 October 1930, 1 February, 4 October 1931, 20 January, 6 March 1932; *Daily Mirror*, 31 January 1973; Long Bay Gaol, 3/6004, No. 188.

5. *Truth*, 8 March 1925, 12 April, 29 June 1930, 7 February 1932, 4 April 1943; *Sun*, 23 April 1971; Long Bay Gaol, 3/6007, No. 659.

6. *Truth*, 19 October 1930, 6 March 1932; *Australasian Journal of Pharmacy*, August 1930, p. 783.

7. *Labor Daily*, 16 and 26 May 1938; *Sun*, 14 May 1939; *Daily Telegraph*, 4 August 1938; *SMH*, 6 and 26 August 1938; *Truth*, 3 July, 28 August 1938.

8. *Truth*, 25 October 1936, 31 January, 8 August 1937; N.S.W. Parliament, 4 August 1937:22-26.

9. *Truth*, 17 October 1943; *SMH*, 25 November 1970; *Daily Telegraph*, 25 November 1970; *Sunday Mirror*, 19 July 1959.

10. N.S.W. Parliament 1954:168-72, 176, 219, report, 70, 71, 173; *National Review*, 19-25 November 1976.

11. *Truth*, 25 February 1945; *Daily Mirror*, 26-27 June 1967; *Sun*, 26-27 June 1967; N.S.W. Parliament 1954: Schedule 92, p. 5.

12. *Truth*, 6 and 13 August 1944; 20 April 1947; *Daily Mirror*, 20 December 1972.

13. *SMH* and *Sun*, 13 August 1965; *Daily Mirror*, 21 September 1965.

14. Victoria Parliament 1959: 15; *Sun*, 16 October 1958; *SMH* and *Daily Telegraph*, 17 October 1958.

15. *SMH*, 13 and 20 July 1963; *Sunday Telegraph*, 21 July 1963; *Daily Telegraph*, 23 July 1963.

16. *SMH, Daily Mirror,* and *Daily Telegraph*, 8 August 1963.

17. *SMH*, 13 July 1965; Totalisator Agency Board of New South Wales 1980.

18. *National Times, 13 March 1978; SMH*, 18 March and 10 November, 1982.

19. Interview with a former member of the N.S.W. Police Consorting Squad, Sydney, February 1981.

20. Interview with former Kings Cross gunman, Sydney, February 1979.

21. *Sun* and *SMH*, 1 December 1977; N.S.W. Parliament, 30 November 1977:10643.

22. *Sunday Telegraph*, 14 October 1979; *Sun Herald*, 2 and 16 September 1979; *Sunday Sun*, 19 July 1979; *SMH*, 10 July 1979.

23. *SMH*, 6 December 1967; *Sunday Telegraph*, 21 March 1976; *Financial Review*, 3 August 1978.

24. N.S.W. Legislative Assembly 1974: transcript, 248, 1190, report, 73; N.S.W. District Court 1978a.

25. *Daily Mirror*, 13 May 1975; *Daily Telegraph*, 16 July 1975; *SMH*, 9 February 1977.

26. Interview with Commonwealth Police, Canberra, January 1979.

27. *National Times*, 21 February 1982; N.S.W. Corporate Affairs Commonwealth-Commission 1969 and 1979; Commonwealth-N.S.W. Joint Task Force on Drug Trafficking 1982:289-92.

28. *SMH*, 10 November 1982; *National Times*, 21 February and 6 June 1982; Joint Task Force, pp. 399-406.

29. *National Times*, 13 June 1982; *Wall Street Journal*, 24 August 1982; Joint Task Force, pp. 304-28; 371-98; 501-02.

30. *Wall Street Journal*, 24 August 1982; Joint Task Force, pp. 290-92.

31. *National Times*, 21 February 1982; *Wall Street Journal*, 24 August 1982; Joint Task Force, pp. 290-92.

32. *SMH*, 10 November 1982; Joint Task Force, pp. 483-90.

33. *Now or Never*, 30 July 1975; *SMH*, 9 July 1975, 2 July 1977; *Sun Herald*, 13 November 1977, 8 February 1981; *National Times*, 5 July 1976.

34. *National Times*, 28 February and 19 September 1982; Royal Commission on the activities of the Federated Ship Painters and Dockers Union 1982:10-103.

35. *Challenge*, October 1979; *National Times*, 17 February 1980; *SMH*, 18, 21, and 25 July 1980, 20 January 1981.

References

Australasian Journal of Pharmacy. 1930. August.
Bulletin. Sydney. Various dates.

Burnaly, I. H. 1980. *The Australian Urban System: Growth, Change and Differentiation.* Melbourne: Longman Cheshire.

Challenge. 1979. Sydney. October.

Commonwealth of Australia, Parliament, 1982. *National Crimes Commission Bill 1982.* Canberra: Australian Government Publishing Service.Commonwealth-N.S.W. Joint Task Force on Drug Trafficking. 1982. *Report Volume 2: Nugan Hand.* Part 1. Canberra: Australian Government Publishing Service.

Daily Mirror. Sydney. Various dates.

Daily Telegraph. Sydney. Various dates.

Financial Review. 1978. Sydney. Various dates.

Hall, Richard. 1981. *Greed: The "Mr. Asia" Connection.* Sydney: Pan.

Kelly, Max. 1978a. "Picturesque and Pestilential: The Sydney Slum Observed, 1860–1900." In *Nineteenth Century Sydney: Essays in Urban History*, ed. Max Kelly. Sydney: Sydney University Press.

————. 1928b. " 'Worse than Physic': Sydney's Water Supply, 1788–2888." In *Nineteenth Century Sydney: Essays in Urban History*, ed. Max Kelly. Sydney: Sydney University Press.

Kruger, Henrik. 1980. *The Great Heroin Coup: Drugs, Intelligence & International Fascism.* Boston: South End Press.

Labor Daily. Sydney. Various dates.

Long Bay Gaol, Department of Corrective Services. n.d. Photo Description Books. N.S.W. Archives.

McCarty, J. W. 1978. "Australian Capital Cities in the Nineteenth Century." In *Australian Capital Cities: Historical Essays*, ed. J. W. McCarty and C. B. Schedvin. Sydney: Sydney University Press.

McCoy, Alfred W. 1972. *The Politics of Heroin in Southeast Asia.* New York: Harper & Row.

————. 1980. *Drug Traffic: Narcotics and Organized Crime in Australia.* Sydney: Harper & Row.

National Times. Sydney. Various dates.

National Review. 1976. November 19–25.

New South Wales (hereafter N.S.W.)

N.S.W. 1920, 1929, 1941. *New South Wales Official Yearbook.* Sydney: 1921, 1930, 1942.

N.S.W. Corporate Affairs Commission. 1969 and 1970. Australasian and Pacific Holdings Limited, Prospectus, 15 September 1969. Notes to Financial Statements, 18 May, 1970.

N.S.W. District Court. 1977 and 1978. *R. v. Frank C. Lawrence, Graham Twaddell and Patricia C. Moylan*, 77/973 and 78/332.

N.S.W. District Court. 1978a. *R. v. Murray Stewart Riley*, 78/781. Transcript.

N.S.W. Legislative Assembly. 1892. *Royal Commission on Alleged Chinese Gambling and Immorality and Charges of Bribery Against Members of the Police Force.* Sydney: Government Printer.

N.S.W. Legislative Assembly. 1912. *Royal Commission of Inquiry Respecting the Question of Legalizing and Regulating the Use of the Totalisator in New South Wales.* Sydney: Government Printer.

N.S.W. Legislative Assembly, 1932. *Police Department Annual Report for the Year 1931.* Sydney: Government Printer.

N.S.W. Legislative Assembly. 1934. *Police Department Annual Report for the Year 1936.* Sydney: Government Printer.

N.S.W. Legislative Assembly. 1936. *Report of the Royal Commission of Inquiry (His Honour Judge Markell) into Allegations Against the Police in Connection with the Suppression of Illicit Betting.* Sydney: Government Printer.

N.S.W. Legislative Assembly. 1937. *Police Department Annual Report for the Year 1936.* Sydney: Government Printer.

N.S.W. Legislative Assembly. 1974. *Royal Commission into Allegations of Organized Crime in Clubs. Transcript.* Sydney: Government Printer.

N.S.W. Legislative Council. 1978a. *Interim Report from the Select Committee on Crime Control Together with the Proceedings of the Committee and Minutes of Evidence.* Sydney: Government Printer.

N.S.W. Legislative Council. 1978b. The Select Committee on Crime Control. *Evidence of Mr. Francis Michael Lynch, Chief Racecourse Inspector for the Australian Jockey Club and the Sydney Turf Club.* Sydney: Government Printer.

N.S.W. Parliament. 1908. *Debates.* Sydney: Government Printer. 15 October.
N.S.W. Parliament. 1923. *Debates.* Sydney: Government Printer. 3 October.
N.S.W. Parliament. 1926. *Debates.* Sydney: Government Printer. 16 November.
N.S.W. Parliament. 1929. *Debates.* Sydney: Government Printer. 22 October.
N.S.W. Parliament. 1937. *Debates.* Sydney: Government Printer.
N.S.W. Parliament. 1954. *Report of the Royal Commission on Liquor Laws in New South Wales.* Sydney: Government Printer.
N.S.W. Parliament. 1963. *Report of the Royal Commission of Inquiry into Off-the-Course Betting in New South Wales.* Sydney: Government Printer.
N.S.W. Parliament. 1977. *Debates.* Sydney: Government Printer.
N.S.W. Parliament. 1979a. *Debates.* Sydney: Government Printer.
N.S.W. Parliament. 1979b. *Royal Commission into Drug Trafficking.* Sydney: Government Printer.
N.S.W. Parliament. 1980a. *Royal Commission into Drug Trafficking.* Sydney: Government Printer.
N.S.W. Parliament. 1980b. *Further Report of the Royal Commission into Drug Trafficking (The Honourable Mr. Justice Woodward).* Sydney: Government Printer.
N.S.W. Police, Crime Intelligence Unit, 1977. "Subject: Confidential report to the Superintendent in Charge of C.I. Branch re Organized Crime – George David Freeman." March 7.
Now or Never. 1975. Sydney. July 30.
Republic of the Philippines, National Economic and Development Authority. 1980. *Philippine Statistical Yearbook.* Manila: NEDA.
Royal Commission on the Activities of the Federated Ship Painters and Dockers Union. 1982. *Interim Report No. 4.* Volume 1. Canberra: Australian Government Publishing Service.
Scott, Ernest. 1937. *Australia During the Great War: Official History of Australia in the War,* XI. Sydney: Angus & Robertson.
Smith's Weekly. Sydney. Various dates.
Sun. Sydney. Various dates.
Sun Herald. 1962. Sydney. October 21.
Sun Mirror. 1959. Sydney. Various dates.
Sunday Sun. 1945. Sydney. Various dates.
Sunday Telegraph. 1963. Sydney. July 21.
Sydney Morning Herald [hereafter SMH]. Various dates.
Totalisator Agency Board of New South Wales. 1980. "TAB Turnovers since 1963." Unpublished manuscript.
Truth. Sydney. Various dates.
Victoria, Royal Commission on Police. 1883. *General Report on the State and Organization of the Police Force.* Melbourne: Government Printer.
Victoria Parliament. 1959. *Report of the Royal Commissioner Appointed to Inquire into Off-the-Course Betting.* Melbourne: Government Printer.
Victoria Parliament. 1982. Board of Inquiry into Casinos, Exhibit 248: Superintendent, Bureau of Criminal Intelligence, "Organised Crime in Victoria – Interim Report." *Transcript.* Melbourne.
Wall Street Journal. 1980–1982. New York. Various dates.

Name Index

Subject Index

Contributors

Joseph L. Albini is professor of sociology at Wayne State University. He has written extensively on organized crime, and his book, *The American Mafia: Genesis of a Legend,* published in 1971, set in motion a new approach to the study of organized crime in the United States.

Menachem Amir is professor of criminology and criminal law at The Hebrew University in Jerusalem. He has written on and consulted with the government of Israel on organized crime problems. In addition to teaching in many universities in the United States and Europe, Professor Amir is the author of *Patterns in Forcible Rape* (1971).

Alan A. Block is professor, Administration of Justice at Pennsylvania State University. His many influential works on organized crime include: *Eastside-Westside, Organizing Crime in New York: 1930–1950* (1983); *Organizing Crime* (with William Chambliss, 1981) and *Poisoning For Profit: The Mafia and Toxic Waste Disposal in America* (with Frank Scarpitti, 1985).

Henner Hess is professor of criminology at the University of Frankfurt in West Germany. His research on the Sicilian Mafia is regarded as the most important work to appear on this phenomenon in this century. His works include: *Mafia & Mafiosi: The Structure of Power* (1973); *The Social History of Terrorism in Italy* (1984); and, *Tobacco: The Legal Drug* (1985).

Hiroaki Iwai is professor of sociology in the Graduate School of Tokyo University, and director of its Institute of Social Relations; he also consults on criminal justice matters with the Prime Minister of Japan. His many writings cover criminal justice issues, organized crime, juvenile delinquency, and problems of urbanization.

Richard Kedzior is a research associate at the International Center for Comparative Criminology, University of Montreal, Quebec Commission for Inquiry into Organized Crime. His current research includes the organization of crime; the social evaluation of sentencing and imprisonment, and credit and check forgery.

Robert J. Kelly is associate professor of criminal justice and special education in The City University of New York and Brooklyn College. His writings include studies of organized crime, prisons, revolutionary and terrorist movements, and topics in the sociology of deviance.

Peter A. Lupsha is professor of political science at the University of New Mexico. He has written extensively on organized crime, international narcotics trafficking, and issues in law enforcement intelligence. His monograph, *The Politics of Drug Trafficking in Latin America* will be published in 1986.

Andrzej E. Marek is professor of criminal law and criminology and Director, Institute of Criminal Law, University of Nicolas Copernicus. His many articles and books, which have been translated into several languages, include: *Criminal Law, Criminality and Its Control in Poland* (1979); and *Prostitution in the Light of Criminological Research* (1985).

Alfred W. McCoy is associate professor, School of History, University of New South Wales. His writings on drug trafficking in Southeast Asia and organized crime are internationally known. His many works include: *Politics of Heroin in Southeast Asia* (1972); *Drug Traffic: Narcotics and Organized Crime in Australia* (1980); and *Laos: War and Revolution* (co-editor, 1970).

Humbert S. Nelli is professor of history, University of Kentucky. His well-regarded works on organized crime among Italian-Americans include: *The Business of Crime: Italians and Syndicate Crime in the United States* (1981); *Italians in Chicago, 1880–1930: A Study in Ethnic Mobility* (1973); and *From Immigrants to Ethnics: The Italian Americans* (1982).

James S. E. Opolot is associate professor of criminal justice at Atlanta University. His research on organized crime includes: *Organized Crime in Africa* (1980).

Pierre Tremblay is a research associate at the International Center for Comparative Criminology, University of Montreal, Quebec Commission of Inquiry into Organized Crime. His current research includes the organization of crime; the social evaluation of sentencing and imprisonment; and credit and check forgery.

James Walston is a professor of sociology, University of Maryland, who teaches in Italy. His publications on organized crime include: *Mafia in Calabria* (1985); *Mafia and Ideal Types of Society* (1980). He is a consultant to the Regional Government Enquiry into organized crime in Rome.